The European Union and the Nordic Countries

Until January 1995 the majority of the Nordic countries remained outside the EU. That changed with the accession of Sweden and Finland. Relations between the Nordic countries and the EU have always been close, though attitudes towards the EU have often varied dramatically between states. The relationship is set to change again, now that Sweden and Finland have joined Denmark inside the EU.

This study brings together a set of contributors from the five main Nordic countries – Denmark, Finland, Iceland, Norway and Sweden – which provide an authoritative analysis of the intricate relations between the EU and the Nordic bloc. The book charts the history of EU/Nordic relations and the national situations of the above countries. The effects of a changed relationship are also explored in terms of economic and monetary union, social and environmental policy, agriculture, fisheries and foreign and security affairs.

The book argues that the impact on the EU by the arrival of Sweden and Finland will be a positive one, and that although the eventual accession of Norway and Iceland will happen, it will necessitate a major shift of public opinion within those countries.

Lee Miles is Lecturer in Politics at the Department of Politics, University of Hull.

The European Union and the Nordic Countries

Edited by

Lee Miles

ROUTLEDGE

London and New York

First published 1996
by Routledge
11 New Fetter Lane, London EC4P 4EE

Simultaneously published in the USA and Canada
by Routledge
29 West 35th Street, New York, NY 10001

Routledge is an International Thomson Publishing company

Typeset in Times by Keystroke, Jacaranda Lodge, Wolverhampton
Printed in Great Britain by TJ Press, Padstow, Cornwall

British Library Cataloguing in Publication Data
A catalogue record for this book is available from the British Library

Library of Congress Cataloging in Publication Data
The European Union and the Nordic countries / edited by Lee Miles.
p. cm.
Includes bibliographical references and index.
ISBN 0-415-12422-0. — ISBN 0-415-12423-9 (pbk.)
1. European Union countries—Foreign relations—Scandinavia.
2. Scandinavia—Foreign relations—European Union countries.
I. Miles, Lee, 1969– .
D1065.S34E97 1994
327.4048—dc20 96-11328
CIP

ISBN 0-415-12422-0 (hbk)
ISBN 0-415-12423-9 (pbk)

Dedicated to my wife, Lesa

Contents

List of figures ix
List of tables x
List of contributors xii
Preface xiv
Acknowledgements xv
List of abbreviations xvi

Part I Introduction

1 Introduction 3
Lee Miles

Part II A history of European Union–Nordic relations

2 The concept of the Nordic region and the parameters of Nordic cooperation 15
Alastair H. Thomas

3 The Nordic countries, the European Community (EC) and the European Free Trade Association (EFTA), 1958–84 32
David Phinnemore

4 The Nordic countries and the European Economic Area (EEA) 47
Sieglinde Gstöhl

5 The Nordic countries and the fourth EU enlargement 63
Lee Miles

Part III The national dimensions

6 Denmark and the European Union 81
Thomas Pedersen

7 Sweden and the European Union: implications for the Swedish party system 101
Anders Widfeldt

8 Finland and the European Union 117
Teija Tiilikainen

9 Norway and the European Union: domestic debate versus external reality 133
Martin Sæter

10 Iceland and the European Union: Non-decision on membership 150
Gunnar Helgi Kristinsson

Part IV The European Union and the Nordic countries: an issue-based approach

11 Monetary integration and the 1995 Nordic enlargement 169
Ian Barnes

12 The impact of the Nordic countries on EU social policy 186
Debra Johnson

13 The Nordic countries and European Union environmental policy 203
Pamela M. Barnes

14 Agriculture, fisheries and the 1995 Nordic enlargement 222
Ian Barnes

15 The Nordic countries and EU membership: the energy factor 235
Janne Haaland Matlary

16 The Nordic neutrals: facing the European Union 245
Lauri Karvonen and Bengt Sundelius

17 The NATO Nordics and the CFSP 260
Clive Archer

Part V Conclusion

18 Conclusion 275
Lee Miles

Bibliography 284
Index 301

Figures

7.1 Swedish public opinion concerning EC accession, 1967–88 105
7.2 Swedish public opinion concerning EC/EU accession, 1989–94 106
8.1 The development of Finnish public opinion concerning membership of the EU, 1987–94 124
8.2 Percentage of 'Yes' opinion in various socio-political groups in Finland, 1987–94 126–127
10.1 Icelandic attitudes towards an application for membership of the EU, 1989–94 156–157
12.1 Public spending on social protection, 1990 188
12.2 European and Nordic unemployment rates, 1977–92 189
12.3 Unionisation of Europe's workforce 191

Tables

5.1 The twenty-nine Chapters for the Accession Negotiations 70
5.2 Brief chronology of the Accession Negotiations between the EU and the Nordic applicants 70
7.1 Result of the Swedish referendum concerning membership of the European Union, 13 November 1994 109
7.2 Distribution of the 'Yes' vote, EU referendum 1994, by party 109
9.1 The relative strengths of the political parties, 1989–94 149
10.1 Reasons for respondents' attitudes towards an application for EU membership in June 1994 158
10.2 Public attitudes towards an application for membership of EU, October 1994, by party affiliation 159
10.3 Public attitudes towards an application for membership of EU, October 1994, by age 161
10.4 Public attitudes towards an application for membership of EU, October 1994, by settlement 162
10.5 Public attitudes towards an application for membership of EU, October 1994, by employment 162
11.1 Real effective exchange rates 1988–93 173
11.2 Sweden's main trading partners in 1993 176
11.3 Finland's main trading partners in 1993 178
11.4 Convergence criteria for EMU (1994) 181
13.1 Examples of where higher environmental standards exist in the Nordic countries 209
13.2 Examples of economic regulators used in Sweden 211
13.3a Finnish trade by imports and by end use of goods 213
13.3b Finnish trade by exports and by industry 213
13.4 Progress in implementing directives applicable to the environment 216
14.1 Farm structures in 1990 224
14.2 Yields per hectare in 1992 224

14.3 Self-sufficiency in agricultural production, 1988–90 224
14.4 Support for Nordic agriculture in 1993 225
14.5 Fish catches in 1991 230

Contributors

Clive Archer is a Research Professor at the Department of Politics and Philosophy, Manchester Metropolitan University, UK.

Ian Barnes is Professor of European Studies and Dean of the School of Economics and International Studies, University of Humberside, UK.

Pamela M. Barnes is a Senior Lecturer in European Union Studies at the School of Economics and International Studies, University of Humberside, UK.

Sieglinde Gstöhl is a Researcher in International Relations at the Graduate Institute of International Studies, Geneva, Switzerland. In 1992/1993, she was an International Institutions Fellow at the Center for International Affairs, Harvard University, USA. She also organised the 'Yes' movement in the referendum campaign on joining the EEA in her home country of Liechtenstein in 1994/1995.

Debra Johnson is a Senior Lecturer in Economics and European Studies at the School of Economics and International Studies, University of Humberside, UK.

Lauri Karvonen is Professor of Comparative Politics at the Department of Comparative Politics, University of Bergen, Norway.

Gunnar Helgi Kristinsson is Reader in Government in the Faculty of Social Science, University of Iceland, Iceland.

Janne Haaland Matlary is a Senior Research officer and Acting Head of the Political Science section at CICERO (Centre for International Climate and Energy Policy Research) and Lecturer in Political Science, University of Oslo, Norway.

Lee Miles is Lecturer in Politics at the Department of Politics, University of Hull, UK.

Thomas Pedersen is a Jean Monnet Associate Professor in European Integration at the Institute of Political Science, University of Aarhus, Denmark.

David Phinnemore is a Lecturer in European Studies at the Department of European Studies, Liverpool Hope University College, UK.

Martin Sæter is a Senior Researcher at the Norwegian Institute of International Affairs and Professor of Political Science at the University of Oslo, Norway.

Bengt Sundelius is Associate Professor at the University of Uppsala, Sweden, Editor of *Cooperation and Conflict* and chair of the Nordic International Studies Association (NISA). He was formerly Director of the International Graduate School at the University of Stockholm, Sweden.

Alastair H. Thomas is Reader in Comparative Government in the Department of European Studies, University of Central Lancashire, UK.

Teija Tiilikainen is a Researcher at the Department of Political Science, Åbo Akademi, Åbo/Turku, Finland. She is also chairperson of the Finnish International Studies Association and the Chief Editor of *Politiikka*, a Finnish journal of Political Science.

Anders Widfeldt is Lecturer in Nordic Politics, University of Aberdeen, UK. He was formerly a Researcher at the Department of Political Science, University of Göteborg, Sweden.

Preface

With the entry of Sweden and Finland into the European Union (EU) in 1995, the Nordic region has entered a new era in its development as three of the five Nordic countries are now full EU members. At the same time, the EU has begun to embark on the policies outlined in the 1992 Treaty on European Union (TEU), which will increasingly affect the Nordic region.

As a result, intra-Nordic relations between the three full members (Denmark, Sweden and Finland) and their contacts with those Nordic countries remaining outside the EU are being reviewed and revised. Thus, 1995 offers both a rationale and a useful opportunity to consider the European Union and the Nordic countries at a critical juncture in their histories and before further EU reforms are agreed at the 1996 Intergovernmental Conference (IGC) on the TEU.

The principal purpose of this book is to provide an evaluation of the relationship between the Nordic countries and the European Union. This is by no means an easy task given the complexity and multiplicity of relations between five sovereign states and an increasingly dynamic European supranational institution. Therefore, this book incorporates a mixture of approaches in order to facilitate a relatively comprehensive examination. Part II includes a chronological discussion of Nordic–EU relations from 1958 to 1995; Part III assesses the national dimensions and Part IV uses an issue-based approach to examine the EU's most influential policies and the implications for them resulting from wider Nordic membership of the EU.

Acknowledgements

The editor would first like to thank each and every one of the contributors to this book for their valuable efforts. The quality of the contributions is, in the editor's view, a true reflection of the professionalism of the contributors. Michael Horton's help with the figures and tables included within the book was also greatly appreciated. Finally, and most of all, the editor would like to thank his wife, Lesa, for her help during the final stages of the editing and for her patience in 'waiting just another minute' during the production of this book. Any errors or omissions are still, of course, entirely the editor's.

Abbreviations

CAP	Common Agricultural Policy
CCP	Common Commercial Policy
CET	Common External Tariff
CFP	Common Fisheries Policy
CFSP	Common Foreign and Security Policy
CMEA	Council for Mutual Economic Assistance
COMECON	See CMEA
CSCE	Conference on Security and Cooperation in Europe
DKR	Danish Kronor
DM	Deutsche mark
EAP	Environmental Action Programme
EC	European Community
ECE	Economic Commission on Europe
ECSC	European Coal and Steel Community
ECU	European Currency Unit
EEA	European Economic Area
EFTA	European Free Trade Association
EIB	European Investment Bank
EMI	European Monetary Institute
EMS	European Monetary System
EMU	Economic and Monetary Union
EP	European Parliament
EPC	European Political Cooperation
ERM	Exchange Rate Mechanism
EU	European Union
EURATOM	European Atomic Energy Community
FIM	Finnish Markka
FINEFTA	Fenno-EFTA Agreement
FTA	Free Trade Agreement
GATT	General Agreement on Tariffs and Trade
GDP	Gross Domestic Product
GNP	Gross National Product
GSP	Generalised System of Preferences

HLCG	High Level Contact Group
HLNG	High Level Negotiating Group
IEA	International Energy Agency
IEM	Internal Energy Market
IGC	Intergovernmental Conference
IMF	International Monetary Fund
IR	International Relations
JHA	Justice and Home Affairs
LO	(Swedish) Labour Federation
MECU	Millions of European Currency Units
MTK	Confederation of (Finnish) Agricultural Producers
NACC	North Atlantic Cooperation Council
NATO	North Atlantic Treaty Organisation
NHO	Confederation of Norwegian Business and Industry (*Næringslivets Hoverdorganisasjon*)
NOK	Norwegian Kronor
Nordek	Nordic Organisation for Economic Cooperation
OECD	Organisation for Economic Cooperation and Development
OEEC	Organisation for European Economic Cooperation
OPEC	Organisation of Oil Exporting Countries
OSCE	Organisation for Security and Cooperation in Europe (formerly the CSCE)
PCBs	Polychlorobiphenyls
SAF	Swedish Employers Federation
SAP	Swedish Social Democratic Party
SEA	Single European Act
SEK	Swedish Krona
SEM	Single European Market
SME	Social Democrats Against the EU
SF	Danish Socialist People's Party
TEC	Total Energy Consumption
TEU	Treaty on European Union
UN	United Nations
WEU	Western European Union
WTO	Warsaw Treaty Organisation (Warsaw Pact)

Part I
Introduction

1 Introduction

Lee Miles

To a large extent, the countries of Denmark, Finland, Norway, Iceland and Sweden have been perceived by others as a 'Nordic bloc' of nation states, sharing a large (if at times rather superficial) consensus on many domestic and international issues. The Nordic countries have historically been confronted with a common set of problems when defining their relationships with the European Community (EC) and later European Union (EU).[1] In particular, these countries have all faced the challenge of securing preferential trading relations with continental Europe, while simultaneously maintaining close contact within their own region through Nordic cooperation.

Since the late 1950s, this challenge mainly focused around dealing with the emerging political and economic might of the European Community and managing their growing economic interdependence with it. Yet, although it may have been a shared problem affecting all the Nordic countries, the starting points of the states have differed due to their individual legacies of economic and political contact with the rest of Europe. Denmark for example, has maintained close ties with continental Europe due to her geographical position as part of the European mainland. In contrast, Iceland's geographical position halfway between the North American and European continents has given it a far more 'Atlantic' flavour and a greater reluctance to be an integral part of a supranational Europe. For the most part, postwar attempts at advanced levels of either Nordic cooperation or complete Nordic participation in wider European frameworks have mostly ended in failure (see Chapter 3).

Rather, the preferred point of departure for the Nordic countries was a rather limited affair. Their initial solution to meeting the challenge of closer economic relations with mainland Europe and the EC lay in European Free Trade Association (EFTA) membership and participation in the later European Economic Area (EEA). Denmark, Norway and Sweden were all founder members of EFTA. For Finland and Iceland, full EFTA membership took a little longer. Finland enjoyed associate status under its special FINEFTA arrangement until it became a full member in 1986 and Iceland joined the organisation in 1970. Nordic cooperation and

EFTA membership seemed to be complementary as all the main Nordic countries were members of both organisations. Nordic cooperation could still deal with primarily intra-Nordic political questions, while EFTA secured trading concessions from mainland Europe and acted as a counterweight to the emerging European Community.

As will be discussed in Part II of the book, the EFTA and EEA solutions proved to have several shortcomings (see Chapter 4). The dawning of these EFTA deficiencies upon the Nordic countries was universal. However, the speed of realisation and the related domestic popularity of any alternative solutions has varied enormously, helping to ensure that the accomplishment of EC/EU membership has remained a piecemeal affair. Denmark and Norway were the first to seek EC membership as early as 1961. Yet, Denmark, which was also the first of the Nordics to join the EC, took twelve years to achieve this and only became a full member in 1973. Sweden and Finland adopted various approaches for gaining an EC accommodation before they finally applied for full membership in 1991 and 1992 respectively and joined the EU in 1995. Even now, the EU question for Iceland remains problematical (see Chapter 10). Thus, although each of the Nordic countries has secured a trading relationship with the European Community since 1972, the questions of how to improve these relationships or whether to seek full EU membership have been difficult ones for all the Nordic governments.

Nor has the achievement of EU membership (once the decision to apply had been taken) been entirely smooth either. Indeed, two Nordic territories perhaps hold the European mantle for causing the most problems for the EU in terms of membership questions to date. Greenland remains the only Nordic or even European province ever to leave the European Community voluntarily after a plebiscite in 1982. In addition, Norway probably holds a double title. First, for the country which has applied the most times and second, as the only nation state which has rejected full membership in a national referendum more than once. In practice, Norway has applied for full membership four times, reached the point of finalising accession terms twice and rejected full membership in a public referendum twice.

Thus, the relationship between the Nordic countries and EU is of considerable analytical interest for both specialists of the Nordic countries and the European Union. In the first place, it represents a complex patchwork of relations, with some Nordic countries being full members (Denmark (1973), Finland (1995), Sweden (1995)), others enjoying a close relationship through the EEA (Norway and Iceland) and some territories merely having free trade agreements (Færoes, Greenland). This has not only complicated relations between the EU and the Nordic countries, but has affected intra-Nordic relations and EFTA membership. Second, the EU issue has been a sensitive domestic problem within the Nordic countries emphasising traditional Nordic social and cultural divides. In Norway, for instance, the 1972 national referendum proved so painful to Norwegian society that the issue of EC membership was virtually a political taboo for almost a decade (see Chapter 9).

For the European Union, the Nordic countries also raise three aspects of special interest. First, the Nordic countries illustrate some of the more deep-seated national concerns over EU membership and its future obligations. Toivo Miljan (1977) for example, identified the Nordic countries as the 'reluctant Europeans' and in many ways, their reluctance on such issues as federalism and the development of comprehensive supranational frameworks still remains. However, their reluctance is now felt inside the EU as full members rather than as non-member states. Thus, as Denmark has shown over the Treaty on European Union (TEU), the Nordic countries' primary rationale for EU membership is still economic and Denmark's profound scepticism regarding a federal Europe is still apparent even after over twenty years of full membership. Second, the Nordic countries also provide a recent indication of some of the problems for the EU in dealing with richer European states and not just poorer ones, when negotiating an enlargement.

Finally, as wider Nordic EU membership becomes a reality, the Nordic countries also bring with them their own baggage which the EU must learn to carry. These countries have their own and, in many ways, common agenda which will come to bear. Policies, such as greater transparency in EU decision-making (see Chapter 5) will be boosted by their membership. The EU's focus will once again become more Northern orientated, reducing the Mediterranean bias evident since the 1981 and 1986 enlargements. However, if the relationship between the Nordic countries and the European Union is to be more fully considered, then clearly the Nordic countries themselves must be further explored.

CONSIDERING THE NORDIC COUNTRIES

The Nordic countries can be compared in many different ways. In historical terms, they represent a mixed bunch of old and new nation states. Sweden and Denmark can be regarded as relatively old nation states in Europe while Norway (1905), Finland (1917) and Iceland (1944) all became independent states this century. However, the Nordic countries do share a common history and the existence of the nation states in the region are very much interlinked. For example, both Norway and Finland have been parts of the Kingdom of Sweden during periods of their history (see Chapter 2).

In constitutional terms, they are all parliamentary democracies some of which are quite old; for instance, Norway's constitution (*Grunnloven*) originates from 1814, even if her existing status as a sovereign nation state only dates back to 1905. Some, however, are new and two Nordic constitutions have been rewritten comparatively recently: Denmark in 1953 and Sweden in 1974 (Petersson 1994a: 23). However, the Nordic countries can be broadly divided into two separate groups. On the one side, the monarchies of Denmark, Norway and Sweden and on the other, Finland and Iceland as a separate group of republics. However, these are only nominal classifications. The division of the two groups does not necessarily correspond to the levels of political influence that their respective executives constitutionally maintain. For instance, it is widely recognised that the Swedish monarch holds the weakest amount of constitutional power regarding the political affairs of the state, while Denmark and Norway still theoretically provide for a prominent role for their monarchs (Petersson 1994a: 24–7). In contrast, the Finnish President has considerable power, particularly in foreign affairs and has comparatively greater political influence than any of the three monarchies.

From a parliamentary perspective, the Nordic countries do resemble one another, sharing more commonalities than differences. In particular, since Denmark and Sweden abandoned bicameral parliamentary systems in 1953 and 1971 respectively, the Nordic countries all operate unicameral parliaments, although even here this has to be qualified as the Norwegian *Storting* is divided into two sections. The Nordic constitutions also contain, albeit to varying degrees, advanced numbers of safeguards aimed at protecting the rights and freedoms of the individual and embodied in strong traditions of open government.

In modern times, this has been translated to mean that Nordic citizens are endowed with social rights based on universality and equality under which they are entitled to direct support from the state. This principle has been one of the main reasons for the development of comprehensive welfare provisions in these countries and Stein Kuhnle (1991) has argued that their commonality has been financially and economically apparent through the existence of their welfare state systems. The Nordic countries share a stronger commitment to state intervention, the maintenance of large public sectors and higher levels of employment in social and educational sectors than most comparable European states. Most noticeably, social rights are based on citizenship and not related to participation in the labour market or levels of income.

In political terms, the Nordic countries also share a basic five-party system, based around a rough socialist–non-socialist divide. It has been widely argued that a system of five parties seems to be a typical configuration for nearly all of the Nordic countries, although this system is under threat in several of them. On the left, there is usually a Social Democratic party and a Communist party, while on the right there is a grouping of non-socialist parties consisting of an agrarian-based Centre party, a Liberal party and a Conservative party. The respective sizes and dominance of the parties do, of course, vary; for example, the Social Democratic parties in Denmark, Norway and Sweden are large political forces, and the agrarian-based Centre parties in Finland and Norway are still very influential.

From this brief overview, it seems that there are an unusually high number of commonalities between the Nordic countries, although for the most part they still remain at a generalised level. As Petersson (1994a: 33–4) argues the Nordic countries share high levels of commonality built roughly around two interconnected main areas – namely a specific type of public policy and a specific type of polity. In short, Petersson assumes that first, the Nordic countries share comparatively similar welfare policies, which are comprehensive and institutionalised and aim to create solidarity; and second, they attempt to unite capitalism, parliamentary democracy and the welfare state through the existence of powerful state machinery and participatory interest groups. This view is reinforced by Elder, Thomas and Arter's (1988: 2–28) assertions that the Nordic countries are indeed 'consensual democracies' enjoying low levels of opposition to the system governing political conflict resolution, a small degree of conflict over the actual exercise of power and are characterised by a high degree of concertation in the determination of public policy.

It can be argued then that the Nordic countries will provide something qualitatively different to the EU and this could be related to the common characteristics of the Nordic countries. In short, the main features of the Nordic countries are:

- *Mature parliamentary democracies* characterised, albeit to varying levels, by long traditions of consensual decision-making and a low degree of opposition to their respective political systems.
- *Competitive market economies* incorporating elaborate corporate procedures for economic policy-making. Their systems encompass the widest possible spectrum of viewpoints through effective parliamentary channels, such as the Swedish Commissions of Inquiry and the 'Remiss Procedure'. There is also an attachment to collective bargaining, which is reflected in widespread membership of representative organisations and low levels of industrial disputes. For instance, trade-union membership includes 80 per cent of the registered workforce in Sweden.
- *Comprehensive welfare provisions and social and environmental standards*. This is politically supported by the Nordic populations and economically by reasonably high levels of GDP per capita. In fact, until recently, there has been strong, traditional public confidence in their economic strength and the merits of state intervention.
- *Common Nordic traditions of open democratic government*, incorporating freedom of information, public accountability and a commitment to human rights.
- *An attachment to national sovereignty and strong defence*. The individual defence policies of the Nordic countries have, however, varied. Denmark, Iceland and Norway are members of the North Atlantic Treaty Organisation (NATO) and Sweden and Finland preferred non-alignment. Indeed, for a long period, the concept of the 'Nordic Balance' predominated; a non-aligned and neutral Sweden being balanced to the

West by Danish, Icelandic and Norwegian NATO membership and to the East, by Finland's sensitive relations with the USSR through the 1948 Fenno-Soviet Treaty of Friendship, Cooperation and Mutual Assistance.

- *'Internationalist' and a shared preference for a free trade global economy*, owing to the sensitivity of their comparatively open export-orientated economies and active participation in international and humanitarian organisations, such as the United Nations.
- *A strong regional affinity promoting a 'Nordic identity' and cooperation through the Nordic Council.* This has facilitated limited sectoral integration – such as the Nordic Passport Union and the Common Nordic Labour Market.

However, there are numerous problems associated with determining universal Nordic characteristics and thus, the concept of a 'Nordic model'. In many ways, the concept is still ambiguous and has been used collectively to describe entities that are to some extent different in kind. For instance, the term 'Nordic model' has been used to identify both political and economic features within these states. Second, the diversity among the Nordic countries also makes conceptualising completely delineated characteristics virtually impossible. There are still many differences among the states and sources of friction, especially among the weaker Nordic countries over Swedish or Danish leadership within the region. Finally, the impact of severe recession during the early 1990s, especially in Sweden and Finland, has led to a widespread reappraisal of their internal features and whether a successful or unique 'Nordic model' exists at all.

FIVE PLUS THREE?

Indeed, it is doubtful whether the Nordic countries can be restricted to an elite club of Denmark, Finland, Iceland, Norway and Sweden. There are also the three autonomous areas of Åland, the Færoes and Greenland which have now gained such a large degree of self-government that they have developed their own political institutions. Åland, for example, has a special status within Finland and shares many linguistic, cultural and economic ties with neighbouring Sweden. Ever since the 1921 League of Nations decision to subject the islands to Finnish sovereignty, it has also been ensured that they also enjoy a considerable level of autonomy. The 1991 Act of Self-government stipulates that the islands are governed by an Executive Council responsible to a parliament (*Landting*). In similar vein, the Færo Islands have gained considerable autonomy from Denmark ever since the 1948 Home Rules Bill. Interestingly, Greenland's status as part of the Danish crown has altered over the years. Originally a Danish colony, it then became part of Denmark due to constitutional reform in 1953, and it was, at this time, given the right of self-determination by the Danish *Folketing* after the 1979 public referendum in Greenland.

Yet, these autonomous regions have led to even further complexities within the context of Nordic relations with the EU and have complicated the question of universal Nordic full membership of the EU. The Færoes elected to remain and have remained outside the EU since the time of Danish accession. Greenland also decided to leave the European Community following a referendum in 1982. In both cases these territories opposed EU membership mainly because of the implications of becoming part of the Common Fisheries Policy (CFP) as an obligation of full membership. Interestingly, Åland did approve EU membership in its referendum in 1994 and has become part of the EU along with mainland Finland from January 1995.

THE OBJECTIVES AND STRUCTURE OF THE BOOK

In this book, the Nordic countries will generally be assumed to consist of the five main sovereign states of Denmark, Finland, Iceland, Norway and Sweden. The book aims to chart the history and discuss the nature of the Nordic countries' relations with the EU. Part II provides a chronological overview of the Nordic countries and their relationship with the emerging European Union. In particular, the Nordic countries are discussed within the triad of Nordic cooperation, EFTA membership and relations with the EU.

In Chapter 2, Thomas examines Nordic cooperation. He argues that it represents a complex web of inter-relationships. Phinnemore goes on to examine the Nordic countries' participation in EFTA and their early attempts at reaching an accommodation with the evolving EC. Gstöhl evaluates Nordic perspectives during the Luxembourg process and the EEA negotiations and argues that it was the political defects of the EEA which finally drove three Nordic countries to lodge full membership applications. In Chapter 5, Miles discusses the evolution of their applications and the nature of the 1993–4 accession negotiations between the EU and Sweden, Finland and Norway and argues that for the most part, the Nordic applicants gained relatively generous accession terms.

In Part III, the national dimensions of the individual Nordic countries are evaluated. The objective of this section is to analyse the differing national perspectives and reactions to the prospect of full EU membership in the near and distant future. In particular, these five chapters not only deal with the individual Nordic countries, but also stress various sectoral problems facing these states as they participate in further European integration. Pedersen, for example, in his chapter examines the years of Danish full membership and argues that Denmark did not become completely committed to a supranational European Union until well into the late 1980s. In particular, he considers whether Danish governmental views can be rationalised in terms of Hermann's theory of foreign policy change.

In contrast, Widfeldt draws attention to the impact of the issue of EU membership on party systems and public opinion and argues that Swedish EU membership will continue to affect (albeit to varying degrees) the unity and popularity of the Swedish political parties. In her chapter on Finland, Tiilikainen draws attention to the influential role of specific interest groups and comments upon the role of the agrarian sector in shaping domestic opposition to EU membership in Finland. In the Norwegian chapter, Sæter stresses the role of external pressures and argues that the successive domestic rejections of EU membership in Norway fly in the face of external realities and that a future reappraisal of the issue is inevitable. Finally, Kristinsson evaluates the dilemmas for Iceland of remaining outside the European Union and discusses why Iceland has continued to not fully consider the merits of EU membership.

Part IV adopts an issue-based approach. It analyses the impact of wider Nordic membership on the policies of the European Union and the implications for the Nordic non-member states. The following chapters deal with specific policy areas, such as monetary integration, social policy and environmental affairs. In particular, Chapters 14 and 15 examine the sensitive issues of Nordic agriculture, fisheries and energy liberalisation which are considered in relation to EU membership. The next two chapters focus upon foreign affairs. The critical questions of why some Nordic countries eventually accepted that EU membership was compatible with their security policies and the potential impacts of the Nordic countries on any future Common Foreign and Security Policy (CFSP) are evaluated. Finally, the conclusion draws together many of these key aspects and assesses the general implications of EU membership for the Nordic countries, their impact on the EU's configuration and how in practice EU–Nordic relations may change in the future.

By taking this approach a number of prevalent themes should become obvious and will be at least partially considered. These critical variables are essential to the determination of past, present and future relations between the European Union, its Nordic member states and the Nordic countries in general. These include:

- *The perceived general performance of the Nordic economies* and their ability to maintain the traditional commitments associated with the 'Nordic model'.
- *The changes in the external environment affecting the Nordic countries*, such as the dramatic changes in Eastern Europe since 1989.
- *The expanding profile of the European Union*, as a result of, for example, the SEM and the TEU, and the growing levels of economic and political dependence of the Nordic countries upon it.
- *The decline of traditional obstacles to EU membership within the Nordic countries*, such as in some cases the maintenance of a credible policy of neutrality.

- *The failure of potential alternatives*, such as Nordic cooperation and the EEA in securing the Nordic countries' long-term interests.
- *The revised and positive evaluation of the estimated economic and political benefits* for the Nordic countries in taking up full EU membership and the changing perceptions of national sovereignty within the Nordic countries.
- *The domestic sensitivity of Nordic public opinion to the issue of European integration and EU membership.*

Nevertheless, there are a number of qualifications which need to be made regarding the assessment of the Nordic countries and the EU attempted here. First, this book was mainly written at the start of 1995 and thus during the early days of wider Nordic EU membership after the Swedish and Finnish EU accessions in January 1995. Therefore, the intention of this book is simply to evaluate relations between the European Union and the Nordic countries up until 1995 and to at least try to begin to assess the impact of these Nordic countries on the EU. At times, then, the book aims to highlight their potential roles since the actual implications are virtually impossible to gauge at this point. None the less, this does not detract from the need to initiate this kind of wide-ranging study and this book will have achieved its aims if it promotes further research in this area.

Yet, regardless of the degree of influence derived from these Nordic determinants, it can be said with some safety that relations between the EU and the Nordic countries have reached a critical new phase in EU development. A delicate period of transition will be necessary for all parties at various levels. Denmark, Sweden and Finland will need to become familiar with the dynamics of wider Nordic EU membership and this will at least partially alter intra-Nordic relations with those countries who are not full EU members. New arrangements will be necessary to incorporate the concerns of Norway and Iceland that they should not be further marginalised as a result of their choice of not taking up the option of full EU membership. Whatever the outcome in the next few years, the Nordic countries will need to confront many new challenges which will determine both their level of influence in shaping the new Europe and help secure their economic and political interests as they near the twenty-first century. A firmer and even closer relationship with the European Union will therefore remain on the agenda of all the Nordic countries regardless of whether they are at present full EU members or not.

NOTES

1 Although the European Community still exists as part of the European Union's three pillar structure as outlined in the Treaty on European Union (TEU), the editor has decided to adopt the following rules:

a) The term 'European Union' will be used for all references to the organisation after the TEU's ratification in November 1993 unless it is a reference to one of the specific European Communities. Where the text is referring in general to the organisation without any specialised reference to a time period then the term 'European Union' will also apply.

b) Otherwise, the term 'European Community' will be used for all references before the ratification of the TEU.

Part II

A history of European Union–Nordic relations

2 The concept of the Nordic region and the parameters of Nordic cooperation

Alastair H. Thomas

THE NORDIC REGION

In current usage the Nordic region encompasses the monarchies of Denmark, Norway and Sweden and the republics of Finland and Iceland, as well as the Færo Islands and Greenland, which have autonomy under Danish sovereignty, as do the Åland Islands under Finland. Norwegian territory includes the island skerries off its long coastline plus Spitzbergen and the Svalbard group of islands far to the north and the uninhabited Jan Mayen Island near the Greenland coast (important in determining Norway's extensive fishery zones). Norway is also responsible for Queen Maud Land in the Antarctic. In Nordic languages the region is referred to as 'Norden', meaning the North, but there is no precise English equivalent. Politically this usage has been consolidated in the second half of the twentieth century but, as we shall see near the end of this chapter, wider international links have gained strength in the 1990s.

Scandinavia is a collective term for Denmark, Norway and Sweden. In a precise geological sense it applies only to the fjord-indented and mountainous Norwegian and Swedish peninsula. Denmark is included in Scandinavia on cultural and linguistic grounds, although geologically part of the north German plain. Danish, the two Norwegian languages *riksmål* and *nynorsk*, and Swedish are all very closely interrelated languages in the North Germanic group. They could be regarded as dialects of a single Scandinavian language as they are all mutually intelligible, even if on sociological criteria they remain the distinct languages of the various national communities. In contrast, Icelandic is rooted in the Old Norse of the Vikings (who settled there in about AD 900) and can be set apart from the other Scandinavian languages. Finnish is entirely unrelated and is a member of the Fenno-Ugric branch of the varied Uralic family of languages, as are the seven Sami languages spoken by the Lapps. In Greenland the Inuit people speak a branch of the Eskimo-Aleutic or Eskaleutic group of languages. The Nordic countries are near-homogeneous in their Lutheran Christianity, although for most people church attendance is infrequent.

THE CHARACTERISTICS OF NORDIC INTEGRATION

Nordic integration has been characterised by numerous small links, often at an inter-personal level and few of them are of major importance singly. But when taken together and cumulatively over the period since 1945, when listed by the Nordic Council (for example, in *Nordiska samarbetsorgan* 1992) they add up to a highly-developed pattern of mutual cooperation and integration. This integration in many small matters has been termed micro-integration (Solem 1977: 165–7) and coincides with Andrén's (1967) 'cobweb theory' of Nordic integration, which emphasises the importance of the many weak links of interdependence which together have made up a strong web of integration. Indeed, since the Nordek negotiations failed in 1970 many more strands have been added to the web and they have been strengthened financially and organisationally.

The process of Nordic integration has accommodated two important reasons for a rather cautious approach. First, regional rivalries, past patterns of domination, and more recent patterns of inequality still have their effects and act as important brakes on the pace of integration – in a phrase, 'familiarity breeds suspicion'. Second, an active and anticipatory style of problem solving within consensual political systems (Richardson 1982; Elder, Thomas and Arter 1988) has produced a general preference for detailed investigations before decisions are taken and has sometimes delayed or stopped the launch of new projects.

As a result, Nordic integration has proceeded dialectically, in a pattern of action and reaction: ambitious schemes have been planned, have failed, and in their wake many lesser schemes have been implemented which add further strands to the web of integration. Thus in the face of their inability to integrate security policy in the aftermath of the Second World War, the Scandinavian governments reacted by forming the Nordic Council in 1952. Protracted discussions in the 1950s to establish a Nordic Customs Union were overtaken by the formation of the seven member EFTA, which expanded inter-Nordic trade within a wider framework. In 1968–70 another attempt at economic integration, Nordek, failed and within two years Denmark (with Britain and Ireland) joined the European Community, while Norway negotiated membership terms, only to see them rejected at a referendum which also shook popular support for party leaders. The non-EC Nordic countries then negotiated free trade arrangements with the EC. To counteract the new division, a flurry of initiatives followed to integrate the Nordic countries in non-economic sectors of policy, this time underpinned by the development of the Nordic Council of Ministers in 1971, with a permanent secretariat to provide its institutional infrastructure. Although such major initiatives met with serious setbacks within their intended sector of cooperation, the setbacks prompted major innovations in other policy sectors. Using neo-functionalist terminology, Sundelius and Wiklund (1979: 59–75, following Schmitter in Lindberg and Scheingold 1971) see the process as one of spill-arounds rather than spill-backs. The following section traces these developments.

Building on their linguistic, religious and historical affinities, the Nordic countries have developed a complex web of inter-relationships so close that they have been described as 'the other European community' (Turner and Nordquist 1982). This common Nordic identity has grown through inter-Nordic trade and migration, through substantial efforts to harmonise domestic legislation across a broad range of sectors, and through extensive inter-Nordic cooperation and interchange of scientific, academic and cultural activity. Much of this has been achieved under the umbrella of the Nordic Council, but the successes rest more on shared culture and common objectives and values than on integrating institutions. Moreover, while the successes have been numerous and extensive, they have generally been low-level. Efforts during the fifty years since 1945 to co-ordinate the 'high politics' of national defence and security or to integrate the Nordic economies with each other have foundered on divergent national interests, but specific failures in high politics have brought renewed efforts to compensate which have developed a network of strengthened links at lower levels.

DISINTEGRATIVE FACTORS

Yet, from a historical perspective, relations between the Nordic countries have been marked more by disintegration than by cooperation. Denmark and Sweden have long histories of distinct national identity and rivalry. Margrethe II, Queen of Denmark since 1972, represents the oldest monarchy in Europe, descending from well before Knud (Canute), the Viking king of England who succeeded to the Danish throne in 1019. From 1375 until around 1523, the whole Nordic region was united in the Kalmar Union. Sweden also reached a border agreement with Novgorod in 1323 which established Swedish rule and culture in Finland. After the breakup of the Kalmar 'union of the three crowns' Sweden increased in power and territory, achieving great power status during the seventeenth century. For the most part, Denmark and Sweden were rivals in sometimes bitter conflict for dominance in the Baltic region until the end of the Napoleonic wars.

Iceland and Norway look back to greatness in the Viking age (about AD 800–1050) but came under the Danish crown in 1380. Norway hoped to gain independence in 1814, but instead endured ninety years of imposed union with Sweden before attaining sovereignty in 1905. Iceland obtained some political and financial autonomy in 1874 and home rule from 1904. The constitution was democratised in 1915 in line with Danish developments, and in 1918 Iceland became a sovereign state, although still linked with Denmark in a shared monarchy and with foreign relations conducted by Denmark. This relationship persisted until the Icelanders declared themselves an independent republic in 1944. Finland was transferred from

Swedish rule in 1809, spent 108 years as a Grand Duchy of Imperial Russia, and became independent in 1917.

Thus Denmark and Sweden are old-established powers, while the independent states of Norway, Finland and Iceland in their present forms are new nations of the twentieth century. Danish and Norwegian nationalism was further strengthened by German wartime occupation from 1940 and liberation in 1945, while the modern Finnish identity was moulded by tenacious self-defence against the USSR in the Winter War of 1939–40 and the Continuation War until 1944, and then against Germany until 1945. Fenno-Soviet mutual understanding of each other's security interests, leading to cautious and gradual enlargement of Finland's freedom of action, was built carefully through the following forty-five years. For the five hundred years to 1945 'the Nordic area experienced continual political disintegration as the present regional structure of five independent nations emerged' (Sundelius and Wiklund 1979: 61).

DIVERGENT SECURITY INTERESTS

The emergence of Nordic countries from subordination to independence helped to create conditions favouring their voluntary cooperation in a Nordic union. Running counter to the disaggregating tendencies of Nordic nationalism, there were stirrings of cultural pan-Scandinavianism as early as 1840. King Oscar I of Sweden–Norway responded to a congress of Scandinavianist students in 1856 by saying that: 'From now on war between the Scandinavian brothers is impossible', and perhaps even hoped to unite the three crowns of Scandinavia in his own person. But when Denmark was attacked by Austria–Prussia in 1864, hopes of a defensive alliance with Sweden came to nothing – an instance of Sweden's recurrent policy of avoiding peacetime alliances which might draw her into European wars. Nevertheless, commercial links between the Nordic countries grew stronger and led in 1873 to the gold-based currency union between Denmark and Sweden which Norway joined in 1875. Although never formally dissolved, by the First World War divergent economic and monetary policies effectively ended it. Until then Nordic cooperative activity was strongest among academics, educationalists and the labour movement (Wendt 1959: 22–30).

In 1914 the kings of Denmark, Sweden and Norway met at Malmö, in the face of looming conflict involving Germany, and resolved that their countries would remain neutral, a hope which was fortunately fulfilled. To extend the cooperation that had been achieved in wartime, in addition to continued intergovernmental contacts, the Norden Association was formed in 1919 in each of the three Scandinavian countries, and it soon extended its network linking commerce, interest groups and individual citizens to Finland and Iceland. In the 1920s it mainly emphasised educational and cultural links.

In the 1930s the Nordic governments continued to pin their faith on neutrality and collective action within the League of Nations, but once again developments in Germany, this time the rise of Nazism, drew them together. The Scandinavian foreign ministers met in 1932 and annually from 1934 to 1940, and ministers of Commerce, Social Welfare, Justice and Education also conferred together. After independence in 1917 Finland initially developed relations with Poland and the Baltic Republics, but was gradually drawn into Nordic links and in 1935 Prime Minister Kivimäki declared that in future Finland would associate with Scandinavia and adopt the same neutrality policy. When Russia applied pressure on Finland in October 1939, Nordic solidarity was expressed in support for Finland, but was insufficient to ward off the wars which exacted such a heavy toll on Finland. The 1944 armistice with the USSR imposed heavy reparations (paid off by 1952). The 1947 Fenno-Soviet commercial agreement and the 1948 Treaty of Friendship, Cooperation and Mutual Assistance seemed to tie Finland closer into the Soviet orbit, but the terms were less onerous than were imposed on Romania and Hungary. While accepting them, Finland was gradually able to develop trade and cultural relationships westwards.

Diverse experiences of the Second World War were crucial determinants of subsequent security arrangements in the Nordic region. Finland's armistice with the USSR imposed neutrality by treaty. Sweden's tradition of neutrality dated from 1809 and had been maintained through the war, despite pressures alike from Allied and Axis powers. Denmark and Norway were occupied by Germany from 9 April 1940, and Iceland by Britain and the USA. However, wartime setbacks to the Danish and Norwegian economies were not recovered until about 1948, whereas Swedish ability to continue trading with prewar partners resulted in a 20 per cent rise in GNP over the six war years. Finnish war losses, both human and material, were devastating, especially where retreating German forces left 'scorched-earth' behind them, and were compounded by the need to settle a large number of refugees from Karelia, the eastern province lost to the RSFSR. The 140,000 Icelanders gained greatly from the presence (and spending) of 40,000 British and US troops. In many respects, then, the war drove the Nordic countries apart, and King Haakon's view on returning to Norway was widely shared, that 'There must be no more talk of Sweden as big brother' (Derry 1979: 352). Atlanticist and pro-British sentiment became more obvious and were strongest in Norway and Denmark, given their recent experiences of German occupation.

SECURITY ARRANGEMENTS AFTER 1945

As early as May 1945 the Swedish prime minister Per Albin Hansson proposed a Scandinavian regional defence agreement, evoking Danish agreement that whatever endangered one Scandinavian country was a threat to all. But this idea did not progress beyond the consultative stage, and fell apart in 1948. While the Swedes saw the plan as an extension of their defensive neutrality and were opposed to any link with Britain or the USA, the Norwegians would accept no alliance which might make US military supplies unavailable in emergency. As this incompatibility became clear, the Norwegians decided to join NATO. Sweden saw a bilateral pact with Denmark as too large a defence liability, so Denmark followed Norway's example, though both governments made the important reservation that they would not allow any foreign power to establish bases on their territory 'so long as it was not attacked or threatened with attack'. Later Denmark and Norway also excluded nuclear weapons and nuclear-powered vessels from their territories in peacetime (though this exclusion did not apply to the US bases already established in Greenland). Iceland was also a founder member when the Atlantic Treaty was signed on 4 April 1949, but with the larger reservations that Iceland alone would decide whether to permit bases or facilities, and would not be liable for any contributions in men or money (Derry 1979: 358). Thus from the 1930s onwards, full sovereignty for the Nordic countries has been compromised by intersecting German, Russian and Anglo-American strategic interests.

Nordic security decisions formed the basis for what came to be termed 'the Nordic Balance': the presence of neutral Sweden between Finland and the Nordic NATO members helped to reduce Russian pressures on Finland, while the reservations of the NATO members helped to keep tensions low in the Nordic region. The Nordic Balance was posited on interdependence between Soviet policy towards Finland, Swedish neutrality, and low-key behaviour by Denmark and Norway within NATO: moderation by all would bring regional stability, to the benefit of all. The idea has been much discussed, with argument mainly revolving around the extent to which the considerations actually influenced policy-making. The Finnish dimension is clearly significant in Swedish foreign policy debates, but it is more difficult to find a similar concern in Danish or Norwegian foreign policy discourse, despite the statement by the Finnish President, Urho Kekkonen, that 'traditionally each Nordic country is accustomed to taking the others into account in its decisions'.[1] The Nordic prime ministers, foreign ministers and defence ministers continue to meet regularly, but they do so outside the framework of the Nordic Council of Ministers, thus illustrating the acceptance of divergent national interests in foreign and defence policy.

FAILED ATTEMPTS AT NORDIC ECONOMIC INTEGRATION

The 1873 currency union disintegrated as the Nordic economies diverged in their development before and during the First World War, and during the inter-war years there were no systematic attempts to integrate the Nordic economies. In the 1950s a Nordic Customs Union was discussed but the plan was overtaken by the formation of EFTA, with the three Scandinavian countries among the seven founder members in 1957–60. Initial Finnish inhibitions (arising from their relationship with the USSR) were overcome in the separate FINEFTA treaty of 1961. Iceland's reluctance to share fishing grounds and her ongoing dispute with Britain over fishing rights initially kept her out of EFTA, but the need for new markets to complement the industrialisation programme, and depression in the fishing industry pushed her into membership in 1970.

To its Nordic members EFTA was a more attractive proposition than the limited Scandinavian customs union because its wider membership included the large and important UK market, as well as Portugal's traditional market for dried and salt cod. What had proved impossible in twelve years of inter-Nordic negotiations was achieved in under a year in the wider EFTA context (Sundelius and Wiklund 1979). The main hope for the proposed Nordic customs union had been to expand inter-Nordic trade, and the EFTA arrangements achieved this to a spectacular extent, especially from 1965. During the 1960s Sweden replaced the Federal Republic of Germany as the second most significant trading partner for Denmark and Norway, and EFTA did much to facilitate the transition of the Nordic economies from an agricultural to an industrial and commercial base. EFTA met the Nordic preference for a broad-based and relatively less restrictive form of trading cooperation. But still the Nordic countries were in one trading bloc with their largest trading partner, the UK, while Germany and other large European economies were beyond the rising tariff barriers of the EC.

Following the failed second attempt in 1967 to join the EC, when the UK had negotiated with Denmark and Norway in tow, the Danish Radical Liberal prime minister Hilmar Baunsgaard proposed a Nordic common market which would involve putting in place a tariff union (excluding agriculture) by 1971 as the first push towards full co-ordination of the four Nordic-EFTA economies (Iceland was not included). There were also proposals for closer cooperation on agriculture and fisheries policy, in industry, research, energy policy, education, and development aid, and to establish funds to finance developments in industrial infrastructure, agriculture, and the fishing industry. The Nordic Investment Bank was planned, for which contributions would be in proportion to respective gross national products, with Sweden responsible for 46 per cent, Denmark 24 per cent, Norway 16 per cent and Finland 14 per cent. This aroused some resentment of Swedish domination (Soloveytchik 1970), and it was eventually established in 1975.

It was clear that Denmark retained the long-term aim of EC entry, and saw Nordek as a bridging exercise which would give wider access to EC markets to all the Nordek countries while retaining Denmark's Nordic links. But the Finns were wary that any move to draw them into a closer relationship with the EC might jeopardise their good relations with the

USSR, since their 1948 Treaty of Friendship, Cooperation and Mutual Assistance was intended against renewed German aggression, and Finland did not want a potentially closer relationship with EC members to be construed as a breach of this Treaty. At the February 1970 meeting of the Nordic Council there were many expressions of goodwill for Nordek, and plans were made to sign the treaties in April. But in March Finnish misgivings led them to withdraw, at which point the Swedes expressed similar worries about their neutrality and the Norwegians their fears of Swedish financial predominance (Turner and Nordquist 1982: 109–10). Baunsgaard suggested continuing the plan as 'Skandek' without Finland, but Norway and Sweden declined, not least because the EC scenario had changed greatly. De Gaulle had retired from active French politics and, while Swedish and Finnish neutrality was still seen as a barrier to EC membership, Denmark and Norway were receiving strong indications that they would be welcome to open negotiations to join the EC.

When Britain and Denmark (with Ireland) entered the European Community in 1973 this brought the advantage that Denmark's British and German markets were within the same trading group. While the 1973 EC enlargement divided the Nordic region, this was compensated in four ways. First, the interests of the non-EC member Nordic countries were met by trade agreements with the EC; Sweden in July 1972, Norway in July 1973, and Finland (with a counterbalancing agreement with Comecon) in October 1973, giving freedom of trade in industrial goods from 1977. Trade between the Nordic countries and the EC increased substantially, so that in 1992 well over half the exports of each Nordic country went to the EC, and over half of Danish and Finnish imports came from the EC. Second, Denmark acted as a bridge from the EC to the rest of the Nordic region, keeping fellow-Nordic governments informed of EC developments. (With Sweden and Finland in the EU from 1995, Denmark may continue to perform a similar bridging role for Norway.) Third, many Swedish and other Nordic firms established bases in Denmark. Fourth, renewed efforts were made to strengthen the Nordic Council as a channel for inter-Nordic cooperation.

The elusive goal of Nordic economic integration was finally achieved on 1 January 1994 with the creation of the European Economic Area (EEA), following intense and extensive negotiations in 1990–1 (see Chapter 4). Once again, however, agreement came only within the much wider context, as a combined EC/EFTA arrangement in which the EFTA countries effectively accepted the full *acquis communautaire* of EC rules. Ironically, this state of affairs was little more than ephemeral. By the end of 1994 referendums in Austria, Finland and Sweden had confirmed their decisions to become full members of the European Union, while (as in 1972) the Norwegian referendum produced a clear-cut decision not to join. This left Iceland and Norway as the remnant of the EEA, linked by EFTA to Switzerland and Liechtenstein, while the rest of Western Europe from Galway to Vienna and Crete to Kiruna was within the European Union. During the Norwegian referendum campaign there were recurrent majorities of opinion against EU membership, but also a consistent majority which expected that Norway would be a member by the year 2000. Following the Norwegian decision not to join the EU, decisions by Norsk Hydro, Norway's largest industrial group, to abandon a 9 billion kroner (£85.2 million) plan to expand and modernise its four aluminium smelting plants in Norway and by the shipbuilding company Kværner possibly to relocate its head office from Oslo to London or Brussels[2] may hasten understanding among Norwegians of the costs of remaining outside the EU; as may disruption of the Nordic passport union, which had operated since 1952, by the appearance of customs posts and passport queues on the Norwegian–Swedish border. Such considerations prompted Denmark to apply in 1995 to join the Schengen agreement and other Nordic countries (including Norway) to consider doing so, despite Danish reservations on this score at the 1993 Edinburgh Summit of EC leaders.

STEPS TOWARDS NORDIC REGIONAL INTEGRATION: THE NORDIC COUNCIL

The Nordic Council was built on the pattern of regular meetings of the Scandinavian section of the Inter-parliamentary Union, dating back to 1907. Following an initiative by Danish prime minister Hans Hedtoft, and with strong support from Sweden and more qualified approval in Norway and Iceland, its first meeting was held in Copenhagen in 1952. The Finns were restrained by Soviet disapproval until 1955, but promptly joined when this obstacle was removed. Cooperation between the five Nordic states was formalised in 1962 in the Treaty of Helsinki.

Nordic Council plenary meetings are held annually and rotate among the five Nordic capitals. Since 1993 there have been additional autumn sessions.[3] Members of the Nordic Council comprise delegations elected from each parliament, since 1984 numbering seven from Iceland and twenty from each of the other Nordic countries. The Danish group includes two delegates from each of the legislative assemblies in the Færoes and Greenland plus sixteen from metropolitan Denmark, while the Åland Islands' assembly also sends two delegates, reducing the mainland Finnish delegation to eighteen. Funding for Nordic cooperation is by national contributions assessed in proportion to each country's share of the total Nordic gross national income.[4]

The Nordic Council acts by adopting recommendations prepared in its standing committees, or by passing specific declarations which are then acted on by ministers and officials in member states. It initiates, encourages and follows up the results of Nordic cooperation by issuing advisory resolutions and statements to the Nordic Council of ministers and to the parliaments and governments of its member states on issues of economic, legal, communications, cultural, and social and environmental cooperation. Recently defence and foreign policies have been added to the list of issues discussed. The agenda also allows for questions to the Council of Ministers and to individual governments. Elected members are allocated to the ten-member presidium or to one of the six standing committees, which cover the five policy sectors just listed plus budget and audit policy. The latter committee co-ordinates consideration in the other committees of budget proposals from the Council of Ministers and supervises the activities funded by the Council of Ministers. The President of the Council is normally the chairman of the delegation from the host country and has held office for the previous year, so that the presidium provides continuity between plenary sessions. It is assisted by the Secretariat, based in Stockholm and staffed by Nordic civil servants who act independently of their national governments. Each national delegation also has its own secretariat based in the national parliament. The committees do much of their work outside the short annual meeting session.

The parliamentary delegations are proportionally representative of the parties in the national parliaments, and four main party groupings operate within the Nordic Council: the Conservatives, Centre, Social Democrats and Left Socialists. Various small parties stand outside these groups, as do the Danish and Norwegian Progress Parties who form a Liberalist Group (*Nordisk Ministerråd* 1992: 22–3). The Centre group is rather diverse, but each of the other groups includes a single main party from each country and provides an important network for exchange of policy ideas and cooperative action. As a result of decisions at the Nordic Council in Reykjavik in March 1995, from the beginning of 1996 the roles of national Nordic secretariats, with their tendency to oppose change, will be reduced and the political planning roles of the cross-national party groups expanded. The chair-holders of the party groups will form a new 'political economy committee' to direct the policy agenda, and this is likely to bring a shift from unanimity to majority decisions – and perhaps, depending on the role of the Council of Ministers, a shift from inter-governmentalism to integrated decision-making.

Parallel to the parliamentary meetings, the government ministers covering relevant policy areas meet as the Nordic Council of Ministers, with a membership which varies according to the policy sector under discussion (as in its EU counterpart). Each country has a single vote in the Council of Ministers, and decisions have been by unanimity of those voting. Unanimous decisions are binding on governments, though in some instances national legislation requires decisions to be subject to parliamentary approval. The basis for the Council of Ministers was formalised in amendments to the Helsinki Treaty in 1971, and since then each national cabinet has included a Minister of Nordic Cooperation, with responsibility to supervise the progress of Nordic cooperation and co-ordinate Nordic policies which are not specifically covered by other cabinet colleagues. Ministers are entitled to speak in debate in the Nordic Council, but without voting rights. In practice their interventions are often decisive indications of governmental willingness or unwillingness to implement proposals. In addition to the framework set out in the Helsinki Treaty, formal cooperative arrangements have been reached in the Nordic Cultural Agreement (1971), the Nordic Transport Agreement (1972) and the Environmental Protection Convention (1974). This flurry of developments arose from the Nordek negotiations, and helped to compensate for the collapse of yet another unsuccessful attempt to integrate the Nordic economies.

Apart from the formation of SAS, the Scandinavian Airlines System, in 1947 and the passport union in 1952, one of the first achievements of Nordic cooperation was the Common Labour Market Treaty agreed in 1954 (and extended to Iceland in 1982) which has enabled over one million people (many of them Finns moving to Sweden) to live and work outside their country of origin without the need for a work permit. Specific recognition of professional qualifications has been achieved to allow freedom of movement to doctors, dentists, nurses and nursing auxiliaries, psychologists, opticians and veterinary surgeons, for example. Since the 1955 Nordic Social Security Convention, a migrant Nordic citizen has also been able to claim social security and other social rights such as health care, child benefits, social assistance, pensions or unemployment pay on the same basis as the country's own nationals. At a very specific level, Nordic hospitals cooperate on kidney transplants – it is especially important to be able to draw on a large population to achieve good tissue matches.

Very many areas of collaboration are organised through various permanent institutions, committees and other cooperative bodies (121 are listed in the 1992 directory of Nordic cooperation, *Nordiska samarbetsorgan*), some financed from the budget of the Nordic Council of Ministers and others from national contributions. Their large numbers and diversity make them difficult to categorise. Many are committees for cooperative medical and scientific research, for example for alcohol and drug research, advanced training in occupational health, or arctic medicine. In science there are institutes for particle accelerator-based research, theoretical atomic physics, physical oceanography, vulcanology, or marine biology (to name a few). There is a Nordic Economics Research Council and links between Natural Science and other research councils, plus research institutes in, for instance, the humanities, the law of the sea, European integration law, building standards and co-ordinating disability services.

As we have seen, the Nordic countries share much cultural common ground. Building on extensive previous activity, the 1971 Nordic Cultural Agreement aimed to strengthen and intensify cultural cooperation and increase efforts in joint education, research and cultural activities. Some of this work is officially encouraged, but much is sponsored by the Nordic Associations, voluntary and professional societies and individuals. For example, there are Nordic cultural institutes, such as at Kautokeino for the

Sami (Lapps), a Nordic Arts Centre in Helsinki and the Nordic Cultural Fund, based in Copenhagen, which supports all aspects of Nordic culture and the arts. Councils also exist to promote specific cultural activities, such as music and art, tourism and for the translation of Nordic literature into other Nordic languages. A Nordic Council literature prize is awarded annually for a literary work in one of the Nordic languages, and a music prize is awarded every second year.

Individual universities and colleges retain the right to accredit awards made in other countries and many students study for part or all of their qualification in another Nordic country than their own. Joint programmes of postgraduate study are offered across the Nordic region, especially within establishments such as the Nordic Institute for Studies in Urban and Regional Planning in Stockholm or the Nordic School of Public Health in Göteborg. In addition, agriculture and forestry have been identified as an area of priority for Nordic cooperation. A Nordic action programme on agriculture and forestry, for example, runs to 1995, co-ordinated by a committee of senior officials established initially in 1979. A contact organisation in this sector was established in 1961 and reorganised in 1984, while the Nordic Gene Bank was set up in 1978 to collect and store economically important agricultural and horticultural plant strains. The Nordic countries cooperate on plant breeding, plant protection, evaluation of pesticides, farm and forestry machinery, and research and development in these areas.

Environmental issues receive high priority in Nordic politics, and the 1976 Nordic Environmental Protection Convention stresses each country's responsibility for its neighbour's environment as well as its own, and gives the right to put forward views on proposed developments. The region receives extensive air pollution on winds from the south-west and south, and the Nordic countries have acted together to initiate agreement among the twenty countries represented in the Economic Commission for Europe (ECE) to reduce sulphur dioxide emissions by 30 per cent.

All seven states around the Baltic have signed a convention to protect the marine environment, and there are bilateral agreements such as the one between Denmark and Sweden to protect the Sound from pollution. A bridge/tunnel to improve road and rail links across the Sound between Copenhagen and southern Sweden was much delayed by concerns about its environmental impact on bird-life and on water circulation through this narrow strait. Since the Baltic has low salinity and very little tidal range, it was feared that these factors might be adversely affected by the bridge. The Swedish government gave the go-ahead in 1994 and work was expected to start in Autumn 1995, with the DKR 19.3 bn (£3.3 bn) cost providing a useful boost to the Danish and Swedish economies (Brown-Humes 1995: 83).

There are also Nordic financial institutions, such as the Nordic Fund for Technology and Industrial Development, the Culture Fund (established in 1976 and reviewed in 1991), and the Nordic Investment Bank (NIB), which finances collaborative private and/or public-sector ventures involving two or more Nordic countries. Projects need to be commercially viable and have included, for instance, Icelandic salmon-farmers working with Norwegian and Færoese partners, and the development of a Nordic telecommunications satellite. Further afield, the NIB has also sought to export Nordic expertise and has funded, for example, a milk-treatment plant in north-east China. Such distant activities are likely to be redirected in accordance with the priorities set at the 1995 Reykjavik session of the Nordic Council (discussed below).

Another integrational activity concerns local and regional cross-border cooperation between local authorities. This rests on a 1977 agreement and covers such local government functions as health care, communications, tourism, education, culture, the environment, or industrial and commercial promotion. Sometimes the result is the shared use of hospitals, schools, mobile libraries or fire services and geographically the areas participating can be quite large. For example, the funds and committees dealing with cross-border regional development include such areas as the West Nordic area (Greenland, Iceland and the Færoes), and even the archipelago between Stockholm, Åland and the county of Turku/Åbo in Finland. One of the earliest areas of cross-border cooperation was in Nordkalotten (the northern region where Norway, Sweden and Finland meet), established in 1971, reviewed in 1985, and extended across the Russian border in 1994 to include collaborative transport, environmental and other activities with local authorities in Murmansk and the Kola peninsula.

In twenty-two policy areas there are contact committees for senior civil servants with similar responsibilities, making it a simple matter to contact their opposite numbers in the other Nordic countries, and to check on policy details and co-ordinate proposed changes on a wide range of issues. This allows integrative initiatives and co-ordination of policy between Nordic countries without the need for a substantial bureaucracy: policies are made by national governments and implemented by their own officials, whether in departments or directorates or at county or *kommune* level as appropriate.

The achievements of the Nordic Council lie, however, not in its institutional structures but in the very many areas in which policy has been co-ordinated between the member countries during its four decades of existence. These include, in harmonising legislation among the Nordic countries, facilitating freedom of movement within the region, and establishing cooperative bodies to facilitate a closely inter-laced network of inter-Nordic cooperation on cultural, educational, and scientific projects, benefit entitlements, labour mobility, regional cross-border cooperation, and collaboration in agriculture, fisheries and forestry.

NORDIC COOPERATION BEYOND 1995

In March 1994, when terms of entry to the EC/EU for Finland, Norway and Sweden were largely agreed, the Icelandic prime minister David Oddsson began to press for a response to the 'new situation'. The initially cool response changed when it was realised that maintaining a clear commitment to Nordic cooperation could have political advantages to pro-EU governments keen to obtain a 'Yes' vote in the referendums at the end of the year. The popularity of Nordic cooperation suggested that if it were accorded a reduced commitment after EU entry, then the referendum vote would be adversely affected. For the first time, therefore, Nordic cooperation addressed the consequences of EU entry, and priority was given to culture, education and research.

In the new situation following the accession of Finland (with the Åland Islands) and Sweden to the EU, the March 1995 Reykjavik Nordic Council resolved that Nordic cooperation could be used as a platform for pursuing Nordic advantage (*nytte*) and to exert an influence on the European agenda, so as to maintain Nordic co-ordination and harmonisation of legislation. Nordic cooperation will focus on three main areas: intra-Nordic cooperation, cooperation with Europe/EU/EEA, and cooperation with the areas adjacent to the Nordic region.

Intra-Nordic cooperation would continue in pursuit of a shared perception of democracy, a healthy environment and fundamental social rights, concentrating where joint Nordic solutions confer advantages which could not be gained from national or broader international measures. This sharper focus would exclude gestures related to wider issues and would emphasise activities where tangible results could be achieved by Nordic action, demonstrate Nordic solidarity, and raise levels of Nordic competence and competitiveness. The new Nordic EU members looked to Denmark's experience of EU membership for advice. In turn Denmark remained keen on Nordic cooperation, partly to contain Swedish assertiveness and partly to solve the domestic issues arising from the Maastricht Treaty exemptions negotiated in December 1992. For example, these included the stipulation that union citizenship could in no way replace national citizenship. But Norway's 'No' revealed the need for customs and immigration control of travellers to and from Nordic countries – breaching the 1952 Nordic passport union. Denmark's response was to apply in March 1995 to join the Schengen agreement. Finland and Sweden were ready to do likewise, and Norway and Iceland also declared themselves ready to operate the necessary immigration controls (Nordic Council 1995b: 8–9).

In the European context, Nordic cooperation would aim to influence the European agenda and the co-ordinated implementation of EU/EEA directives. It would also aim to build a bridge between Nordic members of the EU and the Nordic countries which are involved in European cooperation via the EEA agreement (Iceland and Norway). EU expansion after the 1996 Intergovernmental Conference, with the possible accession of Central European countries, might lead to regional decentralisation within the EU; in that case Nordic experience and achievement would be valuable. Foreign and defence policy was thought a likely area for co-operation, and the proposal for a Nordic nuclear-weapon-free zone might be revived. But in other respects the relationship might be of competitive cooperation, as illustrated by the competition between Finnish and Swedish pulp producers and their joint concern at Danish emphasis on recycling.

In the areas adjacent to the Nordic region – the Baltic Sea and the Arctic, including the Barents Sea – developments exert a major impact on the Nordic countries. A soundly established system of cooperation with the Baltic states and northwest Russia would make a significant contribution to stability and democracy in these regions, and would be based on such factors as the responsible use of natural resources, with due regard for the unique environment and for the interests of the indigenous peoples in the Arctic region.

INTERNATIONAL COOPERATION BEYOND THE NORDIC REGION

Although all the Nordic countries are small by world standards, and two have been neutral since 1945, they have played active roles in international affairs. Beyond the Nordic Council, Nordic governments cooperate in the UN, its specialised agencies, and in other international bodies such as the General Agreement on Tariffs and Trade, the World Bank, the International Monetary Fund, the African Development Fund and the Asian Development Bank. Where appropriate they have joint spokesmen, and have sometimes succeeded, by concerted action, in nominating a Nordic national to senior positions – for example Trygve Lie, the Norwegian first Secretary General of the United Nations, his Swedish successor Dag Hammarskjöld, and the Dane Poul Hartling as UN High Commissioner for Refugees. Martti Ahtisaari, elected President of Finland in January 1994, had been the special representative of the UN Secretary General in Namibia. The three Scandinavian countries all give in excess of 1 per cent of their GNP as official assistance to developing countries and, in line with the 1968 Copenhagen Convention, revised in 1981, they co-ordinate a substantial part of this to finance joint Nordic projects in Kenya, Tanzania and Mozambique. Other important aspects of Nordic internationalism include Finland's role as host of the 1975 Conference on Security and Cooperation in Europe, and the successful Norwegian initiative in 1994 to mediate in Israel/Arab relations. A Nordic voting bloc within the EU may be expected, but its strength is reduced by Norway's 'No'.

PROSPECTIVE SCENARIOS

The Nordic identity is in crisis, argues Wæver (1992). Despite divergent security orientations, the Nordic region was defined by the 'Nordic balance', which implied a lower level of tension than the confrontation and militarisation prevailing in Central Europe. The socio-economic identity of the Scandinavian model depended on the competition between capitalism and communism, to which it offered a 'middle way' (Childs 1980). At a deeper level, and in contrast to the old Europe, the future lay in the rational, enlightened, anti-militarist Nordic society. Now the future develops from the 1989/92 Europeanisation, with its key concepts being political freedom, free markets and integration. Suddenly the sources of the future are found on the continent, not in the North. In the new and wider Europe, Northern Europe will find its place in a 'Europe of the Regions', and its region will centre on the Baltic.

While Wæver's case may be overstated, there is clearly a common concern on the part of the Nordic countries (except perhaps in Norway or Iceland) for the Baltic sea and for the ex-Soviet Baltic republics of Estonia, Latvia and Lithuania. There have been arguments to enlarge the Nordic Council to accommodate the three Baltic republics, but these are opposed on three grounds. First, widening would imply watering-down existing cooperation. Second, the agenda of the Nordic Council will increasingly be about integration with the European Union, and it would be hindered in this if the Baltic republics were members. Third, relations and possible conflicts between the Baltic republics need to be resolved before it would make sense to enlarge the Nordic Council.

It therefore seems more likely that the future lies with a council of the three Baltic republics, with which the Nordic Council could work closely. Both these bodies might also work within the Council of the Baltic States, involving representation from German federal and *Land* governments and parliamentarians with the eventual aim of bringing together everyone around the Baltic Sea from Kiel to St Petersburg. In this scenario, Nordic cooperation will continue in roughly its present form as a set of networks, but it will co-exist with one circle of European Union links and another of Baltic Sea networks. Other potential regional networks include an Arctic region growing out of existing Nordkalot links, and a west-facing set of North Atlantic links between Norway, the Færoes, Iceland and Greenland. The Nordic record indicates that, if thought of in terms of cooperation rather than integration, many such links could co-exist and be made to work.

NOTES

1 Speech by President Urho Kekkonen at the Swedish Institute of International Affairs, 8 May 1978.
2 *The Guardian* (1995), 4/2/95:39.

3 For example, the Nordic Council met in Reykjavik in February 1995 and Stockholm in 1994. Its forty-second session was in Oslo in March 1993 with an autumn session in Mariehamn, Åland, in November 1993.

4 Proportions in 1987 were Denmark: 20.5 per cent, Finland: 20.0 per cent, Iceland: 0.9 per cent, Norway: 21.5 per cent and Sweden: 37.1 per cent of a total budget for the Nordic Council of Ministers of DKR 537 million. The latter figure represents less than 0.09 per cent of Danish national income for that year.

3 The Nordic countries, the European Community (EC) and the European Free Trade Association (EFTA), 1958–84

David Phinnemore

INTRODUCTION

The Nordic countries have rarely been at the forefront of efforts designed to promote integration and cooperation in Western Europe. None gave serious consideration in the 1950s to joining up with the Six in developing integration through the creation of the supranational institutions. Preference was generally given to intergovernmental cooperation and subsequently the pursuit of trade interests through the European Free Trade Association (EFTA). Consequently, prior to 1995, only Denmark was to become a member of the European Community (EC). However, the Nordic countries did not remain aloof from developments in Western Europe. For trade reasons, relations with the EC were, from the outset, often at the top of each country's foreign policy agenda. Hence, for much of the period 1958–84 a primary foreign policy objective of the Nordics was accommodation with Brussels.

The purpose of this chapter is to chart the development of Nordic relations with the EC during the period from 1958 until 1984. The chapter begins by outlining the basic determinants in the policies of the Nordic countries towards European integration and cooperation. Thereafter, it reflects upon Nordic involvement in the early years of EFTA and the individual responses of the Nordic countries to the various attempts made by the United Kingdom to gain membership of the EC. Attention is also paid to the level of support government policies enjoyed. The overall impression to be gained is that for reasons of trade, each of the Nordic governments was generally keen to establish where necessary some form of relationship with the Community. The chapter then deals with the first enlargement of the EC in 1973 and the formal accommodation of the Nordic countries either as members or as signatories of free trade agreements. The development of Nordic-EC relations over the ensuing decade provides the focus for the remainder of the chapter.

POLICY DETERMINANTS

For the Nordic countries, the main factor encouraging involvement in the processes of European integration and cooperation has been economic. Denmark, Finland, Iceland, Norway and Sweden have all traditionally relied on trade for a relatively high proportion of their gross domestic product (GDP). For most of the period 1950–70 exports made up 20–25 per cent of GDP (Miljan 1977: 51). Thereafter the level tended to remain fairly constant, if not rise. Hence, by 1987 exports made up between 22.4 per cent (Finland) and 28.0 per cent (Sweden) of GDP. In the case of Iceland, which relies on fish and marine products for 70–90 per cent of its exports, the share of exports in its GDP rose significantly from 16.1 per cent in 1958 to 25.7 per cent in 1987 (Wijkman 1990: 8).

The major market for Nordic exports has been Western Europe. Between 1950 and 1970 the percentage of these exports taken by the region rose from 69 per cent to 72 per cent (Miljan 1977: 288). Notable increases were to follow. Hence, by 1987, the West European market accounted for 79.6 per cent of Norway's exports (Wijkman 1990: 16). While this shows a marked dependence on the West European market, when the figures are broken down the major determinants in the early integration policies of the Nordic countries become clear. The first of these determinants was the importance of the Nordic market. From 1950 to 1970 the percentage of exports going to this regional market rose on average from 15 per cent to 23 per cent. For the Nordic countries, therefore, there was much to be said for consolidating access to that market. Moreover, any changes in European trade policy by one Nordic country would lead to re-evaluations by the others.

However, a second major determinant was trade with the United Kingdom. During the 1950s and 1960s, the United Kingdom was generally the single most important trading partner in Western Europe for the Nordic countries. While Finland, Norway and Sweden relied on the UK market for 14–23 per cent of exports, Danish dependence, initially at least, was even greater. In 1950 the United Kingdom received 42 per cent of Danish exports. This had fallen, however, to 19 per cent by 1970 (Miljan 1977: 290). Nevertheless, the importance of the United Kingdom as a trading partner could not be overstated. Consequently, the development of each Nordic country's policy towards the EC was often heavily influenced by the development of UK policy.

When combined, the Nordic and UK markets thus accounted for approximately 38 per cent of Nordic countries' exports during the 1950s and 1960s. This allowed the countries to remain outside the EC's Common External Tariff (CET) without adverse effect on their exports. However, the fact that the EC's share of Nordic countries' exports stood at 26–29 per cent during this period meant that access to the markets of the Six was also of considerable importance. This was particularly the case as far as Danish agricultural exports to the EC were concerned. Moreover, were either the United Kingdom or any of the Nordic countries to accede to the EC, the latter's importance would increase considerably. Thus, a relationship with Brussels would have to be created which could secure, to the greatest possible extent, the existing bases for trade between the Nordic countries and the new members of the Community.

While the economic importance of Western Europe was the major factor in forcing Nordic countries to consider and participate in the processes of European integration and cooperation, political factors have acted as significant constraints on actual participation, especially in the supranational EC. Two factors were of particular importance. The first of these – a strong attachment to national identity and national sovereignty – was common to all the Nordic countries and reflected recent historical experiences. Each of the countries, with the exception of Sweden, had suffered foreign occupation during the Second World War and were initially determined to reassert and maintain their identity as independent states. Moreover, Norway (1905) and Iceland (1944) had only gained their independence from Sweden and Denmark respectively, comparatively recently. Consequently, there was considerable reluctance to participate in projects involving a transfer of sovereign powers to supranational institutions. This was accompanied by a sense of traditional detachment from the European mainland and desire on the part of the Danes, the Icelanders and the Norwegians not to undermine the NATO-based and pro-Atlanticist orientation of their foreign policies. In this respect there was considerable convergence with the views of the United Kingdom (Stålvant 1982: 113–14).

The second constraint was specific to Finland and Sweden. Their status as neutrals had traditionally been regarded as incompatible with membership of supranational organisations.[1] For most of the period under discussion therefore, Sweden and, in particular, Finland were unable to consider membership of the EC as a realistic policy option if they wished to retain the credibility of their neutrality policies (Stålvant 1974: 405–28). In the case of Finland, there was a further policy constraint. This was the need to place relations with any Western European organisation, whether economic or political, intergovernmental or supranational, within the context of the country's special relationship with the USSR.

1957–61 TOWARDS A EUROPE OF SIXES AND SEVENS

When the Six established the European Community (EC) in 1958, none of the Nordic countries was inclined to become a member. With the United Kingdom intent on remaining outside the new Community, the economic benefits of joining were limited. Moreover, all the Nordic countries were generally sceptical of the EC's supranationalism. In the cases of Finland and Sweden their status as neutrals prohibited any real consideration of membership. Nevertheless, a desire to see a Europe-wide liberalisation of trade had seen each of the Nordics respond favourably to the United Kingdom's proposal in 1956 for a European free trade area among the members of the Organisation for European Economic Cooperation (OEEC).[2] However, the failure of the subsequent negotiations led the Nordics to focus their attention on developing alternative trade-based arrangements. Initially, consideration was given to reviving the option of a Nordic Customs Union. Yet progress proved to be elusive. Consequently, emphasis was placed on Swedish-UK proposals for a free trade area among the industrialised OEEC member states outside the EC. Hence, in November 1959, following generally positive discussions with other OEEC members, Denmark, Norway and Sweden joined with Austria, Portugal, Switzerland and the United Kingdom (the so-called 'Seven') in signing the Stockholm Convention establishing the European Free Trade Association (EFTA) (Urwin 1991: 96–7; EFTA 1987: 117–38).[3]

The Association was attractive to the Nordics on three grounds. First, the Stockholm Convention provided for a loose intergovernmental structure which failed to raise concerns about 'sovereignty' and 'supranationalism' in the member countries.[4] Second, the primary aim of EFTA was the establishment of free trade in industrial goods between the member states through the removal of tariffs and quantitative restrictions over a ten-year period. For the Nordic countries, this would facilitate the development of trade and provide some compensation for trade lost as a result of the moves towards the establishment by the EC of its CET (Camps 1964: 210–31; Gellner 1960: 15–23). For the Danes, however, the exclusion of agriculture from EFTA's rules was a drawback. Danish farmers were eager to gain access to new markets as a result of their exclusion from the EC's Common Agricultural Policy (CAP).[5] This was compensated for in part by EFTA's third attraction – the promotion of trade relations ('bridge-building') with the EC. However, progress in this area was limited. Despite Denmark being a most persistent and eager advocate of 'bridge-building' between EFTA and the EC, initiatives from the EFTA side were consistently ignored by the Six. Consequently, Denmark was soon converted to the idea that EC membership was the only real European policy option available. This conversion was reinforced by Denmark's failure to make any significant progress in promoting agricultural trade within the Association (Hansen 1969: 40).

Nordic priorities within EFTA were, however, realised as far as relations with Finland were concerned. Early Swedish pressure led to discussions in May 1960 on Finland being granted associate membership of EFTA. The Finns were naturally keen to establish such a relationship given that 34 per cent of the country's exports went to markets of the Seven. However, prior to the establishment of an association, Finland was obliged to conclude a tariff agreement with the USSR granting the latter the same access to Finnish markets as Finland would be granting to the EFTA states. With relations with the USSR thus settled and despite limited enthusiasm from the non-Nordic members of EFTA, the so-called FINEFTA association agreement was eventually signed on 27 March 1961 (Camps 1964: 351–2; Sorsa 1974: 463; Törnudd 1969: 64–5).

Apart from the Danes, the Nordic states generally saw in EFTA an adequate basis for trade liberalisation. However, once the United Kingdom had decided that EFTA did not offer the economic and political influence it desired and the Macmillan government made known its wish to apply for EC membership, the value of EFTA as an alternative to the EC for the other members decreased considerably.

1961–3 MEMBERSHIP, ASSOCIATION OR 'WAIT AND SEE'

The centrality of the United Kingdom to the Nordics' European policies was most clearly emphasised in 1961 when the United Kingdom submitted its first application for membership of the EC. The Danes immediately followed suit by applying on 10 August 1961. The Norwegians also applied but not until April 1962. Political and constitutional reasons lay behind the delay (Lambert 1962a: 350–60; Allen 1979: 45–51). The Swedes, meanwhile, also sought an arrangement with the Six, while the Icelanders and the Finns observed developments with interest.

The Danish government welcomed the United Kingdom's decision to apply for EC membership. Indeed, the Danes had actually been urging the United Kingdom to submit an application (Steininger 1993: 214), since an arrangement between Denmark and the EC was becoming more urgent given the agreement among the Six on the fundamentals of the CAP. Moreover, domestic opinion favoured membership. Hence, the Danish application to the EC was widely supported both within the *Folketing* and among the people. With the exception of the Communists and the Socialist People's Party, all political groups generally welcomed the government's attempt to join the EC. However, the *Folketing* did impose three conditions on the Danish government. First, Denmark was only to seek membership together with the United Kingdom. Second, and in line with the London Declaration of EFTA states in June 1961, full regard had to be given to the interests of the other EFTA states in the negotiations. Finally, the importance of continuing and increasing Nordic cooperation had to be taken into consideration (Closse 1964: 715–34).[6]

As for public opinion, polls in 1961 indicated that 53 per cent of Danes favoured joining the EC alongside the United Kingdom. Only 9 per cent of people were wholly against. However, the decision to apply for membership did lead to the creation of the so-called 'anti-Rome' committees and a tradition of popular anti-EC movements in Denmark. During 1962 support for membership did drop to 41 per cent with the majority of people unsure (51 per cent). By 1963, however, the figure in favour of joining the EC had recovered to 49 per cent, although the 'don't knows' still stood at 44 per cent (Hansen 1969: 30–8).

In the case of Norway, the United Kingdom's application did not receive an enthusiastic welcome since it forced the government to address the membership issue. However, given that the country would be dependent on an enlarged EC including the United Kingdom and Denmark for over 40 per cent of its trade, the government had little choice but to submit an application for membership. Nevertheless, while the decision to apply was taken with less enthusiasm than in Denmark, the prospect of membership alongside a pro-Atlanticist United Kingdom hostile to supranationalism meant that Norway's fears concerning the political implications of involvement in the EC were lessened. Moreover, security considerations pointed towards membership as the most appropriate course to follow given the United Kingdom's application and US support for enlargement (Allen 1979: 45–7; Closse 1964: 734–52).

Within the *Storting* a clear majority (113 out of 150 MPs) in favour of a membership application did exist. However, the governing Labour Party was not united on the issue and there were clear divisions among the Liberals and within the Christian People's Party. Only the Conservatives were wholly supportive of membership. Strong opposition came from the Centre party and the far left, and seemed to reflect popular misgivings about acceding to the EC. Indeed, support for membership among the Norwegian population did little to encourage the government. While more people tended to favour membership, the actual number supporting accession did not rise significantly above 35 per cent during 1961–2 (Allen 1979: 48–50; Turner and Nordquist 1982: 135–6; Hanssen and Sandegren 1969: 50–6).

While Denmark and Norway followed the United Kingdom in applying for membership of the EC, Sweden responded to the events of 1961 by joining Austria and Switzerland in applying for an association agreement with the EC (Nydegger 1962: 1–15; Lambert 1962b: 444–52; Lisein-Norman 1974: 15–31). In doing so, the Swedish Social Democrat government was endeavouring to reconcile the perceived need to create a close economic relationship with the enlarged EC, while maintaining the country's traditional and widely supported policy of neutrality. Hence, jointly with the other two neutrals, Sweden formulated a series of neutrality reservations which would have to be met in any association with the EC (Lange 1962a: 414–19; Lange 1962b: 438–43). Such a cautious approach, however, did not command universal support domestically. While the Centre Party and the Confederation of Trade Unions supported the government, the Conservatives, the Liberals and Swedish industry favoured actual membership of the EC. The left-wing of the Social Democratic Party and the Communists, meanwhile, wished for nothing more than a trade agreement with the Community (Bergquist 1971: 39–56; Hancock 1972: 428).

As for Finland and Iceland, both adopted a 'wait and see' policy towards the EC during this period. For Finland, a trade-based arrangement with the Community would have been desirable had the other Nordic countries acceded to or established an association with the EC. However, given that any moves in this direction were likely to incur the wrath of the USSR, particularly in light of the 1961 'note crisis', Finland failed to make any overtures to Brussels in 1961–3 (Miljan 1977: 260). Iceland, meanwhile, did make its position known to the EC. However, given widespread domestic disagreement over the policy to be pursued, the government refrained from making any formal moves until it was known how the EC intended accommodating the other EFTA states (Eggertsson 1975: 95).

1963–9 REASSESSING OPTIONS

With the collapse of the EC–UK negotiations following de Gaulle's veto in January 1963, all attempts by the Nordic countries to find some form of bilateral accommodation with the Community were halted.[7] Instead, enthusiasm for EFTA was revived. Hence agreement was reached in 1963 on plans to accelerate the envisaged tariff reductions between the member states. These were duly completed three years ahead of schedule in 1966. Moreover, the value of EFTA, particularly to its Nordic members was becoming more apparent as intra-EFTA trade rose. By 1970 the Nordic countries had seen their trade within EFTA increase by 284 per cent (Turner and Nordquist 1982: 133–4). Also, Finland was becoming more directly involved in EFTA discussions. However, the enthusiasm soon dwindled as a result of the United Kingdom's decision in 1964 to impose a 15 per cent surcharge on imports from EFTA countries. This denied the Nordics significant preferential access to the United Kingdom market and thus undermined the main reason for being part of the Association (Urwin 1991: 118, 127).

Consequently, when in May 1967 the United Kingdom reapplied for membership of the EC, the Danish and Norwegian governments were again quick to follow suit. As in 1961, the Danish government warmly welcomed the United Kingdom's application. Moreover, popular support for membership had increased. Opinion polls suggested that 56 per cent of the electorate would vote in favour of joining, while only 7 per cent said they would vote against (Hansen 1969: 30; Sauerberg 1992: 75).[8]

In Norway, enthusiasm for membership within the *Storting* appeared to have increased. During the parliamentary vote in July 1967, only 13 votes were cast against reapplying for membership. Moreover, 1967 represented a high point in public support with figures suggesting that a clear majority of the population would support membership in a referendum. However, much of the support was based on a strong belief that the French would not allow negotiations to take place (Allen 1979: 51–5; Hanssen and Sandegren 1969: 56–7; Brundtland 1968: 169–83).

While Finland and Iceland, as in 1961, maintained policies of 'wait and see' (Stålvant 1974: 408–9; Törnudd 1969: 67–70), Sweden's Social Democratic government's response to the United Kingdom's second application was more positive. On 27 July 1967, it submitted to Brussels an 'open' application for 'extensive, close and durable relations in a form compatible with continued pursuit of Swedish neutrality'. Although not made explicit, the wording was designed so as not to rule out the possibility of actual membership of the EC. This reflected a belief that French policy towards the EC, the 1966 Luxembourg Compromise and France's withdrawal from the military structures of NATO had made EC membership a possibility worth exploring (Mousson-Lestang 1990: 84; Andrén 1975: 55). Moreover, domestic support for membership among politicians appeared to be increasing (Bonham 1969: 149–61).

With de Gaulle casting his second veto on UK membership of the EC in November 1967, attempts by the Nordic countries to develop bilateral arrangements with Brussels were once again halted. For the Danes in particular, this led to a revival in interest in plans for the creation of a Nordic Common Market (Nordek) (Arter 1993: 153). However, this was essentially seen as either a temporary diversion from, or a stepping-stone towards, the main objective of obtaining some form of accommodation with the EC (Miljan 1977: 178–9; Ueland 1975: 1–19).

In a move unrelated to de Gaulle's veto, Iceland applied for membership of EFTA on 23 January 1969. This came against a background of depression in the Icelandic fishing industry, efforts in the 1960s to promote industrialisation within the domestic economy, and the increasing need for access to neighbouring markets to ensure the success of the industrialisation programme. Iceland subsequently negotiated a membership agreement with EFTA involving a ten-year transition period for the reduction of its import duties. This agreement was then ratified by the *Althingi* with thirty-four votes in favour and seven against thus enabling Iceland to join EFTA on 1 March 1970 (Eggertsson 1975: 95–6; Sparring 1972: 396; Hannibalsson 1989–90: 15–17).

1969–73 ACCOMMODATION WITH BRUSSELS

With de Gaulle having resigned the French Presidency in April 1969, the prospects for an enlargement of the EC improved dramatically. For the Nordics, this immediately reduced the importance of the negotiations towards the creation of Nordek, most notably in the case of Denmark. Indeed, once the Finns withdrew from the Nordek negotiations, few attempts were made by either the Danish, Norwegian or Swedish governments to revive the proposed customs union (Urwin 1991: 142–3).

However, de Gaulle's departure also led to a shift back towards supranationalism within the EC. In October 1970 the Community's foreign ministers accepted the Davignon Report on foreign policy cooperation. This had the effect of forcing most of the Nordic countries, particularly Sweden, to consider closely exactly what type of relationship they wished to establish with the EC. Not surprisingly, the Swedish government announced in March 1971 that EC membership was no longer a policy option. Instead, Sweden would seek a customs union with the EC (Miljan 1977: 251–8; Andrén 1975: 55; Lisein-Norman 1974: 33–47). In the case of Norway, the renewed enthusiasm for integration among the Six meant support for membership declined. Indeed, while the Danes welcomed the renewed possibility of acceding to the EC, opposition to membership in Norway was becoming more pronounced. A popular movement opposed to entry was gaining support and splits over membership within parliament and within political parties eventually led to the collapse of the Borten government in March 1971. The incoming minority government of Trygve Bratelli then committed itself to a consultative referendum on the question of accession to the EC (Allen 1979: 84–113).

Despite the prospect of further integration among the Six, the fact that enlargement of the EC now appeared imminent forced Finland to move away from its traditional 'wait and see' policy for the first time. The need to retain access to the UK, Norwegian and Danish markets was vital. Hence, in April 1970 the Finnish government made it known that it wished to conclude a free trade agreement with the EC (Hancock 1972: 429–31; Mäentakanen 1978: 29–30). In Iceland, the success of the country's industrialisation programme was dependent on free trade with the EFTA countries. Hence, fears of losing its duty-free access to EFTA markets if EC enlargement were to go ahead, led the country's coalition government to follow the Finns in November 1970 and present its case to the EC for a free trade arrangement. Despite the defeat of the government in the 1971 election and the victory of a more independent-minded coalition led by the Progressive Party, the application to the EC was not withdrawn (Sparring 1972: 393–5; Gíslason 1971: 20–1).

The actual membership negotiations with Denmark and Norway opened in June 1971. Those with Denmark generally proceeded problem-free (Miljan 1977: 211–15). However, in the case of Norway, continuing disagreement on the fisheries chapter meant that the conclusion of negotiations was delayed until mid-January 1972. Shortly thereafter, on 22 January 1972, Denmark and Norway joined with the United Kingdom and Ireland in signing accession treaties with the EC (Miljan 1977: 211–15; Allen 1979: 114–27).

As far as Finland, Iceland and Sweden were concerned, negotiations towards the conclusion of appropriate agreements with the EC began in December 1971 (Nicholson and East 1987: 145–54). Sweden, for its part, favoured an arrangement based upon a customs union and involvement in the CAP. It nevertheless retained the neutrality reservations it had jointly formulated with Austria and Switzerland in 1961. While the Swedish government dropped its request for CAP involvement early on in the negotiations, it maintained a desire to be involved in cooperation with the EC in a wide variety of non-commercial areas. However, the EC was unwilling to accommodate many of the Swedish requests. Hence, the agreement which Sweden signed on 22 July 1972 was essentially restricted to establishing free trade with the EC in industrial goods (Hakovirta 1988: 128–30; Stålvant 1974: 236–45; Åkström 1971: 421–8; Binswanger and Mayrzedt 1972: 35–42).

The Finnish government, meanwhile, adopted a more minimalist approach than the Swedes. The reason for this was the need to ensure that the proposed arrangement could be reconciled with the country's policy of neutrality. The Finns thus preferred the creation of a simple commercial arrangement with the EC leading to free trade in industrial goods and a maximisation of Finnish timber exports. In addition, access to the EC market was sought for Finnish agricultural goods. The fact that Finnish aspirations corresponded fairly closely with what the EC was willing to offer, ensured that the negotiations proceeded more smoothly than with the Swedes. Nevertheless, the signing of the agreement with Finland was delayed owing to the collapse of the Paasio government in July 1972 and the need to reorganise relations with the Soviet Union in the light of the agreement with the EC. On the latter, Finland concluded a cooperation agreement with the Council for Mutual and Economic Assistance in spring 1973, and thereafter tariff reduction agreements with the individual members. This allowed the agreement with the EC to be signed on 5 October 1973 (Sorsa 1974: 464–70; Stålvant 1974: 419–20; Mäentakanen 1978: 30–1; Muoser 1986: 196–9).

For Iceland, there were two objectives: reciprocal free trade in industrial goods with the EC; and, more importantly, duty-free access to EC markets for fish and fish products (Gíslason 1971: 20–1). While initially the EC was generally understanding of Iceland's position and accommodated this in the free trade agreement signed on 22 July 1972, disputes arising from Reykjavik's unilateral declaration of a 50-mile fishing limit meant that free trade in fishery products became conditional on the question of West German and UK access to Icelandic waters being resolved (Sparring 1972: 397).

The free trade agreements signed by the Nordic countries with the EC were practically identical on most points (Bernitz 1986: 567–90; Moxon Browne 1973: 337–42; Wellenstein 1973: 137–49). Each provided for the gradual establishment of free trade in industrial goods over a period of four and a half years and the removal of all tariff barriers and quantitative restrictions on such trade by 1984. In addition, a joint executive committee was set up to oversee the implementation of the agreements. Each of the agreements, except that with Finland, also included a so-called 'evolutionary clause'. In the cases of Norway and Sweden, this contained provision for the development of relations in areas of 'common interest' not covered by the agreement. In the agreement with Iceland, cooperation was restricted to 'economic matters' only (EFTA 1987: 152).

Once the accession and free trade agreements had been signed, each had to be ratified by the signatory states. In the cases of Denmark and Norway this involved a referendum. In the remaining Nordic countries, ratification was by parliamentary vote.

The first of the two Nordic referendums was held in Norway on 25 September 1972 and followed a long, bitter, intense and closely fought campaign which split the governing Labour Party and indeed the country. In a turnout of 77.6 per cent, the Norwegian people voted against EC membership by 53.5 per cent to 46.5 per cent. Consequently, and although the referendum was technically only consultative, it was immediately made known that Norway would not be joining the EC (Allen 1979: 128–68; Arter 1993: 173–9). The negative outcome of the referendum also brought about the collapse of the Labour government and the creation of a minority coalition led by the Christian People's Party. Its first objective was to secure a free trade agreement with the EC similar to those signed with the other EFTA states. Negotiations towards such an agreement began on 16 February 1973 and were swiftly concluded two months later. Following unanimous approval by the *Storting* on 24 May 1973, Norway's free trade agreement with the EC entered into force on 1 July 1973 (Allen 1979: 169–83; Noreng 1972: 27–40).

In Denmark, the referendum took place on 2 October 1972. This followed a parliamentary vote on 8 September 1972 in which the *Folketing* voted by 141 votes in favour to 34 against EC membership.[9] The subsequent referendum also produced a majority in favour. In a turnout of 90.1 per cent, membership was accepted by 63.4 per cent to 36.6 per cent. This represented an overall majority (57 per cent) of the electorate. With ratification complete, Denmark acceded to the EC as the first Nordic member on 1 January 1973 (Miljan 1977: 182–9; Arter 1993: 164–5).[10]

In Sweden, ratification also proceeded smoothly. The *Riksdag* voted overwhelmingly (298 to 15) in favour of the free trade agreement on 12 December 1972. However, doubts were raised by the Liberal and Conservative parties concerning the adequacy of the agreement as a mechanism for regulating the country's relations with the EC. Concerns were raised over the limited scope of the goods covered by the agreement and the weak commitment of the EC to cooperation in areas other than trade. Consequently, calls were made for a renegotiation of the treaty and for Sweden to become a full EC member (Stålvant 1974: 425). Moreover, it appears that a majority of the elite in Sweden in 1972–3 preferred a closer agreement with the EC, including membership, than that which had been concluded (Hancock 1974: 225–42). Nevertheless, the Swedish free trade agreement duly entered into force in 1 January 1973.

In Iceland, however, the process was not so smooth. The disputes over fishing limits meant that ratification of the free trade agreement was delayed until 28 February 1973. Consequently, the agreement did not enter into force until 1 April 1973. Finland's agreement with the EC eventually entered into force on 1 January 1974 following ratification by the

Eduskunta (141 to 36 votes) on 16 November 1973. Parliamentary support for the agreement came from the newly formed majority coalition government of Kalevi Sorsa (Social Democrats, Centre Party, Swedish Party, Liberals) and the Conservatives. The only parliamentary party to oppose ratification was the communist People's Democratic League (Mäentakanen 1978: 30–1, 35–7; Singleton 1974: 68–71).

1973–84 IMPLEMENTATION AND CONSOLIDATION

With Denmark having joined the EC and the free trade agreements having entered into force, each of the Nordics now had a contractual relationship with the Community. However, this did not mean that the question of relations with Brussels had been resolved for good. As noted, the Swedes were not entirely satisfied with the outcome of their negotiations. Moreover, the majority of the agreements contained evolutionary clauses. There was thus scope for a further development in relations. Also, the Danes had to come to terms with membership.

Denmark's enthusiasm for the EC prior to accession did not translate into active and dynamic membership after 1973. This was despite the net annual gains the Danes were making from the EC by the late 1970s (Turner and Nordquist 1982: 169). Indeed, Denmark was soon regarded as one of the Community's foremost 'foot-draggers', advocating a minimalist approach to integration. This was accompanied by opinion poll findings consistently showing the Danes as having the most negative attitudes towards 'Europe'. Moreover, during Denmark's first ten years as an EC member popular support for membership declined from 57 per cent in the referendum to a low of 31 per cent in 1983. This decline was mirrored by the support given to the anti-EC parties in the first two European Parliament elections. These parties, including the People's Movement against the European Community, polled 32.5 per cent of the vote in 1979 and 31.3 per cent in 1984, gaining a total of five seats each time (Sauerberg 1992: 69; Sørensen and Væver 1992: 13).

In the other four Nordic countries, the general satisfaction with the agreements evident in the overwhelming parliamentary majorities in favour of ratification, was also evident as their implementation proceeded smoothly and according to schedule. Hence, by 1977 most tariffs on industrial trade between the EC and the member states of EFTA had been abolished.[11] The remaining tariffs on mainly sensitive products such as paper, had been removed by 1984. Despite this success, there was little, if any, spillover into other areas of cooperation. Moreover, in spite of calls from EFTA leaders at their Vienna Summit in 1977 for closer cooperation between the EC and the member states of EFTA (EFTA 1987: 155–9), the poor economic climate of the 1970s and the EC's preoccupation with its own enlargement to include Greece and the negotiations on Lomé III meant that little was forthcoming. Nevertheless, this did not mean that the question of relations with the EC failed to appear on domestic political agendas.

In Norway, the question of EC membership remained a political taboo for at least a decade. Nevertheless, Norway was keen to develop links with the EC. Indeed, of all the Nordics, it was Norway which was most prominent in pursuing closer cooperation with the EC, whether multilaterally via EFTA, or on a bilateral basis. Hence, there were proposals in 1976 to use EFTA as a means for promoting cooperation with the Community on economic and monetary questions; Norwegian participation in the so-called 'snake'; and, after 1980, close contacts with the European Political Cooperation (EPC) process. Moreover, cooperation, particularly concerning fishery issues and the reduction of non-tariff barriers to trade, developed on the basis of the free trade agreement's evolutionary clause (Allen 1979: 219–25; Kristinsson 1994: 93; Turner and Nordquist 1982: 168–9).

In Sweden, any discussion of establishing a more developed relationship with the EC soon dried up after 1973 as the Palme government pursued a stringent policy of independence from bloc politics and, after 1976, the country endured a series of weak non-socialist coalition governments which failed to prioritise relations with the EC. The position of governments was made more difficult given the prominence within coalitions of the anti-EC Centre Party. Nevertheless, bureaucratic contacts with Brussels were developed and attempts made to use the free trade agreement's evolutionary clause. Moreover, with a return to office of the Social Democrats in the early 1980s, clear political signals were given that Sweden wished to consider extended cooperation with the EC. Hence, once the Copenhagen Summit of EC leaders in 1982 had agreed in principle to establish an internal market without frontiers, the Prime Minister, Olof Palme, was quick to indicate his government's desire not to be left isolated from developments (Ross 1991: 118–19; Viklund 1989: 30–2; Turner and Nordquist 1982: 167).

In Finland, the question of relations with the EC did not enter on to the political agenda to the same extent. For the most part, the government was satisfied with the implementation of the free trade agreement, except where the EC's restrictive interpretation of certain clauses on trade in steel and paper were concerned (Väyrynen 1979: 12–13). Moreover, the absence of an evolutionary clause in Finland's agreement did not mean that the country excluded itself from the areas of cooperation the EFTA states were pursuing with the Community (Antola 1981: 46–7; Wellenstein 1983: 722–3). Nevertheless, the country's relationship with the USSR meant that Finnish involvement was often more guarded.

In the case of Iceland the continuation of disputes with the United Kingdom and West Germany over fishing rights until mid-1976 clearly marred relations with the EC. Nevertheless, the adequacy of the free trade agreement in providing market access for Iceland's exports was not seriously challenged. This reflected the general consensus among political parties on Iceland's foreign economic policy. However, as the EC's share of Icelandic exports was rising from 16 per cent in 1972 to 54 per cent in 1986 and the Community began to reform its Common Fisheries Policy in the early 1980s, an upgrading of relations could not be ruled out. The favoured approach was multilateral via EFTA (Kristinsson 1987: 247–52; Kristinsson 1989: 22–3).

The increased consideration being given to relations with the EC within the Nordic states was accompanied in the early 1980s by a more positive attitude towards EFTA on the part of the EC. This reflected the fact that politically it was in the interests of the EC to intensify relations with its main trading partner, particularly in a time of economic recession (Church 1991: 11). Hence, recognition that bilateral cooperation after the Vienna Summit in 1977 had only been pursued in a limited number of areas meant that Swedish proposals for the development of a new EC–EFTA dialogue were warmly received by the French Presidency of the EC Council of Ministers. These led to the first EC–EFTA ministerial meeting in Luxembourg in April 1984 and the beginning of a new relationship (Pedersen 1988: 6).

CONCLUSION

One assessment of the Nordic countries' attitudes towards European integration in the period up until the mid-1970s concluded by labelling them all 'reluctant Europeans' (Miljan 1977: 284). Such a conclusion is an accurate reflection of Nordic attitudes towards supranationalism. It accounts for the Norwegian 'No' in 1972 and the minimalist approach towards integration adopted by the Danes as members of the EC. However, it does not appreciate the various approaches made by the individual Nordic countries towards establishing purposeful relations with the EC. Each of the Nordics' policies tended to be shaped by events outside the control of governments. Hence, the position of the UK and the other Nordics and the need to maintain credible neutrality policies tended to determine the timing and nature of individual approaches to Brussels. Moreover, the actual free trade agreements concluded with the EC often fell short of the relationship desired. As a result, the Nordics outside the Community showed little reluctance in subsequently consolidating relations.

NOTES

1 For further details on the neutral countries and European integration during the period 1958–84, see Binswanger and Mayrzedt 1970; Boyens 1963: 401–10.
2 The four Nordic OEEC members – Denmark, Iceland, Norway and Sweden – played essentially peripheral roles in the ensuing negotiations. Denmark, however, was active in advocating the inclusion of agriculture in the proposed agreement. Iceland was perceived as a 'peripheral country' and it was envisaged

that the OEEC would devise special arrangements to accommodate the specific problems with her economy. Finland held observer status in the OEEC and was not involved in the negotiations (Miljan 1977: 116–42; Camps 1964: 93–172).

3 Iceland was not invited to take part in the EFTA negotiations due to an unsettled dispute with the UK over fishing rights and the country's restrictive economic system and illiberal trade policy (Eggertsson 1975: 95).

4 See, for example, Berge 1972: 134–77.

5 The Danish Liberal Party voted against ratification of the Stockholm Convention on the grounds that it was a highly unsatisfactory arrangement for Danish farmers (Hansen 1969: 22–4, 32, 40).

6 While the first and second of these requirements were adhered to, the Danish government responded coolly to Swedish proposals in 1961 for a new treaty on Nordic cooperation (Hansen 1969: 41–2).

7 The Danes were offered the possibility of membership of, or an association with, the EC by de Gaulle. However, the offer was turned down (Miljan 1977: 176).

8 As in 1961, the *Folketing* made Danish EC membership contingent on the UK joining. However, in a change to the conditions previously placed on the government, the reference to EFTA solidarity was dropped thus providing a further indication of the limited importance the Danes now attached to EFTA. In place of the EFTA commitment was an 'expectation' that the interests of the other Nordic countries would be accommodated in arrangements with the EC (Hansen 1969: 42–3).

9 According to the Danish Constitution (Section 20), a referendum would be required in order that the 1972 Accession Treaty could be ratified unless the *Folketing* voted for ratification by a 5/6 majority. According to Section 42 of the Danish Constitution, a 1/3 majority in the *Folketing* may also force a referendum on a bill. Although the outcome of the parliamentary vote in September 1972 meant that a referendum was now constitutionally required, the Social Democratic Party had already indicated in 1971 that it would use its 35 per cent of the seats in the *Folketing* to force a referendum.

10 Having been granted home rule by Denmark in 1979, Greenland left the EC on 1 January 1984. The region's departure followed a referendum in February 1982 in which 52 per cent of the people in a turnout of 74.9 per cent voted against remaining in the EC. The Færo Islands, which also enjoy home rule within Denmark, have remained outside the EC since 1973 (Arter 1993: 166–7).

11 According to its agreement with the EC, Iceland had until 1980 to abolish the equivalent tariffs.

4 The Nordic countries and the European Economic Area (EEA)[1]

Sieglinde Gstöhl

'EVER CLOSER COOPERATION'

It can be argued that two considerations have dominated the history of EC–EFTA relations – namely determining the scope and the level of success of strategies for cooperation between the two trading blocs. In particular, the European Free Trade Association (EFTA) countries were presented with several options in order to deal with the emerging European Community (EC). In short, the scope of EFTA cooperation with the EC could range into four categories; first, no participation in the EC's integration efforts; second, the pursuit of a sectoral case-by-case approach; third, a comprehensive approach covering most of the issue areas of Community integration, or finally, seeking full EC membership. In addition, more than one strategy could be adopted in order to facilitate the scope of cooperation. The EFTA countries could unilaterally or bilaterally adapt to EC rules, co-ordinate their bilateral adaptation to those rules or consider multilateral action between EFTA and the EC. However, in practice, both the scope and success of EFTA strategies depended on the Community's willingness to engage in cooperation.

In fact, the Nordic EFTA countries have over time tried all of these integration strategies in combination with different scopes of cooperation. On the basis of the bilateral Free Trade Agreements, all of them have concluded a varying number of additional bilateral deals with the Community. In the light of the Community's White Paper, an initiative was launched in 1984 to expand this sectoral cooperation under the so-called 'Luxembourg Process', named after the location of the first joint EC–EFTA ministerial meeting. While the greater extent of its results fits into the bilateral-co-ordinated category (separate bilateral agreements that are quite similar for all the EFTA countries), a few agreements were made on a multilateral basis (with EFTA taking a common position and negotiating a single agreement with the EC).

By contrast, most attempts at a comprehensive approach have failed, such as the neutral EFTA countries' co-ordinated initiative for association (1961–3) and Sweden's 'open application' of 1967. There has been only one example of successful comprehensive (and multilateral) cooperation: the complex negotiations on the creation of a European Economic Area (1989–92) which replaced the Luxembourg Process. In spite of the European Economic Area (EEA), however, Sweden applied for EC membership in July 1991, Finland in March 1992 and Norway in November 1992.

The countries of the European Free Trade Association have traditionally been 'reluctant Europeans'. They chose not to participate in the European Community even though they would have qualified for membership early on. For almost four decades, the Nordic EFTA countries tried to maintain their traditions of formal non-involvement while grappling with the EC's growing economic attraction. Yet, since 1990, most of the EFTA countries have considered and even sought EC membership. At first glance, it seems surprising that these countries have pondered full membership at a time when the Community was moving towards a European Union (EU) including not only Economic and Monetary Union (EMU) but also an embryonic Common Foreign and Security Policy (CFSP), especially as this would have substantial implications for national sovereignty.

This chapter focuses on the Luxembourg Process and the negotiations on the European Economic Area in order to explain this puzzle. It deals to some extent with the EFTA countries as a group since in this time period the integration policies of Finland, Iceland, Norway and Sweden can only be understood as a part of EFTA which also included the three Alpine countries (Austria, Liechtenstein and Switzerland). The late 1980s and early 1990s turned out to be a critical transitional period for the Nordic EFTA countries as they moved from bilateral and sectoral cooperation to comprehensive multilateral cooperation and eventually towards full EU membership. This chapter argues that the experience of the Luxembourg Process and the EEA negotiations helped the Nordic EFTA countries overcome their reluctance towards closer supranational integration.

THE LUXEMBOURG PROCESS

EFTA's original aims were to establish a free trade area for industrial goods among its members and to facilitate cooperation with the European Community. In fact, EFTA's whole rationale was to avoid their economic discrimination resulting from the 'ever closer union' of the EC countries. The first success constituted the bilateral Free Trade Agreements (FTAs) which soothed the negative impacts of the British and Danish departure from EFTA. These agreements (except the one between Finland and the EC) contained evolutionary clauses allowing for collaboration outside the trade area. In the following years, a piecemeal extension of bilateral cooperation took place in various fields.

Except for some 'sensitive' products, the EC–EFTA free trade area for industrial goods had been established by 1 July 1977. In May 1977, the EFTA governments therefore announced that it was

> important to ensure that the advantages deriving from free trade are not jeopardized as a result of diverging economic developments and policies. The EFTA Governments are convinced that it would be desirable to develop the existing co-operation within EFTA and – in varying degrees of intensity – between the EFTA countries and the European Community
>
> EFTA 1977: 53

The European Parliament for its part called for closer ties with EFTA (European Parliament 1977). It entrusted Denmark with particular responsibility for relations between the EC and the Nordic countries and considered broader cooperation desirable and feasible if based on 'each other's economic and political freedom of action and autonomy' as well as 'each other's interest in being informed of and consulted on economic and political questions'. The European Parliament even offered to institutionalise political contacts at the level of ministers or officials as well as between social and economic partners and to establish parliamentary relations. It also proposed some substantive areas for closer cooperation such as trade, fisheries, research, environment as well as monetary, economic and social policy. Yet, nothing much happened during the next few years and Denmark's bridge-building role did not materialise. In 1981 the Commission was content to state that an extension of cooperation took place primarily with the individual EFTA countries and that there had been mutual agreement not to institutionalise that cooperation (Commission of the EC 1981: 2).

The Luxembourg Declaration

In the early 1980s the EFTA Secretariat in Geneva was revived by a new, dynamic Secretary-General, the Norwegian Per Kleppe. He helped float ideas of a common multilateral approach instead of each EFTA country focusing on its bilateral relations with the European Community. Moreover, representatives of multinational companies from the EFTA countries had been involved in the preparation of the Single European Market (SEM) project through the European Round Table of Industrialists set up in 1983. They began to push for EFTA participation in the White Paper Programme. The continued calls for closer cooperation from both the EC and EFTA sides were finally heard. A first joint EC–EFTA ministerial meeting took place in Luxembourg on 9 April 1984 in order to celebrate the successful implementation of the Free Trade Agreements and the abolition of the last remaining tariff barriers and quantitative restrictions affecting trade in industrial products. The formal initiative came from the (then) Swedish Minister of Trade and Chairman of the EFTA Council, Mats Hellström, who suggested the idea to his French counterpart and President of the EC Council, Claude Cheysson (Pedersen 1994b: 27).

At Luxembourg, the ministers stressed 'the importance of further actions to consolidate and strengthen cooperation, with the aim of creating a dynamic European economic space' (EC/EFTA 1985: 54). After the economic recessions of the 1970s and the proliferation of non-tariff barriers to trade in the industrial countries, this goal was remarkable. The Community finally began to consider the EFTA countries more as partners than as rivals. For the Nordic EFTA countries further cooperation with the EC was essential as the Community's Single European Market programme presented a serious new challenge. The Luxembourg Process introduced elements of the common market into the EC–EFTA free trade system, created a revitalised political commitment to the EC–EFTA relationship, and enriched it with a multilateral dimension without creating new institutions.

The Luxembourg Declaration was followed by an EFTA summit meeting in Visby on 23 May 1984 where the EFTA governments once more underlined the importance of an intensified EC–EFTA dialogue. In general, the Nordic EFTA countries welcomed this new multilateral aspect. Yet, the benefits of a common EFTA stance were first tested on a very different occasion as the accession of Portugal and Spain to the Community in 1986 called for amendments to the EC–EFTA Free Trade Agreements. Spain insisted on an asymmetrical trade liberalisation in its favour but it could not split the EFTA side and finally consented to equal treatment.

The Luxembourg joint declaration mentioned a long list of mutual interests, such as the desire to improve the free circulation of industrial goods through harmonisation of standards, the elimination of technical barriers, the simplification of border controls and rules of origin, and the prohibition of state aid contrary to the Free Trade Agreements and liberalisation of access to government procurement. It also envisaged cooperation in new fields such as research and development, transport, agriculture, fisheries, energy, working conditions, social protection, culture, consumer protection, the environment, tourism and intellectual property. Finally, concertation of macroeconomic policy, in particular to combat unemployment, was foreseen. Services as a generic term and the free movement of capital and of persons were not mentioned.

In the Luxembourg Declaration the concept of a European Economic Space (EES) was proposed for the first time without being given a clear definition.[2] The EES was characterised as 'dynamic' and subsequently also as 'homogeneous'.[3] From the Nordic point of view, the dynamism would accrue from the expected benefits of removing trade barriers and partly from the intention of both EFTA and the EC to continue to enlarge the scope of their cooperation. The homogeneous aspect was interpreted as referring to the parallel changes in the EC–EFTA relationship which would correspond to the developments in the Single Market (EFTA 1987: 111). Later on, these two basic characteristics of the European Economic Area were interpreted as meaning that the same legal rules should apply in all the EEA countries and that in the future the EEA should develop in step with the Community.

Follow-up of the Luxembourg Process

The EC–EFTA rapprochement took place without great public attention. An informal group of high officials of the EFTA countries and the EC Commission, known as the High-Level Contact Group (HLCG), was set up in 1984 with the remit of organising and supervising the work of the various expert groups. In addition, from 1985, the EFTA ministers also met with a Commission representative annually to review progress. Cooperation under the Luxembourg umbrella eventually covered thirty areas and involved as many expert groups. The HLCG gave priority to the questions of technical barriers to trade, rules of origin, simplification of border formalities and cooperation in research and development. Elements of the free movement of goods thus constituted the main concern.

In May 1987, the first two multilateral agreements between the Community and EFTA as a group were signed at Interlaken: a convention on a common transit procedure and a convention introducing a single administrative document for all trade between the EC and EFTA countries. Both sides reiterated on this occasion that the intensification of their co-operation 'should be pursued in step with the Community's progress towards completion of its internal market' (EC/EFTA 1988a: 44). Two major constraints hampered faster progress. On the EFTA side, a common position had to be agreed on before approaching the EC. In many areas, however, diverging economic interests limited multilateral agreements. On the EC side, Commissioner Willy De Clercq had made clear that EC–EFTA relations should be governed by three basic principles (De Clerq 1985: 5–6):

1 the priority of the Community's internal integration;
2 the preservation of the Community's decision-making autonomy; and
3 the maintenance of a balance of benefits and obligations.

Priority to the EC meant that negotiations with the EFTA side must not affect the completion of the Single Market. Autonomy meant that cooperation with EFTA must be in conformity with EC rules and not interfere with EC decision-making. A balance of advantages and obligations meant that mutual concessions must, by and large, be equivalent (so-called 'real reciprocity'). The Nordic countries in general had no problems with these guidelines. On the contrary, they applied the principle of autonomy to their national decision-making as well.

At the second joint ministerial meeting held in Brussels in February 1988, the three 'Interlaken principles' were confirmed at the highest level. In the run-up to this meeting, Spain tried but failed to introduce the additional principle that 'social and economic cohesion' should be applied in all areas. The joint declaration of the EC and EFTA ministers noted that:

> co-operation should take into account the specific institutional and legal structures of the EC and the EFTA countries. They fully understood the priority attached by the EEC to the completion of its Internal Market and other Community policies. Whilst excluding no area for co-operation from the outset, they felt that the evolution of EC–EFTA co-operation should aim at seeking a balance between the benefits and obligations in the interest of all parties concerned. They agreed that the best way to proceed would be to develop co-operation pragmatically on a multilateral and on a bilateral basis.
>
> EC/EFTA 1989a: 32

The Luxembourg Process required the EFTA countries to reinforce their own cooperation. In some areas, such as the free movement of goods, the EFTA countries first needed to adapt their internal rules and procedures before concluding a bridging agreement with the Community. They introduced, for instance, a new multilateral EFTA procedure for the exchange of information on planned new technical regulations and an EFTA convention for the mutual recognition of test results and proofs of conformity in order to facilitate agreements eliminating trade barriers with the Community. At the culmination of the Luxembourg Process, all the governments finally began to consider EFTA as their 'common platform for cooperation and negotiations with the EC' and recognised 'the importance of a multilateral approach for reaching EES-wide solutions' (EFTA 1989: 34). Indeed, this became evident in the November 1988 EC–EFTA joint declaration, which called for strengthened co-operation in fields going beyond the free movement of goods such as in financial services, processed agricultural products, environmental protection, mutual recognition of tests and certificates, public procurement and indirect taxation (EC/EFTA 1989b: 48–51). Exchanging information would also continue, or be initiated, with regard to, for example, product liability, intellectual and industrial property rights, capital mobility, company law, consumer protection and social policy.

This long list of problems still to be tackled at the end of 1988 showed that the Luxembourg Process was slow, costly and inadequate. Both the Swedish and the Norwegian governments decided in June 1988 that all new national legislation relevant for the Single Market should be considered with a view to voluntary harmonisation with Community law. This parallelism helped avoid any risk that completing the SEM would create further obstacles.

The Nordics in the Luxembourg Process

The overall economic interests of the six countries that constituted EFTA in the mid-1980s (Austria, Finland, Iceland, Norway, Sweden and

Switzerland) were quite similar.[4] This is not surprising since they are all small, highly industrialised and open market economies and thus are more dependent upon, and perceive there are greater benefits from, freer international trade. The EC and EFTA were geographically close and are also each other's major trading partners and sources of inward investment. The EC's share of EFTA trade had been increasing over many years whereas intra-EFTA trade was only of some relevance for the Nordic countries. In addition, the EFTA countries produced similar and easily substituted goods to those of the EC and it was feared that the principal share of the Single Market's trade diversion was therefore likely to fall on EFTA suppliers.

The EFTA countries' trade was generally concentrated on manufactures and intra-industry trade. Yet, there were marked differences with regard to the export shares of manufactures. The Nordic EFTA countries could be divided into two groups according to the commodity composition of their exports: on the one hand Finland and Sweden whose forest-based exports have been declining in relative importance but are still substantial, and on the other hand Norway and Iceland whose exports still rely to a large extent on natural resources, namely petroleum, natural gas, forestry products and fish.

Both the manufactured goods and the resource-based products depend on market access to benefit from economies of scale. Many Nordic industries lacked a strong foothold in the Single Market and the '1992 project' unleashed a high level of merger and acquisition activity (EFTA 1991: 23–9). This redirection of investment to the EC was particularly serious for Sweden which had large industries dependent on economies of scale. By contrast, Norway exported mainly oil and petroleum derivatives to the Community. Its economy has otherwise been characterised by small and medium-sized enterprises. Finland's position was between Norway and Sweden, but its economic structure has been moving closer to Sweden's. Wood-processing products were still important but other industries such as machinery and electronics had caught up. Around 1990 the terms of trade were most adverse for Finland and most favourable for Norway. Finland's main export market in terms of individual countries had been the Soviet Union. The plummeting oil prices in the mid-1980s and the dissolution of the Soviet Union put this to an end. As a consequence, Finnish exports to Western Europe and Finnish foreign investment in the EC increased rapidly in the late 1980s.

Among the Nordic EFTA countries, Norway was the first one to produce a policy paper on the EC's Single Market in May 1987. The Norwegian government regarded it as necessary that Norway adapt to the Single Market 'as far as possible in order to avoid new trade barriers' (*Utenriksdepartementet* 1987: 4). This strategy should be pursued both bilaterally and through EFTA. Furthermore, Norway as a NATO member has always shown a great interest in the European Political Cooperation (EPC). In December

1987, the Swedish government followed stating that it would 'work for the establishment of a common market in Western Europe encompassing all 18 EFTA and EC countries' and 'to strengthen the position of EFTA as a means of achieving this common market' (*Utrikesdepartementet* 1987: 4).

More than any other Nordic country, however, the Finnish government set its hopes on the 'EFTA card': the EFTA countries should reach a common view on as many issues as possible with regard to the Single Market. The bi-polar Cold War structure and Finland's special relations with the Soviet Union imposed external constraints on its integration policy which for a long time made a common approach along with the other neutral EFTA countries the only option for Finland. Iceland had as well relied on EFTA for its integration policy but for different reasons. After years of struggle, Iceland finally managed to have its major interest, the principle of free trade in fish, accepted by the other EFTA countries in 1989. Its main objective was then to extend the free access of its marine products to the EC's Single Market without having to participate in the Common Fisheries Policy which would require Iceland to grant the EC member states access to its fishing resources.

Even though European integration had an impact on Nordic cooperation, the discussions between the Nordic EFTAns and the Community have been conducted entirely through EFTA. Nordic cooperation rested more on cultural ties than on common interests. It had always been rather limited and therefore could not offer a real alternative to European integration. Plans to create a Scandinavian customs union failed and so did efforts for a common security orientation as Denmark, Iceland and Norway chose to join NATO while Finland and Sweden pursued a policy of neutrality. The historical rivalry between the two Scandinavian great powers of Denmark and Sweden and the fact that Finland, Iceland and Norway had gained their full sovereignty only in this century partly explains why Nordic collaboration has been subordinated to cooperation with the EC. It is therefore also less surprising that the early EC membership of Denmark did not play a crucial role in the other Nordic countries' quest for closer EC relations.

During the Luxembourg Process the EFTA countries' common goal of cooperating with the EC dominated their divergent interests. The latter flared up only occasionally when laying down the priorities of cooperation. In the 1980s, EC–EFTA relations focused on facilitating the free movement of goods and left the institutional question aside. There was enough scope for specific bilateral deals besides a few multilateral agreements. The differences between and among the Alpine and the Nordic countries manifested themselves more clearly in the EEA negotiations, where the economic and political stakes were higher while the scope for special treatment was very limited. Nevertheless, the Alpine countries' fears of a Nordic 'ganging up' against them in the EEA negotiations proved to be unfounded as no real co-ordination took place among the Nordic EFTA countries.

THE EEA NEGOTIATIONS

The EEA initiative

By 1988 the EFTA countries had become frustrated by the slow pace and piecemeal character of the EC–EFTA dialogue. Their situation presented itself as follows (Baragiola 1991: 13–15): the abolition of tariffs and quantitative restrictions for industrial goods was somewhat offset by the low level of the Common Customs Tariff and the complicated rules of origin; there was no mutual recognition for technical standards and certificates of conformity; the EFTAns were basically treated as third countries with regard to public procurement, agriculture, capital, services, transport, competition policy and the free movement of persons.

The Luxembourg follow-up had broadened and intensified EC–EFTA cooperation but was still grounded on a case-by-case approach. The Luxembourg Declaration was an expression of political will but the legal basis of cooperation remained the Free Trade Agreements. Lacking a competent institutional body and a timetable, the process relied on political impulses from joint ministerial meetings. Despite a few forays into multilateral dialogue, the relationship between the EC and the Nordic EFTA countries remained on a bilateral footing. The industries in the EFTA countries felt a growing need for more permanent forms of cooperation with the EC to ensure stable and predictable market conditions. Moreover, the *ad hoc* approach was just not sufficiently dynamic to keep up with the implementation of the Single Market.

The Luxembourg Process thus suffered from both substantial and institutional deficiencies. The EFTA countries faced the triple risk of marginalisation as their products would be treated differently, of satellisation since they had no influence on developments in the EC, and of missing the dynamic effects of the market liberalisation (Nell 1988: 573). The lesson to be drawn from the Luxembourg follow-up was the call for an appropriate institutional framework, for a global instead of a sectoral approach and for multilateral instead of bilateral agreements.

The need for more effective, and the desire for more far-reaching, cooperation led in the late 1980s to the discussion of possible scenarios in the EFTA Secretariat and on the occasion of several academic seminars devoted to EC–EFTA relations (for instance, Jacot-Guillarmod 1990: 13–15; Jamar and Wallace 1988). Swedish and Norwegian Social Democrats, and in particular Prime Minister Gro Harlem Brundtland of Norway, had informally approached French Socialist Jacques Delors on this issue (Eide 1990: 413). The idea of institutionalising EC–EFTA relations was then officially launched by the President of the EC Commission in a speech to the European Parliament on 17 January 1989. He suggested looking for a 'a new, more structured partnership with common decision-making and administrative institutions' on the basis of the 'two pillars' of the EC and a strengthened EFTA (Delors 1989: 17).

The EFTA governments could react promptly to this proposal thanks to a summit meeting in Oslo on 14–15 March 1989 which had been convened by the Norwegian Prime Minister Brundtland. They warmly welcomed the initiative and expressed their hope that the negotiations would lead to the 'fullest possible realisation of free movement of goods, services, capital and persons, with the aim of creating a dynamic and homogeneous European Economic Space'. The EFTA heads of governments proposed

> the use of early exchange of information on legislation under preparation, established consultation procedures, mutual recognition of equivalent legislation and common decision-making. This should be supported by equally strong and reliable surveillance and enforcement procedures and common mechanisms for settlement of disputes.
>
> EC/EFTA 1990a: 36

At an informal joint meeting in Brussels only one week later on 20 March 1989 the EC and EFTA ministers discussed the 'Delors initiative' which subsequently came also to be known as the 'Oslo–Brussels process'. A joint High-Level Steering Group (HLSG) was created to examine the possible scope and content of cooperation as well as its institutional aspects. This group in turn set up five joint Working Groups: on the free movement of goods; the free movement of services and capital; the free movement of persons; the so-called flanking and horizontal policies (for example, research and development, education, environment, social policy, company law, statistics) as well as on the legal and institutional questions.

It is safe to conclude that the new launching of the EEA was, in cooperation with the EC Commission, mainly a Nordic initiative pushed for by Norway and Sweden. Switzerland had always been suspicious of a multilateral EFTA approach while Austria was heading towards full EC membership. At the outset, neither the EC nor the EFTA side had a clear concept of the EEA's architecture but both expected it to solve their dilemmas. By offering the EFTA countries an alternative to EC membership, the Community would be able to settle its 'deepening'-versus-'widening' debate and could instead focus on the Intergovernmental Conferences (IGCs) leading up to the Treaty on European Union (TEU). The EFTA countries would be able to avoid both economic marginalisation by taking part in the Single Market and political satellisation by having a say in the decision-making process. Moreover, for Norway, Sweden and Finland the EEA offered a de-politicised version of EC membership.

Course and outcome of the EEA negotiations

The EFTA countries therefore nourished high expectations and aimed at an equal participation in the Single Market and in the process deciding on future common EEA rules. The Nordic countries shared a strong interest in the creation of appropriate institutions. The Norwegian parliament, for instance, had already in 1989 approved specific aims for the EEA process: full access to the Single Market for the Norwegian business sector, elimination of rules of origin and of anti-dumping measures, free access for the export of fish products, common rules of competition in the EEA, high standards and ambitious objectives regarding social and regional policy and environmental issues, full participation in EC cooperation in fields such as environmental protection, research and development, and social, educational and consumer issues, and, finally, the establishment of EFTA institutions (*Storting* Finance Committee 1989: 11–12).

The fact-finding and exploratory talks took one year. An important result was that the *acquis communautaire* should constitute the legal basis of the agreement and the EFTA countries agreed to adopt the relevant EC legislation with some justified exceptions. By 'buying the past', they hoped to be able to influence the future. Moreover, cooperation outside the four freedoms of the Single Market should be broadened and the economic and social disparities between the regions could be reduced (EC/EFTA 1990b: 55). The formal negotiations began in June 1990. The HLSG changed into a High-Level Negotiating Group (HLNG) and the five Working Groups turned into Negotiating Groups. For a while, the Luxembourg follow-up continued in a much reduced form and in parallel to the EEA negotiations before eventually being phased into the EEA process once the EEA agenda went beyond the original Luxembourg remit.

Negotiating the European Economic Area turned out to be a lengthy and exhausting exercise. The EC Commission made clear that the 'Interlaken principles' of 1987 were still valid, which led to hardly reconcilable differences with regard to the institutional structure. Not only the Community aimed at safeguarding its decision-making autonomy but the individual EFTA countries as well. In December 1989, the EFTA side reiterated that 'the establishment of a genuine joint decision-making mechanism in substance and form is a basic prerequisite for the political acceptability and the legal effectiveness of an agreement'(EFTA 1990: 51). In January 1990, Commission President Delors himself told the EFTAns that

> there will have to be some sort of osmosis between the Community and EFTA to ensure that EFTA's interests are taken into account in major Community decisions. But this process must stop short of joint decision-making, which would imply Community membership.
>
> Delors 1990: 9

The bargaining leverage was obviously on the EC's side. The Nordic EFTA countries needed an agreement more than the Community and their expectations did not correspond to what the EC was either able or willing to deliver. The time pressure created by the envisaged entry-into-force in parallel with the completion of the Single Market by the end of 1992 strengthened the EC's bargaining position. The negotiations were further complicated by the fact that the EFTA countries needed to reach common positions. The result of this process was satisfactory with regard to the substance but rather frustrating with regard to the institutions if one compares the initial demands with the final outcome (see for example, Gstöhl 1994: 333–66; Pedersen 1994b: 33–63: Reymond 1993: 449–80 and Norberg *et al.* 1993).

In substance, the Nordic EFTA countries roughly obtained what they aimed for. The EEA Agreement constituted a far-reaching association agreement which basically extended the EC's Single Market to them with the exceptions of the Common Commercial Policy, the Common Agricultural and Fisheries Policy, EURATOM, direct and indirect taxation and the Treaty on European Union. Yet, the EC introduced 'cohesion' as a new substantive element in favour of its less developed regions in the form of a Cohesion Fund financed by EFTA as well as concessions in agricultural trade and fisheries. For the most part, the Nordic EFTAns had no problem with taking over the EC *acquis*, particularly as the legal basis of the Agreement would require that EC and EEA law would need to be developed strictly in parallel in order to maintain a homogeneous market. Moreover, the EC side basically refused permanent exceptions from the *acquis* and granted only short transitional periods and a general safeguard clause instead.

The often quoted 'Alpine-Scandinavian gap' was rather a journalists' myth than a fact. The individual countries' interests diverged between Austria and Switzerland as well as among the Nordic group. A real North–South gap was evident only on very few occasions such as the question of alcohol monopolies, the different legal traditions of the Nordic and the Continental EFTA states and the sensitive issues of Alpine transit and Nordic fisheries. The matters of transit and fish threatened to jeopardise the whole negotiation process and, like trade in agricultural products, finally had to be dealt with separately in bilateral agreements. Other national interests calling for transitional periods were put forward in areas, such as higher standards for health, safety and environmental protection, the foreign ownership of land and of Finnish forests and the free movement of persons in Switzerland and Liechtenstein (House of Lords 1990: 13–15). By following a 'top-down approach', Sweden was the country with the fewest demands for derogations. In contrast to Switzerland, the Nordic countries tended to adopt a maximalist position on substance. Austria supported this strategy since the more Single Market substance was incorporated into the EEA, the closer it came to EC membership.

With regard to the institutions, the EFTA countries' expectations had not been met. As suggested by them, the EEA Council is to meet at ministerial level twice a year in order to provide the political impetus for the further process. An EEA Joint Parliamentary Committee and an EEA Joint Consultative Committee for the economic and social partners have been established as advisory bodies. However, a real joint decision-making mechanism for future EEA rules remained an illusion. It would have implied that the Community accepts EFTA's interference with its own decision-making process. Moreover, the Commission formally retained its exclusive right to initiate, whereas the EFTA countries could only raise a matter of concern at the EEA level at any time (*droit d'évocation*). EFTA experts may not participate directly in all EC committees but are only consulted in the preparatory stage of new measures. The main consultation procedure takes place in the EEA Joint Committee once a proposal has reached the EC Council. Decisions are taken by consensus. As with the Community, the EFTA countries need to speak with one voice. They may only opt out of new rules collectively and at the price of a suspension of related parts of the Agreement.

The institutional set-up of the European Economic Area facilitates the adoption of 'mirror legislation' in parallel to the EC legislation, but it yields the EFTA countries rather limited influence. Maintaining the EC's decision-making autonomy and the sole competence of the EC Court of Justice while trying to grant the EFTA countries some influence on future common rules and to avoid subjecting them to 'foreign judges' was an attempt to square the circle. In particular, the fear of 'foreign judges' posed a domestic problem for Iceland and Norway, mainly for constitutional reasons. In order to save the concept of a homogeneous common legal order, one side had to relinquish some of their autonomy. The EFTA countries consequently gave way to an extensive realisation of the 'two-pillar model' requiring them to establish an independent EFTA Surveillance Authority (ESA) to monitor compliance with the EEA Agreement as well as an independent EFTA Court of Justice. These quasi-supranational EFTA institutions won over the EFTA countries' proposal of a joint EC–EFTA surveillance body and an independent EEA Court ('one-pillar approach'). While the joint surveillance mechanism failed early in the process due to the Commission's resistance, the EEA Court was shattered after the supposed conclusion of the negotiations in 1991 by the objection of the EC Court of Justice. The EEA Agreement was finally signed in Oporto on 2 May 1992 in parallel with the EFTA Agreements establishing the ESA, the EFTA Court and the Standing Committee of EFTA States which was to be EFTA's part of the EEA Joint Committee.

Among the Nordic countries, Norway and Iceland were the most sceptical towards supranational features of the EEA. Finland whole-heartedly supported the EEA as its 'window of opportunity', despite having opposed the initial idea of an EEA customs union favoured by Sweden and Austria. The Swedish wish for a customs union with the EC had failed before in the early 1970s when the Free Trade Agreements were concluded. To some extent one could observe a Nordic East–West division with Sweden on the one hand, increasingly supported by Finland, and the more reluctant Norway and Iceland on the other hand.

In the summer of 1992 the preparation of the entry into force of the

EEA Agreement by 1 January 1993 started within the framework of a High-Level Interim Group (HLIG) and five Interim Working Groups corresponding to the earlier Negotiating Groups. The rejection of ratification by Switzerland in December 1992 resulted in the conclusion of an Adjusting Protocol to the EEA Agreement on 17 March 1993. The European Economic Area finally came into being on 1 January 1994 at a time when the Nordic countries had already started their membership negotiations with the European Community. It has been operating ever since, in spite of some countries switching from the EFTA to the EC side one year later.

The Nordics' applications for EC membership

At the outset, all the Nordic EFTA countries perceived the EEA as a third way between marginalisation and full EC membership. Yet, the more EC membership became a realistic option, the less they were prepared to further bargain for a favourable institutional solution in the EEA. Whereas Austria applied at the very beginning of the EEA process and Sweden in the middle of it, the governments of Finland, Switzerland and Norway waited for the results of the EEA and the Maastricht negotiations before launching their membership applications. Considering the rather limited influence on new EC/EEA rules and the need to establish an EFTA surveillance and judicial mechanism, the Nordic countries increasingly viewed full membership as a viable alternative. For them, there was just no point in transforming EFTA into a 'mini-EC' while accepting a participatory deficit in comparison to full membership in the European Union. In short, the effectiveness of their national policies was undermined by the increasing economic interdependence with the EC. The Nordic EFTA states realised that becoming a member of the European Union was ultimately the only way to secure a larger voice in an increasingly institutionalised Europe.

Yet, the frustration about the lack of a viable alternative to EC membership alone cannot explain the Nordic EFTA countries' accession to the European Union. The EEA negotiations have not been carried out in a vacuum. The policy change was facilitated by the two European 'revolutions' of 1989 and 1992. First, the end of the Cold War has profoundly changed the East–West security climate and in particular, the need for maintaining neutrality policies (see Chapters 16 and 17). Second, additional economic incentives were created by the completion of the Single Market in 1992, the plans for an Economic and Monetary Union, the deep recession in Finland and Sweden and the general crisis of the Nordic welfare model.

CONCLUSION: TAMING THE EFTANS?

Like most of the (former) EFTA countries, the Nordic countries are 'reluctant Europeans' with a preference for intergovernmental cooperation instead of supranational integration. Starting with the founding of EFTA, this traditional scepticism called for arrangements which allowed them to participate in the EC's economic integration while falling short of full membership with its political implications. The Nordic EFTA countries' experience, which spans from the bilateral Free Trade Agreements to the EEA negotiations, constitutes a long-term learning process. Their integration policies evolved from simply maintaining the status quo, to pursuing a sectoral rapprochement and eventually to considering full membership. They exhausted the full scope of cooperation and the strategies of unilateral adaptation, bilateral, bilateral-co-ordinated and multilateral action.

In the late 1980s and early 1990s the Nordic EFTA countries' wish to become pure 'economic members' of the Community led them into a dilemma: the more extensive the substance of the economic integration offered to them in the Luxembourg and EEA processes, the more national legislative autonomy they had to renounce and the more important it became to gain some influence in the decision-making procedures. The EFTAns realised that there was a double trade-off involved in this kind of cooperation: they needed to trade not only autonomy for wealth but also sovereignty for voice.

Even though the actual decision to apply for full EC membership might have been triggered by external events and its timing determined by domestic politics, the Luxembourg Process and subsequently the EEA negotiations have played an important role in preparing this policy change. The insight that the goal of saving as much freedom of action as possible was in the long run better achieved within the EU, helped the Nordic EFTA states to overcome their domestic reservations regarding supranationality, at least at the level of the political elites. It seems quite paradoxical that it was the Nordic EFTA countries' commitment to maintain effective decision-making powers that finally led them to become full members.

For this reason it remains doubtful whether the Nordic countries will suddenly be transformed into 'eager Europeans'. They seem more likely to become 'minimalist' members of the European Union. This reluctance does not refer to their compliance with the EU's *acquis* but rather to their willingness to generate further initiatives in sensitive areas and to introduce greater supranational decision-making. Unless there are strong external pressures, the Nordic enlargement is likely to either slow down the process of deepening political integration or to move Europe further towards a pattern of variable geometry.

NOTES

1 I would like particularly to thank Sven Norberg, former Director of the EFTA Secretariat's Legal Affairs Department and the Swedish Judge at the EFTA Court, in providing a personal account of the Luxembourg Process and the EEA negotiations.

2 As a matter of fact, the Vice-President of the European Commission, Wilhem Haferkamp, had already in December 1983 circumscribed the notion of a European Economic Space as 'a situation in which our industrial producers should be able to consider the whole of Western Europe as their home market' (see Commission of the EC 1983). The term 'Space' due to the unlucky English translation of the French notion 'Espace Economique Europêen' was later changed to the more appropriate 'Area'.

3 The term 'homogeneous' was at EFTA's request in June 1986 (De Clerq 1987: 50).

4 Portugal applied for EC membership in 1977 and finally joined the Community together with Spain in 1986. Finland had been an associated member of EFTA since 1961 and became a full member in 1986. Liechtenstein had been participating in EFTA through its customs union with Switzerland, and in 1991 formally joined as a full member.

5 The Nordic countries and the fourth EU enlargement

Lee Miles

INTRODUCTION

By November 1992, the European Community (EC) had received full membership applications from three Nordic countries. Indeed, once Sweden had applied for full EC membership on 1 July 1991, Finland and Norway followed in relatively quick succession (Finland in March 1992 and Norway in November 1992). The response from the EC was also comparatively speedy and accession negotiations started in February 1993. The purpose of this chapter will be to analyse the various phases of the accession negotiations. By taking this approach, the chapter will link together the international perceptions of the Nordic countries developed in Part II and the domestic pressures within the individual countries which are addressed in Part III.

DECIDING TO APPLY

The reasons why Sweden, Finland and Norway decided to apply for full EC membership between 1991 and 1992 are well documented and explained elsewhere (for example, Ross 1991; Miles 1994a). The Swedish case is of particular interest as her application started the process towards wider Nordic EU membership in the early 1990s (see also Chapters 7 and 14). Several Swedish motives can be identified.

There were the traditional arguments based on growing economic dependency upon EC markets. In short, Sweden was now reliant upon international trade with the EC and its member states for the majority of its imports and exports and neither economic independence nor national sovereignty could be guaranteed by not being a full member (see Chapter 4).

Sweden's economic fragility from 1990 as a result of a severe recession also reinforced the arguments for EU membership. The government argued that the Swedish economy could no longer afford to be excluded given its present weakness and that EU membership would provide at least a partial way of liberalising stagnating sectors. In other words, the traditional

'Swedish model' was coming to the end of an era and EU membership would help to facilitate its transition (Petersson 1994b: 34–43).

The most influential factor in changing Swedish policy was governmental frustration at the slowness of the European Economic Area (EEA) negotiations and the limitations of any future EEA agreement (see Chapter 4). In practice, it was Swedish dissatisfaction with the EEA negotiations during the Swedish 1990 EFTA presidency and the realisation that the EEA only provided for a consultative 'decision-shaping' role for Sweden when determining future SEM legislation that tilted governmental views in favour of full membership. Hence, from 1990 the government stated that the EEA was now only an interim measure until full membership could be achieved (Jerneck 1993: 23–42).

The formal obstacles to EC membership were also removed by 1990. First, the EC's development of a social dimension embodied in the 1989 Social Charter and the introduction of the Fourth Environmental Action programme in 1987 reduced Swedish concerns that full membership would undermine these traditional Swedish priorities. Rather, her government appreciated that full membership provided the opportunity to further influence the development of these fledgling policies. Second, the changes in the European strategic environment allowed for a more flexible interpretation of Swedish neutrality (see Chapter 16). This was officially recognised by Carlsson during his address to the *Riksdag* in June 1991 when he stated that Sweden's neutrality policy was now fully compatible with EC membership (Carlsson 1992b: 2).

The decision to apply was supported by nearly all the Swedish political and business elites, even if this was not completely shared by the Swedish public. The Swedish employers' organisation, the SAF, had supported Swedish EC membership for a long time and was fearful of the economic costs of remaining outside the EU. However, the conversion of the main trade union confederation, the LO, on the grounds that only continued export growth facilitated by EC membership could protect the Swedish welfare state and jobs was also critical (Arter 1993: 224). They maintained influential links with the (then) governing Social Democrats. This meant that the main arms of the Swedish corporate system and both the leading sectoral organisations were in favour of full membership by 1991.

Nevertheless, the decision to apply still surprised the Swedish public. The revision in government strategy was quietly announced as a 'footnote' attached to a 1990 austerity package (see Chapter 7). The potent coalition of domestic elites allowed a considerable parliamentary majority (90 per cent of the *Riksdag*) to approve the government's decision to seek EC membership in December 1990. Consequently, Carlsson lodged the application on 1 July 1991. It also allowed for support for the application to be maintained once the non-socialist Bildt government was installed in late 1991.

For Finland, the conversion to EC membership took longer, but accelerated rapidly once Sweden had taken the plunge and applied in 1991 (Miles 1994a: 63–74). Officially, the Finnish government position was to review the situation once the EEA agreement had been finally agreed. However, the protracted state of the EEA negotiations and the later delays incurred by the European Court of Justice's (ECJ) criticism of the creation of a rival EEA Court led to a revision of Finnish perspectives. Ultimately, the Swedish application was critical (see Chapter 8). In January 1992, the Finnish government sought and gained approval from the Finnish Parliament to seek EC membership.

For Norway, the status of intra-Nordic relations and the scenario that if Sweden and Finland joined, some 80 per cent of the Nordic region would be within the EC was very influential. As Gro Harlem Brundtland, the Norwegian Prime Minister, conceded in her November 1992 address to the *Storting*, Norway was 'faced with a completely new situation now that Sweden and Finland have applied for membership of the EC' (Brundtland 1992: 7). In the Norwegian case, it seems that the decision to apply was driven by political factors rather than on economic grounds for unlike Sweden or Finland, Norway was not experiencing economic recession as her economy was buoyed by her oil exports (Miles 1995b).

Nevertheless, the speed with which the Norwegian government moved the domestic debate on to EU membership was surprising. The previous 1972 referendum on EC membership had created a schism in Norwegian society for almost twenty years and the EC issue became a taboo subject (see Chapter 9). Thus, the EEA received a mixed reaction within Norway. Although the EEA concept was accepted by the Brundtland government at the EFTA summit in Oslo in March 1989, it was rationalised as an alternative to, not a pre-requisite of, EC membership (Sæter 1993: 31–9). However, the next non-socialist government was forced to resign in 1990 on the EEA issue, when the participating Centre Party turned against Norway's involvement. This paved the way for a new minority government of Brundtland's Labour Party. Yet, although the new Norwegian government expressed doubts about the EEA's longer-term viability, it did ensure Norwegian access to the SEM, and consequently the *Storting* approved the EEA by 130 votes to 35 in October 1992.

However, the Swedish and Finnish applications provided a new opportunity and political rationale for contemplating full membership. Brundtland, in particular, argued that a decision on full membership could no longer be postponed. However, the government was wary that there was large domestic opposition, including within the governing Labour Party. Hence the government argued that the application in itself did not guarantee either their support for membership or that accession would eventually happen. At the 1993 Labour Party conference, the application was sanctioned, but only on the condition that a decision on governmental support for full membership would depend on the outcome of the accession negotiations (and especially any deal on fisheries).

The Icelandic reaction to both the EEA and the later three Nordic applications was much slower and in spite of the fact that Iceland was becoming marginalised within EFTA, the EEA and the Nordic Council. Iceland's policy was still to follow the adaptive process of the other Nordic countries within EFTA and remained very cautious (Kristinsson 1994: 93–7). The Icelandic government in 1989 expressed doubts about three of the four freedoms (excluding the free movement of goods). The EEA agreement encountered strong opposition from within Iceland. In particular, the government incurred severe criticism over the bilateral fisheries quotas agreed as part of the EEA process. In the end, the EEA agreement was only accepted by 33 votes to 23 in the *Althingi* and only after some government coercion.

There had been little governmental or public discussion over EU membership as Iceland's agricultural and fisheries interests meant that full membership was not very attractive. In March 1992 a Foreign Minister's report to the Parliament specifically cited the Common Fisheries Policy as the main obstacle to membership and the result has been that there has been hardly any debate on EU membership in Iceland (see Chapter 10).

THE CHANGING RESPONSES OF THE EUROPEAN UNION

The initial response of the European Union to the three Nordic applications was generally positive. Even though these applications proved that the EEA concept had failed to deter future accessions, the European Commission realised that the wider strategic changes in Europe had removed many of the obstacles to wider Nordic full membership anyway. Future EU enlargements were therefore inevitable regardless of the EEA.

The European Commission issued its general strategy for dealing with future enlargement in its 'Europe and the Challenge of Enlargement' report approved at the Lisbon European Council Summit in June 1992 (Commission of ECs 1992b). It became the platform for interpreting the merits of all prospective candidates. The requirements included: the political conditions of a European identity, liberal democracy and respect for human rights; the capacity to implement the EU's political and economic systems; evidence of a functioning market economy and adequate legal and administrative frameworks; and the acceptance of the existing '*acquis communautaire*' and the ambitious goals ('*finalité politiques*') of the TEU.

Yet, the European Commission was only partially successful in defining its position regarding the Nordic EFTA countries as the report included only general criteria applicable to all applicants. The Nordic EFTAns easily fulfilled these, having GDP per capita above the EU average, mature parliamentary democracies and sound human rights records. The Commission recognised that there were few 'insuperable problems' with their membership. The problem was not whether these countries were eligible, but rather the terms on which they should be admitted. The only major concern according to the report, was the compatibility of the Nordic neutrals with the Common Foreign and Security Policy (CFSP Articles J. 1–10 TEU). The report claimed that the Commission would take a strict attitude and seek 'specific and binding assurances'.

There was soon to be a notable change of position on when the accession process should begin, though. The Lisbon Summit in June 1992 specified that the accession negotiations could not begin until the EU had finally ratified the TEU and agreed the Delors-II financial package. In practice, this would delay Nordic enlargement as it tied the opening of accession negotiations to an internal EU solution to the Danish first domestic rejection of the TEU (see Chapter 6).

Yet, the December 1992 Edinburgh European Council Summit decided to open accession negotiations the next year regardless. This marked a major change by the Union and reversed the Lisbon declaration. The Commission's opinions on the Swedish (7 August 1992) and the Finnish (4 November 1992) applications (see Commission of the ECs 1992c and 1992d) had been positive and the EU also recognised that its enlargement policy was fast becoming obsolete and overtaken by events. The Finnish and Norwegian applications in March and November 1992 pressured the EU for a more practical response. In addition, EU internal dynamics were also influential. The EU partly solved the problems with TEU ratification at Edinburgh by accepting the Danish government's demands for a specialised compromise and consequently, the Danes committed themselves to holding a second referendum on the TEU (Worre 1995: 235–58). Finally, further enlargement was central to the incumbent British European Council Presidency and the negotiations were part of a wider compromise between the UK and other member states. Starting accession negotiations was thus agreed in exchange for UK consent to the Delors-II financial package at Edinburgh.

Thus, the speed with which Sweden, Finland, Norway and Austria moved from lodging applications to opening accession negotiations was very quick. For Sweden, the time period was just nineteen months, for Finland, it was barely eleven months and for Norway, it was an amazing four months (Avery 1994: 27–32). Formal negotiations with Sweden, Finland and Austria and the EU began in February 1993, with Norway joining the process in April. It was decided that the negotiations should be conducted between the candidate countries and the EU Council of Ministers (aided by the European Commission's specially created Enlargement Task Force).

Although the Nordic applicants were often viewed as a cohesive group (Nicolaides and Armand 1994: 70–9), the negotiations were mainly bilateral with co-ordination appearing between the respective applicants on mutual issues, such as agricultural support and budgetary contributions.

Nevertheless, EU concessions given to one were usually extended to all, allowing each applicant to target areas for brinkmanship (Miles 1994b: 8–11).

NORDIC PRIORITIES

There were specific issues which the three Nordic governments sought to prioritise during the accession negotiations. These common issues indicate what kind of priorities these countries would develop if they became full EU members. In general, they shared a primarily economic perception of the merits of EU membership and all viewed the political obligations of membership with some trepidation. They were interested in five rough areas, although the degree of emphasis depended on the actual governments. In short, these were:

- maintaining the nature and levels of Nordic support to agriculture and the component regions;
- conserving their stringent environmental policies and standards and the principles of 'sustainable development';
- preserving their generous national social policies and welfare provisions and the development of an EU strategy for full employment;
- guaranteeing that EU membership would not dilute their Nordic liberal democracies and traditions of open government; and
- developing a stronger EU international role for the EU in the Baltic region and closer ties with the Baltic states.

The leadership of the three Nordic countries did champion different issues during the negotiations. The tendency was for those Nordic countries most affected by the specific issue to act as the leader in negotiations with the EU. The others would then be safe in the knowledge that any concessions would be offered to all. Finland, for example, emphasised the transitional problems for Nordic agriculture and the need for EU financial support to overcome these. In the Norwegian case, environmental policy and levels of agricultural subsidies were key issues, although in the additional areas of fisheries and energy liberalisation, Norway acted virtually alone. In contrast, the Swedish government stressed, among others, social and environmental policy derogations, budgetary contributions and transparency in EU decision-making.

THE ACCESSION NEGOTIATIONS – THE FOUR PHASES

The negotiations included four distinct phases (see Miles 1994c) during which the bargaining positions of the Nordic countries became stronger and more resolute. The first phase from February to June 1993 proceeded at a relatively swift pace. This was due to the fact that this stage was dealing with background issues and formulating initial common positions for future negotiation. Generally, the process was buoyed by a sense of optimism on both sides that at last the accession negotiations had formally begun.

For the most part, agreement was expected to be relatively easy, given that a substantial foundation had been laid by the previous EEA agreement (Commission of the ECs 1994a: 1). Of the twenty-nine chapters of the accession treaty (see Table 5.1), chapters 1–11 had already been agreed as part of the 1992 EEA agreement. Chapters 12–16 were partially agreed by the EEA, leaving only chapters 17–29 to be negotiated fully (Granell 1995). In particular, chapters 17–22 dealt with existing policies, such as the regional policy (20) while chapters 23–26 covered new elements (with the exception of the EMS (23)) introduced by the TEU. Hence, by 11 March, Sweden and Finland were able to claim that seven of the chapters were now 'unproblematic' (see Table 5.2).

Yet, the initial optimism was to prove short-lived once the second phase of the negotiations began. This phase marked the start of the actual hard bargaining on the twenty-nine chapters. There was a large amount of posturing on both sides, increasing the sense of frustration at the slowness of the negotiations. At this point, it became obvious why these negotiations to include three Nordic countries and Austria would become more time-consuming than first anticipated.

All four applicant governments were committed to holding a domestic referendum on the outcome of the negotiations. This cast a long shadow over the negotiations and introduced an extra and unpredictable variable. The negotiations needed to consider the impact of policy positions and any eventual deal on the subsequent referendums, especially as there was strong domestic opposition to EU membership in Sweden and Norway. These domestic considerations proved more problematic for the negotiators than any of the major differences in national interests between the Twelve and the Nordic applicants (see Miles 1994c).

This phase of negotiations also began to deal with very sensitive areas, such as agriculture, at a time when opinion polls in these states took a turn for the worse. Sweden and Norway especially showed large domestic anti-EU majorities, with Norway's running at around 45–50 per cent between March 1993 and March 1994 (Ludlow 1994). It was at this point that the 'balance of power' swung towards the applicants as they increasingly dictated the parameters and pace of the negotiations.

In late 1993, the EU Council Presidency and several member states officially raised concern that the negotiations were becoming too protracted and the original deadline for completion of January 1994 was now impractical. With this in mind, the EU's priorities altered from one initially based upon ensuring that the applicants strictly adhered to the EU's criteria to one based on guaranteeing that the negotiations would be finalised. In short, the accession negotiations were as important for the EU as for the applicants. The negotiations were increasingly seen by the EU as

Table 5.1 The twenty-nine Chapters for the Accession Negotiations

Chapters almost fully covered by the EEA:	
1	Free Movement of Goods
2	Freedom to Provide Services and Rights of Establishment
3	Freedom of Movement For Workers
4	Free Movement of Capital
5	Transport Policy
6	Competition Policy
7	Consumer and Health Protection
8	Research and Information Technologies
9	Education
10	Statistics
11	Company Law
Chapters only partly covered by the EEA:	
12	Social Policy
13	Environment
14	Energy
15	Agriculture
16	Fisheries
Chapters in areas covered by the EC, yet not covered by the EEA:	
17	Customs Union
18	External Relations
19	Structural Instruments
20	Regional Policy
21	Industrial Policy
22	Taxation
The 'Maastricht' Chapters introduced by the TEU:	
23	Economic and Monetary Union
24	Foreign and Security Policy
25	Justice and Home Affairs
26	Other Provisions
General Chapters:	
27	Financial and Budgetary Provisions
28	Institutions
29	Other

Source: Granell 1995: 122

Table 5.2 Brief chronology of the Accession Negotiations between the EU and the Nordic applicants

1993	*Decision Taken*
1 Feb (F, Sw)	Opening of negotiations
11 March (F)	Chs 5, 7–12 declared non-problematic
11 March (Sw)	Chs 3, 4, 8–12 declared non–problematic
5 April (N)	Opening of negotiations
28 May (F)	F agree to common positions on safety belts (1), third life assurance (2) and on direct investments (4)

Table 5.2 continued

28 May (N, Sw)	N agree to common positions on safety belts and returnable bottles (1). Sw unable to agree to common positions under Chs 1, 2 and 13
8 June (Sw)	Chs 3, 5, 7–11 and 13 closed
(F)	Chs 3, 5, 7–12 closed
9 June (N)	Chs 7–12 closed
22 July (F)	Agree to common positions on definitions of vodka and Finnish liqueurs (1), radioactive safety standards (13) and energy stockpiling (14). Ch. 21 declared non-problematic
28 July (N)	Agree to common positions on credit institutions' own funds and third non-life assurance directive (2), advertisements for alcoholic products (2), Chs 3 and 10 declared non-problematic
28 July (Sw)	Agree to common positions on third life assurance directive (2), Ch. 21 declared non-problematic
23 Sept (Sw)	Agree to common positions on energy (14), Ch. 17 declared non-problematic
4 Nov (F)	Agree to common positions on Finnish liqueurs no. 2 (1), bathing water quality (13) and customs union (17)
(N)	Agree to common positions on driving licences (5) and financial and budgetary provisions (27) Chs 2 and 21 declared non-problematic
(Sw)	Ch. 2 declared non-problematic
9 Nov	Maastricht Chapters now included in negotiations
25 Nov (F)	Agree to common positions on financial services (2), statistics (10), radioactive waste (13) and CCP (18)
21 Dec (Sw)	Chs 6, 13, 24–26 closed
(N)	Agree common positions on fiscal incentives for motor vehicles (1), hazardous waste (13) and Baltic States (18)
1994	
21 Jan (N)	Ch. 26 closed
8 Feb (Sw, F)	Ch. 17 closed
17 Feb (Sw, F, N)	Joint Declaration on Nordic Co-operation agreed (29)
22 Feb (F)	Agree to common positions on secondary residences (4), fisheries (16), maritime links and Åland Islands (29). All three Nordics agree to common position on Sami people (29)
1 March (Sw, F)	Agreement on Nordic agriculture, regional and budgetary questions, veterinary questions and agricultural quotas
8 March (N)	Agreement on budgetary, agriculture, regional and veterinary questions
15 March (N)	Agreement on fisheries (14) and EMU (23)
30 March (Sw, F, N)	Final agreement on Chs 23 and 28
11–12 Apr (Sw, F, N)	Acceptance by candidates of Accession Treaty and beginning of the ratification process
24 June (Sw, F, N)	Signing of Accession Treaty at Corfu

Note: F = Finland, N = Norway, Sw = Sweden
Source: Modified from Granell 1995: 125–7

a new beacon of achievement after the traumatic problems associated with the TEU's ratification. This point was not lost on the Nordic governments.

The December 1993 preliminary agreements proved the turning point in the accession negotiations. They facilitated further agreement and a belief that the negotiations could finish on time. By 22 December 1993, out of a total of twenty-nine chapters, thirteen of them had been agreed with Norway, fifteen with Finland and eighteen with Sweden. There was also substantial progress on several of the more sensitive areas. The applicants accepted the 'Maastricht chapters' (including EMU and Justice and Home Affairs (JHA)); there was a joint statement on the Nordic countries becoming 'full and active members' of the CFSP and a four-year transitional period on environmental standards was agreed.

There were two particularly influential agreements with regard to the domestic debates in the Nordic countries. First, the granting by the EU of a derogation for Sweden and Norway regarding their 'snus' tobacco trade. Second, the agreement that the Nordic countries could maintain their alcohol monopolies on retail sales (even if these would have to be abolished for the importation, production and distribution of alcohol). Both these derogations were essential if domestic opposition to EU membership was to be overturned. In fact, the announcement of these EU concessions was delayed until December (having been originally agreed in November) in order to raise the domestic profile of the Nordic governments and the belief that they were protecting sensitive national interests. There were also protocols recognising certain exclusive rights for the Sami people and the autonomous status of Åland.

Yet, the third phase between January and March 1994 marked the transformation of the accession process. The progress of December 1993 was reinforced by a new sense of urgency on both sides that the 1 March 1994 deadline for completion needed to be respected. In particular, a new institutional dimension came to the fore. The requirement that the accession treaties were approved by the European Parliament (EP) provided another catalyst for agreement. The postponing of the deadline from January to March 1994 in late 1993 now meant that the negotiations would coincide with the EP's election year. It was essential that the EP should ratify the accession treaties before its dissolution in May 1994, if the applicants were to become full members on 1 January 1995.

For both sides, it was critical that this strict timetable was adhered to. For the EU, failure to do so would represent yet another embarrassment, having failed to meet its own deadlines. For the Nordic applicants, any delay would make it more difficult to convince their sceptical publics in the ensuing referendums. In practice, this proved to be the greatest impetus for final agreement as failure threatened the entire enlargement timetable.

However, for the most part, final agreement was only concluded due to the flexibility of the EU negotiators. At the psychological level, the Nordic negotiators proved to be robust. They consistently used the argument of needing domestic consent to gain new concessions from the EU. For Nordic public consumption, the EU was consistently seen to give way on the main issues. However, this was also quite accurate. When the choice was between financial concessions and matters of principle, the EU usually opted for the former and blatant monetary persuasion. Some member states even accused the applicants of achieving 'daylight robbery' on certain issues such as levels of budgetary contributions (Sweden), agricultural support (Finland) and fisheries (Norway).

THE ACCESSION TERMS – A GOOD DEAL FOR THE NORDIC APPLICANTS?

On 1 March 1994, the main aspects of the final agreement between the EU and Sweden, Finland and Austria were concluded. Agreement with Norway was reached slightly later on 15 March 1994. The intention here is only to provide a brief survey of the accession outcome in order to comment on the nature of the deals for the individual Nordic countries. More detailed assessments are provided in Part IV of the book.

By far the most important aspects of the accession deal for the Nordic countries concerned four economic areas – the degree of agricultural transition, regional policy support, levels of budgetary contributions and the protection of fisheries (for Norway). In all these, the Nordic countries received relatively generous concessions.

Transitional agricultural support

The countries that have joined have reduced their level of subsidies for Nordic agriculture to CAP levels from the day of accession. However, several concessions were made. First, the CAP was expanded to include arctic and sub-arctic agriculture. The Nordic countries gained an explicit recognition from the EU that there were legitimate political and strategic reasons for maintaining aid to the remote agricultural communities in the North.

Second, the EU will financially bear some of the costs of the transition for Nordic agriculture. It will provide compensation amounting to ECU 3.6 billion over four years to aid this transition. The creation of 'Nordic support' involving long-term compensatory national aids for farms situated North of the 62 degrees north parallel provides an additional safety net, especially for Finland (see Chapter 14). Thus, the fall in Nordic agricultural prices to CAP levels was only secured after the inclusion of considerable EU financial incentives.

Third, long-term national support is still to be permitted. Common pricing extends across the EU since accession but there are also digressive national aids to compensate farmers for income loss for a five-year transitional period. The sensitive nature of Finnish agriculture was reflected in the agreement on a complementary national farm package between the Commission and

Finland. In 1995, price support will be paid for milk, wheat, malt barley, rye and starch potatoes, with all other products receiving support based upon hectares and livestock. National support in Finland will also amount to some FIM 3.8 billion in order to keep incomes at 1993 levels (Kettunen 1995). Nevertheless, the outlook for Finnish farming still looks grim and farming prices in Finland still fell more than expected in early 1995. This was less of a problem for Sweden as her government had implemented reforms in 1991. Swedish agricultural subsidies were already comparable or even below those of the CAP (see Chapter 14).

Regional policy support

Nordic regions in unfavourable geographical locations are eligible for Structural Fund support. The EU recognised the handicaps that the Nordic countries faced, especially in terms of the isolation of border regions. The Nordic applicants are eligible for Structural Fund aid under the new Objective 6 criteria based on low population density of less than eight inhabitants per square kilometre. This virtually guaranteed that nearly all of Finland and most of Northern Sweden and Norway will be eligible for funding. The global amount allocated from the Structural Funds (after adjustment for Norway's rejection of membership) for the period 1995–9 is ECU 1,704 million for Finland, ECU 1,623 million for Austria and ECU 1,420 million for Sweden (Commission of the ECs 1995: 3–4).

Budgetary contributions

In spite of much domestic criticism, the Nordic countries gained a relatively generous deal especially when compared to other previous enlargements. The EU, in the short term, will not see a massive new injection of capital. Sweden and Finland will receive limited budgetary rebates and Finland will not be an initial net contributor to the EU budget. The EU agreed to provide budgetary compensations amounting to 2,966 MECU for the 1995–6 period (for the (then) four applicants for adjustments to EU policies and a further 630 MECU for EEA commitments and liabilities, all of which would come out of the EU budget – Commission of the ECs 1994e: 5). In fact, Sweden will only contribute a minimal 50 million ECU in her first year of membership. She also gained a two billion ECU budgetary rebate for the first three years of membership dressed up as a farm adjustment payment (even though Swedish agriculture does not face the large transitional costs comparable to those envisaged for Finland).

However, these deals were essential given the state of public financing in Sweden and Finland. In practice, any large EU budgetary demands could only have been financed out of national public budgetary deficits. This would further complicate their economic problems, especially if they are to meet the convergence criteria set out for future EMU (see Chapter 13).

Norwegian fisheries

The negotiation of chapter 16 proved extremely difficult throughout. The negotiations addressed the four sensitive areas of access to waters, access to resources, management of resources and market access for fisheries. Agreement with Norway was only finally reached on 15 March 1994 after several delays due to disputes between the Norwegian and Spanish governments. The stances of the two governments proved to be the obstacles rather than there being a problem for the whole EU.

The main issue here revolved around the agreement that Spain and Portugal were also to be fully integrated into the Common Fisheries Policy (CFP) by January 1996 (alongside Norway and some six years ahead of the date envisaged in their Accession Treaty) in order to avoid discrimination against them and in favour of the (then) potential member, Norway. To the Norwegian government, this meant fewer restrictions on the numbers of Spanish fishermen operating in Norway's fishing grounds. The government argued that it had already been generous on fisheries under the EEA agreement and declared that the 1994 EEA cod quota of 40,000 tonnes allocated to the EU was sufficient. The Norwegian government stated that it would not concede 'one more fish' and this firm, if politically untenable, position was maintained for domestic consumption.

The outcome was a limited compromise between the Norwegians and the Spanish. Under the agreement, the EU was permitted to fish an extra 3,000 tonnes of cod in Norwegian waters and Norway's sovereign rights to manage fisheries resources would be gradually taken over by the EU by 1 July 1998 (Royal Ministry of Foreign Affairs 1994a: 7). Norway was also allowed to continue to fish for herring for the production of fish oil and fish meat for three years. However, the Spanish government did not achieve its demands of 14,000 tonnes of cod from Norwegian waters. In particular, it did not gain the 7,000 tonnes of its 'historic catch' of cod that it claimed had been lost when it was barred from Norwegian waters in 1981. The flexible attitude displayed by the EU was less obvious in the case of fisheries than in other areas due to heightened national sensitivities. Nevertheless, Norway was successful in defending many of her fisheries interests and, from this perspective, gained a relatively generous deal from the EU.

Overall, the accession terms for the three Nordic countries were by no means as restrictive or financially demanding as many had first expected. There was a general understanding within the EU of the domestic political difficulties faced by the Nordic governments and the economic problems within Finland and Sweden. Most were considered legitimate and were accommodated within the eventual outcome.

DOMESTIC REACTIONS AND EU INTERNAL DISUNITY

The Union's strategy of appeasing the Nordic countries on domestic grounds was, however, only partially successful. Despite the rhetoric of the Nordic governments that a final decision on whether to favour EU membership would depend on the actual accession terms, the domestic impact once these were agreed was minimal. Each Nordic government declared that the negotiations were a success and would be recommending EU membership in the subsequent referenda. Sweden's Prime Minister, Carl Bildt even declared that this was his country's 'most important international agreement of the century'. The reaction in Finland was more qualified with some criticism by Prime Minister Aho that the agreement included 'a little bit of mist in it', although this partly reflected Aho's delicate political position as leader of the agrarian based Centre Party. However, the domestic Confederation of Finnish Industry and Employers, the Central Organisation of Finnish Trade Unions and the powerful Central Union of Agricultural Producers (MTK) all received the agreement with varying degrees of positive approval (Norros 1994: 1).

The final agreements did initially affect public opinion. Swedish opinion polls, for example, showed the previously strong 'No' support shrinking from 42 per cent with the 'Yes' vote rising to 35 per cent. However, the impact was not as large as the governments had anticipated and was short-lived. Much of the agreement had already been leaked and was public knowledge. To some extent, the Nordic electorates were suffering from political fatigue on the issue. In addition, elements of the agreement were ambiguous or had deferred decisions until after EU entry which led to uncertainty.

Furthermore, the accession terms would have negative implications for certain Nordic sectors, such as reducing agricultural subsidies for farmers. These groups remained vehemently against EU membership as they were either traditionally hostile to the EU and/or would suffer most from any accession agreement. Yet, it was unlikely that any realistic solution would have been enough to offset their criticisms, especially those of the Nordic farming and fisheries communities.

Moreover, no sooner had the positive impact of the accession deals been felt, than this was overtaken by internal division within the EU over the institutional impact of enlargement. The practical implications of these intra-EU disputes were only minimally felt within the Nordic countries. However, there was some frustration within the Nordic governments that the positive changes to Nordic domestic opinion resulting from the agreement would be undermined by the divided image of the EU during 1994. The Nordic governments especially viewed the statements by Theodoros Pangalos (the Greek Foreign Affairs Minister and chairman of the last sessions of the fourteen-month accession negotiations) as unfortunate when he officially declared that, 'Now that this is done, now that I have done my duty . . . I honestly want to say that this decision is wrong . . . the EU should not have undertaken new responsibilities before the Community structure deepens' (Granell 1995: 134).

The institutional dispute over future voting rights within the Council of Ministers as a result of the enlargement was also embarrassing for the Union. Ironically, this was not a source of contention between the EU and the Nordic applicants, but became a problem within the Twelve once the accession negotiations had been finalised. On the one side, both the UK and Spain insisted that the blocking minority for the Council's qualified majority voting criteria should remain unchanged at 23. In contrast, most of the member states and the EP argued that it should be raised to 27 in order to maintain the roughly one third 'blocking minority' needed to stop EU legislation. The EP recorded in its January 1993 vote on the Hansch Report that institutional reform would be necessary (Granell 1995: 133) and its political groups rejected any dilution of the 27 vote threshold in March 1994.

The outcome was the 29 March 1994 Ioannina Compromise,[1] but ultimately the dispute was to make little difference. Much to the relief of the Nordic governments the EP convincingly approved the accession treaty (voting for Norway by 376 for, 24 against and 57 abstentions; for Finland by 377–21–61 and for Sweden by 381–21–60 (Miles 1995a: 27)).

CONCLUSION

On 24 June 1994, the accession treaty was signed in Corfu. This marked the end of the negotiation phase and the beginning of the final ratification process. For both the EU and the Nordic countries, the accession negotiations were viewed as a success. The negotiations generated a dynamism of their own and the balance of power did shift in favour of the applicants as the time needed to finalise the negotiations before the EP's dissolution for elections drew closer.

However, the internal dynamics of the negotiations were overtaken by external priorities. The EU did not gain many of the specific and binding assurances which it had previously claimed at Lisbon were essential if the enlargement was to take place. Instead, it gained a successful outcome at a time when the EU was most concerned with confidence building after the TEU's difficult ratification.

There seemed to be a growing asymmetry of perspectives between the EU and the applicants during the negotiations. For the Union, the need for success outweighed the problems of negotiating fine detail. For the Nordic applicants, the future domestic referendums required that their government negotiated firm and detailed terms for domestic consumption. In short, the Nordic governments had to be seen to be protecting national interests. For the most part, the Nordic countries gained somewhat generous terms especially when compared to previous accessions and certainly more than the prior EU declarations would have indicated. All this provided the background for the forthcoming domestic debates and referendums on EU membership. It is the reactions at individual national levels that Part III will now address.

NOTE

1 The Ioannina Compromise was amended following the Norwegian referendum. The 1994 agreement remains outside the framework of the Treaty of Rome. It permits a minority of member states mustering a total number of votes between 23 and 25 to block temporarily a decision taken by qualified majority under the rules. In that case, the council will try to reach a solution that can be adopted by at least 65 votes.

Part III

The national dimensions

6 Denmark and the European Union

Thomas Pedersen

INTRODUCTION

In studies of the recent development in relations between the Nordic countries and the EU there has been a tendency to distinguish sharply between Swedish and Finnish EU policy on the one hand and Danish EU policy on the other. Denmark is cast in the role of an experienced player in the supranational setting, whereas Sweden and Finland are portrayed as the hurried newcomers. None of the descriptions are very accurate especially as membership means various things to different states. In particular, the Danish elite managed to postpone the fundamental decision on supranationality for some fifteen to twenty years. Sweden and Finland's accession to the EU in the 1990s had been prepared by a gradual entry into the Single European Market (SEM) through the EEA (Pedersen 1994b). However, it is to Denmark's evolving relationship with the EU that this chapter directs its attention.

While many would emphasise the continuity in Danish EU policy evident by the continuing reservations as regards certain features of the EU, it could be argued that the recent departure from traditional Danish policy with its emphasis upon confederalism and welfare-oriented motives is more important than specific opt-outs. It can thus be argued that in fact Denmark did not become fully committed to membership of a supranational community until the late 1980s. Danish EU policy underwent a change in 1989–90 which, though not as dramatic as the Swedish and Finnish, was equally fundamental.

In a recent article on Sweden's new European policy, Bengt Sundelius highlights the need for comparative analyses of the redirection in foreign policy that has taken place in several of the erstwhile EFTA countries in relation to the EU. He also suggests an analytic framework for such a comparative analysis recommending Charles Hermann's approach with its focus upon agent-driven activity (Sundelius 1994). Hermann's approach has been applied in another recent article on Sweden's new European policy by Magnus Jerneck (Jerneck 1993). Despite some methodological shortcomings, it thus seems appropriate to try to apply this framework when analysing recent changes in Denmark's European policy with the subsidiary purpose of comparing policy changes in Denmark and Sweden.[1]

The chapter first briefly outlines the historical evolution in Danish EU policy with a view to assessing the change that has occurred as a result of the endorsement of the Treaty on European Union (TEU) and the Edinburgh agreement. The chapter goes on to examine the causes of this policy redirection and finally undertakes a critical assessment of Hermann's model arguing that integration theory might be helpful in filling some lacunae in Hermann's theory of foreign policy change.

EXPLAINING FUNDAMENTAL FOREIGN POLICY CHANGE

Of particular relevance to the debate about recent changes in the European policy of the Nordic countries is Charles Hermann's attempt to differentiate the concept of foreign policy change. Hermann's theory of foreign policy change posits four types of change in a country's foreign policy (Hermann 1990):

1 *Adjustment change.* Changes . . . 'occur in the level of effort and/or in the scope of recipients'.
2 *Programme change.* Changes are made in the methods or means by which a goal or problem is addressed. Programme changes . . . 'are qualitative and involve new instruments of statecraft'.
3 *Problem or goal changes.* 'The initial problem or goal that the policy addresses is replaced or simply forfeited.'
4 *International orientation change.* Apart from changes in methods and goals this kind of change involves the redirection of the actor's entire orientation towards world affairs. Hermann specifies that . . . 'orientation change typically involves shifts in alignments with other nations or major changes of role within an alignment'.

The three latter forms of change are categorised as fundamental change. Synthesising recent contributions to the debate within the discipline of comparative foreign policy, Hermann furthermore suggests four sources of change which may produce a major shift in direction.

First of all, a change may be leader driven. An authoritative decision maker may impress his innovative ideas upon a political system or undergo a significant learning process. The Gorbachev phenomenon could be a case in point. The concept of leader driven change corresponds roughly to Odell's category of 'ideas' (Odell 1982).

Second, change may originate in bureaucratic advocacy. 'A group within the government may become an advocate of redirection.' A proposition echoing the bureaucratic politics tradition in international relations theory. This is an interesting and innovative proposition since bureaucrats are not typically thought of as advocates of change (at least not of radical change).

Third, change may be due to domestic restructuring in the sense that attitudes alter in politically significant sections of society. Drawing his inspiration from the American system, Hermann seems to define the significant societal elites as interest groups. It is thus unclear whether changes in the attitudes of the general electorate are included in his concept of domestic restructuring. Here domestic restructuring is, however, defined in the broad sense.

Finally, external shocks resulting from dramatic international events may be a source of change. The theory does not distinguish between different kinds of events (economic or political). Nor does the concept of shocks explicitly include (external) structural effects upon foreign policy. As such it represents a radical agent-oriented alternative to Waltzean neo-realism.

It can be noted that Hermann transcends the traditional focus in comparative foreign policy upon internal and external forces by adding the variable of leadership. Hermann's empirical references mainly stem from American foreign policy and his model could be argued to be overly influenced by the experience of a great power with a relatively strong executive. Similarly his concept of bureaucratic advocacy may be hard to apply to, for example, the more closed and unitary foreign policy systems in Europe.

Hermann explains that often there will be an interplay between the different sources of change. 'They may work in tandem or one may activate another.' Unfortunately, Hermann refrains from any systematic consideration of possible linkages between the four sources of change, a problem that cannot be pursued here. However, it seems reasonable to expect that, for instance, certain external shocks may produce changes in the attitudes of both a leader and domestic groups.

Hermann's model is an input–output model emphasising the role of the decision-making process. Foreign policy is affected by internal and external factors but leaders have considerable room for manoeuvre and inputs are mediated by a complex decision-making system. Decision-making regarding foreign policy change is not a clean-cut matter. There may be time-lags between, for example, a state's perception of external shocks and its policy response (Jerneck 1993). Hermann argues that the various sources of changes are channelled through a decision-making process with a number of typical stages. Each stage is like a filter which an input must pass before being able to influence policy. As such Hermann's model is reminiscent of Goldmann's theory of stabilizers in foreign policy (Goldmann 1986), only Hermann's theory is much more voluntary and indiscriminate.

Hermann suggests the following stages formulating propositions relating to each stage (Hermann 1990: 14):

1 Initial policy expectations
2 External actor/environmental stimuli

3 Recognition of discrepant information
4 Postulation of a connection between problem and policy
5 Development of alternatives
6 Building authoritative consensus for choice
7 Implementation of new policy

The decision-making process and its modalities is thus at the heart of the theory. One notes the inspiration from the cybernetic understanding of decision-making as a process of steering and control of streams of information. Nevertheless, Hermann's model is basically heuristic, although parts of the model can be used in an explanatory approach; it requires the analyst to penetrate the complexities of the decision-making process and study the welter of minor choices decision makers make before taking a major decision. As such the approach implies some methodological costs. The theory obviously loses predictive power. As a framework for comparative analysis it is also somewhat unwieldy. Yet, the fact that Hermann's model has already been applied in several case studies of Nordic foreign policy is a powerful argument for choosing this model. Besides, a voluntary approach has a certain *prima facie* attractiveness in view of the anomalies confronting structural approaches when it comes to explaining recent developments in European politics (for instance, Rosenau and Czempiel 1992).

What Hermann calls 'self-correcting' change appears to have become more important in world politics, for example the foreign policy changes in Germany under Kohl. It should be noted, however, that these instances of leader driven change have mainly occurred in big states. An interesting question which can here only be dealt with in passing is whether voluntary change based upon leadership (and domestic politics) is equally important in small states, which are often described as units essentially adapting to external structures.

POSTPONING FUNDAMENTAL DECISIONS: INTEGRATION BY STEALTH

Denmark and the creation of the ECSC and the EEC

During the 1950s and 1960s Danish EC policy was largely formulated by politicians and civil servants with only scant interference from the general public (Hansen 1969). In fact, the role of the political leadership appears to have been modest, the most prominent politicians generally preferring to invest their energy in Nordic endeavours. This left bureaucrats and notably the foreign ministry with considerable latitude in the early years of European integration. Recent studies have unveiled some of the reasoning behind the positions adopted by the Danish elite in the early period of European integration (Thomsen 1992). The traditional picture of Denmark as a stalwart intergovernmentalist has been revised. This finding should be seen in the context of new research, showing that the six founder states were mainly motivated by material interests with supranationalism generally being seen less as a goal in itself than as an effective instrument in the pursuit of national interests (Milward 1992). In other words Denmark and the other EFTANs are no longer regarded as special cases.

The Danish 'No' to the ECSC was due more to general economic and political interests than to any philosophical dislike of supranationalism. Newly released documents reveal that Danish representatives adopted a more open-minded attitude to supranationalism than their British counterparts. In the UNISCAN meetings, the Danish representatives went further than their partners in accepting the supranational approach of the Six. In fact, the Danish Foreign Ministry appears to have been sympathetic to the basic neo-functionalist philosophy, according to which sector-specific integration should pave the way for a more comprehensive supranational integration which would be a significant contribution to the maintenance of peace in Europe.

However, economic and political considerations caused the Danish government to opt for a 'wait-and-see' attitude as regards the ECSC. The economic consequences of the ECSC for Denmark were unclear. Besides, the Danish decision makers were cognizant of the political dimension of the ECSC and in influential quarters of the foreign ministry there was a fear that membership of the ECSC might, in due course, lead to the 'absorption' of Denmark by Germany (Branner 1992). The close relationship to the Anglo-Nordic grouping also played a significant part in making Denmark a detached observer to early European integration plans.

The overriding economic and political concern for the Danish government was to avoid a new division of Europe on top of the East–West confrontation. This concern became more acute in the late 1950s, when the Six proceeded to set up a Common Market including agricultural products. There was now a risk that an 'iron curtain' would be drawn between Denmark's two main markets for agricultural exports, the UK and the FRG (Thune 1987). The parallel talks on the creation of a Nordic Common Market added to the complexity of the situation. Danish negotiators pursued various strategies in an attempt to reconcile the country's conflicting interests. The general Danish role was one of bridge-building. The preferred option was the creation of a wider West European Free Trade Area along the lines suggested by the British but combined with a Nordic Common Market and with a parallel programme for extension of agricultural trade. Attempts were also made to obtain a Danish association to the agricultural cooperation in the EC but to no avail (Laursen 1992: 71).

In early 1957 the difficulties facing the OEEC talks made Danish decision makers consider applying for EC membership. The Danish foreign minister even visited the European Commission to make enquiries about the conditions of association and membership. Three considerations explain the eventual decision not to apply. First, a wider European solution was still not totally unrealistic. Second, the Centre-Left coalition government formed in May 1957 implied a consolidation of the Nordic line in the government. Third, while agricultural pro-EC interests had hitherto dominated the domestic political debate in 1957 industry and the labour movement intervened in the debate, voicing strong reservations regarding Danish EC membership (Laursen 1992: 73). After the failure of the Maudling talks Denmark joined the newly established EFTA.

When the UK decided to apply for membership in 1961, Denmark immediately followed suit (Olesen and Laursen 1994). This provoked a serious crisis in the Danish-Swedish relationship. Sweden had tried to make the EFTA countries negotiate a joint association agreement with the EC. In the wake of the Danish application, Sweden launched a proposal in the Nordic Council for a treaty which would confirm and codify Nordic cooperation. The application also produced some domestic political restructuring. Two anti-EC movements were set up, one in Copenhagen called 'The Information Fund Regarding Denmark and the Rome-Union', another in Aarhus called 'The Committee for the Preservation of Denmark's Freedom'. The new movement was very heterogeneous encompassing nationalists, as adherents to Danish decentralist democracy, and veterans from the resistance. However, the French vetoes on British membership in 1963 and 1967 postponed the decision on Danish membership and facilitated a new debate about Nordic integration.

In 1959 EFTA had overshadowed the plans for a Nordic Common Market and the idea had been shelved. In the second half of the 1960s it resurfaced. During the Kennedy Round, the Nordic countries had negotiated as a caucus and an effective one at that. The Danish Social Democratic government considered that since accession to the EC was not imminent a Nordic economic grouping might be economically helpful in preparing the Nordic economies for membership, and politically useful as a means of reinforcing the negotiating position of the Nordics. Denmark thus proposed extending Nordic economic cooperation in 1968 at a meeting of the Nordic Council.

This is not the place to dwell upon the intricacies of the intra-Nordic negotiations. Suffice it to say that unlike earlier attempts the Nordek talks were actually brought to a successful conclusion. However, true to form Finland was uneasy about the whole endeavour and informed her partners on 24 March 1970 that Finland had decided not to sign the treaty after all. The reasons for the Finnish 'No' have still to be examined in depth. For the pro-EC government in Denmark the Nordek attempt was undoubtedly important in domestic political terms, since it made it possible for Danish adherents of membership to point to the absence of real alternatives to EC membership (Christensen 1992: 144).

Denmark's accession to the EC

De Gaulle's abdication in 1969 unblocked the enlargement process prompting an immediate resumption of accession negotiations with the applicants (Petersen and Elklit 1973). The Danish accession negotiations were strikingly smooth lasting only one and a half years. Besides demanding that the Nordic EFTA countries be given arrangements ensuring their continued access to the markets of the new members, Denmark asked for immediate entry into the common arrangements for industrial products and agricultural produce, wanting to avoid a long transition period for the price adjustments on agriculture. In principle, Denmark was granted a transitional period of five years but with an exception for agriculture. Denmark thus obtained immediate financing of its agricultural produce. Besides, Denmark was allowed to retain the three-day rule for travellers' import of wine, spirits and tobacco; after some difficulty, it also obtained a five-year transitional period regarding restrictions on EC citizens' right of establishment in Denmark.

The accession agreement itself was hardly criticised in the ensuing debate, but the issue of membership and its longer-term consequences soon mobilised the general public. After pressure from the Social Democratic Party (which was deeply split on the issue), the Social Democratic government decided to hold a referendum. For the parties which were internally divided this was an ingenious way of removing the EC issue from the debate in the forthcoming elections.

The choice presented to the Danes in the 1972 referendum was basically one between losses in welfare and participation in an intergovernmental cooperation with carefully defined purposes. It was felt in the Danish elite that the population which had only recently been involved in the debate about European integration and was still strongly attached to the vision of a close Nordic cooperation could not (yet) be brought to accept political integration and supranationality.

Significantly, the Danish elite consistently referred to EC policy as 'market politics' and the Danish minister responsible for EC matters held the title 'the minister for European market relations'. This line was in accordance with an already long Danish tradition for giving economic considerations first priority within the European policy (Hansen 1969). In the preliminary debate on the Law of Accession, a leading Social Democrat, Poul Dalsager, placed the emphasis squarely on economics saying that . . . 'the EC is primarily a cooperation of an economic nature', adding that . . . 'an economic assessment of the question must mean a yes . . . ' (*Folketing* 1972: 5280). Jens Otto Kragh, the Prime Minister, while not arguing exclusively in economic terms, nevertheless also placed a strong emphasis on economics. An article by the Prime Minister, published the day before the referendum, starts out with the following statement:

> The issue in tomorrow's vote is whether the Danish population wants a continuation of that market policy, which has constituted the indispensable framework for the longest period of progress, which the Danish society has ever experienced.
>
> (Kragh 1972)

Here EC membership is (falsely) portrayed as a mere continuation of the intergovernmental EFTA policy and membership is linked to a maintenance of a high level of welfare. Similarly, the Prime Minister ends up by issuing a stern warning . . . 'it is no use denying that a no to the EC . . . will inevitably endanger both the welfare state, the employment situation and the living standard'.

Another article by the Social Democratic chairman of the *Folketing*'s market relations committee carries a similar message. Characteristically it starts out by arguing that . . . 'an extended European cooperation will be of fundamental importance for securing full employment and social progress' (Dalsager 1972). None of these mention the EC's supranational features. On the contrary, the EC is portrayed almost entirely as traditional interstate cooperation.

On 2 October 1972 following a highly emotional debate the Danes voted on accession. The appeal to short-term material interests proved effective with the Norwegian 'No' in September having little effect on the Danish outcome. The pro-EC side won the referendum comfortably with 63 per cent for and 37 per cent against.

Denmark and the Single European Act

During the first ten years of Denmark's membership the integration process lost momentum due to a combination of factors. The plans for institutional reform of the EC moved forward at snail's pace giving way to pragmatic cooperation in areas such as monetary policy, foreign policy and Third World aid. This gave the Danish pro-EC elite a breathing space, which could have been used to educate the population on the merits of supranationality. Instead the changing Danish governments chose to dodge the debate on political integration. With the benefit of hindsight it is easy to lament the complacency or outright deceit which seemed to characterise official Danish EC policy of the 1970s. But at the time there was a widespread feeling (not only in Denmark) that federalist plans were dead (Sørensen 1978).

Yet, the 1970s proved to be merely an interlude. In the early 1980s, the momentum towards European Union picked up again due to renewed German efforts and notably a change in the French attitude towards supranationality. The Danish government which had counted upon France to reject ambitious plans for changes in the treaties was caught by surprise, when French President Mitterrand cautiously supported the Spinelli report in two speeches in 1984.

In June 1984 the European Council decided to set up the Dooge committee which was to make proposals for changes in EC cooperation. The majority of EC members wanted major reforms including changes to the treaty itself. This was rejected by the UK, Greece and Denmark; the Danish Centre-Right government was under considerable pressure from the predominantly EC-sceptical Social Democrats. The Social Democrats still argued in classical functionalist terms rejecting the need for strong supranational institutions (Schou 1986). On 28 May 1984 the *Folketing* held a general debate on the Danish position regarding the future of the Community. With a majority of 134 against 30 the *Folketing* adopted a lengthy but important motion from the Social Democrats which read in its entirety (*Folketing* 1984: 7160):

> The *Folketing* decides that the foundation of Denmark's membership of the EC is the preservation of the right of veto and a maintenance of the current division of power between Council Commission and the EP and therefore the *Folketing* rejects the EP's draft Treaty on European Union.
>
> The *Folketing* decides that in the coming years Denmark shall actively work for:
>
> - a determined effort to combat unemployment
> - the carrying out of new common activities in the field of industry, research, technology and energy
> - a coordinated effort to improve the external and working environment in ways that do not hamper a country's possibilities for making progress by national measures
> - a more stringent control of multinational companies
> - maintenance of the principles governing the common agricultural policy
> - an intensified cooperation with the EFTA countries

It can be noted that first, the motion is defensive containing a number of bastions; second, that the motion deals only with the substance of EC cooperation brushing aside institutional concerns. In the Dooge committee which was dominated by adherents of institutional reforms the Danish representative consequently acted with great caution inserting a whole range of reservations in the preliminary report (Council of the ECs 1984). Thus the Danish representative inserted a general reservation expressing serious doubt regarding the approach adopted by the majority of the representatives. The Danish view was that changes in the founding treaties would not solve the fundamental problem which was a lack of political will on the part of governments. It was furthermore argued that the difficulties confronting the EC were, to a considerable extent, due to the fact that existing treaty commitments had not been fully implemented or were not respected. The Danish representative also inserted specific reservations regarding new decision-making procedures (such as, on majority voting).

The outcome of the negotiations at the IGC was subsequently rejected by the Social Democrats and the small radical liberal party, leaving the government in a minority on the issue. In a surprise move the conservative Prime Minister Schlüter reacted by calling a referendum. During the campaign prior to the referendum the Social Democrats mainly criticised the weak guarantees for Danish environmental standards and the enhanced role of the EP, whereas the radical liberals reacted to the chapter on foreign policy cooperation. The referendum was won comfortably by the pro-side, 56.2 per cent voting in favour and 43.8 per cent against the SEA. This defeat made a strong impact on the Social Democrats, whose 'No' to the SEA had anyway been far from unanimous. It helped pave the way for a revision of the party's European policy (Haahr 1993: 211ff). In 1986 the Social Democratic Party issued a policy report which argued the case for a wider European cooperation embracing non-EC states but at the same time expressed sympathy for the idea of a more independent Europe between the super powers (Social Democratic Party of Denmark 1987).[2]

CHANGING COURSE: FROM MAASTRICHT TO EDINBURGH

Yet, the turning point in the Danish attitude to the EU did not arrive until 1990, when seven parties in the *Folketing* with the Social Democrats in a key role agreed on a proposal for changes in the Treaty of Rome. The so-called Memorandum contained a number of novelties: first of all, it says that . . . 'the Community must be strengthened in order that it may constitute a foundation for the political and economic unity of the entire Europe' (SNU 1991). The memorandum supports EMU unequivocally stating that . . . 'the Danish government considers it of importance that the conference on EMU leads to a positive result'. It furthermore proposes the inclusion of new chapters in the treaty on consumer protection, public health, education, energy, telecommunications, and cultural policy attaching subsidiarity clauses to the proposed chapters on education and health and the revised chapter on labour market policy (but not on cultural policy). Finally it proposes the introduction of majority voting in three sectors, namely – environmental protection, labour market policy and framework programmes for research and development.

In November 1989 in the run-up to the European Council at Strasbourg, the *Folketing* adopted a motion reflecting the new willingness in the Social Democratic party to consider a deepening of integration. In the debate the Social Democratic spokesman stressed that with the SEA, Denmark had been exposed to the full force of free movement, but because of the unanimity requirement had not been given the possibility of raising labour market and environmental protection in countries with low standards. The economic problem addressed by the Social Democrats was that there was a risk of Denmark being exposed to social dumping (Haahr 1993).

Significantly, the motion which was adopted by a majority of 110 votes against 18, links the introduction of new decision-making procedures with wider European cooperation. The motion recommends . . . 'new forms of decision-making and patterns of collaboration which open the way for a closer cooperation with the EFTA countries and with the countries in Central and Eastern Europe . . . ' (*Folketing* 1990: 2567).

During a parliamentary debate in 1990 on the revision of the treaties, Svend Auken, at the time leader of the Social Democrats, summarised his party's vision saying that . . . 'we wish both a more open and a more binding cooperation in Europe, and the most useful framework for such a development is a reformed EC cooperation'. Linking a widening to a deepening of integration he added that . . . 'the goal must be a strong, but open community of the European nations' (*Folketing* 1991: 996–7). Clearly, external shocks were causing a major domestic restructuring of Danish EC policy which gave pro-Union segments in the administration a greater freedom of manoeuvre in their attempts to take Denmark further down the road of regional integration. The fact that a number of countries in EFTA and Central and Eastern Europe were moving closer to the EU had changed many Social Democratic politicians' perception of the Community.

Changes in Europe's power structure also affected the Social Democrat attitude to the EU. The party's EC ideologist, Ralf Pittelkow, in a newspaper article described the new EC as . . . 'an alternative to unilateral dependence on Germany' (Pittelkow 1990). In a now famous statement, Ritt Bjerregaard, an influential thinker in the party, asserted that the Danes had once and for all to come to terms with the fact that Denmark was a part of the North German plain.

In December 1991 the European Council adopted the TEU (Laursen 1994). A large majority in the *Folketing* (125 against 30) supported the treaty referring to important concessions to Denmark in areas like consumer protection, majority voting on environmental and labour market issues and the inclusion of the subsidiarity principle in the treaty (Pedersen 1993: 86). Nevertheless, in several respects the treaties went beyond the negotiating position laid down in the memorandum: the inclusion of some important new chapters such as judicial and internal affairs and citizenship ran counter to Danish wishes. Notwithstanding the Danish reservation on the WEU defence integration was made a long-term goal of the EU. Similarly the strengthening of the EU's institutional capacity went beyond what Danish decision makers had wished; the European Parliament being granted a de facto right of veto in a number of areas, a reform that could be argued to change (or at least modify) the institutional balance within the EU system. The Danish position on the latter point had been to extend the cooperation procedure.

By early 1992 Danish EU policy had thus changed significantly. While consensus building at the parliamentary level proved relatively easy, securing the support of the population proved much more difficult. In fact, the pro-Maastricht camp was facing a daunting task having to convert the Danes from members of an extensive economic cooperation centring on the Single Market to adherents of a political Union. Considering the errors of omission made in the preceding years, the closeness of the outcome of the referendum was as surprising as the outcome itself: 49.3 per cent of the voters voted 'Yes', 50.7 per cent 'No' (Svensson *et al.* 1992). Research on the polling result shows that the 'No'-side was mainly concerned about the loss of sovereignty in political areas. Typically, there was considerable support for closer economic and monetary cooperation but little support for giving up the Danish Krone, the latter constituting a much larger political step.

The June 1992 referendum could be seen as a clash between a political leadership strongly supported by bureaucratic segments and influential interest groups and an EU-sceptical electorate. The immediate winner was the slim 'No'-majority in the population, egged on by well-organised anti-EU movements, but in the period from June 1992 until May 1993 the pro-Union coalition skilfully managed to recapture the initiative. This process was in part leadership driven. The Danish foreign minister who was strongly pro-Union did not object to his eleven colleagues issuing a statement from a meeting in Oslo on 4 June to the effect that the process of ratification would continue in accordance with the agreed timetable despite the fact that formally the treaty had fallen. Having refrained from blocking the process of ratification the government initiated a campaign of agenda-shaping. The foreign ministry played an important role in this campaign preparing a 'White Paper' on Denmark and the TEU (see *Udenrigsministeriet* 1992).

The report makes interesting reading. The politically important part of the report is a survey of eight possible solutions to the problem created by the Danish 'No' to the treaty. This survey is preceded by an analysis of the difficulties involved in letting some countries continue as members of the EC while others cooperate on the basis of the TEU. There is also an analysis of what is called 'the extreme solutions'. The extremes are described as on the one hand a Danish withdrawal from the EC and an EEA solution for Denmark, on the other hand full Danish participation in the EU. By excluding the 'extreme' solution of a complete re-negotiation of the TEU the report effectively defines the problem of the Danish 'No' to the treaty as a Danish problem. The subsequent consideration of the eight options does include the possibility of re-negotiation. However, the relevant passage is very short and attention is drawn to the Oslo statement in which the eleven other members refuse a re-negotiation. Besides, the reader is already told discreetly that at least one of these alternatives is not realistic in practice.

Following the publication of this report, seven parties in the parliament including the anti-Maastricht party the Peoples' Socialists, initiated talks on a 'national compromise' on Danish EU policy. The premise underlying the talks was that Denmark should seek a special status *vis-à-vis* the Union, while at the same time trying to convince the other members of the need to introduce more democracy and openness in the EU. Opinion polls showed that a majority of the Danes would vote 'Yes' in a new referendum if Denmark were to obtain 'opt-outs' on key issues like monetary integration, judicial cooperation, defence and citizenship (Svensson *et al.* 1994: 202).

At the Edinburgh summit Denmark negotiated four 'opt-outs' from the TEU in the areas of monetary integration, defence, citizenship and cooperation on juridical and internal affairs. Declarations on democracy, openness and subsidiarity were also adopted by the European Council. The Edinburgh agreement was subsequently approved by a comfortable majority in the second referendum of 18 May 1993. The pro-Unionists managed to convince a majority of Danes that the Edinburgh agreement was significantly different from the TEU. The debate in the run-up to this second referendum differed from the debate prior to the first referendum. Economic arguments came more to the fore (Svensson *et al.* 1994; Svensson 1994).

The significance of the 'opt-outs' must be regarded as limited. The 'opt-out' on citizenship is little more than a clarification of the treaty. The 'opt-outs' on defence and EMU basically recall the reservations expressed at Maastricht on these matters. As regards the third pillar Denmark agrees to 'participate fully' in cooperation (for a conflicting interpretation see Petersen 1993).

Significantly, a final declaration states that the agreement with Denmark 'is compatible with the treaty . . . and does not question its goal'. Thus, Denmark remains bound by the EU's political goals. The main significance of the Edinburgh agreement is that it makes it politically very difficult for a Danish government to give up the reservations on, for example, defence and monetary union without calling another referendum. The 'No' in the referendum of 2 June 1992 thus caused only a minor backtracking in Danish EU policy compared to the programme change introduced with the Treaty on European Union.

Since 1993 new external shocks have changed the parameters of the Danish EU debate. The fact that Sweden and Finland negotiated accession treaties without 'opt-outs' has put the EU-sceptics on the defensive. Moreover, the EFTA enlargement has weakened the anti-EU side by essentially removing the Nordic alternative to EU membership.

THE NATURE AND CAUSES OF THE CHANGE

Danish EC policy in the period from 1973 to 1989 underwent a series of adjustment changes, the basic philosophy behind the Danish policy being sector-specific confederalism. Danish EC policy was far from static during this period, but there was no qualitative change. Whatever proposals were made for increased integration were conceived solely as increases in scope. The turning point in Danish EC policy occurred in October 1990 with the formulation of the Memorandum on the IGCs supported by a broad section of the *Folketing*.

The changes of position expressed in the Memorandum of October 1990 constituted more than just an adjustment change. It was not just a question of Danish politicians working harder for the traditional goals of Danish EC policy although there were elements of continuity in the position adopted prior to the IGCs on economic, monetary and political union for example, regarding the importance of a wider Europe. New methods were introduced, most notably majority voting but also supranational forms such as (guarded) Danish support for EMU and the support for an extension of the cooperation procedure between Parliament and Council.

It is open to question to what extent the change in Denmark's European policy can be referred to as an international orientation change. There were significant changes in a number of issue areas and it could be argued that the Danish political elite now opted for a new role within the 'EU alignment' as a (positive) 'shaper' rather than (negative) 'barrier' (Allen and Smith 1990). Yet, international orientation change implies an alteration in foreign policy as a whole even though the EU constitutes a key part of Danish foreign policy; Danish foreign policy retains an independent dimension.

The concept of programme change thus seems mostly to fit the description of the change in Danish EU policy which took place in 1990. But arguably there was also an element of problem and goal change involved. Whereas hitherto the EC had been regarded as fulfilling a predominantly economic function, Danish politicians were now almost unanimous in praising the political role of the EU. External political shocks appear to have been of great importance as catalysts of change in Danish EU policy as indeed of the change in Swedish European policy. Denmark and Sweden changed their European policy almost simultaneously, that is in the autumn of 1990. The fact that small states with different foreign policy traditions reacted in a similar fashion to external structural changes suggests that realism is helpful in explaining recent changes in the European policies of small states. The Nordic adaptation to the EU can be seen as a typical case of small states pursuing a band-wagoning strategy *vis-à-vis* the strongest power in a power constellation (Germany) (see Kelstrup 1993). From the perspective of adaptation theory, it can be argued that Denmark opted for a new kind of indirect adaptive acquiescence, in which general concessions to a supranational regime are used against a potential threat from an actor (Mouritzen 1988: 64). Yet, the cases of Finland where the response to structural change was delayed and Norway, where there was no response, demonstrate the continuing importance of other factors such as domestic politics.

There were three external political shocks influencing Denmark's

European policy: first, Germany's unification and the perceived need to strengthen the EU as a means of influencing the new power house in European politics (Pedersen 1995c); second, the EU's new role as a moderniser and stable anchor in the new Europe (the European Commission's active profile in relationship to Eastern Europe appears to have had an especially positive effect on the EU's image in Denmark); third, the prospect of a significantly widened EU epitomised by the clamour for membership from the EFTA countries and Central and Eastern Europe. The statements made by Social Democratic politicians which played such a key role in the policy change suggests that all three factors were important. However, the three factors were not accorded equal weight. While the 'German argument' was not controversial among ordinary Social Democrats and the wider public, the linkage between a widening of Europe and support for major reforms of the EU was a perfect tool for building a new consensus within the party.

Although external shocks were highly important sources of change, it would be wrong to overlook other sources of change. Between 1986 and 1990 a significant domestic restructuring occurred which cannot be explained by external shocks alone. Unlike Sweden where restructuring among influential economic interest groups was of great importance, this was mainly a restructuring of the domestic political scene. The Social Democratic party in particular shifted its loyalty in some policy areas from the national to the supranational arena, arguing that there was a need to rectify the imbalances of the single market and the SEA (Haahr 1993: 230). But the restructuring even included the left wing, notably the Socialist Peoples' Party (SF), which appears to have been particularly influenced by the new role played by the Commission *vis-à-vis* Central and Eastern Europe.

Leadership appears to have been of limited importance in the Danish case. Leadership is generally of little importance in the Danish political system, in which minority governments are common and broad solutions are sought especially in foreign policy and European policy. Traditionally, individual factors have been assumed to play a limited role in the foreign policies of small states (Rosenau 1971). However, the case of Sweden, where Carl Bildt appears to have played a certain role in diffusing new ideas regarding the political virtues of regional integration, suggests that even in small states leadership may play a role.

Bureaucratic interests ought not to be neglected as determinants of Danish European policy. As yet we have little concrete knowledge of the influence exerted by bureaucratic segments, a research topic rife with methodological problems. However, a powerful theoretical case can be made for regarding bureaucrats as an important source of pro-integrative change in the EU. Bureaucrats in general have a vested interest in (further) supranational integration since this type of integration causes a shift in the balance of power within the national political system between the executive and the legislative branch of government to the advantage of the executive (Pedersen 1994a, 1995a). Much legislation that used to be discussed in three public hearings in the *Folketing* is now discussed in secrecy by ministers and civil servants gathered in the Council with the EP in a secondary role. Moreover, the present EU system offers promising career prospects and an attractive international working environment. The *Fusionsburocratie* (Bach 1992) still occupies the centre ground in the EU's decision-making system. It is also probably the most important elite network in the consociated EU system. The foreign ministries have a particular stake in a continuing integration process since in most cases they play a key role in preparing Intergovernmental Conferences.

Obviously, it is one thing to argue that bureaucrats have a vested interest in EU integration, quite another to show that bureaucratic advocacy is an important source of policy change. Concrete evidence is admittedly scarce. But clearly the Danish foreign ministry played an influential role in the years prior to Danish accession and after accession it retained considerable influence, for example, in preparing Danish positions at the EU's Intergovernmental Conferences.

INTEGRATION THEORY AND FOREIGN POLICY CHANGE

It seems worth considering whether classical integration theory can shed some light on processes of domestic restructuring in integrating states. The fact that domestic restructuring had a different meaning in the Swedish and the Danish case also raises the question to what extent and in what respect institutional affiliation with an integration system changes the parameters of foreign policy.

As suggested by neo-functionalist theory, states which take part in a regional integration process may experience a constant domestic 'restructuring'. First of all, regional market liberalisation increases the dependence of the society in question upon the regional economy which over time leads to a reduction of policy alternatives (Nye 1971). This is basically a variation on the theme of interdependence. Second, participation in regional integration potentially implies a restructuring of incentives (functional spill-over) and attitudes (political spill-over) at the national level which may lead to a shift of attention and loyalty towards the supranational system of governance (Haahr 1993; Haas 1958, 1964).

The first proposition is relevant to both the Danish and Swedish case, the second mainly to the Danish.

In both countries there was a widespread feeling in 1990–2 that there was no alternative to EU affiliation. Svensson *et al.* in June 1992 asked a sample of Danish voters to state their justifications for voting 'Yes' and 'No' to the TEU. As many as 44 per cent of them said they thought 'Denmark could not cope outside the EU', which comes close to saying that there is no alternative to EU membership (Svensson *et al.* 1992: 93).

In Sweden the exodus of productive capital from the country reduced the alternatives available to Swedish politicians in a very tangible way (Mortensen 1995).

A restructuring of incentives does appear to have influenced the Swedish government's abandonment of the European Economic Area in favour of the membership option (Pedersen 1994b). Yet, the imbalances in the EEA treaty were mainly perceived by the political elite in Sweden which referred to these imbalances in its public rhetoric on the necessity of Swedish EU membership. Societal attitude restructuring was on the other hand clearly in evidence in Denmark in the second half of the 1980s as shown by Haahr (1993).

It would seem that the parameters of foreign policy in an integrating state are not quite the same as those of 'normal' foreign policy. It makes a difference whether we are referring to the European policy of a member state or a non-member state. The relative importance of different sources of change varies in the two types of actors; domestic restructuring and bureaucratic advocacy are more important in the integrating state. If applied to the integration policy of a state already formally affiliated to the regional integration system, Hermann's concept of the nation state is simply too static.

First of all, foreign policy-making in an integrating state is characterised by an almost constant feed-back process which influences decision makers as well as domestic groups. Decisions made by the integration system may restructure the incentives of domestic groups. Moravcsik (1993) has argued convincingly that intergovernmentalism lacks a theory of domestic preference formation. However, his theory is deficient in that it only looks at the input side, turning a blind eye to possible feed-backs from the integration system to member societies.

Second, an integrating state is not only exposed to recurring economic shocks. It also finds itself responding to recurring external political shocks due to the extraordinary interdependence between the political systems of member states. The latter are mainly actor-oriented involving both state-actors and societal actors. They can be defined as actions by states which change the parameters of European policy-making thus inducing learning. Richardson's notion of 'dyadic relationships' and the importance of 'reference societies' may be relevant here (Richardson 1982). Clearly, 'reciprocal behaviour' is more important in the EU context than in international politics in general. For example, the consequences of the June 1992 Danish referendum illustrate that societal developments in a single and even a small state might also affect the parameters of European politics, which shows the extraordinary interdependence implied by EU membership.

In a sense integrating states find themselves caught up in an almost constant cycle of policy change. Following neo-functionalist theory this change will essentially be a programme change in that influential actors in society will change their attitudes regarding the methods whereby their utility-maximising goals are to be realised shifting their loyalty towards the supranational level of political governance. National bureaucrats have a vested interest in the present EU system. Neo-functionalism contains the important additional proposition that bureaucratic segments in an integrating state might undergo a process of socialisation due to their participation in transgovernmental networks (*engrenage*). Bureaucrats taking part in supranational networks tend to go native and become advocates of further integration: witness the conversion of Lord Cockfield, the British EU Commissioner, from a free-market confederalist to an advocate of extensive supranational regulation.

Similarly, the anti-German current which existed in the Danish foreign ministry in the 1950s has since disappeared giving way to French- and increasingly also German-leaning currents, a transformation that should probably mainly be seen as a consequence of growing asymmetries in trade dependence but which could also be related to transgovernmental interaction within the EU.[3] Studies of foreign policy change in integrating states ought to be particularly attentive to instances of bureaucratic advocacy in view of the strong position of bureaucratic actors in the present EU system.

CONCLUSION

This chapter has argued that, like the Swedish, Danish European policy underwent a programme change and also to some extent a change in goals and general orientation in 1990–1. The Swedish change was more dramatic than the Danish implying an abandonment of the traditional 'Nordic model'. But to the extent that it had postponed its decision on the fundamentals of supranational integration, 1991 became a moment of truth for Denmark. While the explanation for this policy of delay should probably in part be sought in domestic politics, the consequence of the decision to postpone fundamental choices was that a combination of structural dependence and attitudinal integration was allowed to build up pressures for continued membership of the EC. The policy of fragmenting the fundamental decision on membership of a supranational community seems to be a wise one.

Traditionally, Denmark had pursued a strategy of keeping its international military (NATO), economic and cultural (Nordic) commitments separate. Notwithstanding the reservation regarding the WEU, the European Union and the parallel process of enlargement inaugurated a gradual fusion of Denmark's external commitments in a single framework, the EU. On the one hand this reduced Denmark's freedom of action, permitting linkages to be made between economics and politics. On the other hand the fusion removed some domestic political obstacles to an active Danish EU policy.

The fusion between the European and Nordic framework does not necessarily imply that the Nordic dimension in Danish foreign policy will disappear. Contrary to conventional wisdom, sub-systems are generally compatible with a dynamic integration process and indeed may serve to consolidate such processes (Pedersen 1995b).

The causes of Danish and Swedish acceptance of the TEU were quite similar. In both cases, external political shocks were important catalysts of change; a crucial shock being the structural change in world politics leading to the unification of Germany. This suggests that Hermann's neglect of external structural determinants is a serious weakness, when it comes to understanding recent changes in European foreign policy. There are thus indications that systemic factors remain predominant in determining the foreign policy of small states despite the fact that domestic politics have in individual cases been shown to be able to disarm systemic pressure.

However, external shocks cannot alone explain the fundamental changes in the European policies of the two Nordic countries. Domestic restructuring was another important factor behind both Danish and Swedish policy change. In Sweden domestic restructuring was channelled through private industry adapting to changing realities in European political economy. Swedish direct investments in the EU thus exerted strong pressure on Swedish politicians to establish closer political ties with the EU (Pedersen 1994b; Mortensen 1995).[4] Thus in the Swedish case domestic restructuring is to a very considerable extent determined by structural interdependence, a factor not included in Hermann's model.

In Denmark the domestic restructuring paving the way for acceptance of the EU involved a broader range of determinants. While a reduction of alternatives due to economic interdependence was a factor of some importance in pushing both the Swedes and the Danes in the direction of EU membership, the Danish restructuring included a change in attitudes and incentives. The absence of a more elaborate concept of learning thus constitutes a serious lacuna in Hermann's model (Levy 1994).

Despite our emphasis upon structural factors and domestic forces, the case of Denmark and the EU also demonstrates the importance of the decision-making process itself, notably the existence of stumbling blocks in the stage of ratification, where entirely new actors invade the scene. Fundamental redirection regarding integration policy can be assumed to be particularly difficult to implement, EU policy constituting an acute challenge to the traditional notion of the incompatibility between democracy and foreign policy. Danish decision makers clearly underestimated the extent to which changes in the EU treaties had become a concern for the ordinary citizen.

All in all, it would seem that important similarities between recent changes in the European policies of Denmark and Sweden leading to affiliation with the EU have been overlooked. The case of the Nordic countries and the Maastricht Treaty generally points to the continuing importance of systemic factors in accounting for the foreign policy of small states.

Having said that, domestic restructuring and bureaucratic advocacy appear to have been more important in the case of Denmark than in the case of Sweden which suggests that there are inherent differences between the nature of European policy change in states that are members of the EU and in states that are not. Comparative foreign policy apparently cannot (alone) account for changes in the European policy of integrating states. There are important dynamics of foreign policy change not accounted for by state-of-the-art theories of foreign policy change as evidenced by our application of Hermann's model. There is therefore a need for more systematic and in-depth comparisons of the EU policies of members and non-members with a view to isolating the peculiarities of states acting within the constraining context of a regional integration system. This amounts to saying that a specific theory explaining the integration policies of states is needed as opposed to 'normal' foreign policy. Curiously, integration theories have never systematically studied integration from the perspective of the integrating state.

More generally, Hermann's notion of governments practising 'self-correcting' change is not easy to reconcile with the operational sovereignty, the regionalised economy and the 'plurilateralist networks' characteristic of the EU (Cerny 1993). This lends some credence to the proposition advanced by Georg Sørensen and others that . . . 'state units in the present international system ought to be functionally as well as structurally differentiated' (Sørensen 1995; Nørgaard 1994). The paradox of the EU is that post-modern nation states appear to develop in the context of a state-centred integration system (Pedersen 1994a).[5] A preliminary solution to this theoretical puzzle could be to distinguish between different types of integration policy.

NOTES

1 Such a comparison may also be undertaken from the perspective of adaptation theory (see Mouritzen 1993).

2 For a comprehensive analysis of the evolution in Social Democratic thinking on the EC in Denmark during the period 1986 to 1990 see Haahr 1993.

3 An intriguing question but one that is not easy to study empirically is to what extent there has been a change in the 'reference society' of the Danish Foreign Ministry in recent years.

4 Interestingly, Mortensen even suggests that in the Swedish case economic interests were more important than the response to changes in the security context.

5 The present EU system can be characterised as a consociated system exposed to a number of conflicting structural pressures.

7 Sweden and the European Union

Implications for the Swedish party system

Anders Widfeldt

INTRODUCTION: A BRIEF HISTORY

When Sweden on Sunday, 13 November 1994 voted 'Yes' to European Union (EU) accession, a turning point was reached in the nation's history. The issue of European integration had been on the political agenda for over 30 years and yet, for the majority of that period Swedish accession seemed very unlikely.

The Treaty of Rome in March 1957 had only a limited political impact in Sweden and full European Community (EC) membership was not on the political agenda. In contrast, the negotiations which led to Sweden becoming one of the founding members of EFTA two years later enjoyed widespread political support. However, when the UK announced its intention to join the EC this totally changed the outlook for the EFTA countries, and once Denmark and Norway decided to follow the British example it became clear that Sweden had to adopt a more clearly defined policy regarding the EC.

On 22 August 1961 this policy was publicly announced by the Social Democratic Prime Minister Tage Erlander when he addressed the national conference of the Metal Industry Workers' Union (Ruin 1986: 301; Andrén and Möller 1990: 163; Gidlund 1992: 31). Erlander declared that Swedish full membership of the EC was out of the question and argued that Sweden's policy of non-alignment would be incompatible with European integration in the long run. Erlander's so-called 'Metal Speech' was highly significant as, in practice, it defined the Social Democratic (and hence, in practice, governmental) policy regarding European integration for almost 30 years. Indeed, even when the Social Democratic leadership eventually altered this policy, opponents both inside and outside the party continued to refer to Erlander's 1961 arguments, maintaining that these arguments were still as valid as ever. This still proved to be the case during the 1994 referendum campaign.

The Liberal and Conservative opposition parties were annoyed at Erlander's declaration, especially as they did not share his assessment of the consequences for the non-alignment policy and argued that he was neglecting the obvious advantages to be derived from membership. They also argued that Erlander had broken the consensual tradition of Swedish foreign policy as he had previously not consulted the opposition parties and thus had made no attempt to formulate a consensus. However, the non-socialist opposition parties were not totally united and the Centre Party, which had declared its intention to form a government with the Liberals and Conservatives, agreed with the views of Erlander (Jonnergård 1985: 170). Not surprisingly, the fifth party represented in the *Riksdag*, the Communist Left Party, remained firmly opposed to the EC and portrayed it as a capitalist project in total contradiction to the party's inherent values.

Thus, a battle line was drawn between the parties which was to remain relatively intact until the early 1990s. On the negative side were the Social Democrats, the Centre Party and the Communists and on the other were the Conservatives (later to be renamed the Moderates) and to a lesser extent, the Liberals. Olof Palme, Erlander's successor as Prime Minister and party leader, was confronted with the issue of further European integration as one of his first major tasks. Palme's governing Social Democratic Party favoured economic integration, but was much less enthusiastic about the prospect of political integration. However, the government became convinced that full membership was undesirable once the EC's Council of Ministers outlined its vision of a future political and monetary union in February 1971. Gullan Gidlund suggests that Social Democratic officials had become increasingly aware that important parts of the party organisation were profoundly opposed to membership (Gidlund 1992). Instead, the Palme government successfully negotiated a bilateral free trade agreement with the EC. This was a necessary step, as the departure of several important EFTA members left the organisation seriously depleted. The agreement was completed in July 1972, and ratified by the *Riksdag* in December 1972, with only the Left Party voting against. The Moderate Party and also, to some extent, the Liberals expressed concern that the option of full membership had not been seriously considered but conceded that the issue was now resolved for the foreseeable future (Gidlund 1992: 44).

After that date, the European issue was removed from the Swedish agenda for several years. The free trade agreement worked effectively and gradually won over many sceptics. The shift from Social Democratic to a succession of non-socialist governments between 1976 and 1982 made little difference. It was not until the late 1980s, when the EC's plans for further integration became apparent, that the EC issue re-entered the political arena.

After the Social Democrats had returned to power in 1982 it became increasingly clear that the trade agreement would no longer be sufficient. Ingvar Carlsson, who replaced Olof Palme after his assassination in 1986, began a gradual revision of party policy towards Europe, although at this time it was not regarded as preparation for membership, but merely interpreted as *ad hoc* measures for dealing with international economic developments.

Two important decisions were taken in 1988 and 1989. First, the Swedish currency, the Krona, was tied to the ECU in 1988 and second, currency flows were deregulated in 1989. The Liberal and Moderate Parties were positive towards these reforms, but believed they were insufficient, especially as the EC had embarked on further integration built around the Single European Market (SEM). They pressed for a more open attitude towards accession, something which became particularly evident after the 1988 election. Sweden, they argued, was now faced with the stark choice of whether to participate in European integration or not. The time had now passed when Sweden could merely choose the specific aspects it desired.

A single obstacle remained in the form of Sweden's policy of non-alignment and neutrality. Sweden has remained outside all military pacts since the early nineteenth century. Ever since the 1960s, a large part of the controversy with regard to EC membership had centred around whether it was compatible with continued non-alignment or not. The Centre Party manifesto from 1981 literally stated that this was not the case, while the Moderates' manifestos from 1973 and 1984 both claimed that it was a possibility (Wieslander 1974, for example).

However, the policy of non-alignment has not been as continuous as might at first seem. While it is undeniable that Sweden has been a non-aligned nation for some 180 years, it is questionable when this became a coherent and continuous policy. Arguably this was not the case until the late 1940s, when efforts to form a Nordic defence bloc failed and Sweden decided not to follow Norway and Denmark into NATO. Thus, it can be argued that Swedish non-alignment was a product of the Cold War, rather than being perceived as a response to a series of relatively independent decisions in varying situations (Andrén and Möller 1990).

From this perspective, the neutrality/non-alignment argument became redundant around 1990 when the disintegration of the Warsaw Pact and later the Soviet Union removed one of the pillars of bi-polarity. In particular, the Swedish Liberal and Moderate Parties reacted quickly, while the initial response from the Social Democratic government was more cautious claiming that it would be unwise to commit Sweden to an integration project whose outcome was still difficult to predict. It came as a surprise, therefore, when the government on 26 October 1990 announced its intention to submit an application for full membership. This was immediately supported by the Moderates and Liberals, who claimed that this was evidence that their view had prevailed (Gidlund 1992: 56 ff).

From now on the EC issue was firmly established on the political agenda. Although the EEA negotiations between the EC and EFTA began in the summer of 1990, this process was largely overtaken by the issue of EC membership after the 1 July 1991 application by Sweden. Thus, the simultaneous EEA and EC/EU accession processes had a bearing on each other. There were those who resented the EEA as much as the EC, since it included similar commitments but incorporated no right to influence further developments. However, many leading sceptics used the EEA treaty as an argument against EC membership and argued that the EEA already supplied Sweden with the necessary tools to participate in economic integration and would therefore cater for Sweden's crucial export industries. This, in many ways, reflected the continuation of the familiar Social Democratic position of favouring economic but opposing political integration. These arguments remained central to the debate surrounding the 1994 referendum.

In December 1990 the *Riksdag* approved the full membership application, with only the Left Party and the Greens voting against. The application was formally submitted by Ingvar Carlsson on 1 July 1991, and once Carl Bildt's non-socialist government later replaced this administration the Social Democrats supported the new government in relation to the EEA and EC negotiations. The accession agreement between Sweden and the EU was finalised on 1 March 1994.

THE DEVELOPMENT OF SWEDISH PUBLIC OPINION ON THE EU

Swedish public opinion regarding EU membership has fluctuated, especially over the last decade, and Sören Holmberg has referred to this development as a 'roller coaster ride' (Holmberg 1994). Of course, there is a close correlation between public opinion development and significant events identified in the previous section, such as the trade agreement in 1972 and the changes in Eastern Europe in 1989–90.

Figures 7.1 and 7.2 display opinion development on EC/EU membership between 1967 and 1994. The data in Figure 7.1 are based on identical wordings of the questionnaires (see Figure 7.1 notes) and are therefore comparable over time. Opinion appears to have been largely positive in the late 1960s, something which is supported by the Swedish election studies from 1968 and 1970 (which indicate, albeit smaller pluralities in favour of a Swedish application – Gilljam and Holmberg 1993: 159). There is a substantial gap in time until the next data point. However, election study data from 1973 (not included in the figure) indicate that the decision in 1972 not to participate in the first enlargement was, for the most, part supported by the Swedish public (Lindahl 1994: 42). Although time points are scarce, opinion was quite stable for several years, with a gradual and marginal increase of negative opinion for the remainder of the 1970s and the first half of the 1980s. However, the period after 1986 has been highly turbulent and began with a drastic shift in favour of membership between 1986 and 1987. The late 1980s were characterised by a positive plurality, although not overwhelming compared with that of the late 1960s.

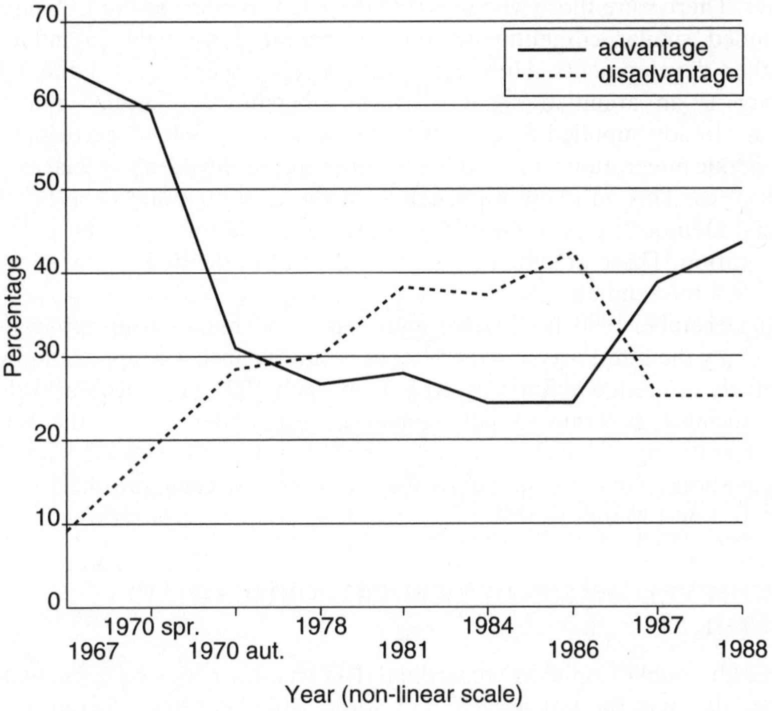

Figure 7.1 Swedish public opinion concerning EC accession, 1967–88
Note: The question asked was, 'Do you believe it would be an advantage or disadvantage for us if Sweden became a full member of the EC?' Don't Knows are included in the percentage bases but not in the figure
Source: Lindahl (1991: 66)[1]

Figure 7.2 shows the development from 1989 until the referendum in November 1994. However, the wordings of the questionnaires were altered on three occasions in order to accommodate the actual changes in the accession process (see notes, Figure 7.2). From December 1991, a full comparison over time is available (until the end of the figure) and it is possible that the final phrasing forced respondents seriously to consider the consequences of full membership as they were asked how they would vote in a referendum. At the same time, respondents were probably aware of the fact that Sweden was now involved in a real accession process.

The plurality in favour of an application peaked in 1990 and this coincided with the Social Democratic government's decision to apply for membership. Thus, just like previous decisions to rule out membership, the Social Democratic decision to reconsider EU entry was in line with, and a response to, public opinion.

However, soon after the 1991 election there was an equally dramatic shift in the reverse direction, so that by 1992, there was once again a plurality

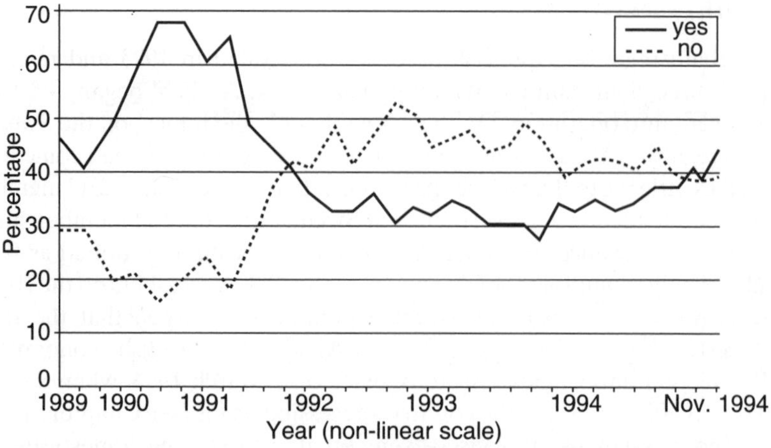

Figure 7.2 Swedish public opinion concerning EC/EU accession, 1989–94
Note: The questions asked were, 03/1989–06/91: 'Do you think Sweden should apply for membership or not?'; 10/1991: 'Do you think Sweden should be a member of the EC or not?'; 12/1991: 'If there was a referendum today, would you vote Yes or No to Sweden becoming a member of the EC/EU?'. Respondents could answer Yes, No or Don't Know (DK). Only Yes and No answers appear in the figure, although DKs are included in the percentage base.
Source: Lindahl (1994: 41)

against full membership. There are several possible reasons for this dramatic opinion change of which only a few are considered here. First, the Social Democrats faced several problems. In the September 1991 *Riksdag* election, the party suffered its worst election defeat since 1928 which resulted in a new government led by the Moderates.

Rutger Lindahl argues that Social Democratic supporters became more critical as party loyalty was no longer a reason to support the government's accession efforts (Lindahl 1992a: 112). Second, Lindahl points out that the sudden and unexpected policy shift in 1990 took most people, and the media, by surprise. It took the media a year to adapt before they started critically to scrutinise the consequences of possible full membership for Sweden. The Danish rejection of the Treaty on European Union (TEU) in the June 1992 referendum also provided further inspiration for EU sceptics.

The dominance of negative opinion existed well into the 1994 referendum year, although the difference narrowed somewhat during 1993. A national Swedish TV exit poll on the *Riksdag* election day (18 September) showed a plurality in favour of Swedish entry – the first to do so for two years. Indeed, when Ingvar Carlsson returned as Prime Minister in October, he claimed that his party's electoral success had increased the chances of a 'Yes' in the referendum. Nevertheless, the finish was going to be very close (see Figure 7.2).

THE REFERENDUM

The debate regarding Swedish accession intensified in 1993 and revolved around three significant events during early 1994. As 1994 began, the EEA treaty went into operation. On the whole though, the impact on the Swedish debate regarding the EU was moderate as EEA membership had come to be viewed as little more than a brief parenthesis before the issue of EU membership was fully resolved. Nevertheless, if Sweden rejected full membership of the EU the relevance of the EEA agreement was still questioned as there would be only a handful of small countries left as EEA members on the EFTA side. However, Swedish Euro-sceptics continued to argue that the EEA provided sufficiently for the continued survival of the Swedish economy.

The second important event took place on 1 March 1994, when Sweden and the EU finally agreed the country's accession terms (see Chapter 5). This was, of course, a highly publicised event, but its effect on the domestic debate is difficult to gauge. In many ways the accession agreement raised as many questions as it answered. Many of the specific agreements on controversial areas, such as defence cooperation, would still be subject to later decisions after Swedish accession. The announcement of the date of the referendum represented the third event and this proved to be the most controversial. Two factors were of particular importance. First, the opinion polls indicated that a referendum in the near future would be very likely to result in a Swedish rejection. Second, there was to be an election to the Swedish *Riksdag* in September 1994. In particular, the Social Democrats and the Centre Party were still deeply divided on the EU issue and both wished to avoid a referendum before the election as this would risk them entering the election campaign wounded after damaging internal splits. It was decided on 18 March that the referendum was to be held on Sunday, 13 November 1994 and this meant that the Swedish people would be aware of the results of the Austrian and Finnish referendums on EU membership when they went to the polls. This 'referendum cycle' was criticised as being designed to maximise the chances of a 'Yes' vote in each of the four countries, especially as Austria, the nation most likely to vote 'Yes' would vote first and the respective nations seemed to follow in correlation with their perceived chances of an outcome in favour of membership. Critics argued that this ordering would maximise the potential for a positive 'domino effect'.

The debate leading up to the referendum date became increasingly intense, but seldom heated. Although the campaign can be said to have started the day that the date was announced, the forthcoming September parliamentary election diverted public attention during the summer and early autumn of 1994. The election campaign was, surprisingly, not centred on the membership issue, even if the electoral success of the Green and Left Parties was largely attributed to their firm opposition to accession.

The arguments in the referendum campaign were diverse, although much of the debate can be attributed to the traditional left–right divide. The 1991

Election Study had already shown that voters' opinions about the (then) EC correlated with an ideological left–right dimension, with the left against and the right generally for accession (Gilljam and Holmberg 1993: 162). However on the individual level, there were many and notable exceptions to this rule.

The non-alignment issue continued to be the focus of attention. The sceptics argued that membership was incompatible with continued neutrality and in fact, the protagonists were not completely unified. Some argued that it was possible for Sweden to maintain a relatively independent defence and foreign policy even as European integration progressed. At the same time, it was also suggested that neutrality had become obsolete after the collapse of the Warsaw Pact.

A further debate concerned the question of continued peace in Europe. EU supporters emphasised that the EU represented the best platform for the maintenance of continued peace in Europe. While the sceptics did not directly deny this, they argued that the EU acted as the cradle for a new military and nuclear superpower, which could constitute a threat to global peace. From an economic perspective it was also suggested by the anti-EU camp that EU trade liberalisation would further discriminate against non-EU countries and especially the Third World.

Another issue within the Swedish debate concerned the control of alcohol, an area where Sweden has a long tradition of strict regulation. Sales and imports of alcohol have been monopolised through the state-owned *Systembolaget* for almost a century and within Sweden there was a declining but still influential teetotal political lobby which feared that EU membership would lead to increased alcoholism in Sweden. The accession agreement did not directly answer these questions and although the *Systembolaget* has been given a reprieve, its long-term future is still in doubt. A connected issue was the fear that the abolition of certain customs regulations would facilitate greater drug-trafficking.

The financial costs of future EU membership were another source of controversy. While it was never denied that Sweden's role as a net contributor to the EU budget would put additional pressure on her already huge fiscal deficit, it was pointed out that some of Sweden's financial contribution should find its way back to Sweden in the form of regional subsidies, and that generally there would also be a positive effect on growth. This debate on the acceptable level and form of Sweden's financial contribution to the EU and its net effect on her economy was very intense. Equally, other contentious areas covered topics as varied as food quality, environmental standards, gender equality and unemployment and in many of these cases no clear solutions were provided within the accession agreement. Although comparisons were drawn with the benefits for individual existing EU members, such as Denmark, this did little to clarify matters, especially as, for example, gender equality can be ambiguous and it is difficult to isolate the specific effects of EU membership.

Table 7.1 Result of the Swedish referendum concerning membership of the European Union, 13 November 1994

	Absolute numbers	*Percentage*
Yes	2,833,721	52.3
No	2,539,132	46.8
Blank ballots	48,937	0.9
Valid votes	5,421,790	
Invalid votes	2,297	
Total votes	5,424,087	
Electorate	6,510,055	
Turnout	5,424,087	83.3

Source: Holmberg 1994/SVT/VALU 94EU

Table 7.2 Distribution of the 'Yes' vote, EU referendum 1994, by party (percentage)

Party	*Yes*	*No*	*Blank ballot*
Left Party	10	90	0
Social Democrats	50	49	1
Centre Party	45	54	1
Liberals	81	18	1
Moderates	86	13	1
Christian Democrats	41	59	0
Green Party	15	84	1
New Democracy	34	62	4

Source: Holmberg 1994/SVT/VALU 94EU

The referendum was the fifth national referendum to be held in Sweden, the previous one being on nuclear power some 14 years earlier (Petersson 1994b: 229). The turnout of 83.3 per cent was higher than any previous referendum (see Table 7.1). There was a slight, if not overwhelming 'Yes' majority, even if blank and invalid ballots are added to the 'No' votes. The distribution of the votes among the parties is shown in Table 7.2.

THE SOCIAL DEMOCRATS

The Social Democrats, by far the largest of the Swedish political parties, have played a key role throughout the history of the EU issue. After all, it was Social Democratic initiatives which for many years killed all possibilities of full Swedish membership, and later it was the same party that suddenly decided in 1990 to lodge a membership application. Even after its historic electoral defeat in 1991 its support of 37.7 per cent was still more than 15 percentage points larger than any other party. Thus, even during lean times its large residual support among the electorate has still made it a central player in the EU debate.

Before 1990, the EC issue caused little distress within the Social Democratic Party. Olof Petersson, for instance, has shown that Social Democratic voters in 1968 and 1970 were neither hostile nor enthusiastic about the prospect of EC accession with around 50 per cent having no opinion on the issue. The Free Trade agreement in 1972 was, however, supported by the majority of the party's voters in 1973 in line with the party leadership. Thus, the issue never became controversial in the party and any proposals favouring full membership were comprehensively resisted by a united Social Democratic Party (Lindahl 1991: 69).

Therefore, until October 1990, the EC issue posed few problems for the Social Democrats, but this was changed by the government's shock announcement to apply for accession – something that was reflected by the fact that the party congress (which had met the previous month) had spent little time debating the EU issue. In spite of the leadership's earlier statements (which hinted at a possible shift away from the previous negative policy stance on EU membership), the October announcement was received with surprise. This historic declaration did not initially seem to be the start of a new and coherent policy on Europe, especially as it was announced as part of an extensive austerity package aimed at improving the struggling Swedish economy. (The policy reversal became widely known as 'the footnote switch' – Gilljam and Holmberg 1993: 159.) At first though, opinion among Social Democratic voters was not entirely hostile to the idea of Sweden submitting a full membership application. However, by 1992 Social Democratic opinion was clearly and universally against accession.

The Social Democratic voters were crucial to the referendum outcome: convincing a sufficiently large number would be essential for a 'Yes' majority, especially as most non-socialist voters already favoured Swedish accession. At the same time, the party leadership needed to be careful. Past Social Democratic experiences (such as in Norway – see Chapter 9) provided a stern warning of the possible problems that could follow the referendum. In order to reduce potential party defections, two separate committees were formed, one for and one against EU membership within the party.

The internal debate within the Social Democratic Party was, to a large extent, focused on the future of the welfare state and incorporated the long-standing divide between welfare traditionalists and modernisers. With some simplification, the modernisers tended to favour accession, while the traditionalists were split. Some 'welfare traditionalists' perceived the EU as a threat to the welfare state, while others argued that the possibility existed to influence and direct the Union towards a more extensive welfare state model. This debate was fuelled by the complementary issue of whether EU membership would have an adverse effect on Swedish unemployment rates.

If the 1990 congress had virtually neglected the EU issue, then this was to be redressed in 1993. A heated debate was anticipated, and therefore it came as something of an anti-climax when it was decided not to deal with European issues at all. The congress was adjourned until June 1994 in order to allow the eventual outcome of the accession negotiations to be taken into account before the final decision was to be made. The decision to recommend that the Swedes should vote in favour of membership was eventually taken with a fairly comfortable majority. At the same time, however, it was confirmed that 'Yes' and 'No' committees in the party would continue to operate independently throughout the referendum campaign. The party leadership was anxious to maintain party unity and the debate at the party congress was more hard than hostile.

For the Social Democrats, the September election to the *Riksdag* was a success, with a Social Democratic government led by Ingvar Carlsson being returned to power (Widfeldt 1995b; Aylott 1995). One of the first official statements of this minority Social Democratic government stated that it intended to agitate for a 'Yes' majority in the referendum. At the same time, Carlsson continued to try and avoid alienating the EU sceptics within the party. As part of this strategy, he included two well-known EU critics in his new twenty-one member government: Margareta Winberg as Minister for Agriculture and Marita Ulvskog as Minister for the Interior.

Despite only limited data, it seems that the Social Democratic voters were a crucial factor in determining the eventual 'Yes' vote in the referendum. A large proportion of Social Democrats were still undecided shortly before the referendum and at this time there was a majority against EU membership. Yet, the exit poll conducted by Swedish national TV (VALU 94) showed that 50 per cent of the party's supporters voted 'Yes', with 49 per cent voting 'No' and 1 per cent casting their ballots blank. Certainly, many Social Democrats decided very late in the campaign to vote in favour of membership.

There seemed to be two plausible reasons for this. First, the party's leading personalities and most notably Ingvar Carlsson were committed to the 'Yes' campaign. Pro-EU campaign material, especially in the closing week, focused on Carlsson and the integrity of the leading pro-EU activists. Second, the success of the Social Democrats at the previous general election was also influential, as this not only bolstered Carlsson's legitimacy, but the formation of an exclusively Social Democratic government also reduced the potential for internal divisions and dissension against the party line on full membership.

THE NON-SOCIALIST PARTIES

All the four parties which formed the coalition government between 1991 and 1994 – the Moderates, Liberals, Christian Democrats and the Centre Party – officially advocated a 'Yes' in the referendum, although there were important differences among them. With some simplification, the four parties can be divided into one group of core enthusiasts (the Moderates and Liberals) and one cohort of recent converts (the Centre and Christian Democratic Parties – Miles and Widfeldt 1995).

The Moderate Party has been the most enthusiastic pro-Europe party since the 1960s. The Liberals have also been positive, but the respective party manifestos indicate that, during the period of the 1972 bilateral trade agreement, the Moderate's 'dream of Europe' remained more intact (Wieslander 1974: 58: 169). The Centre Party's EU policy has largely followed the same path as the Social Democrats (it was against accession until 1990 – Wieslander 1974: 274; Gidlund 1992). The Christian Democratic party also has a history of scepticism (Hasselberg 1994).

When the Social Democratic government announced its intention to apply for membership in October 1990, the Centre Party's position began to shift. Shortly after, the party's *Riksdag* group backed a committee proposal to investigate the possibility of Swedish membership and the party supported the *Riksdag*'s decision in June 1991 to submit the application. Centre leader Olof Johansson, however, did have some reservations and emphasised that Swedish accession must be unconditionally subjected to a referendum and that the policy of non-alignment must remain. Johansson's caution was understandable given the Centre Party's well-organised and mostly EU-sceptical membership. The Centre leadership's strategy was to postpone any party decision until the accession agreement had been settled.

The Christian Democratic leadership also reacted positively to the possibility of accession. The party had adopted a new image in the 1980s, attempting to play down its 'confessional' tag and adopted a pro-EU stance in order to further promote a kinship with the larger continental European Christian Democratic parties. Congressional decisions in 1990 and 1991 manifested this change.

In October 1991, the new non-socialist coalition government stated that full EC membership was a prime objective. It did, however, assert that the eventual accession would be subjected to a popular referendum and that environmental concerns were to be given special consideration in the accession negotiations as concessions to the participating Centre Party. In particular, the need for governmental cohesion demanded special care for the Centre Party. Its large numbers of rural-based supporters were concerned about the consequences for agriculture and regional policy. Thus, the party was sensitive to these concerns especially given its 'movement' tradition (Wright 1971; Pierre and Widfeldt 1992, 1994). On the whole, the Moderates and Liberals did not push the Centre Party too hard and eventually all the parties in government agreed that EU accession needed to be approved in a public referendum. In fact, the EU issue did not constitute the biggest problem for Carl Bildt's government. Other issues, such as the controversial bridge construction between southern Sweden and Denmark, proved much more difficult to handle.

The Centre and Christian Democratic Parties were the most split on the non-socialist side, although it would be too simple to conclude that this division line can be regarded as separating the government parties. On the elite level, all parties were in favour of Swedish membership (even if the Centre Party felt the necessity to handle the issue with care), while on the mass level all main parties were split, albeit to various extents.

Once the accession agreement was finalised in March 1994, the internally split Centre Party faced a most difficult situation and an extra congress on the EU issue was held in May. The debate was long and intense, but the eventual decision to recommend voters to vote 'Yes' in the referendum was backed by a convincing majority. During the summer, the Christian Democratic congress also confirmed its support for Swedish membership, while the Moderates and Liberals confirmed their pro-EU stance at congresses in the autumn of 1993 without much controversy.

Despite the Moderates and Liberals being largely united on the EU issue they both included their own *enfants terribles* (Miles and Widfeldt 1995: 1516–18), although their respective leaderships still enjoyed levels of unity that most of the other major parties could only envy. Enjoying large support from their voters and almost total internal unity, they fought the 1994 election and the referendum campaign with little to worry about except defeat itself. In contrast, the Centre and Christian Democratic Parties faced problems regardless of the outcome.

The arguments among the non-socialist sceptics converged to a large extent with those of Social Democratic sceptics, except that they were obviously less likely to view the EU as a project of the right. None the less, they did not share sentiments similar to, for example, the sceptics within the British Conservative Party. Criticism of the TEU's Social Chapter and Protocol were negligible in Sweden and in fact, some non-socialists shared Social Democratic concerns over the future of Sweden's welfare system once Sweden became an EU member. Non-alignment and alcohol policy also remained key arguments, especially among the Liberal, Christian Democratic and Centre Parties who all include influential tee-total lobbies.

THE CORE OPPONENTS: THE LEFT PARTY AND THE GREENS

The Left Party had been against Swedish EU membership from the very start. The Green Party also followed a similar path, even though the EU issue was not high on the political agenda for some years after the party's formation in 1981. As the Left Party modernised its ideology, the reasons for both parties' anti-EU stances converged and were based around similar concerns for Swedish independence, solidarity with the Third World and scepticism over the future democratic control of the EU structures. However, although these sentiments were widely echoed outside these parties, criticism that the EU was a growth-oriented project remained unique. For the Greens, this was largely based on the notion that economic and industrial growth and high environmental standards were incompatible (Gahrton 1988: 105), while the Left Party gradually shifted away from Marxist-based arguments towards, among other things, more environmentally inspired lines of reasoning against membership (Hermansson 1988: 142).

Indeed, the Green Party's re-entry into the *Riksdag* due to its performance in the 1994 election (5 per cent of the vote) and the Left Party's similar result of 6.2 per cent (its best *Riksdag* result in 46 years) are both partially attributable to their anti-EU positions (Bennulf 1994). These parties were, by and large, united and could justifiably claim long and consistent opposition to the EU and Swedish accession.

CONCLUSION: CONSEQUENCES FOR THE SWEDISH POLITICAL SYSTEM

There are many who would argue that the EU referendum exposed, and even aggravated a crisis within the Swedish political system. Scaremongering tactics of the government (and especially those of the Social Democratic finance minister Göran Persson), such as hinting that severe austerity measures would be necessary in the event of a rejection did at least contribute to this feeling of Sweden having reached a critical juncture in its development. Nevertheless, the long-term effects of the referendum are difficult to predict, especially as the consequences of EU membership for Sweden will only gradually become evident.

Many commentators highlighted the fact that the referendum exposed important regional, class and gender divisions in the country. In regional terms, 'Yes' voters were concentrated in the relatively densely populated areas around Stockholm and the southern third of the country, while the populations of the north and rural areas voted against in large numbers. 'Yes' voters tended be more educated and middle class and in terms of gender, men were numerically more in favour of membership than women (Holmberg 1994). Future Swedish governments will clearly have to be aware of these divisions, although this would have been applicable regardless of the referendum's outcome (Gilljam and Granberg 1994). On the other hand, as the major parties managed to convince the electorate of the advantages of EU membership, this can be interpreted as a sign that they still maintain some level of legitimacy. As Norway's rejection of EU membership illustrated a fortnight later, it is not easy to convince a domestic population of the merits of European integration.

One source of debate has been the method of using a public referendum to settle the issue. The use of a consultative referendum has, after all, been compromised in the past. The 1955 vote, for example, on changing from left to right hand driving resulted in an overwhelming majority against; yet the change was implemented 12 years later without a further referendum.

In 1980, the voters were asked to choose among three proposals on the future of nuclear power; none got a majority and the issue has not yet been resolved (Lewin 1988; Asp and Holmberg 1984).

It is possible that the EU issue has gone some way in reviving the legitimacy of the consultative referendum. Although not binding in constitutional terms (as referendums are only binding when considering changes to the constitution), politicians on both sides assured the voters that any result would be respected. Thus, the electorate had the clear alternative of choosing between joining or not joining the EU, and from this perspective the EU issue seemed well suited for a referendum; much better than several of the previous Swedish referendums.

Regarding the Swedish party system, there are several factors that will become more apparent in the next few years and should enable more general conclusions to be drawn. In Denmark and Norway in the 1970s three consequences were observed – the party systems became fragmented, electoral volatility increased and most parties suffered declining membership (Bille 1992; Svåsand 1992). The problem is that, in the Swedish case, these three phenomena were evident even before the EU became a major political issue. Three new parties, for instance, entered the *Riksdag* between 1988 and 1991 and the Social Democrats suffered a historic defeat in 1991 and enjoyed a remarkable recovery in 1994.

Indeed, all the parties, with the possible exception of the Christian Democrats, have also lost members in the last decade. Therefore, perhaps a more detailed evaluation of political attitudes and behaviour, such as attitudes to the EU, trust in parties and the development of more unconventional political methods may provide an answer.

At the individual party level, the evaluation may be easier. The Moderates and Liberals seem to have few EU related problems, although the latter are facing a crisis of confidence after a poor result in the 1994 *Riksdag* election even if the EU issue is not central to their immediate concerns. This is even more applicable to the Moderates, who are the most united pro-EU party, while the Green and Left Parties' political importance can only be helped by their position as the only parliamentary anti-EU parties in Sweden.

Three parties in the Swedish *Riksdag* face problems regarding the EU issue. During the campaign, the Social Democrats and the Centre Party were extremely careful not to alienate sceptical members and in particular, the former also faced the extra task of convincing their voters to approve EU membership as their electoral strength was a crucial determinant in the referendum's outcome. With some simplification, the two parties did use two differing strategies though. The Social Democratic leadership campaigned energetically for a 'Yes' majority, while simultaneously ensuring that the party's sceptics were free to campaign for a 'No'. The Centre leadership, on the other hand, kept both a lower profile and did less to integrate the party's sceptics. On the face of it, the Social Democratic strategy seemed more successful, as exit poll data suggest that the SAP were more successful than the Centre Party in recruiting sceptics to the 'Yes' fold. However, *ceteris paribus* does not apply; the fact that the Social Democrats did well in the September *Riksdag* election while the Centre Party suffered its worst ever result could explain some of the difference.

There is a continual strain on the Centre and Christian Democratic Parties as, having lost votes and seats in the September election, they now face important and difficult internal debates. EU sceptics will take heart from the VALU 94 figures which indicated that majorities of both parties' supporters voted 'No' in the referendum and that public opinion since joining has moved firmly against Swedish EU membership.

However, the Social Democrats must still hold their breath. Immediately after the referendum, some disappointed sceptics in the party proposed the formation of a break-away Social Democratic anti-EU party and in response, the party leadership included a minority representation of sceptics among its first representation to the European Parliament. There are also plans to cater for the sceptics in the coming European election by allowing them to run their own campaigns and ensuring them representation also in the future.

On the governmental level, the Social Democrats are also faced with problems. The harsh criticism from the European Parliament in January 1995 against the new Swedish commissioner, Anita Gradin, came as an unpleasant surprise. The government also suffers from a credibility problem with regard to its future austerity measures as one of the central reasons for many Swedes voting in favour has been attributed to 'threats' of welfare cuts in the event of rejection. As the 1995 budget illustrated, such measures were unavoidable anyway, something which seems certain to affect public opinion.

In conclusion, then, the picture is diverse. If the effects on party standing are indicative, then there is still hope for the Swedish political system, as there are no immediate signs of an EU-related decline for all parties. But this will ultimately depend on Sweden's fortunes inside the European Union.

NOTE

1. The author would also like to thank Rutger Lindahl, Toivo Sjörén and Eva Lindqvist (the latter two of SIFO) for their advice on and data supplied for Figures 7.1 and 7.2.

8 Finland and the European Union

Teija Tiilikainen

INTRODUCTION

The issue of full membership of the European Union still represents a relatively new and unfamiliar topic within Finnish politics. Indeed, the issue was introduced quickly and unexpectedly into Finnish domestic politics, especially as for the most part, the idea of Finnish EU membership had traditionally been resisted. None the less, guided by their political elites, the Finns underwent a rapid change of attitudes. Indeed, the relative confusion of the Finnish people was reflected in the fact that throughout the period up until the referendum in October 1994, 20 per cent of the population felt unable to take up a position on the issue.

The intention of this chapter is to analyse the domestic debate regarding the issue of Finnish EU membership. First, the historical background of Finnish integration policy will be examined; second, the most notable standpoints and divisions on the issue among the main political parties will be evaluated. Finally, the major domestic arguments and the development of public opinion regarding EU membership will be assessed, culminating with an appraisal of the Finnish referendum results.

A RESERVED WESTERN ORIENTATION

By far the most dominant characteristic of Finnish postwar foreign policy was the maintenance of Finland's policy of concessions with the Soviet Union.[1] This policy was legitimised by the legacy of Finland's recent wartime experiences and in particular, the two disastrous wars Finland had fought against the Soviets in the 1940s. The policy was shaped, with broad political support, by two successive Finnish Presidents who enjoyed supreme constitutional responsibility for foreign policy. The President is responsible for conducting foreign policy although certain international treaties have to be approved by the Parliament under the Finnish constitution.[2] However, Presidents Paasikivi and Kekkonen fully utilised their constitutional powers in order to reinforce their control over foreign policy and used the rationale of maintaining friendly relations with the Soviets to bolster support for their actions.

Nevertheless, the official postwar foreign policy, which was supported by all sides of the domestic political spectrum from the late 1960s onwards never completely lacked a Western orientation.[3] It did, however, have to be compatible with and subservient to Finnish relations with the Soviets. Therefore, Finnish relations with Western Europe were based almost purely on economic considerations. Thus, the objective of foreign policy was to ensure that Finnish economic integration with Western Europe was also accepted by the Soviet Union through the use of special arrangements. Consequently, Finland did not accept the offer of Marshall aid in the late 1940s, but continued to trade with the OEEC countries through the 1957 Helsinki Protocol (Antola and Tuusvuori 1983: 128).

Finland also joined the Nordic Council in 1955 (three years after the organisation was established), but insisted that its membership would not include security policy matters or determine its relations with the superpowers (Apunen 1977: 121). In addition, Finland only participated in EFTA as an associate member initially, as this enabled Finland to claim that her membership excluded features of political cooperation. After an arduous domestic debate, Finland eventually concluded a Free Trade agreement with the EC in 1972. However, in contrast to the other EFTA members the Finnish treaty was more limited and, for example, lacked a development clause (Antola and Tuusvuori 1983: 154).

At least until the mid-1980s Finnish foreign policy enjoyed virtual unanimous political and public approval. During Kekkonen's long presidency, foreign policy was personally identified with the President, who more or less was visibly supported by political elites within the Soviet Union. Political debate and open conflict on foreign policy issues were rare as most domestic political actors acquiesed to the idea that foreign policy remained one of the vestiges of the President. Annual public opinion surveys indicated that the Finnish people also supported the official foreign policy line. Around 90 per cent of the population considered that foreign policy had been conducted effectively up until the late 1980s.[4]

In this somewhat unhealthy climate, the political debate around the 1972 Finnish-EC treaty was exceptional. However, even during this period, the most significant political actors were still careful not to exceed the limits of the existing official foreign policy. Full EC membership was not seriously proposed by anyone and the political debate was limited to the question of whether Finland should conclude a Free Trade agreement with the Community. Indeed, the strongest opposition to the agreement came from the extreme left and even the President's own Agrarian Party opposed the agreement on the grounds of deviating from the traditional foreign policy. Nevertheless, most criticism of the Free Trade agreement was neutered by the fact that the policy of neutrality was balanced by the offering of identical trade privileges to the Soviet Union. Almost two decades were to pass before the issue of European integration was to again feature in Finland, when the Finnish government's integration policy was to alter in the early 1990s.

CHANGING THE OFFICIAL POLICY LINE

Even in the 1990s, the argument that EC membership would be incompatible with the policy of neutrality still proved to be the final obstacle to a more extensive Finnish integrationist policy. The changes in the international system in the 1980s, such as the liberation of Eastern Europe from communist power, partly contributed to a more active Finnish integration policy, but they did not lead to fundamental revision of its contents. The European Economic Area (EEA) appeared to be a natural progression in Finnish pragmatism and consequently Finland supported the concept from the start. The EEA treaty never became a major political issue in Finland, especially as the country was experiencing domestic adjustment towards a more open political culture after the long incumbency of President Kekkonen. The economic advantages of the EEA were generally accepted by all parties and the concept was viewed as compatible with Finland's policy of neutrality. None the less, the official Finnish position towards EC membership remained unchanged until the end of 1990. Full membership was viewed as impossible as this would have undermined the credibility of Finnish neutrality policy.[5]

The first actors to diverge from this long-standing integration policy were from industry and commerce and their demands intensified, although notable figures in Finnish academia, such as Esko Antola, had been proposing closer Finnish-EC relations ever since the early 1980s.[6] For the most part, the main arguments in favour of Finnish EC membership were still mainly of an economic nature. All in all, the demands for a policy change were modest and were only seriously considered after the Swedish intention to apply for membership was announced in 1990.

From this time onwards, the political elites in Finland started to perceive full EC membership as a possibility. This revised attitude surfaced within the internal party debates during 1990 (and in particular after the Swedish policy change had taken place). It became a major force once the March 1991 parliamentary elections were completed (Rehn 1993: 207). Unqualified support for full EC membership came from the National Coalition (the main right-wing party), from the Swedish Party and from the Social Democrats. Of these parties, the first two were represented in the new cabinet and therefore had to support the official policy of prioritising the EEA, which at times made the positions of their leadership difficult. The other participant in the cabinet, the Agrarian Centre Party adopted a more cautious approach towards full membership (despite holding the posts of prime minister and foreign minister). Its main residual support came from the farming and rural communities which vehemently opposed EC membership. The Greens were also deeply divided on the question. Only one party, the extreme Union of the Left, categorically opposed membership.

The membership issue came to the fore after the Finnish government had officially applied for membership in March 1992. Without doubt, one of the reasons for this slow start was the novelty of the whole concept of European integration in Finland and the fact that the issue had traditionally been cloaked in economic terms within the Finnish political debate. The government also faced the internal problem that its Centre Party representatives refused publicly to take a stand on the membership question until the accession negotiations were completed. In practice though, this was dealt with by the government commissioning a set of expert studies; the purpose of which was to evaluate the merits of full membership for Finland. Although the government viewed full membership positively, it avoided a final commitment as long as the expert studies were being conducted.

In accordance with constitutional practice, the government applied to the Parliament for approval to lodge an application for membership, even though many of the party leaders within the cabinet refrained from publicly announcing their positions on the issue.[7] Instead, the cabinet indicated its preferred terms for accession and left its position open until the details of Finnish accession had been finalised. Among other things, this governmental strategy for the accession negotiations allowed the membership issue to at last become open.

TAKING UP POSITIONS FOR BATTLE

Once the accession negotiations began, the battle lines for the ensuing domestic political contest started to be drawn. In general though, the main political elites seemed to be almost unanimously in favour of EC membership, with the notable exception of the Centre Party. However, opposition against membership began to increase both within the party structures and among the general public. Opposition cut across all the traditional political divisions and in many ways can be regarded as proof that civic activism (which many believed had totally disappeared) still existed within Finnish political culture.

Organised opposition to EU membership started in 1992 although it remained heterogeneous in terms of social and political groups. Its main constituents came from the extreme right and the extreme left, while another more unified group were the environmentalists. Opposition also remained strong among women who feared that membership would force a deterioration in their social and employment rights. Without doubt, one of the most visible figures in the anti-EU camp was Keijo Korhonen, a former professor and foreign service diplomat, who had first campaigned against EU membership inside his own party, the Finnish Centre and ran for nomination as the party's candidate for the 1994 presidential election. However, in the face of probable failure, he led the purpose built, anti-EU movement 'The Independent Front of the Finnish People'. Another key opposition figure was Jan-Magnus Jansson, who was one of the leaders of 'The Society for Finnish Independence', and was, with Korhonen, a favourite of the Finnish media during the entire membership campaign.

In addition to this rather *ad hoc* opposition, there was one socio-economic grouping who were also almost universally against full membership, namely the farmers. Despite their relatively minor size in representing only 6 per cent of the entire population, the farmers maintain a prominent and influential position within Finnish politics. The farmers tried to use every possible channel in order to prevent Finland from joining the European Union and in addition to using their interest organisation, the Farmers' Union, the interests of the farming communities were championed within the leading cabinet party, the Finnish Centre.

ARGUMENTS FOR AND AGAINST MEMBERSHIP

The debate concerning EU membership ranged across almost every possible policy alternative starting initially with general economic questions before leading to arguments over security and defence. However, both sides approached European integration from a state centric perspective, with the pro-EU and anti-EU camps rationalising their arguments in terms of the potential impact on the Finnish nation state. A broader European perspective, including a deeper discussion over the merits and future configuration of the EU was extremely rare.

It is, of course, impossible to assess every argument used by either side during the Finnish debate. Yet, some of the major considerations can be identified. The first main conflict between the two camps centred over the potential economic benefits of EU membership for Finland, given that access to the Single European Market (SEM) for the Finnish economy had already been granted as part of the EEA. The issue concerned whether it was necessary for Finland to move from the security of the EEA towards full EU membership. The supporters of full membership argued that influential decisions affecting the European nation states were becoming increasingly internationalised at the EU level and it was therefore essential for Finland to 'be part of where decisions are made'. It was simultaneously argued that continued EEA participation would result in a direct loss of powers for Finland, given that the EFTA countries enjoyed only limited rights in 'shaping' SEM legislation (see Chapter 4). This argument was extensively used by EU membership supporters, especially as both sides recognised that irrespective of the result of the referendum, decisions having a direct impact upon the Finnish economy would increasingly be taken by the European Union.

In contrast, the 'decision-making' argument of the EU supporters was often balanced by the 'independence' argument of the 'No' camp which stressed the potential loss of Finnish independence and became one of the tenets of anti-EU opposition. National independence and state sovereignty have been traditional values within Finnish politics and have been an integral part of neutrality policy and resistance to European integration (Tiilikainen 1994b). These values were stressed by the 'No' camp. In essence, the core of the 'independence' argument was that EU membership would imply a renunciation of the Finnish independence and for example, during the campaign, a parallel was drawn between EU membership and the subordination of Finland into the Russian Empire after 1809. The 'independence' argument centred on political and judicial factors. In political terms, it was argued that the loss of independence would be reflected by the fact that Finland would only be of minor political importance in comparison to other EU member states and thus, its influence within the EU would be minimal. In judicial terms, it was also argued that membership would infringe the legislative and judicial powers of the Finnish parliament and courts and could therefore be viewed as a violation of the Finnish constitution.

Somewhat later in the membership debate a new pair of arguments emerged, which could be loosely defined as the 'Finnish identity' arguments. EU membership supporters tried to prove that EU membership was a logical progression for Finnish foreign policy as Finland had, in fact, always been associated with Western values, such as having a liberal democracy and a market economy. Therefore, Finland was merely maintaining its place within the community of Western European states. The 'identity' arguments, like those of 'independence', were based upon rhetoric, whose primary objective was to ignite the passions of the Finnish public, rather than using developed analytical reasoning as a method of persuasion.

In particular, the benefits of European integration in fostering closer relations between Finland and other EU member states were rarely discussed in detail, while debates over the nature, impact upon and future of the Finnish welfare state (which was one of the main arguments of the opposition in terms of 'identity') remained mostly superficial. Indeed, concerns over the implications of EU membership for the welfare state, were central to the referendum debate. There were universal fears among the Finnish public that the high levels of social and political equality, both in terms of civic rights and welfare provision, would be undermined and even reduced as a result of EU membership. These concerns were especially evident among women. Indeed, the belief that EU membership would lead to a deterioration in the position of women in Finnish society was claimed as the main reason for such large numbers of women opposing EU membership.

The last phases of the Finnish referendum campaigns were characterised by the fact that the security arguments began to work in favour of EU membership. The issue of security, including the future of neutrality policy and bilateral relations with Russia, at first appeared to support arguments that EU membership was inappropriate in the Finnish case. One of the first challenges that EU advocates had to face was the need to persuade the Finnish public that full membership was now compatible with security policy. Although there are many reasons for this abrupt change in political attitudes, and most of these can be identified with alterations at both the Finnish domestic and international level, it seems that the continued instability within Russia combined with the increasing openness and self-criticism in Finnish political culture were central elements.

By the summer of 1993, Finnish foreign policy had been revised and members of the Finnish cabinet started to emphasise security as an argument in favour of EU membership (Salovaara 1993: 20). This was couched in cautious terms and focused upon the general impact of EU membership for Nordic security. Gradually, however, the impact of EU membership upon Finnish security was perceived as a future means of protection and as a way of ensuring friendly relations with Russia. Suddenly, the whole idea of Finnish membership was seen in a new light under which the focus was placed upon being a new avenue for maintaining Finnish security.[8] This had a significant impact upon the results of the Finnish referendum as ironically the security argument turned from being one of the most powerful weapons against membership into one of the most important rationales for it. Indeed, this may prove to be a useful indication of the future nature of Finnish politics during the next decade (Tiilikainen 1994a). With this in mind, the next section will evaluate the development of Finnish public opinion on EU membership, culminating with an analysis of the results of the Finnish referendum on 16 October 1994.

THE DEVELOPMENT OF FINNISH PUBLIC OPINION REGARDING EU MEMBERSHIP: IGNORANCE AND MISTRUST

Until the late 1980s, Finnish opinion polls reflected the general political climate regarding the question of European integration. For the most part, the public supported the official foreign policy, with very little pressure for reforming Finnish policy towards European integration. Their specific attitudes are, however, mostly unknown as there were very few public opinion surveys which questioned the actual details of official foreign policy. Consequently, very little accurate data is available gauging Finnish views concerning EU membership before 1987. None the less, the annual surveys measuring the popularity of foreign policy portrayed high scores in support of existing policy, but to a large extent, these surveys did not test the popularity of potential alternative policy lines. There is, however, one early opinion survey on the EU question, which measured Finnish opinion (even though the questions were limited to just the official foreign policy).

When in 1970, the Finnish government began to refine its policy regarding the EC, public opinion still remained mostly ignorant and uncertain especially as the debate was only concerned with the merits of a free trade Finnish-EC agreement. Half of the Finnish population supported the signing of a free trade treaty, while one in three Finns felt unable to take a stand on the issue. These results indicate that there was limited support for European integration, although this may have been partly buoyed by the comparatively recent failure of the Nordek project which at this time led to an increased interest in closer relations with the EC among the Nordic governments. It can be assumed that levels of Finnish public opinion remained similar and stable until the late 1980s. In principle, public opinion on European integration was positive, yet Finnish EC membership was not viable as it was percieved as incompatible with Finland's neutrality policy.

Thus, when the time came seriously to consider EU membership there was a high level of ignorance among the Finnish public. Regular opinion surveys began in 1987, even though the existing foreign policy of neutrality remained intact. Half of the Finns who were consulted on the EC membership issue could simply not give a credible response (see Figure 8.1). Of the other half, 40 per cent claimed to support EC membership, while 11 per cent opposed it. There were no significant differences between various political or socio-economic groups with respect to how public opinion was divided. Supporters of the small Swedish Party and the higher income groups tended to be more positive towards the EU than other socio-political groups.

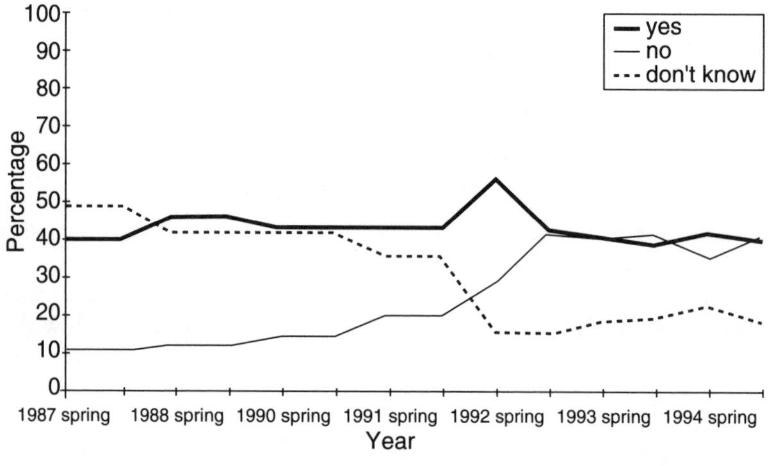

Figure 8.1 The development of Finnish public opinion concerning membership of the EU, 1987–94
Source: Adapted from T. Tiilikainen (1994a)

FINNISH PUBLIC OPINION: RESPONSES TO FOREIGN POLICY CHANGE

If the first 1987 public opinion survey is taken as the point of departure, then the development of public opinion in line with the changes to Finnish foreign policy can be more easily gauged, although the referendum will be treated as a separate and later issue. Curiously, it is noticeable that during the whole period, support for EU membership has never greatly surpassed the level reached in the very first survey. In other words, the change in official foreign policy did not really influence levels of public opinion in favour of Finnish membership. However, the most apparent change that did take place in public opinion was linked to the increasing politicisation of the issue after 1991. It was only then that the Finnish people started to formulate their own views on the question, leading to a huge growth in negative opinion and a decrease in levels of ignorance. None the less, this trend stabilised as the referendum drew closer and by the eve of the referendum, public opinion was, according to the polls, evenly split between those in support of membership and those opposing it (40 per cent each), with some 20 per cent still undecided.

As the issue became more politicised, people's socio-political background clearly played a larger role in determining opinion than when compared with the beginning of the survey period (see Figures 8.2a and 8.2b). Certain socio-political variables were important while others remained surprisingly insignificant. The correlation between political party allegiances and declared viewpoints in the surveys was especially noticeable in the case of two parties. Supporters of the right-wing National Coalition party seemed to constitute the most coherent group in terms of following the party line, with EU support averaging around 80 per cent. The next most cohesive group were the supporters of the extreme Union of the Left, who consistently opposed EU membership at around 70 per cent after 1992. However, supporters of the other political parties were not nearly as unified as far as EU opinion was concerned. The two parties within Cabinet (the Finnish Centre and the Swedish Party), were deeply divided. Their large, constituent membership and residual voting base within the farming communities restricted party allegiance on the EU issue. Supporters of the major party outside the cabinet, the Social Democrats, also remained divided and in spite of the positive stance taken by party leadership. The Greens proved the exception as they declined to take a stand at the party level on the EU question.

If party loyalty is replaced with socio-economic background as the main criterion then similar incoherence is also evident, although there was one social group whose internal opinion on EU membership was united. The farmers displayed virtually complete unity in opposing EU membership. In 1993, support for membership among Finnish farmers was actually measured at 0 per cent, although for the most part the opposition hovered at around 80 per cent of the farming population.

Differences in age or gender played only a minor role as far as variations in Finnish public opinion were concerned. In general though, young people tended to be less critical of EU membership than older age groups within the population. Women were also inclined to take a more negative view and to deliberate longer on the matter; for example, it was estimated that on the eve of the referendum, a third of women were still to decide on

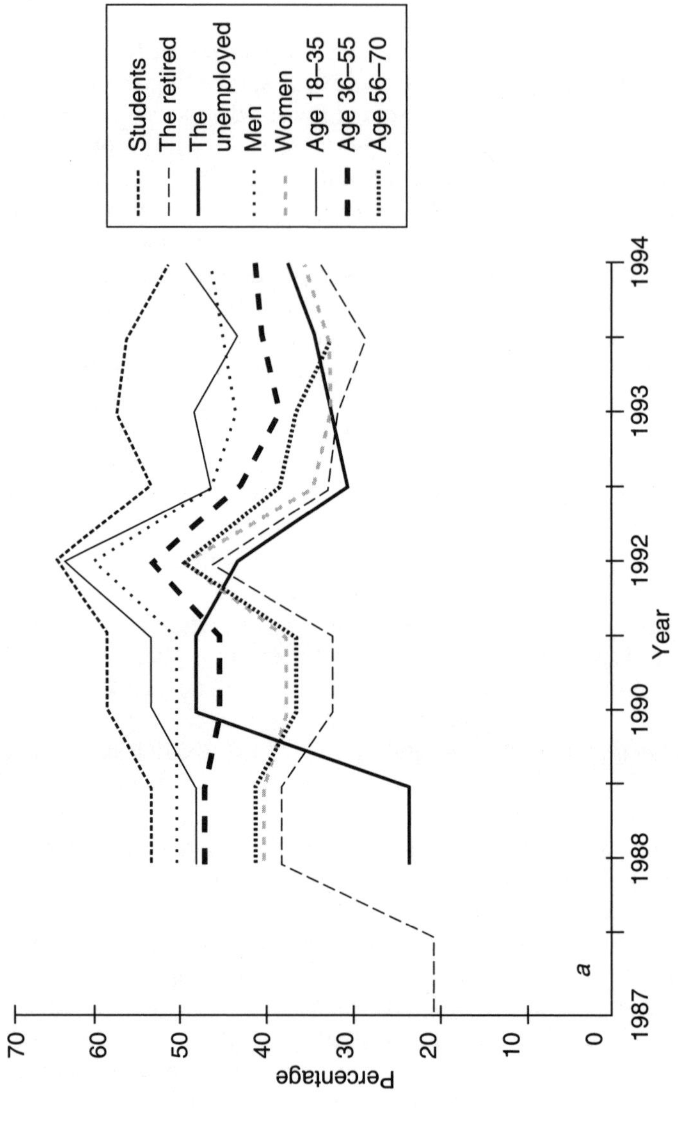
Percentage
0
10
20
30
40
50
60
70
1987
1988
1990
1992
1993
1994
Year
a
Students
The retired
The unemployed
Men
Women
Age 18–35
Age 36–55
Age 56–70

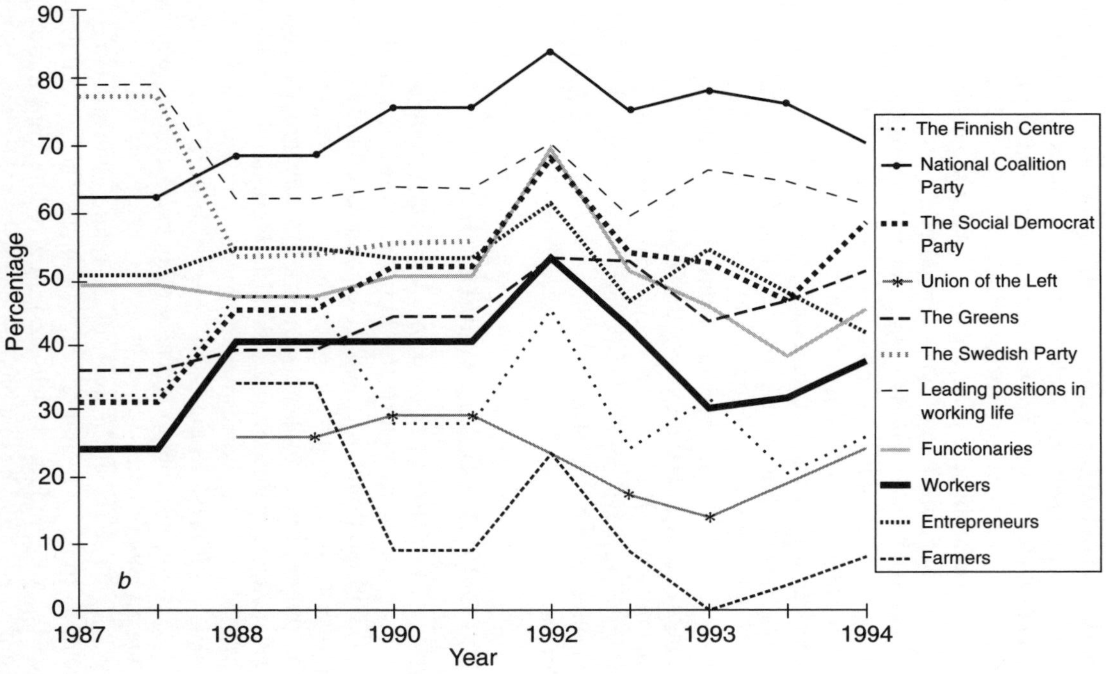

Figure 8.2 Percentage of 'Yes' opinion in various socio-political groups in Finland, 1987–94
Source: Adapted from T. Tiilikainen (1994a)

the membership question (the corresponding figure was only one fifth for men).

There were also rough geographical variations in public opinion. The main geographical division can be drawn between northern (mainly opposed) and southern (mostly in favour) Finland, with the metropolitan areas (which are also predominantly in the south) being the regions most enthusiastic about the prospect of EU membership. This north/south divide was also closely connected with the sources of livelihood in Finland. Farming is more important in central and northern Finland while the occupations are more diverse in urban southern Finland. However, this is not the only factor behind the geographic variations in public opinion, as the rural areas of eastern Finland have tended to be less critical of EU membership than the Western parts of the country, where the number of urban communities is greater. One possible explanation is the proximity of the Russian border, which increases the merits of the security dimension of EU membership for the eastern regions.

All in all, the issue of Finnish EU membership has contributed to the formulation of new types of political divisions within Finland. Their respective stances on EU membership seems to have consistently been the only common factor in maintaining rather diverse coalitions either for or against membership. Rather than traditional political or even socio-economic perspectives dividing the Finns, they have instead been split on geographical lines as a result of a much narrower basis of political and sectoral interests.

A REFERENDUM WITHOUT SURPRISES

Two further heated debates associated with the organisation of the referendum stirred up emotions before the Finnish referendum held on 16 October 1994. Without doubt, they did have an impact on the final result. First, a controversy arose over the order in which the referendums were to occur in the three Nordic applicant countries. Many groups opposing Finnish membership demanded that the Finnish referendum be held either simultaneously or after the corresponding Swedish referendum and not prior to it as planned. Towards the end of the campaign, events in Sweden appeared to be more influential especially among those Finns who were still undecided on how to vote.

The second debate struck at the heart of the referendum and concerned its role in relation to parliamentary decision-making. The central question was whether the referendum, which according to the constitution was merely consultative, should be of a binding character politically, and under this scenario what should be a sufficiently large threshold for approval. Some anti-EU groups emphasised the supremacy of the Parliament with respect to the decision on EU accession, and several Finnish MPs declared their intention to vote against membership irrespective of the referendum result. These concerns increased the uncertainty of the Finnish public over the constitutional significance of the referendum and their votes as the campaign drew to an end.

These rather unique and uncertain circumstances in Finland were reflected in the relatively low turnout (74 per cent) in the referendum (compared to Finnish general elections). According to the random interviews conducted by the media, two of the most frequent reasons for not voting seemed to be first, an inability to decide upon the EU question and second, suspicions about the eventual significance of the referendum. Using a survey on voting behaviour conducted by the Statistics Office one day after the referendum, it is possible to provide a more detailed analysis of the referendum's outcome.

The Finns voted for EU membership by a majority of 57 per cent against 43 per cent in the referendum. The result was sufficient to advise the Parliament even if the victory of the 'Yes' camp was not as large as had been predicted by public opinion polls. The public opinion survey indicates that there was a stronger tendency for voters supporting EU membership actually not to turn out to vote and this perhaps partly explains the smaller than anticipated 'Yes' victory. Indeed, there was only a difference of 400,000 votes between the 'Yes' and 'No' positions, although the pattern in which the public were divided geographically further emphasised this modest majority.

In the referendum, Finland was geographically split between the northern provinces who opposed membership and the southern ones who supported it. However, the division was much sharper than anyone had expected with opposition against EU membership exceeding 50 per cent in the northern provinces of, for example, Lapland, central Finland, Kuopio and Northern Karelia. In the larger cities and towns, there were clear majorities in favour of membership, while there were even greater numbers in the rural municipalities of, in some cases, over 80 per cent against Finnish accession. The supporters of EU membership gained their largest victories in the metropolitan areas (an average of 73 per cent in favour). The highest figures against membership were achieved in Ostrobothnia.

The Statistics Office's survey did not, however, reveal any considerable variations from the predictions and results of the public opinion surveys (Pesonen and Sänkiaho 1994: 52). Positive attitudes towards membership directly correlated with higher levels of income and education and indeed, the degree of income seemed to have been one of the strongest explanatory factors with respect to Finnish voting behaviour. The relationship was especially valid for both sexes and for all of the geographical areas. There were no considerable variations between different age groups with the exception of young men (aged 18–25) (who voted for membership (by 79 per cent)). Also, the prognosis concerning party loyalties held, although the supporters of the leading cabinet party, the Finnish Centre, took a slightly more positive stance towards membership than had been expected and this was probably as a result of the leading position adopted by the party on the issue.

CONCLUSIONS: FULL MEMBERSHIP COMES INTO FORCE

On 1 January 1995, Finland became a full member of the European Union, after experiencing a new and revised form of political debate. First, the Finns had to become accustomed to the fact that the Paasikivi–Kekkonen line was no longer holy or everlasting and that open discussion and disagreement on foreign policy matters was permitted. In practice, Finland has been through a learning process, where new concepts and political thinking entered into domestic politics, leading to an intensive debate on the EU issue.

Once the dominant party-elites had almost unanimously decided to advocate membership, the revised integration policy was strongly recommended to the Finnish people. Compared to the high-ranking pro-EU supporters, the opponents of membership seemed outdated and anachronistic, often referring to traditional political concepts that many Finns no longer associated with. If Finnish public opinion is evaluated overall, then the influence of the political elites appears only mediocre. Even though support of membership remained constant since the first opinion survey in 1987, the fate of Finland was decisively held in the hands of those Finns who ultimately only made up their minds at the very end of the referendum campaign.

Yet, the Finnish referendum caused no great surprises. The Finnish people consented to EU membership by a relatively slim majority and there are clear indications that powerful social interests opposed full membership. The most significant of these were farmers, who dominated the issue of integration in Finland towards the end of negotiations for membership. The unified and hostile reaction of the farmers was reflected by the sharp geographical division of the country in the referendum, stressing that EU membership will require further political and social change within Finland. Membership of the European Union constitutes a final challenge to Finnish agriculture – something that farmers have successfully avoided thus far.

Full membership entered into force in January 1995 unnoticed by the Finnish population. Almost immediately, the Finnish political parties started to prepare for the parliamentary elections, which were to take place in March 1995. Finnish EU membership did not feature among the main topics of the electoral campaign. Only one party, the minor Christian Union demanded Finland's resignation from the European Union. All the major parties took a conciliatory approach towards EU membership and called for a consensus accepting EU membership. More traditional political issues, such as high unemployment, became the main aspects of the electoral campaign.

The Social Democrats emerged victorious from the 1995 general election and went on to form the 'Rainbow government' with a broad party base. The new government included all the main parties, with the exception of the leading party of the previous government, the Finnish Centre. The new government was perceived to be pro-European both in terms of its structure and because of the division of its key portfolios. The Prime Minister, Paavo Lipponen and the Foreign Minister, Tarja Halonen (both Social Democrats), the Minister of European Affairs, Ole Norrback (President of the Swedish People's Party) and the Defence Minister Anneli Taina (National Coalition) are all perceived to be pro-EU membership. In addition, the incumbent President, Martti Ahtisaari (Social Democrat) is strongly in favour of the EU.

The new government has been quick to define its policy towards the EU. First, the government is unenthusiastic about the EU's future supranational development. The government supports intergovernmental approaches to the EU and that the 'three-pillar' TEU-based structure of the EU should be maintained. Second, it favours the further enlargement of the EU to include Central and Eastern Europe. Third, the government has raised concerns over the lack of transparency in EU decision-making and the need for a more developed strategy to deal with unemployment. Fourth, the Finnish government has adopted a minimalist strategy towards the CFSP. It has declared that Finland will remain militarily non-aligned, but will also take an open and positive attitude towards the construction of a new European security structure.

The Finnish people have quickly adapted to their new role within the European Union. A survey conducted in June 1995 showed that the Finnish opinion *vis-à-vis* EU membership remained almost unchanged if compared with the referendum in October 1994 (*Helsingin Sanomat* 18.6.1995). A majority of the Finns were satisfied or very satisfied with the Finnish membership. There have been no significant changes in the division of opinion between the political parties either. After the referendum, the newly established 'Young Finns' party has become one of the keenest supporters of EU membership with almost 80 per cent of their members being either satisfied or very satisfied (34 per cent) with the Finnish EU membership. The Finns are not only pleased with the new political condition, but they also seem to support their national leadership's policy towards the EU. Surveys conducted during spring 1995 indicated high approval rating for both the new government and the president.

The most notable concerns regarding EU membership have disappeared from the Finnish political debate. However, there are distinct limits to the level of Finnish consensus on the EU's future development. Public opinion surveys in 1995 suggest that 59 per cent of the Finns do not favour a single currency. For the time being, it is impossible to estimate the accuracy of these polls as a reflection of Finnish public opinion, given the immaturity of Finnish full membership. However, given that there has been such a radical evolution in Finnish policy from neutrality to full EU membership, then it seems that almost anything is possible.

NOTES

1 This 'policy of concessions' has deep roots within Finnish history and one of its main architects was the leader of the Finnish nineteenth-century nationalist movement, J.V. Snellman. The realist 'policy of concessions' demands that relations with Russia should be cautiously managed in recognition of Russia's political and military power.

2 According to Section 33 of the Finnish Constitution Act (Form of Government Act): 'The relations of Finland with foreign powers shall be decided by the President, but treaties with foreign powers must be approved by the Parliament insofar as they contain provisions which pertain to legislation or which according to the Constitution otherwise require the consent of the Parliament. Regarding war and peace the President shall decide with the consent of the Parliament.'

On 15 December 1993, a special paragraph 33a was added and states that:

> The Parliament participates, as it is given in the Parliament Act, in the national preparations of those decisions taken in certain international organs which according to the Constitution demand parliamentary approval.
>
> If the decision meant in the subsection 1 does not with respect to its contents demand parliamentary approval, or the giving of a decree, the Council of State can decide upon its national preparations and upon its approval and entering into force without any hindrance resulting from Section 33.1.

3 The most significant opposition to the foreign policy of Paasikivi and Kekkonen came from the Finnish Social Democrat Party. However, it did eventually accept this policy and joined the government in 1966.

4 The annual surveys were conducted by *The Planning Commission for Information on National Defence* (the survey results are summarised by Alanen and Forsberg 1989).

5 This position was still held by Prime Minister Harri Holkeri (National Coalition Party) until 1990. After the March 1991 parliamentary elections, the new agrarian-conservative government made the softened policy-line more apparent.

6 Associations, such as *The Delegation for the Finnish Business Life* and *The Finnish Foreign Trade Association* were the first to advocate membership.

7 In accordance with constitutional practice, the Finnish government submitted a report to Parliament which declared its intention to apply for EU membership. This report (submitted on 27 February 1992) was amended by the Parliament before the final government notice was resubmitted and approved by 108 votes to 55.

8 A vital platform for the ensuing Finnish debate was achieved by acknowledging the TEU (and in particular, the CFSP) as the basis for the accession negotiations and declaring an open agenda on security matters. This stance was supported by both the Finnish President Mauno Koivisto and by Prime Minister Esko Aho during 1992.

9 Norway and the European Union

Domestic debate versus external reality

Martin Sæter

INTRODUCTION

On 28 November 1994, the Norwegians for the second time rejected EU membership despite the government's strong appeal for a 'Yes'. The margin was this time smaller: 52.2 per cent against and 47.8 per cent for, whereas in September 1972 the figures were 53.5 and 46.5 respectively. As in 1972, the referendum also took place after a long and intense debate that was almost a repetition of the previous one. Participation was even higher, as the record turnout of 87.9 per cent shows. The dividing lines in the population were almost exactly the same. Several of the political parties – including the governing Labour Party – were split on the question of membership, as they were in 1972. And, most importantly, the road to membership was again effectively blocked by a referendum majority vote. Although the referendum was only consultative, the government had also made it perfectly clear that it would consider the outcome as politically decisive.

However, there are striking differences, when compared with 1972. Unlike the first referendum, the second Norwegian 'No' to EU membership did not produce anything like a crisis in Norwegian politics. The party structure was kept intact, and there was no question of the Labour government resigning from office, as it did in 1972. Neither was there a repetition of the ban on further discussion of the membership issue – agreed on by the parties in 1972 in order to bring the political system back to 'normal', but resulting in a taboo of the question for fifteen years.

On the contrary, after the second referendum the Norwegian government underlined even more strongly than before the need to adapt Norwegian policy to the EU as far as possible, with just one limitation: formal Norwegian membership. This it can do because there is no basis in the *Storting* for an alternative government or policy line, and because opinion polls after the referendum – despite the EU defeat – show a considerably strengthened support for the governing Labour Party. It may also be added that the EU debate this second time seems to have left much less bitterness in the population than it did in 1972. The discussion on EU adaptation and full membership seems to have become a normal part of the Norwegian political process. At the practical political level, the minority Labour government seems able from case to case to mobilise sufficient parliamentary support for the continuation of its EEA/EU policy. To compensate for Norway's non-participation in formal EU decision-making, it seeks as close a presence as possible in EU institutions at all levels.

How is this seemingly paradoxical trait of Norwegian EU policy to be explained? How can the government continue its EU-oriented policy of adaptation despite the fact that the majority of the people have again rejected what would seem to be the logical outcome to this kind of policy, namely full membership?

The answer no doubt has to do with the fact that whereas at each application (1962, 1967, 1970 and 1992) it was the external factors that accounted for the government's decision to apply, it was the domestic process that decided the 'No' outcomes of the referendum results. The fact that the results of both referendums contradicted the recommendation given by the government does not necessarily prove the government 'wrong' in having made repeated applications. There are both external and internal determinants of action. The government is exposed to both kinds of pressure, having to cope with the multilateral politics of security, interdependence and integration at the international level, as well as with domestic forces and influences. Popular opposition movements, in contrast, may concentrate exclusively on domestic concerns, the responsibility of direct democracy being more or less limited to the national level. A 'negative' referendum result may or may not decide what should be the alternative to the option recommended. In 1972, the voters in Norway knew what was the alternative: a free trade treaty. In 1994, they had no such authoritative guidance: the question posed was just 'Yes' or 'No' to EU membership. And, consequently, the 'No' result left it to the government itself to decide how to carry on within the limits of non-membership. This means a big difference from 1972, in the sense that ways and forms of the future policy of adaptation is now a theme for continuous debate.

The strong similarities between the first and the second rounds of public membership debate in Norway – also in terms of outcomes – were probably largely due to the fact that there was in the meantime almost no debate on the issue at all. The second debate to a large extent took the shape of a revival of the arguments and antagonisms of the first one, lacking a proper adjustment to the significant changes that since 1985 were rapidly transforming the external setting. 'When the EC issue was again put on the agenda, it was just as if the lid laid on the previous debate was lifted' (Aardal 1994a: 7). In the following an attempt is first made to explain why the result of the first referendum had such a decisive impact on the second one, and second to show how Norwegian EU policy and EU debate at long last seems to be catching up with the realities of Europe.

THE 1972 TRAUMA

Traditionally, foreign and security policy was in Norway, like in most other West European countries, primarily the domain of the government. The multilateral trade policy negotiations and the establishment of European economic integration frameworks were until the 1970s regarded as parts of foreign policy-making, into which it was not customary for the *Storting* to meddle. The main guidelines in foreign and security policy were generally regarded as expressing a national consensus. Constitutionally, there was no obligation for the policy approval by referendum either.

The late 1960s and early 1970s signified a change in the people–government relationship generally. These were the years of great 'anti-authority' student and grassroot protests in Europe, which no doubt had an impact on the political climate, and should be kept in mind when considering the character of the EC debate in Norway at the time of the first referendum.

The referendum struggle in 1970–2 marked a broad popular protest against the exclusive competence of the government to handle questions of foreign policy and international economics generally and against EC membership specifically. The debate was probably the hardest fought political battle that has ever taken place in this country since the dissolution of the union with Sweden in 1905 (see Allen 1979). It had a profound impact on political life in Norway as a whole, causing the downfall of two governments and splitting political parties, organisations, institutions, groups and even families into opposing and often hostile camps.

There was a widespread feeling that the membership question was being forced upon the Norwegian people from outside and by the government and some leading circles in Norwegian society, including bureaucratic and industrial elites and party leaders. The government's threat to resign in the event of a negative referendum result had the effect of strengthening this feeling and consequently also opposition against membership.

The negative referendum outcome caused something like a political earthquake in Norway. The legitimacy of the government was broken, not just regarding this specific case, but also more generally. The impression in many quarters was that the people, in an almost revolutionary way, had reasserted its threatened sovereign power. The 'No' in a way became part of the Constitution, standing above the government, the *Storting* and the political parties. This notion was strengthened by the taboo-like silence that followed on the issue. Neither the succeeding governments nor the political parties dared to contest the verdict of the people. As late as 1987, the Labour government in its parliamentary report on Norway and Europe, in what almost seemed to have become an exercise of duty by any Norwegian government, repeated that Norwegian policy would build on the result of the 1972 referendum.

THE EXTERNAL DIMENSION

The main priority in Norwegian foreign and security policy after the Second World War was always the 'Atlantic' relationship, built around NATO membership and a strong reliance on the United Kingdom and the United States. However, the first application for membership indicated that there was potential for conflict in the Norwegian political system concerning stronger orientation towards the European Community. The opposition was not limited to the internal dimensions. Externally, membership meant a potential break with the traditional 'non-supranational' Nordic and EFTA approaches, which had made it possible to reconcile neutral policy with alliance interests and Nordic cooperation with West European integration. As a consequence, it was felt by many Norwegians that Nordic cooperation might be jeopardised by opting for EC membership.

It was not easy for the government to explain to the Norwegian people why the UK suddenly switched from strong opposition to the EC to applying for membership, and why Norway should automatically do the same. But de Gaulle's rejection of British membership in January 1963 quickly removed the issue from the political agenda. In 1967, when the UK renewed its application – this time also followed by Norway and Denmark – there was almost no debate at all in Norway around the membership question, probably because the prospect of British success was generally – and correctly – regarded as very poor. In a situation where EC integration was almost dead-locked and where there was the notion of a gradual relaxation of tension in the East–West relationship, there proved instead to be a broad willingness in Norway to support the Danish-initiated plan for a comprehensive Nordic economic union (Nordek). However, as was the case in 1960, when the EFTA was established, the Nordic scheme for integration in the early 1970s – at least for Norway and Denmark – was subordinated to geographically more comprehensive West European frameworks.

For Norway not to follow the UK's example would in the government's view demonstrate a potential parting of roads as regards the Atlantic connection in general and security in particular. However, what the government and its supporting elites presented as continuity in foreign and security policy, appeared to many Norwegians like a break with traditional values. The opposition to membership was to a large extent of a national-conservative nature, especially regarding the external dimension. The question of national sovereignty loomed large in the debate. Centuries of foreign domination had fostered strong nationalist sentiments, which tended to favour the opponents in their argumentation for national sovereignty and independence. The country's economic and social development had produced deeply rooted cultural and moral norms, which many people now felt to be threatened by the prospect of a remote and supranational Brussels.

Whereas the government's motivations for applying for Norwegian membership in the EC were predominantly due to foreign and security policy considerations and related to Norway's place within the frameworks of Western cooperation generally, the motivations among the voters for turning the membership proposal down were more mixed and can be explained by the nature of Norwegian politics at large.

THE DOMESTIC DIMENSION

There was a clear majority in the *Storting* in favour of Norwegian membership in 1972. However, parliamentary support was never strong enough to guarantee the three-quarters majority required by the constitution (paragraph 93). In the 1970–2 campaign, the voters increasingly disagreed with their respective party leaderships on this question, voicing their attitudes outside the parties through the activities of popular mass movement. The composition of the *Storting* no longer reflected the relative support of the political parties within the electorate. These were the main reasons why a referendum was regarded as a necessity.

During the 1970–2 campaign, in contrast to what happened in 1992–4, the pro-EC Labour Party dramatically lost support, mostly to the advantage of the anti-EC Socialists (later to be called the Socialists Left Party). The Centre Party (agrarian in origin), came out on the 'No' side, but not as definitely as in the 1990–4 round. The Christian People's Party was in both referendum campaigns seriously troubled by internal disagreement regarding membership, and even more so was the Liberal Party, which splintered over the issue. The Conservative Party remained fairly intact as a staunch pro-EC party.

GENERAL CHARACTERISTICS OF THE EU DEBATE IN NORWAY

To the question why the membership issue was and is so hotly debated in Norway there is no single answer, but rather several partial ones. A leading expert in the field of political behaviour, Professor Henry Valen, points to 'the interplay of history, geography and social structure' (Valen 1994: 13). Historically, Norway's comparatively recent independence, after long periods of union with Denmark and Sweden, may explain some of the special traits about the debate; others may be explained by the large geographical distance to mainland Europe. The country has traditionally pursued a policy of non-involvement in European conflicts. The centre–periphery dimension is another explanatory factor. Domestic politics unavoidably reflects economic inequalities and conflicts of interest stemming from the huge geographic extension of the country from south to north and the gap in living conditions between the populous and industrialised areas of the south and the thinly populated rural and coastal districts. Furthermore, throughout the EU debates there were unusual but strong alliances between farmers and fishermen, urban radicals, and partisans of linguistic, religious and teetotalist 'counter-cultures'. Valen finds that on most of these dimensions there has been a remarkable stability since the early 1970s.

Bernt Aardal, another specialist in the field, further explains the particular intensity of the Norwegian EU debate by pointing to a number of antagonistic features, mutually reinforcing one another and thus tending to heighten the intensity of the struggle for and against. There are the tendencies to, first, polarise for and against as diametrically opposed values; parties discussing the same issue arrive at completely different conclusions; a common stand on the EU question legitimises broader cooperation even between political enemies. Second, to link every issue to over-arching values, focusing on topics of central importance in Norwegian political history and cultural life: for example, the centre–periphery and the rural–urban dimensions; primary versus processing industries; national versus foreign or supranational government; welfare state versus free market liberalism. Third, to become total or universal in scope: all important aspects of politics are included; feelings are mobilised; traditional opposition against the established centres of power joins with new 'anti-authoritarian' movements (Aardal 1994a: 7).

The victory of the opposition against membership was in 1972 as in 1994 the result of a strong mobilisation across the whole spectrum of Norwegian political life. Because the Community was, and still appears to be, a rather remote and unknown creature to ordinary people the question of what attitude to take as regarding membership became a matter of belief, exposed to manipulation by both sides. As often is the case, it proved easier to argue for the well-known and tangible than for the less known and remote. Mostly, the debate took place on the premises of the opponents (see Nelsen 1993a).

Internal silence and external adaptation

It is not difficult to understand the shock experienced not only by the government and the Labour Party elites but also by those of the Liberal and the Conservative Parties when on 26 September, there was a 'No' majority of 53.5 per cent. Throughout the whole postwar period, there had been a high degree of consensus among the major parties as regards the main guidelines in foreign and security policy, including European economic cooperation schemes. Now the majority of the Norwegian people had vetoed what its leaders had defined as a vital part of this consensus policy line. The Bratteli government resigned and the new Korvald government was authorised to negotiate a free trade treaty with the EC.

MAKING MEMBERSHIP A NON-ISSUE

The primary task of the successor coalition government was to restore order and confidence in the Norwegian political system and to demonstrate towards the outside world that Norwegian foreign and security policy would remain stable despite the failure of the EU application. All official discussion on the membership question was effectively stopped. And to avoid any speculation about Norway 'drifting' towards neutralism, the importance of the NATO dimension of Norwegian external policy in general and the bilateral relationship with the United States in particular were strongly emphasised by the new government as well as by the Labour Party now in opposition.

The establishment of the bilateral Free Trade treaty with the EC proved to be relatively non-controversial. The management of the trade relations with the Community was for the most part left to the bureaucrats. The Norwegian economy was expanding, thanks not least to the oil and gas activities. Everything seemed to function well – even without membership. There was no pressure from outside to re-open the membership question. The climate of détente and the prospects for broader East–West cooperation suited Norway and the other Nordic countries well. The policy co-ordination through the European Political Cooperation (EPC) was seen as a positive contribution in this context.

This kind of 'normalisation' based on taboo (see Sæter 1993) proved to be remarkably stable for many years, due primarily to the fact that the European integration process during the 1970s and early 1980s was marked by stagnation and therefore did not call for controversial new adjustments on the part of Norway. As long as this was the case, there was no pressing reason for the government to re-open the membership question. Given the growing divergences between the United States and the EC as regards the East–West situation, there was also the risk that such a step might involve security which would be undesirable for Norway (see Sæter 1993).

With the new start in the EC and with the end of the Cold War and the bloc division of Europe in the latter part of the 1980s, however, the external situation changed in such a way as to enable the membership issue to again appear on the Norwegian political agenda, although only gradually and in the context of the revived wider European process of integration. Although almost unnoticed in the public debate, Norway had since 1973 been participating in the development of the multilateral frameworks of integration at the practical level (see Sæter and Knudsen 1991: 194–214).

EXTERNAL ADAPTATION

Despite the rejection in 1972, and the following silent treatment of the membership issue, at the practical level, the EFTA economies increasingly adopted the market norms of the EC. Until 1973, EC and EFTA conducted separate free trade areas. Since the UK together with Denmark (and Ireland) joined the EC in 1973 the remaining EFTA countries entered into free trade agreements with the Community with the objective of establishing one common free trade area; the existence of EFTA became ever more firmly tied to the European integration process centred around the EC. By the end of 1983, this common EC–EFTA free trade area was completed.

The joint Luxembourg Declaration of 9 April 1984 marked a second major step in the direction of integrating the EFTA countries with the EC (see Chapter 4). The objective was to create a 'dynamic' common European economic space, later to be called the European Economic Area (EEA), linking the integration policies of EFTA countries inseparably to the dynamics of the EC. It went without saying that the realisation of the EEA meant adapting the EFTA countries to the more far-reaching integration aims of the EC. Through the EEA they were in a way defining themselves as partners in an integration process led by the EC. This process initiated by the Single European Act (SEA) of 1986, covered both economic and political aspects of the policies of the member states including the Single European Market (SEM) (see Chapter 4). The technical nature of the Luxembourg Declaration explains why it did not raise any public debate in Norway. Its major function was to serve as a legitimation for the future EC–EFTA negotiations which started after the consolidation of the EC had taken place through the adoption of the SEM White Paper and the SEA.

THE EEA PROCESS: A PREPARATION FOR THE NEXT MEMBERSHIP ROUND

The first really significant step away from the 'policy of taboo' towards the re-opening of the debate on the EC in Norway followed in May 1987, when a Parliamentary Report entitled 'Norway, the EC and European cooperation' was presented by the Foreign Ministry. Contrary to what had been expected in some circles, however, the government in this report still did not deal explicitly with the question of membership, confining itself to identifying 'the tasks and challenges facing Norway in relation to the EC on the basis of the present form of association' and thus providing 'the basis for a more comprehensive debate on Norway's position in Europe and the country's role in European politics' (Royal Ministry of Foreign Affairs 1987: 3).

The omission of what most people thought to be the critical question of full membership serves, however, to explain why even this long-announced European Report provoked little discussion domestically. Although the report presented a comprehensive analysis of the different dimensions of European integration politics as well as a broad and informative discussion of the aims and rationales of government strategy, namely the policy of adaptation to the EC and its Single Market 'as far as possible', it might be said that the report indirectly contributed to delaying the debate on membership still more.

The government's main argument for not raising the question of membership again was without doubt the same as before, namely the fear that such a step would re-open the kind of disastrous debate that took place in 1972. Speaking in the European Parliament (26 October 1988), Prime Minister Gro Harlem Brundtland argued that:

> The 1972 debate left us with a trauma which still has not been overcome. Community policies represent challenges for Norway regardless of the form of our relations. It is important that Norwegian society is ready and able to discuss these challenges without being eclipsed by a new and premature debate on Norwegian membership of the Community. . . . Our policy approach to the challenges of European integration is to lay the foundation for a new domestic awareness of the European dimensions of our national interests.
>
> Royal Ministry of Foreign Affairs 1988: 3

Obviously, some of the reasons why the membership question was not discussed in the 'European Report' were of a tactical nature. Given that the governing Labour Party remained split on the question and that there was no sufficient majority in the *Storting* supporting a renewed application, the Labour Party stuck to the 1972 referendum result as the official platform for the approaching 1989 parliamentary elections, as otherwise there was a risk that the anti-EC Socialist Left Party would win votes from the Labour Party. The government's official argument was that only the results of the multilateral EEA adaptation process could provide a basis on which it would be possible at a later stage to judge if membership might represent a better way to take care of Norwegian national interests.

The decision to give EFTA a prominent role in the process of adapting to the EC was also a prudent tactical move. Norwegian participation in EFTA had traditionally not been controversial domestically. Everything taking place through the multilateral EFTA framework – and especially where there was Nordic agreement – could be expected to be politically acceptable at the domestic level. The parallel participation of neutral countries served as an additional guarantee to sceptical people that the EFTA/EEA approach would not mean giving up national sovereignty in vital areas, and that it would not imply any fundamental change in security matters.

Nevertheless, the government in its policy of adaptation had to balance between those on the one side who were afraid that the adaptation strategy might bring about *de facto* Norwegian EC membership and those on the other who were opposed to any kind of policy orientation that would be likely to hinder or exclude Norwegian membership as a long-term prospect. It also had to take into consideration the interests of other EFTA states.

A question of crucial importance to people in Norway in connection with the EEA negotiations was whether the EEA could be seen as a lasting arrangement and not just a transitionary one leading to membership. For obvious reasons nobody could give a definitive answer to this question, at least as long as the negotiations on the EEA treaty were not concluded. The Labour government brought Norway into these negotiations in 1989 and argued that the EEA was not about membership and that this question, as stated in the European Report, would eventually have to be decided on the basis of experience gained by EEA participation. It had a united party and a strong majority in the *Storting* behind it in its approach. The coalition government taking over after the general election in the autumn of 1989 – consisting of the Conservative Party, the Centre Party and the Christian People's Party – agreed on a platform strikingly similar to that of its predecessor, stressing a number of conditions and reservations linked to the over-arching aim of preserving national sovereignty.[1] These conditions and reservations tried to secure a viable national consensus for the adaptation policy towards the EC. However, because they proved themselves to be rather unrealistic when faced with the requirements of the EC system, they indirectly contributed to making the later EEA agreements look like a series of retreats on the part of the government. The Centre Party had cold feet after one year and withdrew from the coalition, taking up – together with the Socialist Left Party – the fight against the EEA. The Labour government, replacing the coalition government once more in the autumn of 1990, had the difficult task of bringing the negotiations to a, hopefully, successful end (Sæter 1993: 31–5). An illustration of this domestic balancing act was the need to gain EEA support both from the Conservative Party, which saw the EEA as a step towards membership, and from the Christian People's Party, which was pro-EEA but anti-membership.

What proved to be the most difficult issue during the negotiations was the institutional question, particularly as regards certain aspects of judicial enforcement. The problem was in short how to reconcile the supranational political and legal structures of the Community with the traditional, international law-based approaches of the EFTA countries. Disagreement on this almost caused a breakdown in the negotiations in the summer of 1991, when the EC Court of Justice rejected the draft treaty. At the beginning of 1992, however, there was agreement on a final treaty text on the European Union (EU), which was signed in Oporto on 2 May 1992 and was to be put into effect from 1 January 1993 (see Chapter 4).

The treaty opened up the EU markets to the EFTA countries on the basis of reciprocity. Nothing, however, could hide the fact that it was a treaty between unequals, signifying in reality a subordination of the EFTA countries to the SEM rules and the decisions of the EU (Sæter 1993).

The setbacks suffered by the government in the EEA negotiations, as compared with its initial platform, weakened the credibility of the government's position not only with respect to the EEA but also regarding the EU generally. The opponents' fear of the EEA as the backdoor to EU membership was further strengthened by the fact that, even before the EEA treaty was signed, Austria and Sweden had applied for membership and Finland and Switzerland had made known their intention to do so. This placed the Norwegian government under a time constraint. Not surprisingly, the suspicion grew among the opponents of membership that the Norwegian government would follow suit as soon as the situation allowed for it. Moreover, the anti-EU attitudes were at this stage growing stronger all over Europe, stimulated by the Danish rejection of the TEU.

Under such circumstances, it was a considerable achievement by the government when it succeeded in having the EEA treaty ratified by the *Storting* by a vote of 130 to 35 on 16 October 1992. The following month, the Labour Party concluded its long internal party deliberations and gave a clear mandate to the government to start negotiations for a Norwegian full membership application. There was a condition though, that there should be full freedom of opinion and choice both individually and in party and trade union organisations. On 19 November 1992, the *Storting* approved the proposal, by a majority of 104 to 55, that Norway should apply for membership under the pre-conditions that negotiations with the EU were to be conducted in parallel with those of other Nordic applicants and that the people through a referendum should be consulted on the outcome (Royal Ministry of Foreign Affairs 1992: 101). The government delivered its application on 25 November 1992. The negotiations started in May 1993 and were finalised in March 1994.

THE SECOND REFERENDUM FAILURE

When looking back, the impression is that the second EU referendum struggle was decided even before it had really begun. The crucial test seems to have been the general elections in September 1993, which to a large extent focused upon the question of membership. The anti-membership Centre Party, as the most pronounced defender of national 'self-determination', triumphed by gaining votes from all the other parties and securing together with the Socialist Left Party and the Christian People's Party a solid blocking minority in the *Storting*.[2] However, the Labour Party, the only party realistically capable of building a pro-EU government, increased its strength, drawing votes from membership sympathisers who usually supported, for the most part, the Conservative Party. This was in sharp contrast to what happened in 1972 when the Labour Party suffered great losses among the voters.[3]

During the period from the general election to the referendum, there appeared to be no fundamental change in the overall balance between the sides, even if at the individual level there may have been frequent shifts of attitude. Neither the membership negotiations themselves nor their final outcome seem to have influenced public opinion very much (Valen and Aardal 1994a: 2). A pro-membership effect on EU opinion in Norway was registered by polls in the hypothetical case of Finnish and Swedish membership. But even this estimated impact did not materialise at the referendum.[4] 'Put pointedly, one can maintain that the EU issue was decided by the *Storting* elections in 1993. The 'No' side got an enormous lead which the 'Yes' side proved unable to catch up' (Valen 1994: 13).

The anti-EU popular movements no doubt played a crucial role in maintaining the strength of the opposition to membership. The biggest one, the *Nei til EU* ('No to EU'), numbered more than 140,000 members from all sectors of society, a record size in a small nation of four million. It worked very effectively under the able leadership of Kristen Nygaard, a retired university professor. The pro-EEA but anti-membership SME-movement ('Social Democrats Against the EU'), established in October 1993 and led by a Labour parliamentarian, Hallvard Bakke, restructured the pro-EU membership policy of the government in the sense that it highlighted the risk of a formal splitting of the Labour Party if anti-membership views were perceived as being neglected by the party leadership and the government. More unexpectedly, in September 1994 an anti-membership movement was also organised on the Conservative side (*Borgerlige mot EU*), the initiative being taken primarily by leaders of small and medium-sized firms and industries in the northern and western parts of the country. The Confederation of Norwegian Business and Industry (NHO) reported that only about half the number of member enterprises would feel the impact of a 'No' to be directly negative for themselves. The larger enterprises were as a rule more pro-EU than smaller ones (Valen and Aardal 1994b: 5).

The referendum result of 52.2 per cent against and 47.8 per cent for membership did not really come as a surprise to anyone. The level of participation, however, was unexpectedly high: 88.9 per cent, the highest ever at any election since the introduction of the general right of vote in 1913 and almost 10 per cent higher than in 1972. It was equally high across the entire country, contrasting with the lower turnouts usually produced by the northern-most counties (*fylker*). The degree to which the result tended to confirm the voting patterns of 1972 was also surprising. Of the nineteen existing counties, fourteen showed a 'No' majority, as they did in 1972. One single county (*Ostfold*) switched from 'No' to a 'Yes' by slight margin. All the five 'Yes' counties are to be found in the south-eastern part of the country, around the *Oslo Fjord*. The 'No' majority was largest in the northern-most counties and was even larger than in 1972. In the county of *Finnmark*, 74.5 per cent voted against and 25.5 per cent for, whereas the figures in 1972 were 70.4 and 29.6 respectively. Generally speaking, resistance against membership continued to be strongest in the agricultural and fishing districts in the peripheral parts of the country, an exception being the county of *More* and *Romsdal* in mid-Norway with an increase in

'Yes' votes from 29.2 per cent to 38.4 per cent, probably reflecting the interests of an export-oriented fishing industry.

The 'No'-side was strengthened by some tendencies that are more difficult to explain, especially as they are linked to gender and age. First, in contrast to 1972, there was a marked divergence between men and women in their attitudes towards EU membership, polls showing that 37 per cent of male voters were in favour, compared to only 24 per cent for women. The 'No' dominance among women was especially strong in the public sector. Second, among the voters under 30, 55 per cent voted 'No' and only 26 per cent 'Yes'. Also voters above 60 were generally more negative towards membership than those between 30 and 60.[5]

On the pro-side, perhaps the most significant development was the increase in relative strength of the Labour Party coupled with an increase in the pro-membership percentage of Labour voters.[6] This trend has continued after the referendum, thereby contributing to making it possible for the Labour Party to continue its policy of EU adaptation almost as if this second referendum had not taken place.

AFTER THE REFERENDUM: THE PROSPECTS FOR NORWEGIAN EU POLICY

The Norwegian government was quick to underline that the goals of its policy towards the EU remained unchanged, except for the constraint following from the referendum 'No' as regards membership. Prime Minister Gro Harlem Brundtland made this clear in her speech at the OSCE conference in Budapest on 5 December 1994:

> The Norwegian government regret that the majority of the Norwegian people voted against membership, but we respect this decision. At the same time we will continue pursuing our goals with all the means available, with the exception of the one excluded by the referendum. We will continue to be a part of the European internal market. We will stick to an economic policy that is in accordance with the aims of the Maastricht Treaty. We will make use of every opportunity to actively participate in international cooperation.
>
> Royal Ministry of Foreign Affairs 1994c: 9

These signals were further strengthened by the Foreign Minister Björn Tore Godal in his foreign policy statement to the *Storting* on 19 January 1995:

> The EU and its member states will continue to be Norway's most important economic and political cooperation partners in the years to come, regardless of the form of association Norway has with the Union. Our possibilities of safeguarding our national interests are so strongly influenced by the actions of the EU and its member states that we have no alternative to an active European policy.
>
> Royal Ministry of Foreign Affairs 1995: 3

As regards economics, there is a clear majority in the *Storting* in favour of maintaining the EEA as the basis for managing future relations with the EU. Consequently, through EEA legislation, Norway is bound to be even more closely linked to the EU system, as a 'homogeneous economic area' is built on the rules of the SEM. Important in this context is the Norwegian government's decision to sign the European Energy Charter, which links this vital sector of the Norwegian economy to an energy policy based in essence on the rules of the SEM (Matlary 1993: 63–86).

In the security field, the Norwegian government – watching somewhat nervously the accelerating reduction of NATO military functions and of allied defence commitments in the north – stresses more strongly than ever the need to have an additional security guarantee through association with the EU and its 'defence component', the WEU, not least with respect to dealing with Russia in the important strategic northern areas. This policy line meets with little opposition at the national level.

A question of vital interest to Norway concerning the future is what its position outside the EU would be like if the WEU project fails. This is likely to happen if by 1996 there is no agreement between the UK and the major continental EU powers as regards the WEU's future role and status in relation to the EU and NATO. A WEU failure would be bound to affect NATO negatively, because it would demonstrate the impossibility of reconciling 'European' and 'Atlantic' orientations. The likely consequence of this would be an EU even more dominated by continental powers. Without EU membership, Norway – in contrast to Sweden and Finland – would find itself in a weakened and more peripheral position in terms of security matters. Under such circumstances, the argument of EU membership as a means of improving security would be almost certain to gain in strength.

The fields covered by the so-called 'third pillar' – justice and home affairs (JHA) – did not play any significant role in the referendum campaign. The main reasons for this may be the predominantly intergovernmental character of JHA cooperation and the fact that the Nordic countries have since the 1950s developed cooperation among themselves, to the obvious benefit of all. Had all the three Nordic applicants become EU members, the transition from a Nordic to a European framework of JHA cooperation could have taken place smoothly with few domestic political controversies.

The referendum's 'No', however, has turned the JHA pillar into a potentially problematic issue at both national, Nordic and European levels. A straightforward adoption by the neighbouring Nordic countries of the new EU external border control rules would imply the re-introduction of customs barriers along the Norwegian-Swedish and the Norwegian-Finnish borders. In reality this would put an end to the existing Nordic cooperation in the fields of JHA and in all likelihood create huge practical problems for the border authorities of these neighbouring countries. Politically still more significant would perhaps be the psychological effects on ordinary

Norwegian travellers from being treated as 'third country' citizens when crossing the border to Sweden.

There are seemingly only two ways of avoiding such a deteriorating situation: either to make the existing Nordic rules compatible with EU rules in JHA fields, so that Norway would in practice fall inside a common EU/Nordic border, or to ensure that Norway becomes an EU member. The latter option has been ruled out for the foreseeable future by the referendum. Therefore, the Norwegian government prefers the former, knowing that such a 'Nordic' choice is unlikely to be met by serious opposition in domestic political quarters. It is still too early to know what the EU stand on questions of this kind will be.

Despite the outcome of the referendum, strong forces are thus pulling Norway further along the road to EU integration. The Norwegian government evidently does not take the 'No' for a final answer. On the contrary, it deliberately and explicitly does what it can to bring Norway as close as possible to the EU. As long as it operates 'below' membership, it can count on a sufficient case by case majority in the *Storting*. The question is of course under what circumstances the question of membership will again be on the agenda.

The next opportunity will perhaps occur in connection with the treaty revision of 1996. As part of any future institutional re-arrangement, the EU would probably then be able to deal with the question of Norwegian membership again, provided that Norway accepted the terms already agreed on as well as the outcome of the treaty revision. There is the possibility that the EU at this stage would even encourage Norway to join in a new round of enlargement together with other 'remaining' West European states: Malta, Cyprus, Switzerland, Iceland, and, possibly, some ex-Yugoslavian republics.

To the Norwegian government, a renewed application would seem worthwhile only if it is regarded as having a fair chance of success. At the domestic level, one can expect a growing recognition of the fact that Norway, even without membership, is becoming increasingly dependent on EU policy-making, and that there is really no feasible alternative to this other than membership. More importantly, however, developments in the EU itself over the next few years, especially in connection with the 1996 revision, will probably have a decisive impact on opinion formation in Norway as regards membership.

If in the context of the revision the image of an EU extending to the Central and East European countries and forming the core of an all-European system of cooperation and security is reinforced, then this would probably contribute to swinging one of the opposition parties, namely the Socialist Left Party, over to the pro-side. Under this scenario, this would tip the balance both in the *Storting* and in public opinion in favour of membership.

Hypothetically, at least, the Norwegian political parties could use this 1996 revision opportunity to re-state their positions on EU membership in time for the general election campaign in the autumn of 1997, making these elections also serve as a kind of national EU litmus test. Depending on the outcome, a third referendum could possibly be held shortly afterwards.

Such a scenario may at first sight appear unrealistic, given the recent referendum result. But in view of the fact that similar referendums on the new treaty will probably be taking place simultaneously in several of the member countries themselves as part of the ratification procedure, it becomes more plausible and more likely. One thing seems certain: a new Norwegian membership debate will take place on premises laid down by the government rather than by the opposition and reflecting to a much higher degree the current agenda of European politics at large.

NOTES

1 According to the platform document, the so-called *Lyseby Declaration*, the EEA treaty must be given the status of international law; EEA rules must be adopted by the national parliament; a common EEA court must include members from EFTA countries; formal EEA decisions must be made unanimously; the EFTA countries must be equal parties to the EEA treaty and have the right of initiative and of 'real' influence as regards both formal decisions and the law-making process. Furthermore, a number of reservations are made concerning specific areas: border control must be maintained; a common agricultural policy is not to be considered; each country must be given the right to maintain higher standards of health, labour security and environment; national control over the management of resources and the environment must be maintained on a reciprocal basis; some kind of labour migration control is to be maintained; the use of fiscal duties for social, environmental and health purposes must be permitted.

2 During the campaign, the leaders of the Centre Party and the Socialist Left Party maintained that they would not automatically follow the result of the referendum, arguing that according to the Constitution it was the *Storting* that had to interpret the council given by the people through the referendum.

3 Of the 165 seats in the *Storting*, the Centre Party won 32, the Socialist Left Party 13, the Christian People's Party 13. Added up this makes 58 anti-membership votes, 16 more than required for blocking according to paragraph 93 in the Constitution. The Labour Party took 67 (4 more than in 1989), the Conservative Party 28 (37), and the Progress Party ('pro EC but against the Union') 9 (21). The study of the 1993 elections made by Henry Valen and Bernt Aardal shows that half the number of those who in 1989 voted for the Conservative Party were anti-EU membership in 1993. On the pro-side there was a considerable leak to Labour from the Conservatives, the Progress Party and the Socialist Left Party. On the no-side, the 1993 leak to the Centre Party as compared with 1989 votes was 20 per cent from both the Conservatives and the Socialist Left Party and 17 per cent from both the Labour and the Progress Parties (Valen and Aardal 1993: 3).

4 Given Finnish and Swedish membership, the polls undertaken by *Opinion* from February to April 1994 show a slight majority in favour of membership, from May to September they reversed into a minority, and then in October a majority (of 5 per cent) again. However, when the precondition of Finnish and Swedish membership was not explicitly given, there was all the time a solid majority against membership (*Aftenposten* 15/10/94):

Unqualified question

	Nov	Dec	Jan	Feb	Mar	Apr	May	Jun	Aug	Sep	Oct
No	57	56	52	48	49	48	47	52	48	50	45
Yes	28	26	32	37	31	33	29	28	31	28	35
Don't know	15	18	16	15	21	19	23	20	22	22	20

Question given Finnish and Swedish membership

No	57	45	42	39	38	37	41	44	43	47	41
Yes	28	32	36	41	41	42	36	35	42	39	46
Don't know	15	23	23	19	21	21	23	21	16	14	13

Respondents: 1005, figures are percentages

5 Results of *Opinion*'s August poll, 1994, see *Aftenposten* 20/08/94: 2. As regards gender differences between 1972 and 1994, especially the public sector see also T. Bjørklund, 'En reprise fra 1972?', *Dagbladet*, 30/11/94: 3, commenting on the Market and Media Institute's referendum day poll.

6 In August 1994, 43 per cent would vote for membership, 31 against and 26 were undecided. The trend is still more pronounced under the condition of Finnish and Swedish membership: 61 'Yes', 26 'No' and 13 'Undecided' (*Aftenposten* 20/8/94: 2).

Table 9.1 The relative strengths of the political parties, 1989–94 (percentages)

Party	*General election, 1989*	*General election, 1993*	*September 1994*	*October 1994*	*November 1994*
Socialist Left	10.1	7.9	8.5	8.7	9.0
Labour	34.3	36.9	38.2	25.0	36.9
Liberal	3.2	3.6	3.8	3.9	4.4
Centre	6.5	16.8	19.7	18.8	18.5
Christian People's	8.5	7.9	7.5	8.0	7.4
Conservative	22.2	17.0	15.7	18.2	18.0
Progress	13.0	6.3	4.4	4.1	4.1
Others	2.2	3.7	2.2	3.4	1.8

Source: Valen and Aardal 1994a: 4

10 Iceland and the European Union

Non-decision on membership

Gunnar Helgi Kristinsson

INTRODUCTION

With a sparse population consisting of only 260,000, Iceland can be regarded as either the smallest of the European small states, or a relatively large micro-state. It became a sovereign state in 1918, and a republic in 1944 when the union with Denmark was dissolved. Iceland conducts an independent foreign policy, but foreign policy issues tend to cause domestic political divisions and policy-making is usually cautious on that account.

The cautious approach to policy-making is reflected in the Icelandic approach to European integration. The Icelandic government has never seriously contemplated membership of the European Union. It has emphasised favourable trade relations rather than close political ties. In 1989 Iceland, along with the other EFTA states, began a negotiation process with the EC which led to the formation of the European Economic Area in 1994. Yet, neither the government nor most of the political parties had at that time formed any clear policy on Iceland's objectives or strategies in the negotiations. In fact, Prime Minister Hermannsson (Progressive Party) stated serious reservations at the Oslo meeting of EFTA leaders in March 1989 concerning three of the four freedoms; all except the free movement of goods (*Althingi* 1990: 203).

As regards the issue of full membership, the cautious approach is epitomised in a 'wait-and-see' attitude. At the national conference of fishing enterprises in 1994, Prime Minister Oddsson (Independence Party) explained that although there were important interests at stake for Iceland in maintaining good relations with the EU, there was no immediate problem:

> Even if the European Union will not open up new membership negotiations until the turn of the century, this will cause no problems for us. We can continue to rely on the EEA agreement, and no issue areas outside the agreement press for an early application for membership. As before, membership would hinge on whether the EU accepted Iceland's demands in the fisheries area. The best alternative in the present situation is to watch closely the development of the EU in

coming years and explore systematically, among its member states, whether and how it might in the future accept the prerequisites for Iceland's membership.

Oddsson 1994

VULNERABILITY OF DOMESTIC POLITICS?

The hesitancy of the Icelandic government in forming an active integration strategy can be considered from two different angles; one which focuses on Iceland's vulnerability and another focusing primarily on domestic politics. The two approaches are not incompatible, but they can lead to different conclusions as to why Iceland so far has chosen not to apply for membership of the European Union.

Small states may generally be regarded as more vulnerable in international relations than larger ones.[1] This alone, however, does not prevent integration. Integration may in fact be a way of controlling vulnerability (Webb 1983). Indeed, states in the same general size category as Iceland can be found both among applicants (Malta) and member states (Luxembourg) of the European Union. What distinguishes Iceland is the nature of its economy. A single natural resource, fish, constitutes around three-quarters of its exports of goods. Any threat to the fishing sector is a threat to the very basis of the economy. The European Union, at the same time, has formulated rather far-reaching arrangements in the fisheries sector (the Common Fisheries Policy), according to which control of fishing resources is to a large extent a European Union prerogative. Given Iceland's small population and lack of political clout in an international context, fears of what might happen in the event of Icelandic membership are understandable. A cautious approach is easily rationalised. Rather than trying to influence the course of events, it could be prudent to wait for results and seek adaptation afterwards.

On the other hand, it is possible that such fears are over-stated. Foreign policy is traditionally among the more sensitive issue areas in Icelandic politics. The word independence strikes a key note in Icelandic political rhetoric. Nationalistic sentiments have been employed by different political forces on the left and right alike. Foreign policy is the potential source of conflicts within the parties as well as between them, and needs to be handled with care. Seen in this light, the Icelandic approach to European integration could reflect party strategic considerations rather than vulnerability.

BACKGROUND

Special interest coalitions often play a key role in foreign economic policy (Gourevitch 1978, 1984). In Iceland the rural areas and sparsely populated regions have held a very powerful position in political life throughout this century, on account of a skewed electoral system. Partly allied with the labour movement, rural representatives were responsible for the emergence of an interventionist state in the inter-war period, which among other things put severe restrictions on foreign trade. State intervention continued on a large scale in the postwar period, preventing for the most part Icelandic participation in attempts to organise free trade in the Western world.

A turn-about in the small (by Nordic standards) Social Democratic Party in the late 1950s, however, upset the balance of forces. An alliance of the Social Democrats and the large Independence Party (centre-right) changed the electoral system in 1959 and introduced free trade as the basic principle of foreign economic policy during the 1960s. The left socialist People's Alliance supported the change in the electoral system, but along with the rural Progressive Party resisted the free-trade policies pursued by the coalition government of the Independence Party and the Social Democrats in 1959–71.

Apart from liberalising foreign trade, the coalition government of the 1960s considered various alternatives for linking the country with international trade cooperation. Membership of the European Common Market was among the alternatives considered in 1961–3, but liberalisation of capital movements and the opening up of labour markets was considered too great a risk for the small Icelandic economy. The government favoured association, although a formal application was never made, thereby creating a great deal of political controversy. Association was abandoned as an objective after the rejection of British membership in 1963, and the government opted for less controversial forms of trade cooperation instead. Thus, Iceland acceded to GATT during the Kennedy round in the 1960s, joined EFTA in 1970 and made a free trade agreement with the EC in 1972.

The ratification of the free trade agreement in 1972 marked an end to the conflict over foreign economic policy in Iceland for the time being. A left-wing government took over in 1971, including among others the Progressive Party and the People's Alliance. Rather than abandoning the free trade policies which the two parties had opposed during the 1960s, the government continued the free trade negotiations with the EC and ratified the agreement. Thus, relative consensus prevailed over foreign economic policy from 1972 until 1989, when it was upset by the EEA process.

Although the turn towards free trade in 1960 was undoubtedly a major landmark in Icelandic political history it did by no means create a very liberal economy. On the contrary, state intervention remained at a relatively high level (Kristinsson, Jonsson and Sveinsdottir 1992). A largely state-run financial system was complemented by severe restrictions on capital movements and strict currency regulations. Strict price controls were maintained, along with a ban on agricultural imports, and competition policy hardly existed until the 1980s. The labour market was highly organised, while mostly closed to foreigners, and working-days lost through strikes were far greater than in most European states. A very active – albeit slightly chaotic – industrial policy aimed primarily at supporting the still politically strong regions. Although the change in the electoral system in 1959 had altered the strength relations between parties in parliament, it had done so without radically reducing the overweight of the regional constituencies. This was achieved by dividing the country into eight constituencies with proportional representation, where far more votes were needed per seat in the only substantial urban centre in the country (Reykjavik and the surrounding Reykjanes) than in the rest of the country. The resulting imbalance in the representation of political parties was corrected through an additional member system, designed to maintain the imbalance in the representation of regions. In the election of 1991, to take an example, the distribution of seats between parties was roughly in proportion to the distribution of votes, but the distribution of seats within them was highly favourable to the regions. Reykjavik and Reykjanes, with 64 per cent of the electorate, elected only 46 per cent of the seats in parliament. The effect of the system on the parties – where the parliamentary parties usually play a major role – is to make it very difficult for them to take a stance on any issue dividing the urban Reykjavik and Reykjanes area and the rest of the country.

While some liberalisation of the Icelandic economy had got underway during the 1980s, it was almost inevitable that the EEA and the internal market would upset the relative consensus on foreign economic policy which had prevailed since the early 1970s. To be sure, the first steps in the EEA process were taken under a left-wing government of the Progressive Party, the People's Alliance and the Social Democrats, but it seems clear that what kept Iceland in was partly hesitancy to break with the other EFTA countries, and partly the strong commitment of the Social Democrats to the issue. After the election of 1991, the Social Democrats felt that its coalition partners could no longer be relied on to see the issue through, and formed a new coalition government with the Independence Party.[2] In the ratification process in 1993, the People's Alliance and the Women's Alliance (formed in 1983) turned against the EEA, as did a majority of the Progressives. After the ratification of the EEA, parliament agreed unanimously – in May 1993 – to take up bilateral discussions with the EU on future relations, in view of the ongoing membership negotiations of Iceland's EFTA partners. It was made clear, however, that this did not amount to a decision on a membership application – neither for nor against. The EEA came into effect in the beginning of 1994.

THE DIFFICULT QUESTION OF MEMBERSHIP

As the other EFTA states – one after another – applied for membership of the European Community between 1989 and 1992, very little public discussion took place on an Icelandic application for membership. The partners in the new coalition formed in 1991, the Independence Party and the Social Democrats, decided to concentrate on seeing the EEA through, rather than confusing the issue by raising the question of membership at the same time. In March 1992 the Social Democratic leader and foreign minister, Hannibalsson, none the less pressed in his report to parliament for an open discussion and a systematic study by government institutions of the costs and benefits of membership.[3] His main argument was connected with the negotiations on membership about to start between the other EFTA states and the EC. His proposal, apparently, was rejected by his coalition partners and no systematic survey of the issue was carried through at this time. The Independence Party was not prepared to revise its earlier stance that membership was 'not on the agenda'. Thus, not sending in an application at this time was a non-decision rather than a decision not to.[4]

During the membership negotiations of the other EFTA states, the discussion in Iceland remained muted by the fact that no political party and no interest organisation had come out in favour of membership. After the conclusion of the Norwegian membership negotiations in March 1994, the government none the less decided it was time for a study of the costs and benefits of membership. Several university institutions were asked for reports on particular aspects of the issue. The reports, which became public in the second half of 1994, were generally positive in the sense that the benefits of membership were considered to outweigh the costs.[5] They warned of a tendency towards isolation in the international arena if the other Nordics were to join but not Iceland. Similarly, Iceland's lack of influence within the EEA – whereby it would have to adopt decisions which it had taken no part in shaping – was regarded as an argument for applying for full membership of the EU. Full membership was also considered to compare favourably to non-membership from an economic standpoint.

The main problem with regard to membership has to do with fisheries. In fact, there is broad consensus on this among both opponents and proponents of an application for membership. The main difference between the two sides lies in their evaluations of the likely outcomes of membership negotiations. Proponents are optimistic on what Iceland can achieve, opponents pessimistic (Kristinsson 1991, 1994).

The Common Fisheries Policy (see Chapter 14) has several aspects which make it unattractive to most Icelanders. Formally, the EU takes over control of the resources. While this would not necessarily lead to greater access for foreign fishermen within the Icelandic 200-mile zone it would transfer the important decisions on allowable catches to Brussels. Similarly, the revision of the policy, due in 2002, creates an uncertainty Iceland can ill afford in a vital economic sector such as fisheries. Finally, the right of establishment would grant foreigners the right to invest in Icelandic fisheries, which presently is totally forbidden. Inside the EU this could pave the way for 'quota jumping', whereby foreign firms could invest in the Icelandic fisheries sector and possibly gain a share in its fishing quotas.

Any membership negotiations between the EU and Iceland would have to deal with these issues satisfactorily if a membership treaty were to stand a chance in an Icelandic referendum. Clearly, the EU would have no real interest in damaging Iceland's vital economic sector. On the other hand, it would also be very reluctant to create a precedent for granting an applicant major exceptions from the *acquis communautaire*. How far the relevant loopholes can be found within the present CFP or precedent in the membership terms of the present member states is difficult to tell. It is also difficult to tell how far some system of adjustment periods, temporary (and possibly renewable according to specific criteria) derogations and political commitments might resolve the issue. It all depends a lot, of course, on political will. The crux of the matter is, however, that these questions can only be answered in the actual negotiation process.

PUBLIC OPINION AND THE POLITICAL PARTIES

The public attitude towards an application for membership has been surveyed frequently since 1989. The results may be seen in Figure 10.1. The development of public opinion may conveniently be divided into three periods. In the first period, from 1989 until the election campaign in the spring of 1991, support for a membership application was greater than opposition, although a large share of respondents was also undecided. In the second period, from 1991 to March 1994, the balance changed decisively in favour of those opposed to an application for membership. In March 1994, the balance turned again in favour of membership, but the support declined steadily throughout the year.

The positive attitude towards membership in 1989–91 was not based on any widespread discussion of the issues involved, since very little public debate had actually taken place. Rather, it reflected a vague positive feeling towards Europe, usually not based on a great deal of information. The sociological and political distribution of respondents into opponents and supporters was by no means random, however, but broadly similar to the one which prevailed in the subsequent periods (Kristinsson 1990).

During the election campaign of 1991, a very negative discussion took place in Iceland concerning membership. Progressive Party leader Hermannsson strongly hinted that the Social Democrats and the Independence Party could not be trusted to keep Iceland out of the EC. He even went so far as to suggest that the election could be considered a referendum on the issue. The Independence Party and the Social Democrats angrily claimed innocence of such charges. Even so, in the final weeks prior to the election, the other parties continued with their campaign against membership, while neither the Social Democrats nor the Independence Party made any attempt to argue in its favour. In this political climate, which prevailed to some extent after the election, public support for an application fell dramatically.

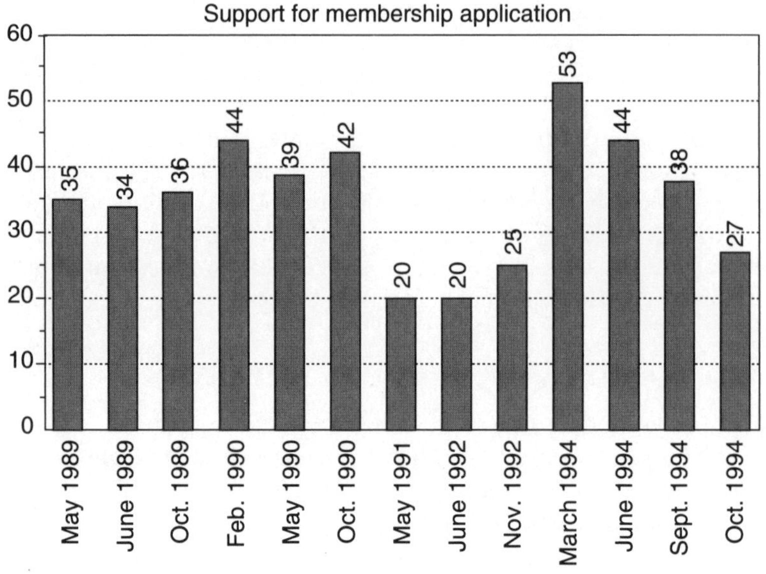
Support for membership application
60
50
40
30
20
10
0
35
34
36
44
39
42
20
20
25
53
44
38
27
May 1989
June 1989
Oct. 1989
Feb. 1990
May 1990
Oct. 1990
May 1991
June 1992
Nov. 1992
March 1994
June 1994
Sept. 1994
Oct. 1994

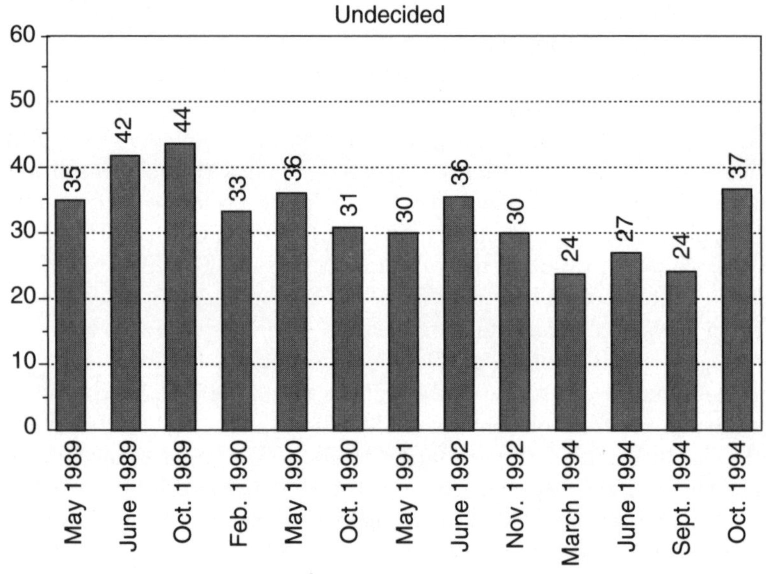
Undecided
60
50
40
30
20
10
0
35
42
44
33
36
31
30
36
30
24
27
24
37
May 1989
June 1989
Oct. 1989
Feb. 1990
May 1990
Oct. 1990
May 1991
June 1992
Nov. 1992
March 1994
June 1994
Sept. 1994
Oct. 1994

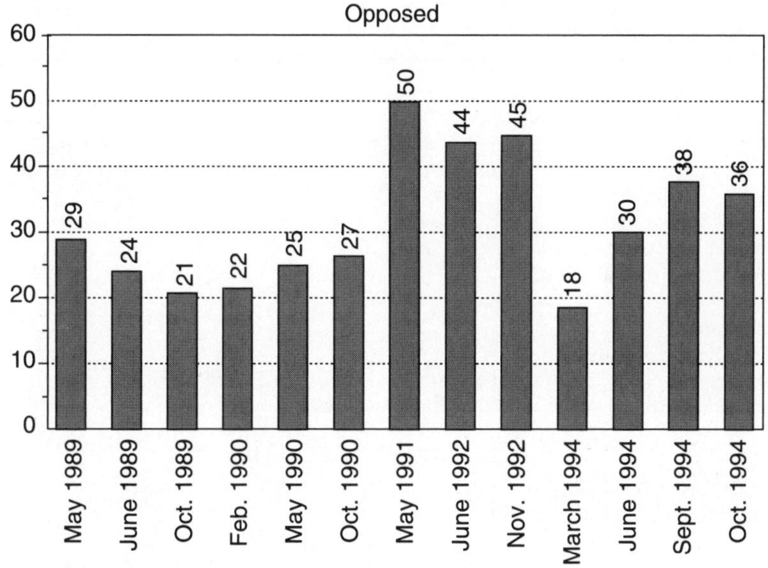

Figure 10.1 Icelandic attitudes towards an application for membership of the EU, 1989–94 (percentage)
Note: The wording of the question in the Gallup survey was slightly different from the others
Sources: Based on data from the Social Science Institute, apart from May 1991 (the Icelandic Election Study), and March 1994 (Gallup)

The next turning point came in March 1994 after Norway had concluded its membership negotiations with the EU. It was always known that the course taken by Norway might influence the discussion in Iceland. This was partly because Norway is considered a major competitor in European fish markets, and partly because Norway was the last of the other Nordic states to negotiate a membership agreement. The spectre of isolation which Iceland seemed to be facing as the only Nordic state outside the EU seems to have been conclusive for the change in public opinion. Table 10.1 shows a classification of the reasons both supporters and opponents of membership gave for their position in an interview survey in June 1994.

Almost half of those giving reasons for an application mentioned the need to participate and avoid isolation, while a quarter mentioned economic reasons. The reasons given by those opposed to membership were more varied. The difference in size between Iceland and the EU was the most common reason, along with a concern with independence. It is interesting to note that only 13 per cent of those opposed to an application mentioned the treaties and the fisheries issues, which have been in the foreground in the public debate. This, however, underestimates the importance of the fisheries issue, since concern with the fisheries probably lies behind some of the other reasons given as well. Thus, when the question was posed in the same survey whether membership would be acceptable if the EU yielded to

Table 10.1 Reasons for respondents' attitudes towards an application for EU membership in June 1994

Respondents for application

	Number	*Percentage of all*	*Percentage giving reason*
Participate/avoid isolation	172	37	49
Economic improvement	86	19	24
Increase freedom/openness	30	7	8
Inevitable future	27	6	8
Good generally	22	5	6
Apply to test EU attitude	11	2	3
Other reasons	7	2	2
No reason given	103	22	–
Total	458	100	100

Respondents against application

	Number	*Percentage of all*	*Percentage giving reason*
EU colossus – Iceland small	78	25	31
Independence/self reliance	73	23	29
Wait and see	41	13	16
Treaty of Rome – fisheries	32	10	13
Against concentration on Europe	17	5	7
Dislike EU	8	3	3
Other reasons	3	1	1
No reason given	62	20	–
Total	314	100	100

Note: The question posed was: Why do you consider an application desirable/undesirable?
Source: Data obtained from the Social Science Research Institute, University of Iceland

all of Iceland's main fisheries demands, support for membership rose from 44 per cent to 66 per cent, and opposition was reduced from 30 per cent to 14 per cent. This may indicate that opposition to membership in Iceland is to some extent pragmatic in nature rather than ideological.

The two coalition partners which had guaranteed acceptance of the EEA in Iceland reacted differently to the new situation which emerged after the Norwegian negotiations were concluded in March. The Independence Party emphasised that the Norwegian deal on the fisheries would be unacceptable to Iceland, and that in any case the question of membership could not become actual until after the conclusion of the intergovernmental conference of the Union scheduled in 1996. The party leadership made a determined effort to 'cool' the issue, stressing that although membership at some future point should not be excluded there was ample time to consider the alternatives. The Social Democrats, on the other hand, increasingly argued in favour of membership, and at their party conference in June adopted the policy that Iceland should 'aim at full membership of the European Union'. While this was an important step, since no political party had before supported membership, its significance was reduced by the faltering fortunes of the party in the summer and autumn of 1994. The party suffered a split, as one of its ministers (Jóhanna Sigurðardóttir) resigned from the party in protest at its right-wing policies, aiming at the formation of a new political force. Later in the autumn, another of its ministers also had to resign following a series of accusations of political misconduct.

The decline in support for membership after March 1994 can be attributed partly to a rather negative debate in Norway concerning the fisheries issues, but more importantly to the strong stance taken by the Independence Party leadership against any immediate moves on the issue. Public attitudes towards membership in October, divided by party affiliation are shown in Table 10.2.

Table 10.2 Public attitudes towards an application for membership of EU, October 1994, by party affiliation (percentage)

Party	*Support application*	*Undecided*	*Against application*	*Total*	*Change in support June–October*
Social Democratic	74	14	12		+11
Independence	35	33	33		–16
Progressive	25	24	51		–10
People's Alliance	23	38	39		–11
Women's Alliance	22	39	39		–17
(Jóhanna Sigurðardóttir)	22	34	45		(not applicable)
All respondents	27	37	36	100	–11

Source: Data obtained from the Social Science Research Institute, University of Iceland

Support for membership has decreased in all the parties except the Social Democrats between June and October. Among supporters of the Progressive Party, the People's Alliance, the Women's Alliance and Jóhanna Sigurðardóttir (not yet a party) there is a clear majority against an application for membership. Supporters of the Independence Party, on the other hand, are divided into three roughly equal groups; for, undecided and against membership. The Independence Party faces a particularly difficult problem in its policy towards European integration. The balance between opponents and supporters of membership is more precarious than in the other parties. Many of its supporters are becoming increasingly restive on account of its failure to take a lead on the issue. On the other hand, there are also staunch opponents of membership within the party, particularly in the regional constituencies, which are vastly over-represented in the parliamentary party. A decisive move, either for or against membership, could easily lead to an open split in the party. It might also restrict its alternatives with regard to coalition formation with other parties. The delaying tactics adopted by the leadership therefore have a sound basis in party strategic considerations.

OLD TIMES – NEW TIMES

In the other Nordic countries, promotion of the issue of EU membership has had something of an elitist character. Support for membership has been far greater among the political elites, for example, the parliamentary parties, than among the population at large. In Iceland, the opposite has been the case. Support for membership is far greater among the electorate than in parliament. The only parliamentarians for membership in Iceland are the Social Democratic ones, and a very small number of Independence Party MPs.

The elitist character of the opposition to membership in Iceland is easily comprehended against its sociological background. The Icelandic power structure was moulded in an earlier period, characterised by the political domination of the regions, strong nationalism and very strong interest organisations in agriculture and the fisheries. This is also the main political basis for opposition against membership of the European Union. At the same time, urbanisation has continued (two-thirds of the population now live in Reykjavik and Reykjanes), young people are more internationally oriented than before, and over 80 per cent of the population is not employed in fishing (4 per cent), fish processing (7 per cent) or agriculture (6 per cent) (Ólafsson 1990: 34).

From the start, interview surveys have shown a strong relationship between age and attitudes towards membership. Older people, socialised in a strongly nationalistic political climate, have great difficulty in accepting the central premises of European integration. Younger people, on the other hand, accustomed to much closer contacts with foreign countries and cultures, find the idea much easier to accept. This can be seen in Table 10.3.

A majority of those under 40 taking sides support membership, but a majority of those over 40 are against it. The age factor is not merely a sociological curiosity, but a very important factor in the handling of the issue in Iceland. Most people in positions of power in Iceland are over 40, including the members of parliament. Within the political parties, the parliamentary parties are quite dominant, and individual parliamentarians in fact enjoy considerable freedom of manoeuvre. Their personal feelings on the matter of membership, therefore, are a factor of great significance. This is one of the reasons for the predominance of opposition towards

Table 10.3 Public attitudes towards an application for membership of EU, October 1994, by age (percentage)

Age group	*Support application*	*Undecided*	*Against application*	*Total*
18–24	39	36	28	
25–39	34	37	29	
40–70	19	36	45	
All respondents	27	37	36	100

Source: Data from Social Science Research Institute, University of Iceland

membership in parliament. Among all parties, the younger members – not yet in positions of influence – tend to be more interested in membership.

The overweight of the regions in parliament is another factor of great significance. The regions, with merely a third of the electorate, hold a majority of seats in parliament. Opposition to membership is much greater in the regions than in the urban Reykjavik and Reykjanes constituencies, as shown in Table 10.4.

In the urban constituencies of Reykjavik and Reykjanes, supporters and opponents of membership are roughly equally balanced, although there is a slight majority against in Reykjavik and a slight one for membership in Reykjanes. In the regions, however, opponents of membership outweigh supporters two to one. The latter are the voters electing a majority of MPs. Even in the Independence Party and the Social Democratic Party, which depend primarily on the urban electorate for support, a large number of MPs are regional representatives. Thus, in the election of 1991 the Independence Party received 73 per cent of its votes in Reykjavik and Reykjanes, but only fourteen of its twenty-six seats (54 per cent). The Social Democrats received 74 per cent of their votes in Reykjavik and Reykjanes, and six out of ten seats.

A further insight into the divisions between the old power-structure and modern society can be gained by looking at the attitudes of respondents by employment (Table 10.5).

The primary economy, agriculture and the fisheries, is clearly opposed to membership. The balance is also clearly against membership among unskilled and skilled manual workers. Non-manuals are more opposed than supportive of membership, but the difference there is not so pronounced. Employers and specialists, on the other hand, are those among the economically active population with by far the most support for membership (although it should be noted that there is also strong opposition among this group). Among those not economically active there is also considerable support for membership. A large number of students in this category may explain a relatively high level of support there.

The industries seem to be deeply divided on the issue of membership. On

Table 10.4 Public attitudes towards an application for membership of EU, October 1994, by settlement (percentage)

Settlement	*Support application*	*Undecided*	*Against application*	*Total*
Reykjavik	30	36	34	
Reykjanes	34	35	31	
Regions	21	37	42	
All respondents	27	37	36	100

Source: Data obtained from the Social Science Research Institute, University of Iceland

Table 10.5 Public attitudes towards an application for membership of EU, October 1994, by employment (percentage)

Employment	*Support application*	*Undecided*	*Against application*	*Total*
Farmers/fishermen	17	33	50	
Manual workers	24	41	35	
Skilled workers	24	38	38	
Non-manuals	26	42	32	
Employers/specialists	39	25	36	
Not economically active	34	31	35	
All respondents	27	37	36	100

Source: Data obtained from the Social Science Research Institute, University of Iceland

the one hand, the powerful organisations of farmers and the fisheries are very reluctant to consider the membership alternative. On the other hand an increasing number of important business leaders in other sectors, even in the fish-processing industry, have publicly come out for membership. One of the employers' organisations – the Chambers of Commerce – formally decided to support membership in December 1994 and there appears to be increasing pressure in favour of membership among employers. This could create a serious problem for the Independence Party, which traditionally has close ties with the business community. Consideration for the Independence Party and the unity of employers, however, may also be a factor weighing heavily on employers generally against taking a formal stance on the issue.

EXPLAINING A NON-DECISION

Explanations of non-events are inevitably fraught with difficulties, unless their significance is such that they were indeed events. Iceland's abstention on the membership issue in 1989–92 was undoubtedly a major event in its political history, as the country thereby parted company with the other EFTA states (except Switzerland) despite the fact that at least a *prima facie* case can be made for membership, as was later shown by the University of Iceland reports. The vulnerability thesis – that membership is unacceptable on account of the fisheries – does not satisfactorily account for the handling of the issue in Iceland. Iceland's failure to participate in the EFTA round of membership negotiations in 1992–4 was not based on a systematic study of the issues involved nor a general political debate on the issue. Indeed, it would seem that the vulnerability thesis can only be verified in an actual negotiation process on membership. The failure of an application to emerge, or any significant preparations for such a move taking place, therefore has to be based on something else besides vulnerability. Domestic politics seems to be the most likely factor.

The relationship of forces between supporters and opponents of membership in Iceland is clearly advantageous to the latter. This is not based on a simple head-count, since supporters have often outnumbered opponents in the opinion polls. It is based primarily on the strategic distribution of support and opposition in the population. Opponents are strong in the politically dominant regions, in the powerful organisations of agriculture and the fisheries, and among the age groups over 40, filling most positions of influence in the political system. The numerical strength of those in favour of membership is not reflected in the political system, as they are concentrated in the Reykjavik–Reykjanes area, among people under 40, and without any interest organisations to promote their cause (at least until December 1994 when the Chambers of Commerce came out in favour). The predominance of the parliamentary parties in the political arena – at the expense of general membership structures – makes an application for membership less likely to be placed on the political agenda in Iceland. The issue was conveniently by-passed through a non-decision.

Yet, the issue of membership does create an uncomfortable situation for those of the parties with concentrated support in the Reykjavik–Reykjanes area. This applies to the Independence Party, the Social Democrats until June 1994, when they came out for membership, and possibly Jóhanna Sigurðardóttir, who is for placing the issue on the agenda without taking a clear stance on application.

PROSPECTS

How the issue of Iceland's membership of the EU develops can be influenced by short-term factors as well as long-term factors. Long-term factors are likely to pull towards membership. One such factor is the age difference in attitudes towards membership. Although fashions can easily change, particularly among young people, it seems likely that within the next decade or so a new generation of leadership will take over in Icelandic politics, with a much more positive attitude towards European integration than the one presently dominant. Similarly, a change in the electoral system is on the agenda, and at least a partial adjustment in the weight of votes seems only a question of time. This will alter the balance of forces within the parties, and possibly also reduce the significance of the interest organisations in agriculture and the fisheries.

A number of long-term factors, however, may also work against the membership option. For one thing, Norway's rejection of membership in November 1994 reduces the significance of the isolation argument for membership. It matters a great deal for Iceland, for example, in the context of Nordic cooperation, that one of the larger Scandinavian states is not joining the EU for at least a considerable period of time. Another long-term factor which may work against membership (but not necessarily against an application) is the continuing problem of the fisheries. The willingness on the part of the EU to offer satisfactory solutions to the Icelandic fisheries problem is by no means a sure thing. Given the small size of Iceland's population, its membership could be regarded as a burden rather than an advantage by at least some of the EU member states. Thus, it could be that EU leaders might make it clear to Iceland, either in the preparations for an application or during membership negotiations, that satisfactory arrangements in the fisheries sector will not be forthcoming. This would almost automatically exclude Icelandic membership.

Among the short-term factors which could affect the membership issue, the situation within and between the political parties seems of greatest importance. Some of the parties are more likely to accept an application for membership than others. The Social Democrats have already come out in favour of membership. There is some pressure within the Independence Party in favour of an application, and this could grow stronger, for example, if the employers' organisations decide to increase their pressure or if the balance between Reykjavik–Reykjanes and the regions were radically altered within the parliamentary party. Jóhanna Sigurðardóttir is still pretty much an unknown quantity, but she has been careful not to exclude the membership option.

Among the remaining parties, the opposition to membership seems likely to remain strong, although there are dissenters within all of them. The position adopted by the Progressive Party is probably most important. After a change in leadership in the party in the spring of 1994, the party seems to have become more pragmatic than before on the issue of membership. The new party leader, Asgrimsson, is – to be sure – against membership, but primarily on account of the fisheries. This leaves him an escape route, for example, in case of unforeseen developments, to apply for membership and put the willingness of the EU to accommodate Icelandic fisheries' interests to the test. Asgrimsson serves as Foreign Minister in a new coalition government formed by the Independence Party and the Progressive Party after the election of 1995. Experience shows that the Progressives tend to adopt a more pragmatic attitude towards European integration when in government than in opposition (the same holds true for the People's Alliance – Stephensen 1994). An immediate change of policy under Asgrimsson's leadership is not likely, however, and the new coalition partners seem in close accord on the issue of membership.

A final factor which could affect the outcome concerns the electorate. Attitudes towards membership are not particularly stable and individual events or party propaganda can make a considerable difference. This increases the risks involved for the political parties, since membership might in fact have to be put to a double test among the electorate. On the one hand an eventual membership agreement would almost certainly be put to a referendum, and on the other it would require a change in the Icelandic constitution, which can only be made if parliament passes the proposed change twice, with an election in between. Popular movements, rather than the political parties, might in fact be decisive in determining the fate of the issue. It is known that contacts are being established among both proponents and opponents of membership across party boundaries. So far, however, these have not led to the establishment of formal organisations.

NOTES

1 'The vulnerability dimension of interdependence', according to Keohane and Nye (1989: 13), 'rests on the relative availability and costliness of the alternatives that various actors may have.' They continue: 'Vulnerability can be defined as an actor's liability to suffer costs imposed by external events even after policies have been altered.'

2 The Progressive Party and the People's Alliance at the time declared, however, that the passing of the EEA would not be a problem if the left coalition continued (Hardarson 1993: 452).

3 Utanríkismál. Skyrsla Jons Baldvins Hannibalssonar utanrísráđherra til Alþingis 1992.

4 Non-decision-making, according to Bachrach and Baratz (1970: 44) is a 'means by which demands for change in the existing allocation of benefits and privileges in the community can be suffocated before they are even voiced; or kept covert; or killed before they gain access to the relevant decision-making arena or failing all these, maimed or destroyed in the decision-implementing stage of the policy process'.

5 The reports referred to here were made by the Centre for International Studies, the Social Science Research Institute, and the Institute of Economics.

Part IV

The European Union and the Nordic countries: an issue-based approach

11 Monetary integration and the 1995 Nordic enlargement

Ian Barnes

INTRODUCTION

There is a close relationship between the exchange rate and the financial systems of the European market economies. In the early 1990s, it seemed that the link between the European Union's (EU) European Monetary System (EMS) and the movement to European Monetary Union (EMU) was inevitable. The member states adopted a strategy at the December 1991 Intergovernmental Conference (IGC) at Maastricht which was designed to move the EU towards a single currency by 1999. This was then incorporated into the treaties via the Treaty on European Union (TEU). Whilst EMU proved to be highly controversial for some of the member states, it was a strategy which was embraced by the Nordic applicants. They had shadowed the Exchange Rate Mechanism (ERM) of the EMS for a period prior to entry to the EU, and gained early experience of the problems of trying to cope with the process of monetary integration.

The governments of the Nordic countries had seen the shadowing of the ERM as a source of strength. However, the wisdom of the strategy was brought into question during the periods of extreme exchange rate instability in 1992 and 1993. The Nordic countries became victims of the speculative attacks associated with the general uncertainty about the future of EU integration, and of the movement towards monetary union. This cut the ties between the Swedish Krona and the Finnish Markka and the ERM. It caused concerns about the survival of the EMS in any meaningful form, and raised doubts about whether EMU would ever be achieved.

This chapter considers the issue of EMS membership by the Nordic countries, and their likely participation in Stage Three of EMU. It argues that the enlargement of the European Union in 1995 will further complicate the process of monetary integration. Despite the fact that the member states' economies display similar characteristics, the EU has become increasingly heterogeneous after each phase of enlargement. Full monetary integration is best fostered between economies with similar structures, and by governments co-ordinating monetary and fiscal policies. The divergence that has emerged has led to a situation where it is possible to speak of a multi-speed Europe. This point was dramatically illustrated by the decision of the new member states to adopt divergent tactics with respect to the EU's Exchange Rate Mechanism. On joining the EU, Austria opted to join the ERM, whilst Sweden and Finland decided to remain outside it. Both Finland and Sweden are relatively small economies, with a thin market for their currencies. Their currencies are vulnerable to sharp movements when faced with speculative pressures. For example, following devaluation in 1992, the Markka fell by 24 per cent by March 1993, only to recover in the period to February 1994, so that the overall devaluation was only 11 per cent (Akerholm 1994: 10).

Finland and Sweden displayed their commitment to EMU when they accepted the *acquis communautaire*. However, their ability to achieve the convergence criteria set out in the TEU is in some doubt, although Finland is in a stronger position than Sweden. Until the EMU convergence criteria have been achieved, Finland and Sweden's commitment to EMU will not be fully tested.

THE EUROPEAN MONETARY SYSTEM (EMS)

The EMS was established in 1979 in an attempt to replace the wildly fluctuating floating exchange rates of the 1970s which had been mainly caused by the weakness of the US dollar. As the foreign exchange markets lost faith in the dollar, there was a flight into the quality currencies such as the German mark – a scenario which was to be repeated in 1995, as dealers moved out of the dollar into the Japanese yen and the German mark.

The purpose of the EMS was initially to create a zone of exchange rate stability in order to promote trade. Later the EMS came to be regarded as being central to completing the Single European Market (SEM), especially as exchange rate instability was seen as a significant barrier to trade. In the longer term, it was hoped that the EMS would provide a platform for EMU, as the EMS helped to fix the values of currencies in relation to one another, and could lead to the introduction of a single currency. In addition, the autonomy that member states enjoy with regard to monetary and fiscal policy would be severely limited. There are three main features of the EMS which offer the prospect of both partial and full membership. These are:

- *The European Currency Unit (ECU)* This is a composite of the EMS currencies weighted according to their importance in trade. The ECU is the central rate of the exchange rate mechanism of the EMS and is used as the nominal currency for EU transactions and as a means of settlement between the EU's monetary authorities. The currency composition of the ECU did not change with the enlargement of the EU in 1995. Article 109g of the TEU stipulated that 'the currency composition of the ECU shall not be changed'. From the start of the third stage (of EMU) the value of the ECU will be irrevocably fixed.

- *The Exchange Rate Mechanism (ERM)* The ERM is a pegged but adjustable system of exchange rate management. Originally, exchange rates were fixed within a narrow band of 2.25 per cent either side of the ECU and Finland and Sweden shadowed these rates between 1991 and 1992. (The exception to this arrangement was a wider 6 per cent margin which operated for a transitional period, and applied to Spain, Portugal and the UK.) From August 1993, the ERM became a much looser system, with the bands being set at 15 per cent either side of the ECU. In effect, currencies could diverge from one another at the top and bottom of the range by a maximum of 30 per cent.

  All members of the EU are part of the European Monetary System. However, ERM membership is largely optional, despite the longer term belief that it will provide the basis of the move towards a single currency. In January 1995, Austria chose to become a part of the ERM, fixed at a rate of 13.7167 schillings per ECU. Both Finland and Sweden opted to leave their currencies floating, taking the view that it was important that they should wait until they were able to resolve the fundamental problems associated with their economies. In the case of Sweden, these were largely associated with excessive budget deficits, whilst the problem for Finland was, among others, the very high level of unemployment.
- *The European Monetary Institute (EMI)* This was established on 1 January 1994, and it replaced the European Monetary Cooperation Fund (EMCF). Article 100f of the TEU sets out the functions of the EMI. These were broadly to assist with the operation of the EMS and prepare the way for Stage Three of EMU by promoting convergence of monetary policy.

  Closer cooperation in monetary policy is a major objective of EU membership of both Finland and Sweden. Both will be able to take advantage of the monetary support which may be on offer to EMS members. Finland and Sweden must now consult and exchange information with the other member states, as well as taking into account their foreign exchange markets. The existing bilateral agreements with these states were replaced by those operated under the auspices of the EMI.

THE PROBLEM OF MANAGING EXCHANGE RATES

Official intervention in order to maintain the value of a currency is normally conducted via the national central banks and their agents using foreign exchange reserves to buy the national currency. There are three sources of funds. The first is national reserves. In Europe there are multiple currencies, none of which is backed by sufficient reserves to fend off a sustained speculative attack. Finland and Sweden were both forced from a policy of shadowing the ERM because of inadequate foreign currency reserves.

The second is borrowing from the private sector markets. On 18

September 1992, Sweden borrowed ECU 8 billion via a syndicated loan to replenish its currency reserves. At the height of the ERM crisis in September–October 1992, the weak currencies borrowed $30 billion. This is, however, a limited source of funds which depends upon the risks that the private sector is prepared to take (International Monetary Fund 1993: 13). Finally, there is the combining of reserves. The EU appeared to have adequate facilities, but these proved to be insufficient to meet an all out attack on specific currencies by speculators. EU currency reserves are not pooled in a complete sense. Even with the massive reserves available to the Bundesbank, it is not possible to defend the weaker ERM currencies.

An alternative or supplementary action that can be adopted in defence of a currency is, of course, the use of interest rates as this makes it more expensive to borrow money for delivery of forward contracts, illustrates a government's willingness to defend a currency and if successful, can attract inward flows of capital. The use of the interest rate weapon can have negative effects on an economy though, for instance, raising interest rates can make a recession worse than it might have been due to the substantial cost attached to servicing high interest rates.

The Swedish response to the 1992 exchange rate crisis showed the limits that can be placed on the use of an interest rate strategy. Between 21 August and 16 September, the marginal lending rate went up from 13 per cent to 500 per cent. This quickly fed into inter-bank one month funds, where rates rose from 16 per cent (7 September 1992) to 70 per cent (17 September 1992). This in turn consolidated pressures on a banking and financial system which was already in difficulties, and in addition led to a major fiscal shortfall.

The liberalisation and reform of national financial sectors was also a common feature throughout Western Europe during the period leading to the completion of the EU's Single Market. Markets became more liquid, increasing financial flows across borders, and capital flows were almost totally liberalised. At the same time the linking of information systems allowed fund managers to make simultaneous decisions based on equivalent information. Under these conditions the control of capital flows is difficult and far greater than the capacity of any one country to cope with, especially if there is a speculative attack against its currency. At the height of the speculation against the pound in 1992 for example, the turnover in the London money markets rose to around £300 billion a day.

THE NEW NORDIC MEMBERS AND THE EMS

Finland and Sweden both decided to shadow the exchange rate mechanism of the EMS prior to their membership of the EU, and in part it reflected their wish to prepare for full membership. In addition, the ERM enjoyed a high degree of credibility, appearing to offer both currency stability and a good record on combating inflation. A great deal of this reputation was derived from the anchor currency, the German mark. However, even in this most successful phase, the ERM was criticised. The ERM currencies often appeared no more stable than other currencies, the inflation rates were similar to those found world wide and the economic growth rates of the ERM states were not particularly good in the 1980s. The domination of the system by the German central bank, and its obsession with controlling inflation, was deflationary, but the EMS's stability was also achieved with the assistance of capital controls. Once these were removed the ERM was subject to increased pressure. Finally, the stability of the ERM currencies in the late 1980s was that of nominal rates (those quoted in the money markets) but changes in consumer prices in member states meant that real exchange rates moved (the exchange rate after the effects of inflation have been taken into account – see Table 11.1).

Table 11.1 illustrates that the majority of economies experienced periods of deteriorating competitiveness caused mainly by domestic inflation, such as in Italy, or by the revaluation of nominal exchange rates as in the case of Germany. Periods of improved competitiveness were due to a devaluation of nominal rates, which impacted on real rates as in the case of the UK, or by achieving low rates of inflation, for instance, the Netherlands. Any competitiveness problems that Finland and Sweden had while shadowing the ERM were as a result of decisions that had been made prior to membership (see Table 11.1).

The 1992–3 ERM crisis came about because of a lack of belief in the durability of the ERM and the move towards EMU. In a situation where it was believed that there would be no devaluations within the ERM, then one currency is as good as another. In these circumstances, if higher interest rates can be obtained in one country then there is every reason to invest in

Table 11.1 Real effective exchange rates 1988–93 (1987=100)

	Year					
Country	*1988*	*1989*	*1990*	*1991*	*1992*	*1993*
Austria	95.3	92.4	92.5	90.3	91.8	95.4
Belgium	97.4	96.1	100.5	100.2	101.3	101.2
Denmark	99.6	97.3	103.0	100.0	101.4	103.9
Finland	103.4	107.9	112.5	104.8	85.5	75.7
France	97.6	95.2	97.5	93.4	94.6	97.1
Germany	100.5	98.3	104.1	102.6	106.1	112.5
Ireland	94.7	86.8	88.4	82.7	81.4	76.0
Italy	97.8	102.3	109.0	109.8	108.0	88.6
Netherlands	97.3	91.9	93.2	92.7	96.4	101.0
Spain	105.0	113.2	122.3	126.5	128.9	117.0
Sweden	103.7	110.4	112.2	110.7	111.2	84.8
UK	105.7	110.0	105.4	109.2	106.7	96.9

Note: A fall in the index is equivalent to an increase in price competitiveness
Source: Economic Commission for Europe 1994: 49

that country. However, once doubts emerge within the system, then usually investors will move into the safest currencies, for example the German Deutsche mark.

THE SHARED PROBLEMS OF THE NORDIC COUNTRIES

There are significant similarities in the way that the economies of the Nordic countries were managed into the 1990s. The Nordic countries typically had high levels of taxation, and state spending. In 1993 for example, state spending was 71 per cent of GDP in Sweden, and 62 per cent of GDP in Finland, compared to an OECD average of 42 per cent of GDP. The high level of welfare spending which they sustained, was heralded as 'a third way' between communism and capitalism and was not a problem for these countries as long as their economies were expanding and they had low unemployment. However, this did cause significant difficulties during the 1990s recession. High levels of unemployment led to a situation where there were unsustainable burdens on state spending and problems for both fiscal and monetary policy (Economist 1993). For example, the unemployed received benefits equivalent to 90 per cent of wages in Sweden in 1994. These high levels of benefit could be afforded when unemployment was only 1.5 per cent during the 1980s. However, once the level of unemployment started to rise significantly, major problems occurred. It led to mounting levels of debt as a result of budget deficits and these countries were required to maintain balance of payments surpluses for the foreseeable future, in order to meet their interest payments. The new members also endured domestic problems associated with financial liberalisation and rapid credit expansion culminating in a full-blown Nordic banking crisis in the late 1980s and early 1990s. This helped to create a picture of continued uncertainty, which impacted upon the exchange rate.

The Nordic countries had shared the experience of shadowing the ERM without adequate support. Sweden made the decision to shadow the ERM in May 1991, whilst Finland took the same path in June 1991. In the case of Finland, the rate chosen was inappropriate and a 12 per cent devaluation took place against the ERM in November 1991. Sweden and Finland were only shadow-members of the EMS and this made it difficult for their governments to convince the foreign exchange markets that the values of their currencies were sustainable. Their linkage to the ERM forced both governments to put up interest rates to real levels that were among the developed world's highest. They were in a very much weaker position when compared to the full members of the ERM in the early 1990s as they remained outside the collective support networks of the EU central banks. It was much more difficult for these countries to mount a defence against the market speculators, once it was believed that the rate was no longer sustainable. In 1992, both Finland and Sweden were forced to cut their links with the ERM.

Yet, Denmark, the only Nordic country to be a full member of the EMS, was able to keep its currency in line with the Deutsche mark throughout most of the 1980s and 1990s. This was in spite of Denmark's decision to negotiate itself an 'opt out' from the final stage of EMU and the fact that Danish public opinion was strongly against participation in the single currency. Denmark was fortunate in remaining largely outside the turbulence that affected many of the ERM currencies. In August 1993, after the near collapse of the ERM, and the move towards 15 per cent margins, the central bank was able to declare that 'The government and the Nationalbank agree that the present circumstances provide no grounds for changing the Krone's rate against present core ERM countries' (Financial Times 1995b). The Krone's rate was stable against the Deutsche mark during the period up to the 1995 enlargement and even whilst there was further turbulence as a result of the devaluation of the Peseta and Escudo in March 1995. The reason for this was the reputation of the Danish currency and that Denmark was moving closer towards meeting the convergence criteria set out by the Treaty on European Union.

SWEDEN'S INTERNATIONAL ECONOMIC RELATIONS

Sweden shadowed the first attempt at EMU in the 1970s. However, in 1977 Sweden cut this link in an attempt to gain control over its own economic policy. In 1982 the Krona was devalued by 25 per cent. After that time the Swedish authorities maintained exchange rate stability by tying the Krona to a basket of currencies. A major constituent of this basket was the US dollar. However, in the 1980s, as Sweden's trade with the EU increased and the dollar slid downward in value, this link became less appropriate. From May 1991 the Krona was fixed to a band 1.5 per cent either side of the ECU. Linking the Krona to the ERM was part of an attempt to bring down the rate of domestic inflation and the ERM appeared to offer a stable exchange rate relationship with key trading partners (UK and Norway), who had also linked their currencies to the ERM in 1990. Increasingly, Sweden came to rely upon its trading links with the rest of the EU (see Table 11.2).

Sweden's experience linked to the ERM was not a happy one. The Krona was associated in the minds of the foreign exchange markets to the Finnish Markka. So that when the Markka was under pressure, the Krona was also in difficulties. The Swedish economy also faced competitiveness problems. Part of its cost crisis was related to its welfare system. In addition to this, being tied to the ERM meant that Sweden had to accept the high interest rates caused by German reunification. Sweden maintained the Krona's artifically high value longer than was necessary in order to avoid being criticised for a premature devaluation of its currency.

The link between the Krona and the ERM was maintained in September 1992, despite the fall of the Markka, and currencies within the ERM itself. This was achieved at a very high price. The Krona was defended by the use

Table 11.2 Sweden's main trading partners in 1993

Country	*Exports (percentage)*	*Imports (percentage)*
Germany	14.4	17.8
UK	10.2	9.3
Norway	8.1	6.4
USA	8.4	8.8
Denmark	6.6	7.3
Finland	4.6	6.2
EU–12	53.2	54.8

Source: Financial Times 19/12/1994, Sweden III

of high interest rates, and heavy borrowing. Marginal interest rates reached a staggering 500 per cent for a short period. Whilst this was a technical device, it did have an impact on longer term domestic interest rates. In addition, crisis budget measures had to be introduced.

Despite this defence, on 19 November 1992 massive outflows of capital threatened to wipe out the central bank's reserves. The Swedish government was forced to abandon its strategy of shadowing the ERM and immediately the Krona sank by 11 per cent against the Deutsche mark (Economist 1992a). The Krona's downward path continued, and by October 1993 it had depreciated by 21 per cent against its previous ECU parity.

It was unfortunate for Sweden that its attempts to further its exchange rate links with the EU should have come about at a time of severe recession in Europe. This caused severe problems for its public finances, and effectively removed the potential for early participation in the third stage of EMU. In 1989, when unemployment was low and economic growth was satisfactory, Sweden had a budget surplus of 5.5 per cent of GDP, which was the largest in the OECD area. By 1993, Sweden had a budget deficit of 14.5 per cent, which was also the highest in the OECD area. The deficit had been reduced for 1994 and was estimated to be 11.2 per cent.

The reason for this rapid deterioration in public finances was that powerful automatic budget stabilisers were at work. Sweden's welfare system was geared to low levels of unemployment. In the 1980s, Sweden had a remarkable record on unemployment. The rate was normally less than 2 per cent of the labour force, and never rose above 3.5 per cent (Economist 1992b). By 1993, it had risen to 8.5 per cent and even with the recovery in 1994 it was still at 7.2 per cent (Economist 1995). These rates of unemployment understate the extent of the problem, however, because nearly 5 per cent of the workforce are on training schemes. Budgetary balances for Sweden are highly cyclical. For every 1 per cent fall in GDP the Swedish government's budgetary balance declined by 0.75 per cent of GDP. This was caused by high levels of social security payments and the impact of falling tax revenues.

FINLAND'S INTERNATIONAL ECONOMIC RELATIONS

Despite its links with the former Soviet Union, the Finnish economy became increasingly tied to the Western European market economies from the 1950s onward (see Chapters 3 and 4). Finland joined the GATT in 1950, and became a full EFTA member from 1986. For many of the Western market economies the collapse of the Soviet Union had largely political implications. However, the impact of these events was more wide ranging for Finland where the economic implications were of great significance.

Trade arrangements between Finland and the Soviet Union had remained largely unchanged in the period from the late 1940s to 1990. They were managed by a clearing system, which was highly beneficial to Finland. The bases of trade were five-year agreements which matched imports for exports. Where there were imbalances, exports were increased to compensate on an annual basis. In theory, although not in practice, there could be an adjustment with the payment of convertible currencies. This therefore avoided any exchange rate risk associated with the rouble. The arrangement was based upon exports of largely investment goods from Finland in exchange for predominantly oil and energy products from the Soviet Union. It meant that when oil prices rose the market for Finnish goods, from some sectors of the economy, benefited significantly. These bilateral arrangements led to a degree of complacency on the part of Finnish industry.

Trade with the Soviet Union amounted to 25 per cent of Finnish exports after the second oil crisis (1979–81). The trade declined by 75 per cent between 1985 and 1991, as a consequence of falling oil prices. This reduced the capacity of the Soviet Union to import. In the same period exports to Western markets increased by 22 per cent. However this was poor with respect to the growth of these markets in a period when they were expanding rapidly. Problems can be attributed to a mixture of factors including the structure of the Finnish economy as well as a fundamental lack of competitiveness. It was difficult for Finland to switch from Soviet to Western markets because of the lack of flexibility within the country's industrial structure and the fact that a significant part of it was obsolete.

The situation deteriorated further with the collapse of the Soviet Union, which led to the use of convertible currencies. The clearing system was abandoned in 1991, by which time many customers could no longer afford Finnish goods. Exports to the centrally planned economies of Eastern Europe fell by a further 65 per cent in the course of 1991. The impact of the collapse of this trade was particularly severe on those larger firms who were fully involved in the Soviet market. The collapse of exports to the East led to an 8 per cent decline in domestic demand. Added to this the recession in the West led to a total decline in industrial production of 10.5 per cent in the year and Finnish GDP fell by 6 per cent (Economic Commission for Europe 1993: 122). At the same time unemployment rose to 13 per cent, and more than 6,000 businesses went into liquidation.

Unemployment was to rise even further to 18.6 per cent in 1994. The extent to which Finland became dependent on Western markets is illustrated in Table 11.3.

The collapse of the IMF's Bretton Woods System in 1973 had led to the adoption of a currency index system of fixing the Markka to other currencies. This was reinforced by the 1977 Currency Act which introduced a system of maintaining the currency within limits around a trade weighted basket of currencies. This policy required keeping a tight control on domestic credit and international capital flows. As with a number of other countries, Finland also went through a period of financial liberalisation. The impact of this was that monetary policy instruments became much less effective, and exchange rate policy more difficult to manage.

The Finnish record of exchange rate management was not impressive in the period of the late 1980s and early 1990s. The period 1987–9 was characterised by increased pressure on the currency. Its feature was a lack of certainty about the direction that policy should take. In 1989 the Markka was revalued in order to curb inflation. However, this contributed towards the over-valuation of the currency, which made the 1990s recession worse than it might have been. Finland chose to shadow the ERM in June 1991 but an enforced devaluation reduced the value of the Markka by 12 per cent in November 1991.

Prior to the partial collapse of the ERM in September 1992 the Finnish Markka and the Swedish Krona were in difficulty. In April 1992 a wave of currency speculation threatened to drain Finland's foreign exchange reserves and force a devaluation. The Nordics were helped by the other European central banks and by adopting very high interest rates. This pattern of speculation showed that small central banks were highly vulnerable outside the ERM. Any sign of weakness placed their currency under attack. It meant that austerity measures had to be introduced with cuts in public spending.

The French referendum on the TEU caused further pressure on the weaker ERM currencies. Finland was sucked into this turmoil and on 8

Table 11.3 Finland's main trading partners in 1993

Country	*Exports (percentage)*	*Imports (percentage)*
Germany	13.2	16.4
Sweden	11.1	10.2
UK	10.5	8.9
USA	7.8	7.3
Russia	4.5	7.6
EU	46.9	47.2
EFTA	17.0	19.0

Source: Financial Times, 1994: 2

September 1992, despite very high interest rates, the Markka was forced to devalue. Finland ran out of reserves in its attempts to prop up the Markka. Once the currency was cut free its value fell by 12.5 per cent in a day. As a shadow member of the ERM the cost of convincing the markets had been too high, especially in the light of its past performance. Devaluation helped to make the economy more competitive and exports grew by 26 per cent in the first half of 1993. The general economic recovery continued into 1994.

THE CASE FOR FULL MEMBERSHIP OF THE EMS

The decision by Finland and Sweden not to participate in the ERM on joining the EU was to be expected, given their recent negative experience of shadowing it. In order to succeed the Nordic countries need to increase exports as well as resolve some of their domestic problems. Membership of the ERM should be an easier option, given that the system now permits wider margins and the two countries can avail themselves of a full range of support, as they are now EU members. Currency stability should assist trade by making pricing more predictable, and provide a useful source of discipline to the domestic economy. Membership of the ERM will also stabilise the extent of the debt that is held outside the two countries. Some 30 per cent of Sweden's debt is denominated in foreign currencies, whilst it is 60 per cent for Finland. Any domestic monetary relaxation will lead to devaluation, but will not reduce the burden of their debt.

However, the case against their membership of the ERM stems from the fact that the Nordic currencies are seen as part of the wider picture of non-sustainable ERM currencies. Weakness in the Markka also has implications for the Krona. Neither Finland nor Sweden has adequate reserves to cope with membership of the ERM in a period of exchange rate turbulence. As long as they are classed as weaker currencies, they will be subject to speculative attacks which their reserves are inadequate to cope with. Also both countries have shaky industrial structures, and currency depreciation is a helpful device to maintain competitiveness. However, this is a solution which can have inflationary consequences, unless there is adequate control of domestic incomes.

MOVING TOWARDS EMU

The TEU envisaged that there would be three stages in the EU's move towards the introduction of the single currency. The first stage has taken place, and involved the completion of the Single Market with freedom to move goods and capital by 1 January 1993. The second stage commenced on 1 January 1994. This stage is designed to prepare the ground for the establishment of the single currency. Member states should become full members of the EMS at this stage.

Crucial to the success of Stage Two are the convergence criteria, which determine the suitability of currencies for Stage Three of EMU. The adoption of the criteria was designed to ensure the transition to EMU would not cause a sudden monetary shock to the participating currencies and as a reassurance to Germany that the EMU would not be inflationary. As a consequence, the real convergence of economies was not part of the calculation, and unemployment, national income levels and growth were not among the criteria. The criteria require that:

1 planned or actual government deficits should be no more than 3 per cent of GDP at market prices, and the ratio of government debt of 60 per cent of GDP at market prices;
2 for one year inflation rates must be within 1.5 per cent of the three best performing economies;
3 for one year long-term interest rates must be within 2 per cent of the three best performing economies; and
4 the currency should have remained within the ERM for the two previous years without devaluation. This was originally interpreted to mean the 2.25 per cent band, which was in existence at the time when the TEU was negotiated. However, Article 3 of the protocol on Convergence Criteria states that member states shall have '. . . respected the normal fluctuation margins provided by the exchange rate mechanism for at least two years'. No mention is made of the width of the margins, so that the 15 per cent margins agreed in August 1993 may well apply. The EU has the flexibility to choose which bands it wishes. Table 11.4 sets out the situation with respect to the criteria, immediately prior to the 1995 enlargement.

As Table 11.4 shows, at the time of the 1995 enlargement only Luxembourg met the criteria. Sweden's budget deficit was expected to be 11.2 per cent of GDP in 1994. This led to a rising level of debt which reached 94 per cent of GDP by the end of 1994. The problems were not as severe for Finland; however, the trend was away from convergence rather than towards it.

Government deficits

The major hurdle to achieving the ERM targets is achieving a ratio of 60 per cent of government debt to GDP. It is difficult to envisage that sufficient debt will be paid off for Sweden to meet this target unless there are substantial cuts in welfare payments and the state is able to privatise parts of the economy to generate the funds. Reducing the value of the debt significantly by inflation within the economy is an option which is contrary to the spirit of the exercise.

However, the TEU (Article 104c) offers the possibility of progression even if government deficits exceed the 60 per cent if either the ratio has declined substantially and continuously and reached a level close to the

Table 11.4 Convergence criteria for EMU (1994)

Country	*Inflation rate (percentage)*	*Budget deficit (as percentage of GDP)*	*Long-term interest rates (percentage)*	*Public debt ratio*	*Number of criteria fulfilled*
Austria	3.1*	4.2	6.8*	58*	3
Belgium	2.4*	5.8	7.8*	146	2
Denmark	2.2*	4.4	7.9*	82	2
Finland	1.7*	4.6	9.0*	72.5	2
France	1.7*	5.5	7.5*	50*	3
Germany	3.0*	5.6	6.9*	41*	3
Greece	11.1	13.1	18.9	118	0
Ireland	2.5*	2.3*	8.1*	92	3
Italy	3.9	10.6	10.6	122.2	0
Luxembourg	2.3*	1.3*	7.8*	10*	4
Netherlands	1.9*	3.8	7.0*	81	2
Portugal	4.6	7.1	10.8	66.7	0
Spain	4.6	7.0	9.8*	64	1
Sweden	2.0*	11.2	8.2*	94.0	2
UK	2.4*	6.9	8.2*	50.3*	3

Note: * convergence criteria achieved
Sources: Financial Times 1995b: 8; OECD (1995)

reference value. Alternatively, progression can take place if the excess over the reference value is only exceptional and temporary and the ratio remains close to the reference value.

The third stage of EMU could commence as early as 31 December 1996. In this case the Council will decide by a qualified majority that a critical mass of at least eight states have met the convergence terms. If this is achieved these states can move to a single currency. This always looked to be an unlikely prospect, even before the currency crisis of 1992. However, the enlargement made the prospect even more distant because the willingness of Austria to participate fully in the EMS was offset by the two new Nordic member states, who were not even prepared to join the ERM. In addition to this they were some way away from achieving the other convergence criteria.

A failure to achieve the above target will mean that Option Two comes into effect. There is no need for a critical mass of states to meet the convergence terms. All that is required is that the European Council confirms in mid-1998 those who have met the criteria for adoption of the single currency. This means that EMU can commence on 1 January 1999. In practice it is likely that at least three states will achieve the convergence criteria as these would be the three states which would form part of the bench mark for inflation and interest rates. Indeed at least two of the new members of the EU may be well placed to join EMU.

OPERATING WITHIN EMU

To make EMU work, the process of economic and political integration will have to develop further than it has today. All states will need to accept that there are going to be severe limits to their national sovereignty in that the responsibility for a great many decisions currently taken by national institutions will be moved to the EU level. It will be difficult to sustain the very high levels of welfare spending which are a feature of the Nordic countries. Inflation rates will have to be harmonised so that the process of adjustment will be minimised. If inflationary expectations among the work forces do differ it will be politically difficult to impose wage restraints, which is the approach the Nordic countries have traditionally followed. Finally, all member states should join the EMU arrangements at an exchange rate which reflects their levels of productivity and competitiveness. The exchange rate on commencement of EMU may prove to be the ultimate stumbling block, because it will be easy for workers to judge their relative position in the wages league. This may provide the stimulus for inflationary wage settlements in those regions where productivity is relatively low.

Optimum currency areas

In some circumstances, the exchange rate is an important policy device, in that it assists (sometimes speedily) the adjustment of an economy. In an economy experiencing a balance of payments deficit there is likely to be unemployment; whilst there is a tendency towards inflation in those which operate a surplus. A major problem for EMU is the inflexibility of the system, which could lead to severe problems for parts of the EU. The question in economic terms must be whether the EU represents an optimum currency area and whether there are any sufficiently large benefits for trade that may offset the costs of being unable to devalue.

For monetary union to be beneficial it requires that economic shocks must be symmetrical, so that a common strategy can be adopted to combat the problem. That is, if there is an event such as a recession caused by global conditions it should have broadly the same impact on all parts of the monetary union. However, because of the diversity of the EU there may be some shocks which are asymmetrical, and which impact only on certain economies. If there are major asymmetrical shocks, then there needs to be measures to compensate for this, for example easy movement of labour, flexible wage rates or large resource transfers into the area in difficulty by means of benefit payments, or tax breaks. Finland's problems in the 1990s partially resulted from the asymmetrical shock of the collapse of their market in the Soviet Union. No other market economy suffered to the same extent, and it was appropriate that the Markka was devalued. This was needed to help competitiveness, and to reorientate trade towards the

West. For the future, Finland's heavy reliance on the exports of wood products (about 40 per cent of exports) may be a problem if this market goes into serious decline.

Other possible sources of asymmetrical shocks facing both Sweden and Finland are the burden of public sector debt and the burden of welfare stabilisers, given the size of the state sector and the extent of state benefits. If interest rates rise significantly the cost of servicing the debt will rise, placing greater strains on the national budgets. A similar situation will occur with a rise in unemployment. Either benefit payments will have to be cut, or taxation will have to be increased significantly, to pay the bill. Either option is unattractive, as it can only help to worsen the domestic problems in the short term.

The recovery of the EU economies in the mid-1990s may well help to mask the problems associated with the burden of the welfare stabilisers. However, in the longer term the problem will return, unless there is a significant improvement in the structures of the Nordic countries. Even Denmark, which enjoys a stronger economic position than the other Nordic members, faces a problem of its competitive position being constantly eroded by states with lower social provision. This suggests that EMU membership may mean that there is little alternative to equalising welfare provision throughout the EU. However, it is unlikely that the Nordic countries would wish to lower their standards significantly, and many of the member states cannot afford to raise theirs.

The very fact that the Nordic countries are not poor means that the EU is unlikely to transfer significant resources to them via the budget. The EU's priorities are likely to lie with the poorer states to the South, and in the future, to the East. Membership of EMU will not therefore be an attractive option until the Nordic countries have economies which are similar in structure to the rest of the member states.

In June 1995, the Swedish government submitted its draft convergence programme to the Advisory Committee on EU Affairs in the *Riksdag* and submitted the programme to the EU for consideration in July, reinforcing its commitment to be part of the EMU (Ministry of Finance 1995: 1). The aim of the programme is to describe how Sweden can participate in the third stage of the EMU, and enjoys the broad support of the main Swedish political parties. However, the programme is ambitious and requires that public finance is reinforced by approximately 8 billion Krona in both 1997 and 1998 in order to reach the reference value of the convergence criteria for the deficit in public finance. The programme is also reliant upon a considerable amount of income for the government from the successful privatisations such as from Nordbanken. It remains to be seen whether this revenue will be forthcoming.

HOW MIGHT NORWAY HAVE FITTED IN?

Norway shadowed the ERM from October 1991 to 10 December 1992. However, the tie with the mechanism was then cut, because of pressures from the foreign exchange markets. Despite the inevitable linking of the Nordic currencies in the minds of the foreign exchange markets, Norway was in a stronger position than the other Nordic applicants, because of its oil exports. A return to the ERM at a later date was considered to be a viable option, and the krona did not deteriorate significantly against the ECU following the end of shadowing. However, on 6 May 1994 there was a policy change, and the currency was floated. By this time the Krone was trading at 5 per cent below its former central rate against the ECU. The aim was still to join the ERM, should EU membership become a reality. Failing this, it was hoped to stabilise the currency against other European currencies.

Norway's decision not to join the EU did not lead to a significant loss of credibility for the currency. However, despite its ability to meet the convergence criteria, the suitability of EMU membership for Norway would always have been in doubt. This was because of the high reliance of the economy on oil exports, and a manufacturing sector which amounted to only 15 per cent of GDP. Any significant change in oil prices meant that there would have been a considerable asymmetrical shock, resulting in either substantial balance of payments surpluses or deficits.

CONCLUSION

The experience of the early 1990s shows that the path towards monetary integration will not be an easy one. A number of problems with the operation of the EMS became apparent, and progress towards EMU was not satisfactory. The member states have only considered their individual national self-interest when trying to set monetary policy, so for example in the early 1990s Sweden and Finland became the victims of high German interest rates. Even if they become members of the ERM, Finland and Sweden will have to bear the ultimate cost of defending their own currencies. The setting of targets for EMU is deflationary, and there are doubts about the desirability of using the EMS as a platform for achieving EMU. For monetary integration to work, there needs to be real convergence between the European economies. This is especially the case for the new Nordic members, who are only now adjusting to EU membership.

When the Finnish and Swedish EU accession became a reality in 1995, they were not well regarded in an economic sense. Finland and Sweden were two heavily indebted Nordic countries which had severe problems adjusting to the global economy. Past experience suggests that they may be cautious in their strategy towards ERM membership. They will also find it difficult to meet the strict criteria for EMU, although Finland is better placed than is Sweden in this respect.

It may not be appropriate for the new members to show open dissent concerning the EU's strategy towards monetary integration. However, Finland and Sweden will probably join the significant number of states who fail to achieve the EU convergence criteria. With relatively few states adopting the single currency, there is a danger of a two or three speed Europe. There may be the inner core of economies who have low inflation. Beyond this would be a bloc of states which were waiting to join EMU, and perhaps states like Denmark wishing not to be members under any circumstances. It will be politically damaging if the core of highly integrated economies are seen as being superior to the other member states. Overall, the Single Market may suffer as a result of fragmentation, caused by differing exchange rate regimes within the EU. The problem that faces high quality currencies of the EMU is that they may be seen as a refuge in times of monetary turbulence. For those that remain outside EMU, there will be higher transaction costs to pay in their dealings with other states.

12 The impact of the Nordic countries on EU social policy

Debra Johnson

INTRODUCTION

The accession of Sweden and Finland to the European Union (EU) has occurred at a key turning point in the evolution of social policy, both in the acceding states themselves and within the European Union. For many years Sweden and Finland have operated a generous social welfare system against a background of consensus between the main economic and social partners and low levels of unemployment. Workers have, through membership of trade unions, exercised influence over important areas of company and national economic policy. This system has also resulted in the highest levels of taxation within the OECD area. In view of rapid social, economic and political change, especially the escalating unemployment of the 1990s, the 'Nordic model' has faced increasing challenges in recent years. Such developments place the Nordic countries under severe pressure to adapt their traditional, and for a long time very successful, social policies.

The European Union's social policy by necessity is much less developed and comprehensive than that of individual member states and the two new Nordic members in particular. Social policy action in the early days of the European Community concentrated upon free movement of labour with some workplace health and safety initiatives. It was only with the introduction of the Single European Market (SEM) Programme that social policy took on a more central role within the European Community. The Social Charter and the related Social Action Programme and the Social Protocol of the Treaty on European Union (TEU) were developed to broaden the appeal of European integration and were primarily concerned with the protection of worker rights. However, following the re-emergence of doubts about Europe's competitiveness in the global economy and a surge in unemployment, the emphasis of EU social policy appears to have shifted from protection of rights to achieving the appropriate balance between job creation and boosting Europe's competitive position.

Sweden and Finland have therefore entered the European Union at a time of rapid change in their own domestic circumstances and of refocusing of EU social policy. The Nordic countries have a well developed social policy tradition and, despite recent pressures, a strong commitment to the maintenance of high social standards, both in terms of social welfare and of workers' rights. The aim of this chapter therefore is to highlight these traditions and to identify common ground and points of departure between Nordic and EU social policy as it is currently evolving. This provides a preliminary input into the potential for the Nordic countries to influence EU social policy.

NORDIC SOCIAL POLICY TRADITIONS

For decades, the Nordic countries have managed to combine the world's most developed welfare states with some of its highest living standards and, until the early 1990s, levels of unemployment were among the lowest in the OECD area. The Nordic welfare system is comprehensive and universal – that is, qualification for benefit is based on residence or citizenship rather than on participation in the labour force or means testing. This has raised the acceptability of the welfare system to all social groups. The benefits themselves are relatively generous and have some redistributive effect. Consequently, the public sector, both in terms of employment and expenditure, plays a much bigger role in Nordic countries than elsewhere in Europe.

Figure 12.1 demonstrates the dominant role played by public spending on social protection in the Nordic countries. In 1990, public spending on social protection in Sweden was equivalent to one third of GDP compared to 15 per cent in Portugal. Given the difference in living standards between the two countries, it is apparent that these figures hide even bigger disparities in the scope and scale of welfare provision. Figure 12.1 is based on 1990 figures for social protection when Swedish unemployment was 1.5 per cent. Given the subsequent rise in Swedish and Finnish unemployment, social protection accounts for an even greater proportion of Nordic GDP in the mid-1990s.

The Nordic welfare system is under attack. First unemployment has risen rapidly since 1990 (see Figure 12.2) thereby increasing the burden on the welfare state. For many years, Nordic unemployment levels were significantly below those in the rest of Europe. Between 1970 and 1990, for example, Swedish unemployment never rose above 4 per cent and for most of the time ranged between 1.2 and 3.5 per cent. During this period EU unemployment was two, three or even four times greater than the Swedish figures. However, by 1994 Swedish unemployment had multiplied to 8 per cent, still below the 1994 EU average of 11.4 per cent but historically high by Swedish standards. Finnish unemployment had escalated to over 18 per cent, second only to Spain in the EU. The Finnish labour market has been hit not only by the recessionary factors which faced all EU countries in the early 1990s but also by the collapse of its trade with Russia which has traditionally been a mainstay of Finnish economic prosperity.

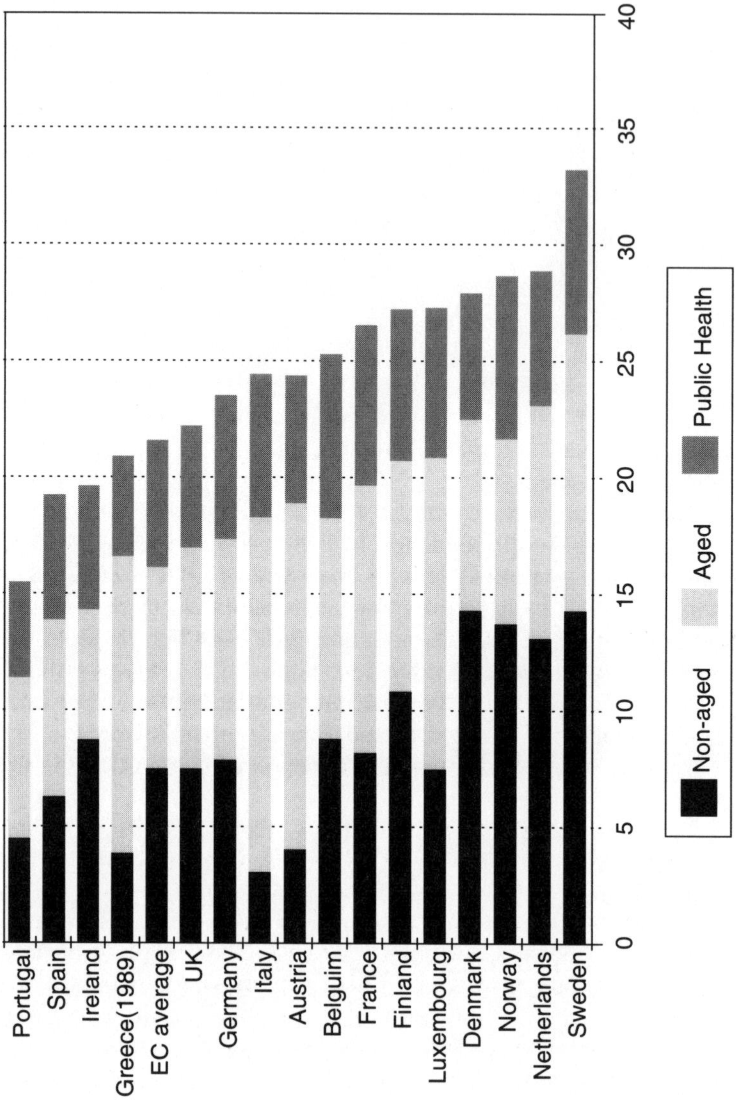

Figure 12.1 Public spending on social protection, 1990 (percentage of GDP)
Source: OECD

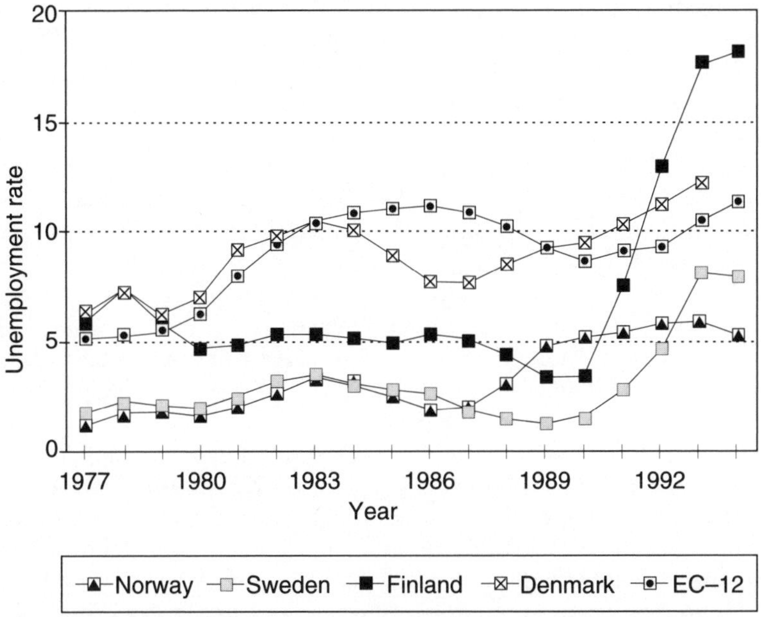

Figure 12.2 European and Nordic unemployment rates, 1977–92 (percentage)
Source: OECD

Second, the convergence criteria for economic and monetary union as set out in the Treaty on European Union require much tighter controls on public debt and the budget deficit than those prevailing in the new Nordic members of the European Union. Although committed to the principle of EMU, the Nordic countries are in no great hurry to move ahead. A concerted attempt to satisfy the convergence criteria would have serious consequences for the welfare states of the Nordic countries which are already under review as a result of the escalating costs of rising unemployment.

The Nordic countries have been more successful in preserving industrial peace and in achieving high workplace standards than in the European Union generally. They have achieved this by allowing the state only a limited role in industrial relations. As a result of Basic Agreements[1] negotiated between employers and trade unions earlier this century, a corporatist system of government has emerged in which consensus and collaboration between the state and the centralised organisations of capital and labour have resulted in relatively conflict-free industrial relations and agreement on key social and economic issues. Although the Basic Agreements have evolved over the years and significant adjustments have been made to their operation,[2] the Nordic tradition of relatively centralised and consensual industrial relations remains strong.

In commenting upon the European Commission's 1993 Green Paper on European Social Policy (Commission of the ECs 1993c), the Danish government reaffirmed its commitment to a system of collective agreements in preference to regulation and pointed out that 'in the field of labour law, it is important that the regulation at European level takes place with due regard to the principles of subsidiarity so that existing national structures are not interfered with. The ultimate aim is not a harmonisation of labour law systems in Europe.'[3] The memorandum elaborates on the advantages of the Danish system which requires a widely organised labour market 'with organisations on both sides which are ready to reach agreement by giving concessions'. The Danish Labour Ministry argues that this model has made a major contribution to social progress and is highly flexible. 'It has the great advantage that the parties feel a higher degree of commitment because they have themselves negotiated the necessary compromises. This means that the parties prefer to solve their disputes without any intervention on the part of the State.'

Sweden and Finland bring similar traditions to the European Union plus a high level of commitment to employee involvement in the workplace. The Nordic co-determination model has evolved out of the collective bargaining system outlined above. Rights to employee involvement tend to derive from union membership. The much higher level of unionisation which prevails in Nordic countries than elsewhere in Europe (see Figure 12.3), confers legitimacy on the system. In its attempts to introduce greater employee participation in the workplace, the European Commission has tended to reflect the more individualistic approach of member states and has emphasised basic legal rights. Such an approach could place the Nordic tradition under pressure. However, if the Commission sticks to its intention to respect different national approaches to industrial relations, the Nordic countries may be able to continue as before.

In short, the accession of the Nordic countries has strengthened the third dimension of industrial relations in the European Union. The biggest single tradition is that of regulation which has dominated in France, Germany and Italy and which has influenced the European Commission's approach to social policy to date. This tradition accords a central role to the state and legislation in governing industrial relations and in ensuring basic rights for workers. Labour market legislation in such countries is comprehensive and covers issues such as working time, holidays and employee representation.

This contrasts with the UK approach which accords the state only a minimal role in industrial relations and the social partners an increasingly small, if not non-existent, influence in the determination of policy. Some labour market regulation does exist to establish minimum health and safety standards in particular but other terms and conditions of employment are left to bargaining between employers and employees. Although superficially operating similar systems in terms of the role of the state, any similarity between the UK and Nordic models ends there. Although eschewing the role of the state in legislating for high levels of labour standards, the Nordic countries have managed to attain some of the highest

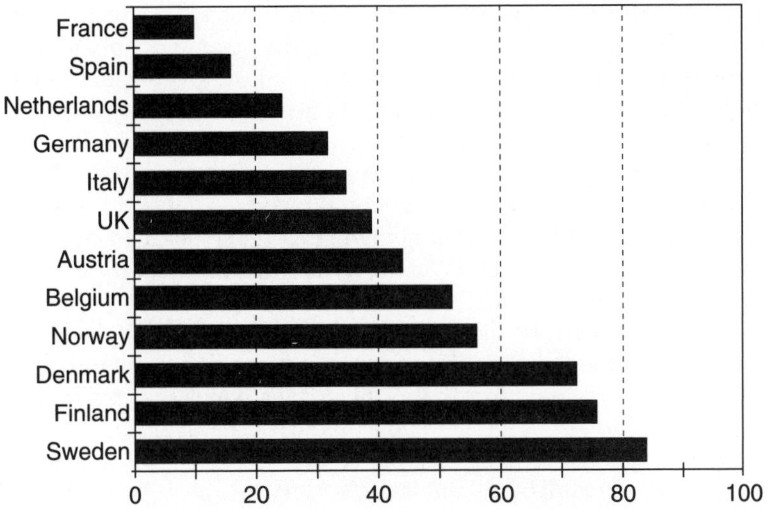

Figure 12.3 Unionisation of Europe's workforce (percentage of union members in the workforce)
Source: OECD

standards in the Union. They are likely to argue for flexibility in methods used to attain high standards but will not question the need for high standards themselves.

EU AND NORDIC APPROACHES TO SOCIAL POLICY

A constant theme in European Union social, and indeed in all, policy initiatives in recent years has been the need to respect the principles of subsidiarity and of diversity of national systems, cultures and practices where this does not conflict with the completion of the Single Market. This respect for national diversity is of paramount importance to the Nordic countries. Prior to the latest enlargement, the European Union already contained a variety of social policy and industrial relations traditions. The accession of Finland and Sweden has added to this richness and diversity.

In the general EU debate about social policy, a commitment to high social standards has consistently been accompanied by a determination to avoid social dumping – that is, the need to ensure there is a minimum level of regulation of workplace rights and health and safety standards. In the absence of such standards, it is feared that member states with high standards might be pressured to lower their standards in order to compete. The Nordic countries are firmly on the side of those countries which wish to avoid the dangers of social dumping. Having consistently taken this line in the debates leading to the formulation of EU social policy, Denmark reaffirmed its position clearly in its memorandum on the Green Paper on Social Policy which it views as providing a framework for social policy 'which tries to reconcile economic and social objectives in the context of a situation with growing unemployment and the need to maintain competitiveness without resorting to social dumping and without any deterioration of the living and working conditions of the workers'.

Finland has rapidly confirmed its agreement with this position. In a statement to parliament less than two months after joining the EU, the Finnish government made a strong commitment to the social dimension and to the avoidance of social dumping in particular, stating 'The use as a means of competition of employment terms which fall short of the basic social security level for workers must not be permitted' (Ministry of Foreign Affairs 1995). In the accession negotiations, the applicant states stressed their commitment to the social chapter and more majority voting to enable the Union to deliver the social chapter. The Norwegian rejection of EU membership had nothing to do with the social dimension, if anything Norway was anxious to achieve a more active EU social policy. Prime Minister Gro Harlem Brundtland laid out Norway's position on this, 'You will find Norway in a group wanting more effectiveness on these kinds of concerns' (Financial Times 1993).

The EU's emphasis on social policy and on health and safety issues in recent years has shifted from harmonisation towards the establishment of minimum standards. The Nordic countries are firmly committed to the attainment of these minimum standards and are anxious to ensure that this commitment does not preclude them introducing higher domestic standards. Again the emphasis is on subsidiarity. In the Finnish Guidelines on European Policy (Ministry of Foreign Affairs 1995), the government states, 'Finland will support the development of the social dimension in both working life and the traditional social security sphere in such a way that only the minimum level is jointly agreed, and Member States may exceed it if they so wish, and that modes of implementation remain within national power of decision.' This approach is entirely consistent with the position of Sweden and Denmark.

THE EVOLUTION OF EU SOCIAL POLICY

During the mid-1990s, EU social policy is undergoing a reassessment in response to the challenges of mass unemployment and an ageing population. In order to appreciate the extent of the changes, it is necessary to trace the evolution of social policy. The improvement of living and working conditions was an explicit objective of the Treaty of Rome but the specific articles relating to social policy in the Treaty were not a sufficient basis for a comprehensive, integrated social policy.[4] Although the Treaty articles touched upon several aspects of social policy, in many ways they remained vague and ambiguous. Not surprisingly therefore, apart from some initiatives on mutual recognition of qualifications and health and safety, social policy was largely neglected in the first fifteen years of the Community's existence.

Growing economic tensions with resulting employment problems resulted in a more active social policy during the 1970s. In 1974, the Council adopted a Social Action Programme containing forty initiatives aimed at achieving full and better employment, promotion of employment and training programmes and work designed to improve living and working conditions. This was an attempt to develop an integrated and coherent social policy but the programme was never fully implemented. However, more health and safety directives were adopted during the 1970s and key directives relating to equal pay and equal treatment for men and women in the workplace were adopted in the second half of the decade. Initiatives to promote employee participation at the workplace were also introduced during this period but made little progress.

Despite the passage of further health and safety directives and more breakthroughs in the treatment of women at the workplace, many other initiatives (for example, part-time work, temporary work and directives relating to employee consultation and participation) failed to make much progress as the 1980s unfolded. However, in November 1985 at Val Duchesse, the Commission revived the 'social dialogue' involving the social partners. Nevertheless, social issues were largely ignored in the 1985 Single Market White Paper (Commission of the ECs 1985). Health and safety directives continued to be introduced without controversy but little else was achieved. The Commission became increasingly concerned that the success of the Single Market required the support of both employers and employees. The Single Market was essentially about removing barriers to trade within the Community and allowing the forces of competition to yield benefits in terms of greater competitiveness and efficiency. Without a widening of its appeal, Commission President Jacques Delors in particular believed the single market programme would lose support.

'Social consensus is an essential factor in maintaining sustained economic growth' (Commission of the ECs 1989a). In addition, the liberalisation introduced by the single market revived fears of social dumping resulting in downward pressure on labour conditions. The Commission chose to combat such dangers by introduction of the Community Charter of the Fundamental Social Rights of Workers which was signed by eleven member states (the exception being the United Kingdom) in December 1989. The Charter was not a legally binding document but a 'solemn declaration' which attempted to establish basic minimum rights at the workplace.[5]

Uncontroversial in eleven member states, the Charter remains unsigned by the United Kingdom which maintains that it increases the costs of European business at a time when it is coming under increasing pressure from low labour cost countries in the Far East. The United Kingdom kept to this position during the negotiations on the Treaty on European Union, resulting in the transfer of the Social Chapter of the Treaty into a Protocol attached to the Treaty – a compromise which allows the other member states to continue their work on implementing the Treaty. Since the Treaty has come into force, emphasis has been placed on attaining agreement of all twelve to social policy proposals before invoking the Protocol procedure. The sustainability of the United Kingdom 'opt out' in the long term is doubtful, especially if other member states amass evidence of companies migrating to the UK because of its less stringent labour laws.[6] The UK opt out will end if there is a change of UK government.

In order to give legal backing and to implement the principles of the Social Charter, the Commission introduced a Social Action Programme (Commission of the ECs 1989e) containing forty-seven proposals for directives and regulations. By the end of 1993, although some aspects of the Programme required further progress, all the proposals in the Programme had been presented by the Commission and the majority had been adopted. More significantly, unemployment, which had been on a steady downward trend, reaching a trough in 1990, was clearly on the rise again as a result of the recession in Western Europe. In addition to the normal concerns about cyclical unemployment, Europe also experienced a crisis of confidence arising from the recognition of the globalisation phenomenon and the fear that Europe will increasingly have to compete with low labour cost countries from the Far East.

In order to confront the new challenges posed by these circumstances, the European Commission issued its Green Paper on Social Policy. It was essentially a consultative document on the future strategy of Europe's social policy and formed the basis for the Social Policy White Paper (Commission of the ECs 1994c) – the main guidelines for the Union's social policy in the coming years. The Green and White Papers were based on the assumptions that member states are facing growing demographic, technological, fiscal, human and industrial pressures which will require significant adaptation in existing policies. Technological change is leading to shifts in employment patterns and the role of work in society as witnessed by the growth of part-time and temporary work contracts in particular. Unemployment, the ageing of populations, changes in family structure and growing poverty is placing the welfare state under extreme pressure and increasing demands for health care. Issues of social justice, equality of opportunity, the role of education and training, changing workplace relationships and workers' and womens' rights are also high on the agenda. These social issues are closely intertwined with questions of socio-economic cooperation and competition on an international level and how Europe is able to adapt to the changing nature of production.

In short, Sweden and Finland have entered the European Union at a time when the latter's social policy is at a critical juncture: the Social Action Programme is almost complete, the Treaty on European Union has opened up new possibilities in the social field and the changing socio-economic situation has prompted a new look at social and economic policies. The Green and White Papers represent, really for the first time, an attempt to incorporate all aspects of social policy in one integrated policy approach and deal with social welfare issues as well as labour market policies.

In view of the far-reaching nature of the White Paper, the following elements of the White Paper have been chosen as areas which have particular resonance for the Nordic countries or in which the European Union may learn from Nordic experience and practice. These areas are health and safety; social welfare; active labour market policies; social dialogue; and improved access to and transparency of Union legislation.

HEALTH AND SAFETY

Occupational health and safety represents the most active and least controversial sphere of EU social policy. The introduction of qualified majority voting through the Single European Act and the use of broad 'daughter' directives which establish the broad principles and objectives of legislation rather than the detailed technical specification of workplace health and safety requirements have resulted in an acceleration of workplace health and safety regulation at EU level since 1988.

However, the Nordic countries interpret workplace health and safety as more than the physical and technical aspects of the workplace environment: it also covers the way work is organised, including job content, working hours, employee participation and the psycho-social aspects of the workplace. In Sweden, the Work Environment Act, which came into effect in 1978, talks about the work environment in the following way:

> Technology, work organisation and job content shall be designed in such a way that the employee is not subjected to physical or mental strains which can lead to illness or accidents. Forms of remuneration and the distribution of working hours shall also be taken into account in this connection. . . . Efforts shall be made to ensure that working conditions provide opportunities of variety, social contact and cooperation, as well as coherence between different working operations. Furthermore, efforts shall be made to ensure that working conditions provide for personal and vocational development, as well as for self-determination and professional responsibility.
>
> Swedish Work Environment Act, Chapter 2, Section 1

Such a broad interpretation of health and safety implies that the European Commission attempts to introduce social legislation under Article 118A are consistent with Nordic practice. Article 118A allows qualified majority voting for health and safety matters rather than unanimity. The directive on working time (Commission of the ECs 1993a), for example, which the Commission introduced under 118A fell completely within the parameters of Nordic health and safety policy. This directive has, however, been subject to a legal challenge from the UK government which claims that the directive deals chiefly with working conditions not health and safety and that Article 118A is therefore an inappropriate legal base for the directive.

The Social Policy White Paper identifies the need to make progress on existing health and safety proposals.[7] In this, the Commission can reasonably expect support from the Nordic states provided they remain free to introduce higher standards within their territory.

SOCIAL WELFARE

EU policy on social welfare to date has been aimed not at harmonising social welfare systems[8] but at migrant rights. There is a consensus among member states that a Single Market can co-exist alongside a variety of social protection systems and there are no plans to harmonise the systems. However, the White Paper identifies a number of common trends and policies within member states, including rising unemployment, changing family structures, and the need to contain the escalation of health care costs – problems which are shared by the Nordic countries.

Little in the way of concrete policy in the social welfare field is offered by the White Paper but it does speak of member states agreeing to 'foster the convergence of their social protection policies' (Commission of the ECs 1994c). The Commission's role is to analyse the development of social protection policies within member states and to evaluate them so that each can benefit from the experience of others. The Nordic countries offer wide and varied social protection schemes from which other member states can learn, including in particular more generous provisions for parental leave, especially paternal rights, than exist in the rest of Western Europe. However, in view of cost problems, EU member states are unlikely to follow the Nordic social welfare example. Rather the most likely chain of events is that the strains on the budgets of the Nordic countries will lead to a scaling down of their welfare systems.

ACTIVE LABOUR MARKET POLICIES

Labour market policies can be divided into two: passive policies which have the objective of assistance, usually to the unemployed, and active policies which aim to promote employment generation, usually through training schemes or other initiatives to improve labour market flexibility. The White Paper aims to shift the balance of labour market policies away from passive to active policies. 'For too long, Europe has focused on the management of unemployment instead of promoting job creation as the top priority' (Commission of the ECs 1994c). The White Paper then goes on to talk about the need for more active labour market policies.

The Nordic countries have decades of experience in promoting active labour market policies. In Sweden public spending equivalent to 1.72 per cent of GDP goes on active labour market measures, compared to 1.2 per cent in Denmark and 0.72 per cent in the OECD area as a whole.[9] Denmark justifies its relatively high spending on active labour market policy in the Ministry of Labour's response to the Green Paper thus:

> Unemployment is the most serious problem in Denmark and the Danish government firmly believes that an active labour-market policy in conjunction with specifically targeted industrial and education/training policies is a pre-requisite for a successful economic policy. This is why Denmark is spending a very large share of the GNP on labour-market and education/training measures, and increasingly on active labour-market policy measures.[10]

Behind the Danish active labour market policy is the view that economic growth will be insufficient to absorb unemployment and that enhancement of skills through education and training will play an important role in the fight against unemployment.

The new Union members, Sweden and Finland, also have a tradition of an active labour market policy. The main objective of Finland's labour market policy is to match the quantity and quality of the labour supply with the short- and long-term demands of the labour market (Ministry of Foreign Affairs, 1993a Annex 5 (6)). In order to achieve this, the Finnish government offers training to the unemployed and those in danger of becoming unemployed and provides pay-related subsidies to facilitate integration of the unemployed into the workplace and to shorten periods of unemployment. Since 1988, the Ministry of Labour has raised funding to help speed up structural change and to adjust the labour market to structural change.

Until the early 1990s, Swedish unemployment levels rarely rose above 2 per cent. Sweden achieved this partly through its active labour market policy programme which enabled labour force participation to increase from 73 per cent to over 84 per cent of the working age population in the two decades leading up to 1990 without a surge in unemployment. However, by 1994 unemployment had risen to over 8 per cent. Accordingly labour market policy has been stepped up and is aimed at promoting economic restructuring: its main task is to prevent the emergence of long-term unemployment; to improve the match between labour supply and demand and to place people in work. In the absence of jobs, the unemployed are placed in active labour market programmes. Cash benefits are only available as a last resort. Active measures taken by Sweden include job placement, vocational counselling, job clubs, employment training, relocation grants to boost geographical mobility (declining in importance), relief jobs (temporary work for the unemployed), recruitment subsidies, youth traineeships, in-house employment training to encourage employers to take advantage of periods of low activity to improve the skills of their employees, educational leave replacements and a general hiring grant which is equivalent to a 15 per cent reduction in payroll fees in 1994 for employers who have increased their number of employees since October 1993. Well-developed schemes also exist to encourage employment of the educationally handicapped.

The EU's White Paper does not propose a comprehensive active labour market policy at Union level. The White Paper alludes to the active labour market policies in place or proposed in individual member states and to the diversity of different national systems. Rather the White Paper talks of developing 'the added value of Union-wide action, and mutual support, in exploiting the diversity of Member State experiences. . . . It means looking at the possibilities to "pick and mix" different elements of policy and good practice from different national systems.' The Commission also talks of increased compatibility between the systems of member states to ensure they do not conflict with overall Union objectives or standards or do not distort competition or inhibit the development of free movement of people within the Union (Commission of the ECs 1994c). Given their experience with active labour market policies, the Nordic countries will provide valuable role models for other member states.

The above does not preclude Union-level initiatives. The Union has developed its own training programmes through the Leonardo and Socrates programmes and, through the Structural Funds – especially the European Social Fund – will make its own contribution to the development of a skilled, adaptable and mobile labour force. The Community Support Frameworks (CSFs), strategies negotiated with member states for the use of Structural Funds, have concentrated on three priority areas: improved access to, and quality of, initial training and education; a systematic approach to continuing training to increase competitiveness and the adaptiveness of the workforce; and to increase employment opportunities for the long-term unemployed.

SOCIAL DIALOGUE

Over the last decade, the European Commission has used the concept of the 'Social Dialogue' – that is, extensive consultation of the social partners in the formulation of social policy initiatives and issues – as a key element in bringing forward social policy proposals. The Single European Act formally embedded the commitment to social dialogue into the Treaty of Rome (Article 118B) – a development which was taken further in the Social Agreement of the Treaty on European Union.

The social dialogue represents a commitment to consensus in decision-making. The White Paper talks of a 'European social model of consensus, reconciling economic effectiveness and social solidarity' (Commission of the ECs 1994c: 42) and identifies collective bargaining as 'a flexible instrument in creating consensus'. The Commission has issued a Communication on the future role of the social dialogue (Commission of the ECs 1993d) which it clearly wants to develop further. The institutional, consultative framework is to be restructured and the social dialogue generally is to be broadened. This is regarded as particularly important at a time when the Union is desperately trying to find a way of reconciling high social standards with the maintenance of competitiveness in an increasingly global economy.

A strengthening of the social dialogue represents a movement towards the Nordic way of conducting social policy. Consensus and consultation have been the hallmark of industrial relations and discussion of social issues which extend beyond the workplace. However, the social dialogue has become more problematic in the Nordic countries in recent years and the Nordic countries have a much greater degree of unionisation than other EU states – a factor which gives the dialogue greater legitimacy and credibility than is possible in member states where unionisation is low.

THE IMPROVED ACCESSIBILITY AND TRANSPARENCY OF UNION LEGISLATION

One of the big challenges facing the European Union, not just in the social policy field but generally, is the need to ensure that directives agreed at Union level are transposed into national law, implemented and enforced (Commission of the ECs 1993d). It is too early yet to assess how the new Nordic members perform in this area, but the long-term Nordic member, Denmark, has, despite its reputation as a reluctant EU member, the best record of all member states in transposing and implementing EC directives into national law. With their respect for the rule of law and their commitment to high social standards, the Nordic countries are likely to act in a communitarian fashion when it comes to implementation.

A key characteristic of the Nordic polity is its commitment to openness and transparency in decision-making. The European Union has been severely criticised for its poor performance in this respect. The White Paper hopes to rectify this in the social field by providing better information about social rights and opportunities through a variety of means and will use the EURES database to disseminate information about living and working conditions in member states in an attempt to promote labour mobility. The Nordic countries will press the EU to ensure that these and other measures are indeed taken to improve openness and transparency. In its Guidelines on European Policy the Finnish government stated that Finland bases her own actions on the greatest degree of openness and strives for this also in the drafting of legislation and decision-making within the EU (Ministry of Foreign Affairs 1995). A similar commitment to openness can be expected from Sweden where most government documents are open to press and public scrutiny at any time.

CONCLUSION

The Nordic countries have some of the highest social standards and strongest commitment to these standards in the world. On the face of it, they could be expected to act as leaders in efforts to strengthen EU social policy. This is far from certain. Whilst firmly in the camp of those member states wishing to prevent the emergence of social dumping and the use of low social standards as a competitive weapon, the Nordic countries have an equally strong commitment to the principle of subsidiarity and for respect of different national cultures and traditions. The Danish Labour Ministry's response to the Green Paper stresses 'the basic principle that the individual Member State formulates and is responsible for its own social policy'.

Although details of their social policy varies, the broad principles of the policy have more similarities than differences among the Nordic countries. They will, therefore, cooperate in this, as in other fields, when it comes to positioning at European Union level. Furthermore, although the Norwegian population turned down EU membership in a referendum, the Norwegian government intends to carry out an 'active Europe policy' (Royal Ministry of Foreign Affairs 1994b). Norway intends to do this through the European Economic Area Agreement (EEA) which contained some elements of EU social policy. However, in view of the long tradition of Nordic cooperation and Norway's continuing commitment to it, Norway's views on social and other aspects of EU policy will be heard indirectly within EU social policy formation forums.

The EU has gained two new members with a strong commitment to social welfare, high standards of health and safety and long traditions of industrial democracy. As such, the Commission is unlikely to encounter opposition from the new members on social policy initiatives unless it tries to intervene in social policy matters which do not have a genuine transnational dimension and, in so doing, transgress the principle of subsidiarity.

The approach to social policy within the Nordic countries and the EU is also moving closer together. The EU, albeit in a limited way, is concerning itself with a broader range of social policies than in the past. Common concerns, especially over rising unemployment, have caused the EU to move towards the Nordic tradition of an active labour market policy designed to create jobs. Nordic traditions of openness and transparency will have an influence in the campaign to increase openness and transparency in the European Union. Within the Nordic countries themselves the old consensus which helped maintain industrial peace and which gave rise to the well-developed welfare state has not broken down but become more complex. Factors like the demise of the extreme centralisation of collective bargaining and the emergence of government sponsored wage policies are pushing the Nordic states, in some ways, towards the traditions of the rest of Western Europe. Will the two groups meet in the middle?

NOTES

1 In Sweden, the Basic or Saltsjöbaden Agreement was concluded in 1938 between the Swedish Employers' Confederation (*Svenska arbetsgivareföreningen* – SAF) and the Swedish Trade Union Confederation (*Landsorganisationen I Sverige* – L.O.); Norway's Basic Agreement was originally established in 1935; and Denmark's main agreement (the *Hovedaftalen*) in the early 1900s.

2 There has been movement away from centralised bargaining throughout the Nordic area. For example, in Sweden in 1990, the SAF decided to abandon centralised wage bargaining and from 1993, negotiations have been carried out at sectoral level between national employers' associations and national trade unions.

3 Commission of the ECs, Contribution to the Preparatory Work for the White Paper on Social Policy, *Social Europe 2:94*, Reply from the Danish Government to the Commission concerning the Green Paper on European Social Policy, Danish Ministry of Labour, published in *Social Europe*.

4 Treaty of Rome provisions relating to social policy included Articles 48–51 (free movement of workers); Articles 52–58 (rights of establishment); Articles 59–66 (freedom to provide services); Articles 117–122 (social provisions, including closer cooperation in matters relating to employment, labour law and conditions, training, social security, health and safety, right of association and collective bargaining, equal pay without discrimination on the basis of gender); and Articles 123–128 (establishment of the European Social Fund charged with the task of 'rendering the employment of workers easier and of increasing their geographical and occupational mobility within the Community' – Article 123).

5 The basic rights established by the Charter included the right of EC workers to work in any member state; the right to fair remuneration; the right to improved living and working conditions; the right to adequate social protection according to the arrangements prevailing in each member state; the right to freedom of association and collective bargaining; the right to vocational training; the right of men and women to equal treatment; the right of workers to information, consultation and participation; the right to health and safety protection at work; the protection of children and adolescents; the guarantee of minimum living standards for the elderly and improved social and professional integration for the disabled.

6 It is conceptually very difficult that a relocation decision is an example of social dumping. In 1993, Hoover decided to move its factory from Dijon in France to near Glasgow in Scotland: 600 French jobs were lost and 400 jobs were gained in Scotland. This is often quoted as a clear example of social dumping in action. Although different labour conditions were a factor in Hoover's decision to move, it is not at all clear that they were the decisive factor. Shortly after the Hoover decision, Rowntree made the reverse move resulting in a net loss of jobs in Glasgow and a net gain in Dijon but without the same political fallout.

7 Draft directives on health and safety in the transport sector (OJ C 271 – 16.10.93), physical agents (OJ C 77 – 18.3.93); chemical agents (OJ C 165 – 16.6.93); travel conditions of workers with motor disabilities (OJ C – 21.1.92) and work equipment (modification) (COM(94) 56 final – 14.3.94).

8 In its Recommendation on the Convergence of Social Protection Objectives and Policies (Commission of the ECs 1992 92/442/EEC OJ N L245 26.08.92), the Council acknowledged that a Single Market can co-exist with the diversity of social protection systems in the Union.

9 Figures from OECD Surveys quoted in Lyck, L. (ed.) (1992).

10 Commission of the European Communities, Contribution to the Preparatory Work for the White Paper on Social Policy, *Social Europe 2:94*, Reply from the Danish Government to the Commission concerning the Green Paper on European Social Policy, Danish Ministry of Labour, published in *Social Europe*.

13 The Nordic countries and European Union environmental policy

Pamela M. Barnes

INTRODUCTION

The Environmental Policy of the European Union (EU) has the potential to be the most important integrative mechanism in the protection of the European environment. The inclusion of a chapter on the environment in the 1987 Single European Act (SEA) and the additional articles in the Treaty on European Union (TEU) have given environmental policy a firm legal basis within the European Union. The accession of Sweden and Finland, which both maintain high levels of environmental awareness could be seen as an important step forward in ensuring that potential becomes reality. However, the main argument of this chapter is that the 1995 Nordic enlargement will be a disappointment for many environmentalists within the EU and that the new Nordic EU members will not be a catalyst for a significant improvement in environmental standards. The objectives of this chapter are: first, to outline the achievements of the European Union's environmental policy; second, briefly to review and identify the differences between the environmental protection policies of Finland and Sweden and the European Union; and third, to assess the impact of the new Nordic members on the future development of the EU's environmental policy.

THE BENEFITS OF EU MEMBERSHIP

EU membership was attractive for the Nordic countries for several reasons. Environmental problems which transcend national boundaries may be dealt with more easily. This seems especially relevant given the joint Swedish and Finnish governmental concerns over the environmental damage inflicted on their countries as a result of acid rainfall and wind-blown sulphur deposition from the United Kingdom and Germany.

In addition, the European Union is unique among international organisations because of its permanent political and judicial system. The continuity of its decision-making processes makes it easy to raise specific environmental concerns. In contrast, most alternative international forums for discussing environmental matters are either little more than talking shops with few powers of enforcement or have to be specially convened to deal with issues as they become urgent. This means that their decisions have little effect. As new member states, Finland and Sweden are fully integrated into the Single European Market (SEM) which requires the removal of trade barriers. Environmental standards on products which are traded must therefore be harmonised and this both benefits consumers (by increasing the range of products available) and facilitates trade.

A number of programmes which are designed to help with the environmental clean up of the countries of Central and Eastern Europe have also been established which are channelled through the European Union. This EU assistance, which may stabilise environmental degradation in Russia is an advantage for Finland given its long border with Russia. Pressures on the EU's Budget are growing as it attempts to deal with the increasing problems of regional backwardness and unemployment and Finland, in particular, will also be able to ensure that this EU commitment remains strong. However, EU environmental policy is not without its problems which have undermined its effectiveness. Finnish and Swedish concerns were evident during the accession negotiations that their higher environmental standards would be compromised. A number of derogations or transition periods were agreed during which Swedish and Finnish national standards will continue to apply. For example Sweden has a total ban on the production of polychlorobiphenyls (PCBs), which are used in electrical appliances and its recycling. This ban will remain until such time as the EU legislation is effective.

In December 1994 the EU reached a compromise position on the Directive on PCBs. The year 2010 was set as the final date for decontaminating or eliminating equipment using PCBs in order to allow for the southern and poorer EU members to adapt to the new legislation. Certain commitments were also made by the EU–12 to review other existing environmental legislation to identify and raise standards to those of the new members.

However, further disappointments may also emerge for the environmentalists of Finland and Sweden. Although EU accession should not lead to an erosion of the national environmental standards of Finland and Sweden, it may in fact make it more difficult for the EU to proceed on an integrated and coherent environmental path. The danger exists that instead of providing a force for a significantly improved environmental performance, the higher environmental standards of the new members will work as a disintegrative force on EU policy.

Pressure from environmental groups in Finland and Sweden in particular may lead to protectionist measures being taken by their governments, where national environmental regulations act as non-tariff barriers to trade. The potential for the development of 'environmental nationalism' will be damaging for the EU for a number of reasons. First, it could undermine the EU's objectives as outlined by the Treaty on European Union (TEU) which stated that its task would be 'to promote throughout the Community a harmonious and balanced development of economic activities, sustainable and non-inflationary growth respecting the environment' (Article 2, TEU). Second it may lead to a distortion of the Single European Market (SEM) by allowing discrepancies to develop between product and emission standards and thereby leading to unfair competition and new barriers to trade. Third, it will complicate further enlargement of the EU. Most notably, the next wave of enlargement will include the countries of Central and Eastern Europe (CEEC), which have severe environmental problems. If, as a result of pressure from Sweden and Finland, environmental standards have been radically improved, then many of these countries will have great difficulties in becoming EU members.

Nevertheless, this is not to argue that EU environmental protection policies should not develop. The EU is committed to a '. . . more progressive and better co-ordinated policy and strategy for the environment and sustainable development . . . ' (Commission of the ECs 1992f: 5). The future development of environmental policy will require careful management in order to achieve all the objectives of the EU. This may result in a slower pace of environmental improvement than the new Nordic member states would readily support.

THE DEVELOPMENT OF EU ENVIRONMENTAL POLICY

European Union Environmental Policy first came into existence in 1972 and was framed within the limited context of supranational cooperation. None the less, it has been the impetus for improved levels of environmental protection in some of the EU member states. However, Finland and Sweden have gradually developed their own individual environmental policies which are primarily the result of the industrial and agricultural concerns of the two countries. It is inevitable that there will be some transitional difficulties for Finland and Sweden to become fully integrated into the EU's policy. For both countries, the problem will be one of adaptation to the EU's procedures and also of accepting that the EU has a role in the development of their national environmental policies.

The 1957 Treaty of Rome did not include any articles which specifically mentioned environmental policy. The primary objective of the EU in the 1950s and later 1960s was economic growth rather than environmental concerns. However by the end of the 1960s it was apparent that faster rates of economic growth were resulting in higher levels of pollution and that the damage inflicted upon the European eco-system was reaching crisis point. The pollution of one country was increasingly affecting others. Hence, the supranational nature of EU cooperation gave the organisation an unparalleled opportunity to improve the existing environmental situation and build a policy for the future protection of Europe.

Initially EU environmental policy was developed through a series of

Environmental Action Programmes (EAPs) as a response to an increased global concern about environmental degradation, and that economic growth resulting from SEM could lead to a worsening of environmental problems. An agreed EU policy would be essential in order to deal with these concerns and there was a growing confidence within the EU about the possibility and effectiveness of joint action.

By 1987 four Environmental Action Programmes had been agreed, and a considerable body of environmental legislation had been introduced. The national governments had accepted that the EU had a responsibility to protect the environment. Thus, a considerable portion of national environmental policy was being determined within the framework of joint action. Therefore when the SEA amended the Treaty in 1987 a chapter on the environment was added, providing a legal basis for new measures.

More than two hundred environmental laws have been adopted by the EU since 1972. EU environmental policy has enjoyed a wide impact, including not just pollution control, but also measures aimed at protecting human health and preserving the environment. Standards have been set on air and water quality, transport pollution and chemical emissions and outline waste management procedures have been introduced. The need to incorporate environmental protection objectives into all areas of policy-making has been formally recognised in the TEU. However, in practice, the opportunity to introduce high levels of environmental protection is being undermined by the failure of the member states to implement policy measures effectively.

TOWARDS SUSTAINABLE DEVELOPMENT?

Since the 1987 United Nations Commission on the Environment, global developments in environmental protection policy have gathered momentum. The EU's contribution to this global debate revolved around the 1992 Fifth Environmental Action Programme and the concept of sustainable development. According to the European Commission, 'sustainability is intended to reflect a policy and strategy for continued economic and social development without detriment to the environment' (Commission of the ECs 1992f: 3). The Nordic countries, led by Norway, have also played an active role in these developments.

The Fifth EAP provides the basis of the EU's environmental policy to the year 2000 and beyond, although it does not contain a definitive list of environmental laws for future introduction. Instead it outlines a long-term strategy for environmental protection, and stresses that in order to achieve its goals, laws must be combined with the introduction of other measures such as eco-taxes, subsidies, tradable permits and financial assistance for environmental projects.

At the same time as the Fifth EAP was finalised, several changes were made by the TEU to the chapter on the environment that are likely to have a mixed impact on environmental protection. Yet, the rhetoric of the commitment to environmental protection has been strengthened. In particular, Article 2 of the TEU stipulates that achieving sustainable development is now a stated objective of the EU. The legal basis of environmental protection measures was also strengthened by the use of the term 'policy' in the TEU for the first time. In addition, by extending the use of qualified majority voting in the Council of Ministers to decisions about environmental legislation the possibility of one member state delaying the passage of legislation has been removed. Furthermore, the powers of the European Parliament within the EU's decision-making process were extended by the TEU and as it is considered to be the most environmentally concerned of the EU institutions, have a positive impact on the environmental protection policies of the EU.

However, two developments have left the potential for undermining environmental policy as a result of the TEU. A number of key areas, such as member state decisions on energy choices and the use of fiscal instruments to protect the environment still use unanimous voting procedures in the Council of Ministers. Second, by extending the principle of subsidiarity from the TEU's environment chapter to all EU policy areas, the decentralising tendency of the principle has been emphasised. This leaves opportunities for the member states to 'claw back' the responsibility for environmental protection from the EU.

Other important concepts for environmental policy included in the Treaty are the principles that prevention is better than cure, damage should be rectified at its source, and that the polluter should pay to remedy damage. The notion that environmental objectives must be incorporated within all other areas of EU policy has also been added since the Single European Act and the TEU also contained the precautionary principle that measures should be taken to protect the environment from potential damage, without clear scientific evidence being required. The TEU's environmental articles are unlikely to be altered during the 1996 Intergovernmental Conference (IGC) review. However, there are related areas, such as enhancing the powers of the European Parliament where Treaty changes would further enhance environmental objectives and lead to a 'greening' of the EU's decision-making process.

THE ENVIRONMENTAL POLICIES OF THE NORDIC COUNTRIES

Each of the Nordic countries has specific environmental concerns which are the result of its own national geographical location, resource endowment and industrial heritage. Therefore, each country has different and clearly defined national environmental objectives. None the less, joint environmental action has played a very prominent role in the collaboration between Denmark, Finland, Iceland, Norway and Sweden within the

Nordic Council. About one-third of its deliberations concern shared environmental problems. Among the most notable developments arising from this cooperation has been a co-ordinated programme of ecological research. A number of joint Nordic Action Plans also cover areas such as air and sea pollution, and for promoting the development of cleaner technology, waste and recycling.

As a result of the differences in their national environmental policies and the influences of the Nordic Council's collaboration on environmental protection, environmental standards in Sweden and Finland were higher than those set in the EU's legislation in a number of important areas (see Table 13.1). Indeed, concerns that these higher standards might be eroded was an important feature of the 1994 accession negotiations (see Chapter 5).

Swedish national environmental policy

Awareness of the need to develop effective environmental protection policy has a long history in Sweden. Its government was responsible for the initiative that led to the first major United Nations (UN) Conference on the Environment held in Stockholm in 1972. Along with Norway, Sweden was also influential in the 1979 UN Economic Commission for Europe (ECE) agreement on Long Range Trans-Boundary Air Pollution. These early environmental concerns were also responsible for the establishment of a national Swedish Environmental Protection Agency in 1967. This agency is the central body responsible for overseeing the protection of all parts of the ecosystem, while the county administration and the local environment and health protection boards provide more detailed supervision.

In addition, a comprehensive body of Swedish environmental legislation exists. This is governed by a number of principles, such as prevention being better than cure and a commitment to remedy environmental damage at its source. Where possible, legislation also encourages the use of recycling and in the area of physical planning environmental impact assessment is an important new development. Although using eco-accounting as a policy-mechanism is still relatively immature, the Swedish government has gradually increased its usage as a tool in policy formulation.

Clearly, there are areas of overlap when the objectives of EU and Swedish policy are compared. The search for a policy of sustainable development 'that meets the needs of the present without compromising the ability of future generations to meet their own needs . . . ' (World Commission on Environment and Development 1987) is common to both. The policy instruments in use do, however, differ. Both Sweden and the European Union have in the past relied on legal instruments to protect the environment. Yet since the Swedish taxation system was reformed in 1991, Sweden has introduced several economic regulators which may be divided into the two broad categories of taxation and subsidies. The EU has been

Table 13.1 Examples of where higher environmental standards exist in the Nordic countries

Country	*Increased control of heavy goods traffic*	*Use and marketing of dangerous substances*	*Labelling and classification of dangerous substances*	*Substances which deplete the ozone layer*	*Dangerous waste*	*Lead in petrol/ exhaust emissions*	*Use of economic regulators*	*Approval of pesticides*
Sweden		*		*		*		*
Finland		*						*
Norway		*	*	*	*	*	*	*

Note: In the negotiations for accession to the EU environmental policy fewer problems of transposition were posed for the Finns than for the Swedes. The two main areas of Finnish concern were:

1 the higher priority placed on control of the sulphur content of certain fuels than in the other states; and
2 the concern to protect and maintain control over the environmental practices of their forestry sector.

Source: Adapted from European Parliament (1994) Pimenta Report

evaluating the effectiveness of a range of legal and economic policy instruments ever since the adoption of the Fifth EAP in 1992 and the future framework of EU policy will also be based on an increased use of economic regulators to protect the environment.

As part of a 'least cost' solution to protecting the environment and at the same time ensuring a rational use of natural resources, economic regulators have a valuable role to play. However the heated controversy which surrounded the introduction of an EU tax on the carbon content of energy sources during the early and mid-1990s, showed how difficult the use of such instruments is at the supranational level. In 1995 the EU had still not reached agreement on the introduction of a carbon tax.

In contrast, carbon taxes are in place in most of the Nordic countries (Sweden, Finland and Denmark). The Finnish tax is minor in relation to other energy taxes and its main purpose is to raise revenue for environmental protection. The Swedish tax is more substantial at a level of 0.25 Swedish Krona per kilogramme of carbon dioxide. As Table 13.2 illustrates the Swedish carbon tax raised SEK 9.108 million in 1991/1992 and in the fiscal year 1992/1993 this increased to SEK 1.1 billion. However, this revenue was not used for environmental protection, but was included as part of general taxation revenue.

Sweden has also successfully used economic incentives to ensure stricter control of emissions from cars (see Table 13.2). This has led to sulphur and lead emissions from national sources in Sweden being reduced to prewar levels by the mid-1990s and Sweden becoming an ardent sponsor of lower sulphur emissions. However the main problem of airborne sulphur pollution from Eastern Germany, Poland and the UK remains. It is expected that the Western German standards will be in place throughout the whole of the country by the year 2000. The problem for the Swedes and the rest of the EU therefore remains of how to pressurise the UK government to raise its standards. As both Germany and the UK are EU members this will provide additional support for the Swedish case, although their limited progress may in practice inhibit the development of higher EU standards. There is also an extra opportunity for concerted action by the EU–15 to help Poland curb its sulphur dioxide emissions, in preparation for EU membership.

Rules on exhaust emissions

The Swedish rules were set out in the 1991 Vehicles Emissions Ordnance. However, the system of taxes and duties on environmentally friendly cars established by this Ordnance are prohibited under Directive EEC 70/220 'on the approximation of laws relating to measures against air pollution from motor vehicles'. Nevertheless, more recent EU rules in 1993 covering emissions from petrol or diesel engines have brought EU and Swedish standards for new cars closer towards one norm. It seems that the main difference between Swedish and EU standards now lies with the standards

Table 13.2 Examples of economic regulators used in Sweden

Regulator	*Income 1991/1992 in millions SKr*	*Used as part of general taxation revenue*	*Used for environmental protection*
Carbon dioxide tax	9,108	*	
Sulphur tax	289	*	
Air transport tax	165	*	
Nitrogen dioxide surcharge	Refundable		
Tax on commercial fertiliser and pesticides	137	Partly	Partly
Tax differentiation on			
1 Leaded/unleaded petrol	+0 –0	*	
2 Environmental classification of oils	+0 –0	*	
3 Environmental classification of new cars and buses		*	
Surcharge on batteries	30		*
Beverage packaging tax	145	*	
Administrative fees	119	*	

Source: Swedish Government (1994)

for older vehicles which have travelled over 80,000 kilometres. The existing Swedish higher standards were introduced to meet the needs of the US market, where large numbers of Swedish built Volvo and Saab-Scania automobiles are exported. More stringent rules on diesel engines, however, are to be introduced into the EU by 1996 which should help to redress the balance somewhat. Indeed, new developments such as proposals from the German government and the European Parliament may raise the standards further so that the differences may be eliminated.

Chemicals

The Swedish policy on chemicals differs from that of the European Union in a number of respects. Swedish rules are based on a long history of legislation imposing controls on the chemicals sector and they generally contain stricter measures governing the manufacture of chemicals than in the EU. First, the manufacturer is responsible for examining and documenting potential risks from chemicals. Second, the onus is on the manufacturer to show that the chemical is non-hazardous. Third, the application of the substitution principle means that anyone who handles chemicals is responsible for replacing hazardous substances with less hazardous ones where it is possible to do so.

There are also stricter rules on the labelling and classification of chemical substances and products in Sweden than are set in EU legislation. In particular, Sweden has introduced more stringent rules on arsenic, cadmium, pentachlorophenol and organic compounds. Under the Swedish Act on Charges for Environmentally Hazardous Batteries, a charge may be made to cover the costs of collecting and finally disposing of batteries which contain cadmium.

Substances which deplete the ozone layer

Sweden has also introduced a stricter programme dealing with the phasing out of all substances that deplete the ozone layer than the EU. All ozone depleting substances have to be labelled as environmentally hazardous and, in addition, Sweden regulates both the consumption and the production of the ozone-depleting substances.

Agri-environmental measures and approval of pesticides

The Swedish agricultural sector is characterised by a tradition of environmental protection and generous national aid for agri-environmental requirements. For example, over 2.6 million hectares of agricultural land are covered by forms of environmental measures. There is also a large emphasis placed on longer-term management of physical resources in order to take account of ecological, social and economic considerations within the Swedish planning legislation. In 1986 the so-called 'Halving' programme was introduced in order to cut the use of sprays and pesticides in agriculture. The target for 1991 was to reduce by 50 per cent the number of approved sprays. By 1994, these approved pesticides had fallen from 700 to approximately 350 varieties. Consequently, the Swedes were concerned that as part of EU membership they might be obliged to accept those EU products which they had previously banned.

Finland's national environmental policy

Finland had fewer problems in adapting to EU environmental policy than Sweden. As a result of the European Economic Area (EEA) agreement most of the EU environmental legislation started to be adopted in Finland in 1993. This included air and water pollution control, noise, chemicals, waste management, industrial emissions and legislation on biotechnology.

The impact of Finnish EU membership on environmental policy is likely to be less than that of Sweden. The government of Finland is committed to ensuring that where stringent Finnish standards exist, it will work towards improving comparable EU standards. This was seen as being particularly important in order to ensure that its stricter environmental rules did not hinder Finnish companies trading with the EU.

The most important and shared environmental problem for Sweden and Finland identified during the accession negotiations concerned acid rain. For the Finnish economy, with its heavy reliance on the pulp and paper industry and its exports (see Table 13.3 (a) and (b)), curbing sulphur emissions was critical if damage to productive forestry was to be prevented. Consequently, derogations from Directive 75/716 (and its 1987 and 1993 amendments) on the approximation of laws relating to the sulphur content of certain liquid fuels were agreed. Finland maintained stricter rules on sulphur content, the right to utilise light fuel oils with a sulphur content of 0.1 per cent, and the usage of economic regulators as a means of promoting low sulphur content fuel oils. During the accession negotiations special transitional arrangements (which allow for Finnish rules to be maintained until EU rules are brought in line) were also agreed.

The advantages of EU membership were apparent to the Finnish timber industry in particular. The forestry industry accounts for almost half of Finnish net exports (see Tables 13.3). Owing to growing EU pressure for the introduction of minimum levels governing the recycled content of

Table 13.3a Finnish trade by imports and by end use of goods (1993)

Commodities	*Percentage*
Raw materials and production necessities	59.2
Consumer goods	20.4
Investment goods	14.9
Fuels	4.5
Other goods	1.0
Total	100

Source: As Table 13.3b

Table 13.3b Finnish trade by exports and by industry (1993)

Exports and industry	*Percentage*
Fabricated metal products, engineering industry	35.9
Paper industry	27.9
Chemical industry	10.6
Basic metal industry	8.8
Wood industry	8.1
Textile and clothing industry	2.3
Other industries	6.4
Total	100

Source: Statistics Finland, Finnish Government 1994

paper products, the Finnish Forest Industries Association wanted to be certain that the Finnish government would be able to influence future EU legislation. The Finnish timber industry will be subject to a stricter environmental standard and this will be coupled to replanting programmes aimed at improving timber stocks and overcoming the problems of carbon dioxide emissions. In addition, a review of the annexes of a number of EU directives dealing with flora and fauna were also required in order to take account of the specific nature of the Finnish ecosystem.

Finnish agri-environmental concerns

The Finnish agricultural sector is affected by several specific problems relating to the country's geographical location (north of 60 degrees latitude north). The Finns have introduced a number of specialised national measures aimed at both protecting the environment and supporting their fragile agricultural sector. When the 1992 reforms of the European Union's Common Agricultural Policy were adopted, a series of accompanying agri-environmental measures were also included. Of these measures two schemes were outlined in EU Regulation 2078/92 which will directly affect Finland. First, the support for agricultural production methods must be compatible with the requirements of the protection of the environment and the maintenance of the countryside. Second, it included an aid scheme for forestry measures and agriculture.

Among the first group of schemes which may be financed are those where farmers undertake substantially to reduce their usage of fertilisers, plant protection products, or keep within any agreed reductions. Farmers may also apply for funding to change to more extensive forms of production, such as forage production or to maintain existing extensive production methods. Coupled with this, farmers are to be encouraged to use other production methods which are compatible with the requirements of protecting the environment, such as rearing local animals which are in danger of extinction. The aid scheme for forestry includes support for the upkeep of abandoned farmland or woodland. Aid will be given to farmers who 'set aside' for at least twenty years, especially if the land is being used for purposes connected with the environment, for example biotope reserves or natural parks.

In general, the measures outlined in EU Regulation 2078/92 to improve environmental protection are compatible with the thrust of Finnish agriculture. Following EU accession in 1995, an indicative annual amount for support of ECU 135 million was agreed for Finland for these schemes. However higher standards existed in Finland for the classification, packaging and labelling of pesticides and plant protection products. There were also stricter Finnish controls on the cadmium content of fertilisers and many of the concerns about lowering environmental standards in agriculture remain.

THE EEA AGREEMENT

The EEA agreement came into effect in January 1994. In accepting the terms of the EEA, the EFTA countries were committed in principle to adapting their environmental legislation in line with that of the European Union. However, environmental policy in the EEA agreement mostly covered those areas where trade would be distorted by continued differences in environmental standards. For the most part, the EEA agreement was a source of concern for environmentalists within all of the Nordic EFTA countries for three main reasons. First, there was no role for the EFTA governments in the environmental decision-making process. Second, under the terms of the EEA, derogations from some environmental legislation were agreed for only two years and it remained unclear what the position would be after this period had expired. Third, it was feared that the measures required to complete the SEM might cause a reduction in environmental standards. Although the time period covered by the derogations was extended to four years as a result of Finnish and Swedish EU membership, the first and third concerns remain.

THE ACCESSION NEGOTIATIONS

Two underlying principles governed the EU's position during the accession negotiations with Sweden and Finland. An environmental 'opt out' of the type that was agreed for the UK and Denmark at the Edinburgh European Council summit in 1992 would not be offered. The EU did, however, acknowledge that higher environmental standards did exist within the applicant states and that some of those concerns would be covered by transitional arrangements. In contrast, Nordic acceptance of EU environmental legislation was based on the view that '. . . the directives establish minimum standards to be achieved by the member states, but do not prevent any country from implementing more stringent requirements . . . ' (Ministry of the Environment and Natural Resources 1993: 2). It was obvious that in those areas where Finland and Sweden maintained stricter regulations than those that existed in the EU, the Union could not be forced to meet those standards during the negotiations. It was equally clear that Finland and Sweden could not be expected to lower their existing standards and, consequently, a 'third option' was sought. In December 1993 it was agreed that Finland and Sweden could maintain their higher standards until 1999. At the end of the transitional period, the *acquis* will be applicable within all of the member states. During the four-year transition period the EU agreed to undertake a review of EU legislation in order to search for technical solutions to the problems of raising environmental standards in all the member states. Nevertheless, there still remains some ambiguity over what will then take place after the temporary period has expired.

THE IMPLEMENTATION OF EU ENVIRONMENTAL POLICY

The Finnish and Swedish governments have made commitments to their electorates that they will ensure that policy is effectively implemented. Their objective is to enable a stronger environmental consciousness to be developed, which will act as a springboard for future environmental improvement within the EU. The introduction of EU measures aimed at monitoring environmental performance will also allow the Nordic governments to gain the opportunity to secure the environmental 'high ground' and foster domestic support for EU membership.

Prior to Finnish and Swedish EU accession, not all member states had demonstrated a commitment to achieving an environmentally sustainable level of development (see Table 13.4). Environmental protection continued to be regarded as an 'extra' tacked on to economic policy, rather than as an integral part of the EU's operation. Implementation and enforcement of EU legislation were only prioritised on the environmental policy agenda during the 1990s.

The TEU included additional provisions for the protection of the environment. It did not, however, deal with some of the most pressing concerns regarding the implementation, monitoring and enforcement of environmental legislation. In particular, the TEU did not deal with the problems of unequal national implementation of environmental laws. The principle of subsidiarity in the EU's decision-making process was extended during the Maastricht IGC, although a lack of clarity about its practical application remained. There is a danger that applying the principle to environmental policy may result in distortion of trade as

Table 13.4 Progress in implementing directives applicable to the environment

Country	*Directives applicable on 31.12.1993*	*Directives for which measures notified*	*Percentage implemented*
Belgium	117	107	91
Denmark	117	115	98
Germany	119	108	91
Greece	119	100	84
Spain	117	106	90
France	117	111	95
Ireland	117	103	88
Italy	117	95	81
Luxemburg	117	108	92
Netherlands	117	108	92
Portugal	117	106	90
UK	117	106	90

Note: not all Directives included in the table
Source: Commission of the European Communities (1994) 11th Annual Report on EU law p. 83

differing environmental standards emerge within the EU. Following this line of thought, Finnish and Swedish membership will only exacerbate these problems.

The unresolved issues of control and monitoring are more urgent. The inclusion of these states as members before the 1996 Intergovernmental Conference does possibly allow the issue of implementation to be given a higher priority in discussion. However, probably the most important development regarding the monitoring of environmental legislation was the 1993 decision to establish the European Environment Agency in Copenhagen. Its primary function is to provide reliable and independent sources of information on environmental matters so that the EU can determine policy based on an informed choice. The decision to base the European Environment Agency in Denmark was the result of protracted negotiations within the European Union. However, given Denmark's existing reputation for environmental awareness it seemed an appropriate choice within the EU–12, especially as its geographical location is in close proximity to the EFTA countries and could bolster any chances of pursuing environmental cooperation between the two blocs. The importance of the Agency's Danish location became more apparent after it began to operate in late 1994. The first task of the Agency was to complete a report on the state of the European environment which was originally initiated in 1993 by the Commission Task Force responsible for setting up the Agency. The work of the European Environment Agency was reviewed in November 1995 and it became clear that the information supplied by the Agency was crucial to the evaluation of the EU legislation during the preparations for Swedish and Finnish membership.

UNDERMINING ENVIRONMENTAL PRIORITIES

In general, it was expected that Sweden and Finland would collectively work together (along with Denmark) as a group within the EU and act as a catalyst for more stringent environmental protection measures. However, Sweden and Finland maintain individual environmental concerns and this fragmentation of interests may reduce the effectiveness of their co-ordination efforts. As a result there will not be substantial pressure radically to improve environmental standards in the short term following the entry of Finland and Sweden.

Norway, which seemed the most environmentally concerned of all the Nordic countries rejected EU membership in its 1994 public referendum (see Chapter 9). None the less, although Norway is a small country, 'its international environmental role is considerable' (OECD 1993a: 143) especially in promoting sustainable development and, indeed, Norwegian standards are in general more stringent than those of Sweden or Finland in many areas (see Table 13.1). Consequently, the possible erosion of their high environmental standards was a major factor which influenced the vote of the young and Norwegian women in the referendum. In many ways the potential for a new and more radical thrust to future EU environmental policy was lost as a consequence of the negative outcome of the Norwegian referendum.

However, the commitment of Sweden and Finland to Nordic cooperation remains strong. The influence of Norway's approach to environmental protection will still indirectly affect the development of EU environmental policy as all three Nordic EU members will still consult Norway on EU environmental matters. In the past, the most significant environmental results have been achieved by a coalition of Norway and Sweden in the Nordic Council. Furthermore, EU membership will also help to alter the nature of Finland and Sweden's environmental agenda, especially as the interests of the EU's poorer Mediterranean members may slow the overall progress of the EU's environmental policy.

Nevertheless, the nature of collaboration within the Nordic Council is very different from the requirements of EU membership for the Nordic countries. Within the EU, environmental legislation is supranationally adopted by all the member states, whereas bilateral agreements on shared problems are the main characteristic of the Nordic Council. As a consequence of Swedish EU membership and the potential weakening of cooperation between Sweden and Norway resulting from it, the environmental focus of the Nordic Council may also be undermined.

Environmental priorities in Sweden and Finland may also change because of the economic difficulties confronting the two countries. Historically the Nordic countries enjoyed lower levels of unemployment than the EU–12. For instance, Sweden's unemployment rate was only 1.5 per cent in 1990; by 1993 this had risen to 7.7 per cent. For Finland the problem was even more severe; the unemployment rate peaked in early 1994 at about 19.2 per cent, before falling to 18.2 per cent by September 1994 (OECD 1995). At the time of their accessions to the EU, the GDP per capita of both countries was below that of the EU average; Sweden's being 98 per cent of the EU average; Finland's 86 per cent of the EU average.

They may also find it difficult as small countries to influence the EU's decision-making process. There are opportunities within the EU for a Nordic bloc to emerge, led by perhaps Denmark due to its experience as the longest serving Nordic EU member. In addition, as a member of the Nordic Council, the Danish government has been prepared to introduce measures with its Nordic partners before their adoption by the EU. For example, when Norway and Sweden introduced stricter vehicle emission standards than the EU's in the late 1980s, Denmark followed suit in 1990. However, the cohesiveness of a Nordic bloc may be undermined by national rivalries between Denmark, Finland and Sweden in other issues. The Danish food industry, for example, is competitive in sectors which receive relatively little support from the EU, such as, pork, eggs and poultry. Several Danish food companies invested in other Nordic countries during 1994 raising fears among Swedish and Finnish companies.

Some environmentalists envisage the new Nordic members cooperating closely with the German government on environmental issues. However, although Germany is still committed to high environmental standards, this commitment has been somewhat eroded since the environmental degradation of the new Eastern *Länder* became more evident. The high costs of cleaning up the new *Länder* has resulted in Germany adopting the lower range of standards permitted by some existing EU legislation.

The countries of Sweden and Finland also favour 'small' government and are opposed to any centralising tendencies which might be favoured by federalists within the EU. This may undermine the attempts to create an environmental policy which will raise the standards of environmental protection throughout the EU. By placing greater emphasis on maintaining their own national standards, the Nordic countries are diverting attention away from attempts at improving EU environmental policy overall. The Finnish and Swedish governments have already clearly stated their intention not to allow their existing environmental protection standards to be eroded. 'It is politically inconceivable that Sweden would accept a lowering of . . . standards . . . ' (Ministry of Foreign Affairs 1993b: Annex 1). Hence, although there was a general acceptance within the EU–12 that higher environmental standards in Finland and Sweden were permitted, as long as they do not distort the Single Market, the potential for market distortion and the danger of growing 'environmental nationalism' remains.

THE POTENTIAL FOR NORDIC ENVIRONMENTAL INFLUENCE

Despite these considerations, the new Nordic member states still remain a potential force for changes in the future. The presence of Finland and Sweden within the EU has bolstered the calls for a more effective environmental protection policy. However unless it is possible to mobilise support from all the member states for better implementation and enforcement procedures, then there will be no radical shift of emphasis and the dangers of fragmentation remain high.

The openness of the consultation process within the Nordic countries on environmental legislation may provide additional support for new EU initiatives. One such initiative was the establishment of the Consultative Forum to provide information and allow debate between all groups interested in environmental developments. It began in 1994 and by March 1995 had produced an outline strategy of policies dealing with sustainable development.

Of more importance will be the impact of the Nordic countries on the calls for increased democratic control of environmental policy-making by the European Parliament (EP). Whilst the Nordic countries might join the group of EU states which will resist increasing the EP's powers, there are several ways in which the EP could become more involved in environmental policy-making with Finnish and Swedish support. First, the EP could take the major role in overseeing the calculation of the true cost of environmental degradation when drafting policy. Second, the EP could help ensure that sufficient resources are available for environmental protection measures.

The SEA introduced the requirement that environmental objectives should be taken into account in all policy areas and since 1990 the national governments have been introducing measures in accordance with this. Indeed, Finland and Sweden were among the first countries in the early 1980s to introduce specialist ministries to deal with environmental policy. They therefore have developed a series of 'best' practices dealing with consultation and implementation which could be incorporated into the EU.

New pieces of legislation have been adopted which use new strategies for encouraging the operation of market forces as a means of protecting the environment, such as the EU's eco-labelling scheme and the registration of manufacturing companies' sites for the EU's eco-management and audit scheme (EMAS). These schemes are voluntary initiatives and the immediate response of companies to the eco-audit scheme in some member states has been cautious. Yet, companies in Sweden, Finland and Denmark have been among the earliest users of environmental auditing techniques within Europe and the cautious attitudes within the EU may alter as the scheme receives more support from Finnish and Swedish companies. In addition, the proposals for EU directives on civil liability for environmental damage and integrated pollution prevention will be supported by the two countries as the overall principles underlying these directives are an accepted part of their existing policies.

CONCLUSIONS

EU Environmental Policy performs several functions. Through its commitment to sustainable development it protects the EU's economic resource base and enables the EU to try to improve the living conditions of citizens within its member states. It is therefore crucial that the development of EU environmental policy should not be undermined. Changes are taking place as a result of the SEA and TEU which are slowing the process of environmental degradation in the EU, and Finland and Sweden have the potential to assist with this progress. There is, however, a danger that their presence within the EU may undermine the objectives which have been set to achieve higher levels of environmental protection for EU citizens.

Finland and Sweden have reputations as countries with long traditions of environmental awareness and this is reflected in their comprehensive national environmental policies. Their EU membership will not however result in a radical revision of EU environmental policy. Indeed, there are several areas where their impact on the process of improving environmental protection will be reduced because of their own specific national interests.

The EU's decision-making process is the result of consensus building with the consequence that environmental improvement has been gradual. The EU has been able to bring pressure to bear on some member states that are not as fully committed to raising environmental standards as others and, consequently, the process of environmental degradation has been slowed. This progressive improvement will be interrupted if some countries are allowed to maintain much higher standards. The incentive to improve will be lost if the gap appears to be widening between the member states' environmental standards and the process of environmental improvement needs careful management. Otherwise the overall impact of the additional membership of the two Nordic countries will be to undermine, rather than enhance the environmental policy of the European Union.

14 Agriculture, fisheries and the 1995 Nordic enlargement

Ian Barnes

INTRODUCTION

Agriculture and fisheries are controversial policy areas for both the European Union (EU) and the Nordic countries. The two policy areas are linked, in the sense that they are concerned with food supply, and are heavily regulated. The Common Agricultural Policy (CAP) and the Common Fisheries Policy (CFP) are governed by the same part of the Treaty. Article 39 of the Treaty of Rome states that there should be a rational development of production and the optimum utilisation of the factors of production, in particular, of labour. There should be a fair standard of living for agricultural workers. Markets should be stabilised and supplies available. Products should also reach the consumer at reasonable prices.

The way that Article 39 operates with respect to the two policy areas does, however, differ. The CAP was a central part of the early development of the EU, and as such was quickly put into place. It heavily favoured domestic producers against imports and sought to achieve self-sufficiency, wherever practical. However, it has not functioned in a satisfactory manner, largely because of its budgetary cost, and the problems created by over production. Significant progress with respect to this problem did not come until the MacSharry reforms agreed in 1992. These reforms reduced price support in return for direct payments to farmers. The aim was to move EU prices nearer to world market prices, so as to meet the obligations which were agreed as part of the Uruguay Round of the General Agreement on Tariffs and Trade (GATT).

The Nordic applicants had generally operated with farm prices which were even higher than those to be found within the EU. The problem facing the Nordic countries was not only to reduce prices to levels comparable to CAP norms, but also to meet the even stricter requirements of the GATT. In this respect, Sweden moved into line comparatively early in anticipation of EU membership. Finland and Norway did not. The 1995 enlargement extended the EU further to the north and as a consequence, new arrangements were needed to cope with this. However, the main problems of adjustment fell upon Finland.

The CFP came into existence later, and was initially concerned with problems of creating an EU-wide market for fish. In 1970, a condition set by the original six member states was that there should be common management of fish stocks. This helped to deter the Norwegians from membership in the 1973 enlargement, and again in 1995. The shared management of resources became of major significance once exclusive economic zones were extended to 200 miles in the mid-1970s. Whilst the cost of the CFP has rarely been a major issue, the EU's record of managing the conservation process has not been good. However, the decision of Norway to remain outside the EU meant that the CFP changed little as a result of enlargement.

This chapter argues that in the case of agriculture the 1995 enlargement had little consequence for the EU but assisted the process of change in the Nordic countries, which was desirable. In the case of fishing, the EU would have benefited if all the Nordic applicants had joined. Once Norway rejected full membership an opportunity was missed for the EU to improve its quality of management of fish stocks. The CFP has relatively few implications for Sweden and Finland.

AGRICULTURE AND ENLARGEMENT OF THE EUROPEAN UNION

Agricultural production in the EU has been characterised by its relatively high production costs and a significant level of protectionism. The aim of the CAP has been to achieve self-sufficiency, and thus the dominant force in policy-making has essentially been political rather than economic. The CAP has been a divisive area between EU members and between the EU and low cost agricultural producers who sell on the world market.

The 1995 enlargement took place against a background whereby the EU had agreed to limit its agricultural production and reduce its prices to world market levels. These reforms were important because of the anticipated conclusion of the GATT Uruguay Round and because they would satisfy the US, which was generally hostile to the CAP. Among the Nordic countries both Denmark and Sweden were better placed in terms of farm structure and average yields to compete under the new CAP regime. Their average size of holding was larger than the average for the EU-12 (see Table 14.1). Crop yields are also higher in Sweden and Denmark than in Norway, Finland or on average the EU, reflecting better production conditions in those countries (see Table 14.2).

Despite the fact that Finland and Sweden have harsh climates, especially in the regions close to the Arctic Circle, they are more than self-sufficient in certain products (see Table 14.3). This is a result of protectionism and high prices encouraging production, rather than these countries having any significant comparative advantage in agriculture.

The Nordic countries are also surplus producers in a number of important

Table 14.1 Farm structures in 1990

Country	*Agricultural area per farm in hectares*	*Area under cereals of farms engaged in this kind of production in hectares*
Denmark	17.3	11.1
Finland	12.8	5.8
Norway	10.2	11.1
Sweden	29.0	14.0
EU–12	16.5	8.9

Source: Commission of the ECs, 1992c and 1992d

Table 14.2 Yields per hectare in 1992 (hundreds kg)

Country	*Wheat*	*Total cereals*
Denmark	61.7	43.7
Finland	36.2	36.3
Norway	35.3	28.1
Sweden	60.1	46.1
EU–12	50.6	47.8

Source: Eurostat 1992: 242–5

Table 14.3 Self-sufficiency in agricultural production, 1988–90 (percentage)

Product	*Finland – degree of self-sufficiency*	*Sweden – degree of self-sufficiency*	*Sweden and Finland – total production as a percentage of total EU–12*	*Denmark – degree of self-sufficiency*
Beef	110	95	3.2	209
Butter	184	122	6.8	194
Cereals	131	123	5.5	140
Eggs	133	105	4.2	72
Pigmeat	111	112	3.5	351
Potatoes	108	89	5.3	97
Sugar	81	110	3.8	265

Source: Commission of the ECs 1992c and 1992d

sectors (see Table 14.3). These surpluses have contributed, in a modest way, to the malaise of subsidised exports being dumped on to the global market. This has helped to depress world prices, and caused hostility from those countries who have a comparative advantage in agriculture.

The acceptance of the *acquis communautaire* requires the adoption of EU production quotas in sectors like milk, and that 'set aside' should be used to restrict production of crops such as wheat. It also means that prices are set on an agreed EU-wide basis. Whilst decision-making shifts from the member states to the EU, much of the long-term cost of supporting the sector falls on the EU budget. This means that the disposal of surpluses is no longer directly the concern of the new members.

The price reductions in the Nordic countries as they moved towards the GATT regime were of an even greater magnitude than those required by the EU (see Table 14.4). All three of the Nordic applicants not only gave greater support to their farmers than the EU (see Table 14.4, the extents of the producer subsidy equivalent), but also passed on a great deal of that cost to the consumer (see the levels of the consumer subsidy equivalent). This was achieved by high import tariffs, which operated in a similar way to the EU's variable levy.

Table 14.4 Support for Nordic agriculture in 1993 (percentage)

	EU–12	*Finland*	*Sweden*	*Norway*
Assistance to producers (producer subsidy equivalent)	48	67	52	76
Implicit tax on consumers (consumer subsidy equivalent)	39	66	45	60

Note: Producer subsidy equivalent is the net total of agricultural support given to farmers. Consumer subsidy equivalent is the implicit tax that has to be born by the consumer as a result of artificially high food prices.
Source: OECD 1994

Whilst the EU's global trading partners consistently complained about the extent of support given to its farmers, it is apparent from Table 14.4 that of the Nordic applicants, only Sweden had moved close to the position of the EU.

Prior to joining the EU, the applicant states were divided as to their position with respect to the EU's farm system. Sweden was broadly happy with the EU's position, whilst Finland would have liked the EU to agree a similar support level as its own. However, any attempt to harmonise the price system upwards would have simply resulted in the problems of surpluses within the EU becoming much worse. Harmonising the prices downward benefits the consumer, but at the expense of the farmers. The new member states could avoid their farmers suffering the effects of price reductions if the EU agreed for subsidies to be paid nationally. This can only be transitional aid as the offering of long-term aid of this type is regarded as being anti-competitive within the EU.

Finland

Finland is one of the most northern countries in the world, but agriculture is possible for most of the country. This is because of the influence of the gulf stream which raises the average temperature by about 6 degrees centigrade. The growing season is, however, relatively short, varying from 180 days on the south coast, down to 130 days in Lapland (compared to 220 to 230 days in Denmark). Farmers make up 7 per cent of the workforce, but they only account for 2.5 per cent of GDP (down from 10 per cent in the 1960s). The average size of farms tends to be small, but forestry is important and this by its nature tends to have much larger holdings. If forestry is added to the sector, the overall contribution to the national income rises to 5.4 per cent of GDP (Aaltonen 1993: 32).

Prior to membership of the EU, the central goals of Finnish Agricultural Policy were not dissimilar to those of the EU. These were to maintain self-sufficiency in food supplies, to ensure an equitable income for farmers whilst guaranteeing food prices at reasonable levels and to develop the industry and maintain the rural population. In order to achieve these goals Finland used a combination of price and income support, along with a variable levy against imports. The variable levy was utilised in order to ensure that imported farm products could not undermine the domestic target price (Kettunen 1993: 32).

Despite similar problems facing both Finnish and Swedish agricultural sectors, the two countries had different agendas with respect to farm price support. Sweden had already started to take action with respect to its very high farm prices, which dated back to 1990. In contrast Finland had delayed its response until it became clear that it was to become an EU member. As a consequence Finnish prices were 60 per cent higher than those in the EU, prior to membership. Finland had allied itself with Austria and Norway in the entry negotiations, rather than with Sweden. But little help could be expected from Denmark, who had benefited from the CAP, because of her superior organisation and better climatic conditions.

The influence of farming groups in national politics is greater than the size of the farming population might suggest, because 35 per cent of the population still live in the rural areas. Many believe that farming is an important counter to rural depopulation. In the membership negotiations it was recognised that Finnish prices would have to come into line with those in the rest of the EU. However, it was hoped that extensive help might be available in order to compensate for this income loss. The negotiations resulted in Finland being divided up into areas which had differing levels of agricultural and regional assistance available to them.

As soon as the European Parliament approved Finland's membership of the EU in May 1994, a reform package was introduced by the Finnish government. This was implemented as of 1 January 1995. The adjustment process was a difficult one because of the high levels of support enjoyed by

Finnish farmers and the extent to which the country had relied on a high tariff to protect its farming industry.

In order to cushion the effects of membership of the EU, Finland was able to negotiate a five-year transition period, where national aid was made available to supplement that given by the EU. The adoption of the CAP increased the cost of farming to the national budget, but the consumer gained. Farm prices were expected to fall by 40 per cent in 1995, which significantly reduced the incentive to produce. The cost to Finland's budget of adopting the CAP was expected to be considerable. To compensate the farmers for the move to EU support prices, national direct income support measures were introduced which cost FIM 6.5 billion. This increased the direct level of help to farmers from FIM 35,000 per person employed to FIM 85,000. The EU was expected to make a transfer to Finnish agriculture of FIM 2.9 billion. This was offset by a loss of contributions from Finnish agriculture of FIM 1.6 billion, giving a net addition to revenue of FIM 1.3 billion. When this is set against the expenditure on income support of FIM 6.5 billion, the increase in net budgetary expenditure was FIM 5.2 billion. However, despite the increased national budgetary costs, the level of farm incomes was expected to fall by 20 per cent (OECD 1995: 41).

The transition arrangements should cushion the effects of membership for a period of time, but there will be hard times for the farmers in the South. Domestic budgetary pressures will limit the amount of state aid that is likely to be on offer. There is a belief that the number of farms will decline from the 120,000 in existence in 1993, to 70,000 after the turn of the century (Financial Times 1994).

To an extent, rural decline should be offset in the more remote areas by regional aid. On top of the normal EU support, 56 per cent of land qualified for help under a special Nordic category (the new Objective 6 criteria of the EU's Structural Funds), and 85 per cent of this has been designated a Less Favourable Area (LFA). Objective 6 is designed to help those sparsely populated areas in the north of the country. However, where assistance is available to promote structural change the danger is that this does not maintain population levels. More direct help is available to maintain farmers via the application of LFA status, which covers 85 per cent of Finland.

MTK, the Finnish agricultural workers' union, believed that the fall in prices was too sudden and allowed little time for farmers to prepare for the consequences of the new support regime. During the membership negotiations Norway, Austria and Finland indicated a preference for the system of border rebates, which had existed prior to the completion of the Single Market in 1993. They criticised the way that assistance was given. Despite the fact that 85 per cent of land is eligible for help, they believed that the way that the land was divided up into regions was unfair. This was because the 15 per cent of farm land in the South, where cereal production and horticulture is located, was excluded from this additional aid. The level of aid was believed to be three times greater in Schleswig-Holstein in Germany, where the average yield was 6.8 tonnes per hectare, compared to 3.1 tonnes per hectare in Southern Finland (Financial Times 1994).

Sweden

Sweden is another country with some areas which face harsh agricultural conditions. In the northern regions of Sweden the growing season is 110 days, which is about half that in southern Sweden and Denmark. Northern Sweden traditionally received extensive support from the government and as such was very much against EU entry. Sweden's agricultural policy was substantially changed as a result of the reforms which were agreed by the Swedish Parliament (*Riksdag*) in 1990. These reforms pre-dated membership of the EU, and came about because of general dissatisfaction with the performance of the sector in the 1980s. The reforms were introduced because prices were high, which penalised consumers, and had encouraged a substantial surplus production in certain sectors (Swedish Board of Agriculture 1993: 1).

The aim of the policy was to move to similar production conditions as other sectors of the economy. The reforms were introduced on 1 July 1991 and were to be phased in over a five-year period. They aimed to abolish export subsidies and special aid for the storage of production subsidies. Yet, the income levels of farmers in the north of the country were also to be sustained. However, as these were radical steps from the regime that had previously existed, transitional measures were introduced to reduce the short-term impact elsewhere. Payments were made for milk farmers to cease production, and assistance was offered to convert land to non-agricultural use.

In 1993, further reforms were introduced to bring the Swedish system of support into line with that of the EU, and to anticipate the outcome of the GATT. These introduced direct income payments for cereals, as well as maintaining headage payments for beef cattle and sheep. Export subsidies were temporarily re-introduced, and a further reduction in cereal prices did not take place. Whilst the 1990 reforms aimed to deregulate the sector, the 1993 reforms reversed this trend. This meant that the sector was prepared for EU membership in 1995 (OECD 1994: 30). In this respect, EU membership held back the pace of reform, rather than encouraging its progress.

Agri-money systems

The EU has endured constant problems with its attempts to keep a common system of pricing in place with the changes that occur in national currencies. In order to cope with this the EU introduced a 'switch over' system of compensation. The logic of this system was that prices moved upward in such a way as to always keep in line with those in member states with the strongest currencies (this is a problem that should be solved with the introduction of a single currency). The currency upheavals in 1993 led to the 'switch over' mechanism being suspended, and it was formally abandoned in December 1994. It was replaced by a new mechanism of price compensation for states facing currency changes. This was believed to be essential in order to ensure that prices were harmonised throughout the EU. However currency instability in early 1995 put stress on the new arrangements. Whilst the new arrangements were not as generous as previous ones, they did increase farm prices in those countries with weak currencies. The fact that the Markka and the Krona are not members of the Exchange Rate Mechanism, and were among the weaker currencies in the EU in the early part of 1995, was therefore beneficial in terms of CAP prices.

FISHING AND ENLARGEMENT OF THE EUROPEAN UNION

The operation of the Common Fisheries Policy had the potential to be one of the most important aspects of the 1995 enlargement process. The Norwegian rejection of full membership was, to a large extent, influenced by the potentially negative aspects of the CFP. However, once the enlargement had taken place without Norway the CFP was reduced to being only an issue of minor importance. Fisheries would appear to be one of the most promising areas for the EU policy makers. Due to modern technology, new methods have been introduced which significantly increase the size of fish catches and as fish stocks are finite this inevitably led to a resource crisis. Fish are migratory which suggests that international control may be effective.

The CFP relies on the objectives set for the Common Agricultural Policy (CAP) in Article 39 of the Treaty of Rome. However, these objectives were further refined in Article 1 of Regulation 170/83, which set in place the new regime as being

> the protection of the fishing grounds, the conservation of the biological resources of the sea and their balanced exploitation on a lasting basis and in appropriate economic and social conditions.

The CFP has at its heart the notion that the fish stocks, within the 200-mile exclusive economic zone (EEZ), are a shared resource. All member states of the EU are subject to the rules of the CFP which was introduced in 1983, for a twenty-year period. The rights to catch quotas were allocated on a national basis, according to a formula which favoured countries like the UK with significant stocks within their national territorial limits. Despite its comprehensive nature, the CFP has failed to resolve the problems of over-capacity of the fleet and a chronic depletion of fish stocks. Attempts to balance catches with available stocks, in order to achieve a sustainable catch level, have not been successful. This has been largely due to the failure of the EU to reduce catch quotas, and the non-compliance of member states with respect to EU regulations. In general, therefore, the CFP has an indifferent reputation and has little to recommend it to potential members who have substantial fish stocks.

The positive benefits for the Nordic countries arising from participation in the CFP was that it offers free access to the EU's Single Market. It also includes effective market support arrangements which have not proved to be excessively expensive. Assistance from the Structural Funds is also available for re-structuring measures and for appropriate aquaculture projects. All member states are expected to comply fully with the considerable body of EU legislation which governs the fishing industry, in all aspects. Three of the five Nordic countries (Denmark, Iceland and Norway – see Table 14.5) have a substantial interest in the fishing industry. Yet, of these, only Denmark is a full EU member and it would appear that this is likely to remain the case for the foreseeable future.

Table 14.5 Fish catches in 1991 (1,000 tonnes)

Country	*Catch*
Denmark	1793.2
Finland	82.6
Iceland	1060.0
Norway	2595.9
Sweden	245.0

Source: Eurostat 1994: 294

Norway and the CFP

Norway is a substantial stakeholder in the fisheries management process. Unlike the member states of the EU, Norway has retained control of its national EEZ and has organised conservation on a national basis. Common stocks have been managed on a bilateral basis, with the EU and other neighbouring states.

Norwegian membership would have created the prospect for great change to the CFP, and perhaps even greater controversy. The fishing industry is important to Norway, where the industry contributes 6 per cent of the country's exports and landings are in the region of 2 million tonnes per year. The addition of the Norwegian fleet would have added 17 per cent to the EU fleet tonnage, and increased the number of fishermen by 10 per cent. Norway's conservation policy was not only more stringent than that of the EU, but also more effective. Membership of the EU threatened to weaken this national system of fisheries management, but had the advantage of offering tariff free access to Norway's most important market.

Norway is also sensitive to the issue of maintaining its fish stocks because of their importance for employment within its remote Northern communities. The fisheries issue was a major cause of the Norwegian public rejecting EU membership in a referendum in 1972 (see Chapter 9). As part of the European Economic Area (EEA) agreement with the EU Norway agreed to permit the Cohesion countries to catch 7,250 tonnes of cod in 1994, rising to 11,000 tonnes in 1997 (known as Cohesion Fish). Spain and Portugal were to gain 90 per cent of this, to be shared equally between them, whilst the balance was to be shared between Ireland and Greece. The total amount of Norwegian fish that the EU was entitled to as a result of the EEA agreement was 2.9 per cent of the stock, which was about 40,000 tonnes, in 1994. This was expected to rise as a result of better management of fish stocks to a total of 51,000 tonnes overall.

The 1993–4 accession negotiations with Norway resulted in the amount of Cohesion fish awarded to Spain and Portugal being increased, to a total of 14,100 tonnes, first by an increased quota, which was to be generated by the better management of fish stocks. Second, extra fish were to be sought from Russian stocks, purchased by use of the EU budget. Norway's rights to manage its fish stocks would be transferred to the EU by 1 July 1998 and the EU would have taken over fisheries negotiations with the Russians, at that time. After the transition period, there would be free access to EU markets.

The benefit of Norwegian membership for the EU was that a greater area of the North East Atlantic fishing grounds would have been under EU control. It would have added a strong advocate of conservation to the debate within the EU about conservation, and it would have helped to meet the EU's needs for greater access to fish stocks.

However, the 1994 accession negotiations on fisheries included certain negative features. First, they were used to the advantage of the existing members of the EU, at the expense of applicant states. Second, the bargaining with the use of 'paper fish' (that is fish that did not actually exist at the time of the negotiations) was a dangerous practice, given that the anticipated fish may not materialise in reality. This was typical of 'lowest common denominator' style of decision-making which had damaged the CFP in the past. Finally, they were used by Spain and Portugal to gain full membership of the CFP, which they were not entitled to until after the expiration of the twenty-year agreement in 2003. Whilst this appeared to be a reasonable price to pay in order to win agreement to the enlargement from Spain and Portugal, it was a promise which had to be honoured when Norway rejected membership. It meant that Britain and Ireland in particular, had to accept the Spanish fleet into areas where they had not been allowed under the transition arrangements.

The result of Norway's decision not to ratify its membership of the EU was that the system of bilateral negotiation concerning management of joint fish stocks continued as in the past. This allowed for the swapping of catch quotas, with EU vessels fishing in Norwegian waters, but subject to very careful supervision.

Iceland and fisheries policy

The Nordic country that is most dependent on fishing is Iceland. This is a country of 267,000 people where the fishing industry contributes 80 per cent of exports by volume, and half the export revenue by value. Fishing contributes 20 per cent of GDP and employs 14 per cent of the workforce (Financial Times 1995a: 3). Iceland had had a long fight with a number of the EU member states to establish its sovereignty over its own 200-mile fishing limit; once this was won, they became reluctant to surrender control again. It joined the EEA in 1994, which gave the EU some token presence in their fishing grounds only. In February 1995 the Social Democratic Party became the first Icelandic party supporting the idea of membership of the EU (see Chapter 10). This was not, however, a widely supported cause. When Norway declined EU membership the position of those who wished to keep independence was strengthened.

Iceland has not, however, had the same degree of success as Norway in maintaining fish stocks. Total stocks of cod in Icelandic waters have fallen from 2.5 million tonnes in the 1950s to 600,000 tonnes today, which is about half of what is regarded as sustainable. There was a need for substantial cuts in cod quotas from 250,000 tonnes in 1993 to 150,000 tonnes in 1995. The fleet has sought alternative species such as shrimp and capelin, and to make up catches by fishing outside their territorial limits, leading to protests from the Norwegians in the Barents Sea.

Sweden and the CFP

Sweden was a net importer of fish, and the catching side of the industry contributed only 0.06 per cent to GDP. The problems of over-exploitation of the Swedish fishing grounds were similar to those faced by the EU, although in its opinion on Swedish entry into the EU the Commission thought that Sweden's inspection arrangements were probably adequate (Commission of the ECs 1992c: 27). The Swedish fleet requires the same kind of restructuring as that of the rest of the EU. This means the scrapping of part of the fleet to bring the catching capacity into line with the availability of fish stocks. Like Denmark, Sweden has an industry which is devoted to catching and processing fish for industrial purposes. While this amounts to a third of all landings in the early 1990s conservationists question whether this industry is desirable. This is because of the impact it has on the maritime food chain, and the damage it does to stocks of edible fish.

Finland and the CFP

Fish farming is a relatively small industry in many of the EU's member states, and where there is a coastline it generally takes second place to catching. Finland is unusual in this respect, fish catching contributes only 0.03 per cent of GDP, compared to 0.07 per cent by aquaculture. In 1991 there are 4,120 fishermen of whom 1,350 are full-time (Kettunen 1994: 10). The addition of the Finnish fleet to that of the EU was estimated to add only 0.6 per cent to the EU's fishing fleet (Commission of the ECs 1992d: 32). As with the rest of the EU, the fish catching industry suffered from over-capacity although, curiously, Finland had only established an eight-mile fishing limit at the time of its membership application. Whilst the monitoring of catching arrangements appears to have been satisfactory there was no national licensing system, except for salmon. This is an essential part of the CFP's control arrangements. In addition, Finnish regulations forbade the discarding of fish, which is contrary to the situation in the EU. The EU insists that under-sized fish, and those which are caught in excess to quotas are discarded, because this discourages the deliberate catching of illegal fish.

CONCLUSIONS

The problems facing the CAP and the CFP are fundamentally different. The CAP is expensive to operate and there are difficulties in reducing surplus production. In contrast, there is a shortage of fish due to inadequate conservation. In both cases the new Nordic members did not help to resolve the EU's problems. They both had agricultural surpluses and had managed their fish stocks poorly. Both countries face rural depopulation, and the difficulty of maintaining remote populations dependent on fishing. However, the new members faced different problems of adjustment to the price regime of the CAP. But, Finland has only herself to blame for her failure to reform agriculture in the early 1990s. The fact that the adjustment to the CAP is to be so severe meant that farming and its supporters are likely to continue to feel hostile to EU membership in the future.

In the early stages of membership the weakness of the Krona and the Markka has been a positive advantage for farmers. It has meant that prices denominated in national currencies have moved in their favour. For the medium term, however, the rising cost of the CAP may mean further pressure for the member states to accept the full costs of the policy themselves. Pressure for this will increase if there is an expansion of the EU into Central Europe.

The 1995 enlargement represented a missed opportunity for the EU with respect to fisheries. The EU's CFP will continue to face a crisis as long as there is a failure to match the capacity of the fleet to sustainable catch levels. As an EU member Norway may have encouraged an improvement in the standard of resource management which would have been a general benefit. Outside the EU Norway will be free to preserve its fish stocks in a way which is appropriate to its needs. However, the prospects look less good for Iceland. The squandering of their fish stocks demonstrates that national ownership of resources does not guarantee their rational development. For both countries to consider, or reconsider EU membership, they would need to be reassured that the EU can manage their fish stocks at least as well as they manage them themselves.

15 The Nordic countries and EU membership

The energy factor

Janne Haaland Matlary

INTRODUCTION

The three Nordic countries that applied for membership of the EU in the late 1980s – Sweden, Finland and Norway – share many similarities. However, in the field of energy they are entirely different. Energy policy has not figured as a prominent theme in the accession debates in general – only in Norway did it become a major factor in the spring of 1992.

Finland and Sweden are energy importers, whereas Norway is the world's second largest net exporter of energy. In fact, the influx of oil revenue has made Norway particularly insulated from the needs of the common competition policy and has created a large public sector. Also Denmark has indigenous reserves of oil and gas, but on a much smaller scale than Norway. The Norwegian reserves were upgraded in early 1995, and are today very significant.

This chapter will first provide an overview of the energy sector of the three Nordic countries with particular emphasis on Norway. It will then examine the recent developments in EU energy policy that are of particular relevance for these countries, before finally analysing the importance of the energy factor in the Norwegian accession debate. The importance of this is two-fold: first, oil revenue has placed Norway in an economic situation that is different from that of other EU countries and its Nordic neighbours; and second, the so-called 'oil directive' proposal from the EU figured prominently in the Norwegian national debate on the consequences of membership.

THE ENERGY SECTORS IN NORWAY, FINLAND AND SWEDEN

Energy is a 'strategic good' in the sense that states need to be concerned with energy supply. Two of the countries to be discussed here, Sweden and Finland, are in the position of having to develop an energy strategy for imports. Both countries have a nuclear sector which is one way of ensuring domestic energy supply, and both countries explore the possibilities for importing more natural gas. Norway is a potential source of gas supply, yet there is so far no major gas line from Norway to these countries. Finland relies increasingly on Russian gas while Sweden cannot phase out its nuclear energy because of the uncertainty of future imports. The energy policy interests and needs of these two countries therefore differ fundamentally from those of Norway, whose main concern it is to remain unrestrained by EU policy in this field. Norway has typical energy exporter's interests, while Sweden and Finland probably will favour the further development of the Internal Energy Market (IEM) as well as a more prominent role for the EU in energy policy.

Norway

In Norway the 'oil age' started in 1977, when commercial production of oil from the North Sea continental shelf started to flow. Both oil and gas production have increased steadily and in 1993 total production amounted to 139 mtoe (million tons of oil equivalent). Of this, oil made up about 110 mtoe, and natural gas the rest. Almost all of this petroleum was exported since Norway is virtually self-supplied with hydroelectric power. Exports made up 37 per cent of total export earnings; and petroleum production amounts to 15 per cent of GNP. Norway is the world's second largest net exporter of oil and has 80 years' reserves of gas.[2] Total reserves were upgraded in early 1995.

Norway's contracts for gas sales to EU countries imply that sales will double from today's level of almost 30 BCM to 60 BCM after the turn of the century. Norway will then be the main European supplier of gas to EU countries along with the Netherlands.

In Norway, energy policy in the petroleum sector has always separated the granting of concessions, which is the task of the government, from the sale of petroleum, which is deemed an entirely commercial activity. Thus, even if the state held a strong hand in energy policy, it left the sale and marketing of petroleum to market actors, notably to Statoil, the fully state-owned oil company. Thus it has been able to avoid a political debate over preferential oil sales as various countries have approached the Norwegian government and asked for energy exports on political grounds. However, even if the marketing and sale of petroleum is a strictly commercial activity, this does not mean that free market rules reign in the domestic organisation of the petroleum sector. Statoil has a privileged place, and this has been an issue in the negotiations for EU membership on the part of Norway. This will be discussed further in the last section of this chapter.

In its negotiations with the EU for membership Norway was keen to ensure that EU energy policy does not deal with the so-called 'upstream' area; that is, with the concession policy and the pace of exploration. In its accession agreement Norway got a special guarantee that the EU would not extend its energy policy to a common policy on the management of natural resources, which was to remain firmly in the hands of national governments. However, Norway voted against joining the EU in a referendum on 28 November 1994.

Norwegian energy interests in the petroleum sector are thus very much determined by the resource situation. However, in the electricity sector Norway passed a law liberalising the sector in 1990 which pre-empts the Commission's internal energy market proposals for electricity. Here the supply sector is to be organised in such a way that 'natural monopolies (the transmission or grid function) are separated from activities subject to competition (production)' (Kristensen 1993: 3). Thus competition is secured in both the production and the distribution phases. This deregulation resembles EU proposals in the sector, and is typical of the general trend towards privatisation and deregulation in many European countries.

All aspects of petroleum policy are thus firmly in the hands of the government, while the electricity sector is deregulated. It has been especially important for Norway to ensure that the EU does not develop a common policy for concessions, rate of depletion, or any other aspect of oil and gas production policy.

Norway's environment and climate policy can easily be seen as the opposite to energy policy. As a major oil producer Norway has common interests with other producers such as OPEC, although there is no formal cooperation between the two. Norway has instead always underlined its place in Western Europe and is an associate member of the International Energy Agency (IEA), which was organised as a response to OPEC's action in the first oil shock in 1973–4. None the less, Norway has a major interest in oil exports, and thus in a stable, relatively high oil price and in a strong market share for oil. But as a major gas exporter Norwegian interests may partly coincide with environmental interests because gas is a relatively 'clean' fuel that can replace coal to a great extent on the continent. The Norwegian interest in being a major actor in international environmental and climate policy can possibly be reconciled with the gas interests. Like the other Scandinavian countries, Norway has adopted a carbon (CO_2) tax.

For Norway it is important that common European energy policies do not develop beyond the crisis management of the International Energy Agency (IEA) and beyond a common environmental policy as well as energy market rules. Thus one is positively interested in such policies but wary of regulations that may affect the national sovereignty of reserves and conditions for the rate of depletion. This concern in energy policy has been important in the Norwegian evaluation of the pros and cons of EU membership.

Finland

Turning now to Finland, energy policy concerns are quite different. Finland relies heavily on gas imports from Russia and has no domestic resources of fossil fuels. Nuclear energy makes up 18 per cent of TEC (total energy consumption), and some electricity is hydro-generated. Coal use fell by 20 per cent between 1990 and 1992 and this largely accounted for a decrease in CO_2 emissions by 5 per cent.

In 1993 Finland signed a contract for additional supplies of gas from Russia. There has traditionally been an extensive trade relationship between Finland and Russia, where energy was bartered for Finnish industrial goods. After the demise of the USSR, much of this trade has disappeared. However, there is gas infrastructure in the form of a pipeline from Russia through Karelia to Helsinki, and thus there is a natural continuation of the gas imports from Russia. The existence of infrastructure is a prerequisite for gas imports, and a long-standing issue between the Nordic countries has been a wish on the part of Sweden and Finland to have a pipeline built from Norway to these two countries. However, there has never been sufficient gas imports in these plans to make such a pipeline economical. Thus, as long as Finland remains unconnected to any other gas source than Russia, increased quantities must come from this source. Import dependence for oil and gas will thus have to be balanced against the acceptability of nuclear energy. Supply security is therefore, in general, the foremost energy policy issue in Finland and as environmental concerns increasingly come up the agenda of energy policy in all countries, these concerns complicate this picture. Whereas the foremost Norwegian concern is to ensure national freedom of action in framing an exploration and export policy for oil and gas, both Finland and Sweden need to be concerned with import dependence and the cost of the latter.

The 'Finnish Energy Strategy' from 1992 sets out three goals: security of supply, market efficiency and limitation of emissions. Carbon taxes and 'no regrets' policies are developed in detail here. Environmental concerns figure prominently in the energy and other policy of Finland as well as Sweden, but one must also consider the supply situation as perhaps the key energy policy issue. In addition to gas imports, Finland, like all non-producers in Europe, is dependent on oil imports.

Sweden

Sweden has an important share of its energy from nuclear electricity generation, which together with hydro-generation make for reductions in CO_2 emissions as well as a high degree of domestic energy supply. Whether to reduce the nuclear sector was the subject of a 1980 referendum and the majority favoured reduction. However, this has not been implemented. Instead, an agreement between various corporate and political actors in the energy sector was reached in 1991, deciding that the phasing out of nuclear energy would be postponed until an appropriate time, probably by the year 2010. This has been interpreted to mean an informal reversal of the referendum. The condition for implementing the referendum decision is now that CO_2 policies are to be met by other means. This appears very unlikely to happen, as nuclear-generated electricity makes up 44 per cent of Sweden's large electricity sector. In the first part of 1995 the Swedish government set up a new energy commission that was mandated to study all aspects of Swedish energy policy with a view to assessing whether and when nuclear energy could be phased out. The government is still bound by the referendum, but such an inquiry could possibly form the basis for calling for a new referendum on the issue. The energy policy challenge is like that of Finland; how to balance energy imports with domestic production of energy?

In the climate policy plan, various measures, including a CO_2 tax, have been adopted. To develop hydro power further appears untenable from a political point of view, especially as environmental concerns are very important in Sweden. Also, it is impossible to substitute with large imports of natural gas, since the infrastructure is lacking. Sweden imports small amounts of natural gas from Denmark and all of its oil. The gas pipeline comes into Southern Sweden from Denmark, but does not extend to the Stockholm area. Denmark would in all events not be able to supply very large quantities of natural gas to Sweden. A pipeline from Norway has been proposed several times, but there is no immediate prospect of this. In order to be economical it would have to include Finland as well, but with the Finnish gas imports from Russia it does not appear that there would be a large enough market to warrant such a pipeline.

From the above it is seen that there are no energy policy issues that unite the Nordic countries. It is only in Norway that the emerging energy policy of the EU has been a major issue in the accession debate, and here one has been wary of all attempts on the part of the EU at developing a common energy policy. Sweden and Finland have looked at the Commission's attempts at market deregulation as positive, especially if they lead to lower energy prices and greater openness in terms of transportation. These are key issues where energy importers have shared interests, but where energy exporters may see both advantages and disadvantages. Yet, before the importance of energy policy in the Norwegian accession debate is discussed it is necessary to examine the development of the Internal Energy Market which is at the core of the discussion of energy issues in the EU.

THE EVOLVING EU ENERGY POLICY[1]

Until the advent of the Single European Market in 1985 there was no common framework for energy policy in the EU. Historically there were two treaties that dealt with energy – EURATOM and the European Coal and Steel Community (ECSC). The former sought to ensure that research on nuclear energy in Europe would be a common undertaking, and thus also to promote nuclear energy as the domestic energy option. The latter attempted to create a common market for coal and steel in Europe, and this was very important for integrating the war-torn Europe and its two main protagonists, France and Germany. But none of these efforts were really successful in the sense that they led to a common policy for energy as such. While nuclear energy has remained a major source of domestic production of electricity in some countries, especially in France, there is no common European policy in promoting the nuclear option. In coal, there has been a policy for each coal-rich country, and here the Commission has been unable to intervene to a large extent. Most important is however the fact that oil became the dominant fuel in modern economic life in the postwar period, and it increased its share in Europe very fast in the 1960s and 1970s. The EU did not, however, develop any common oil policy or attempt to do so at the time. The so-called first 'oil shock' in 1973–4 came as a surprise, and in its aftermath the EU started to develop common guidelines for energy policy, usually valid for a five-year period. However, these guidelines were least common denominator outcomes, as all the member states had to agree on them.

When the Single Market came on to the agenda in 1985, however, energy policy was first thought to be too difficult to include. However, one soon realised that one could not hope to achieve a 'level playing field' in areas such as transport, industry, etc., without more competition and openness in the energy area. It was therefore decided to include energy in the general Single Market work, and to create an internal energy market.

Thus, since 1988, when this was decided, the Commission has developed what is termed an Internal Energy Market (IEM). The concept of the Single Market presented the energy field with a major challenge. The often monopolistic national energy segments faced dismantling, and the national energy policies must follow suit in the prising open of energy markets. Thus the task of the European Commission was a formidable one indeed, since European energy markets were considered to be some of the most difficult to change as they have been characterised by a heavy government hand in the form of strong, national energy policies. This was the reason energy was at first left out of the Single Market concept altogether, only to be added as late as 1988.

An EC 'inventory' of proposals relating to energy policy from about 1988 reads as follows.

Proposals that aim at a freer market

Harmonisation of indirect taxation, price and investment transparency, competition for public procurement, common carriage, integration of grids for electricity and gas, application of competition legislation in the upstream part of oil and gas exploration and production, restructuring of state aid for coal.

Proposals that demand an EU-level energy policy

Security of Supply: integration of grids, plans for an EU policy of supply security by the year 2005, the European Energy Charter; the official merging of energy and environmental policy from 1990, amendment proposals for the inclusion of energy in the treaty text. This also includes measures pertaining to the internal market as such that have direct bearing on energy policy. Foremost among these is a directive on public procurement which includes also the energy sector (Commission of the ECs 1988).

The IEM proposals within the scope of DG XVII (energy directorate) were introduced as a package late in 1989: price transparency in the electricity and gas sectors was the subject of a communication in March 1989 (Commission of the ECs 1989b), and open access proposals for gas and electricity were set forth at the same time (Commission of the ECs 1989c and 1989d), along with plans for the monitoring of large investments in the energy sector. The transit directives were adopted in 1989 and 1990 respectively. They were very controversial, especially that concerning gas transport. (The reason why the question of transmission of especially natural gas is so controversial is that the gas grid is dominated by a handful of companies, often national monopolies, which set the tariffs for transport in bilateral negotiations between the seller of gas and themselves. These prices have been closely guarded secrets in the European gas market, and the transmission companies, as they are called, have also been at liberty to deny access for others.)

NORWAY'S INTEREST

In the European debate over gas transmission there has been no official Norwegian participation, but it is clear that the Norwegian interest lies in safeguarding the status quo; that long-term gas contracts remain possible. This may be jeopardised if the gas market develops to resemble a free market where gas can be traded in short-term contracts that typically last only up to two to three years. Today, European gas contracts last up to thirty years, and this is thought necessary so that both seller and buyer may rest assured that the large investments that are needed to develop an offshore field and to build a pipeline are made. Thus, both gas suppliers and gas transmitters have an interest in retaining the present structure of the European gas market, although Norwegian gas sellers also see that greater market flexibility 'downstream', that is, in the continental market, may be useful for them too. Today Norwegian gas is sold at entry point in Europe, and there is little Norwegian integration in the market structure beyond this point.

However, the issue of gas transmission in Europe was not a debate that 'hit the headlines', as it were. It was a debate that was followed very closely by energy experts, but which did not figure in the public domain very much.

NORWAY AND THE 'CONCESSION DIRECTIVE': A SUCCESSFUL 'TWO-LEVEL' GAME?

The most controversial energy directive proposal from the Norwegian point of view was launched in May 1992. This directive aimed at 'going upstream' in order to apply the competition legislation of the EU regarding concession policy (Commission of the ECs 1992g). The aim was to ensure equal treatment of applicants to exploration and production licences for oil and gas, and to abolish special national treatment which existed in Denmark and Norway, but no longer in the UK, the third production country in Europe.

The 'concession directive' proposal stated that concession policy should be 'non-discriminatory and transparent and impose no conditions on access to or the exercise of these activities which are not technically warranted by the objective of optimum exploitation'. The major point was to bring also the 'upstream' or production part of the energy sector into the remit of the competition legislation and thus make the internal energy market apply also here. However, this proposal met tremendous opposition from Norway, a non-member.

Robert Putnam's celebrated essay (Putnam 1988) on how governments play at least two games simultaneously when they negotiate on an international arena comes to mind when one wants to understand how Norway could come to play such a prominent role in the case of the 'concession directive'. Currently there is much attention given to the metaphor of the 'two levels' in international relations theory as well as the study of the EU-states interaction. Sometimes this is referred to as 'two-level games', but the usage is not precise. Putnam's main point is that one should think about the state as being a gate-keeper between the domestic and the IR (International Relations) level, and that this position allows it to take into account consequences at both levels when formulating strategies of political action.

This metaphor conveys the notion that states act at two levels simultaneously – the domestic and the international; and that they need to take into account implications of their strategies at both levels when they formulate them. For example, if a state wants to deregulate its domestic energy sector but faces severe domestic opposition to this, it may be easier to accomplish when it can invoke some international regime rule, for example, in the EC. Further, if able to, a state may shape the international regime rules for itself then in turn invoke them, thus by-passing domestic opposition while having formulated optimal rules for itself at the IR level. Also, when acting on the IR level, the state must reckon with the need for domestic ratification of what it agrees to, and thus is constrained by that.

The Norwegian government could, and did, argue that it 'needed' an understanding attitude from the Commission with regard to the 'concession' directive since the question of membership was to be decided by a referendum and since there was major opposition to the EU. This probably explains why it was possible to achieve an addendum to the negotiated agreement between Norway and the EU that stated that Norway would retain full sovereignty over natural resources.

The persistent Norwegian position on the proposed 'concession directive' was put in very negative terms. The Prime Minister for example, stated that 'We do not view the introduction of this proposal to be an overly hospitable move shortly before Norway might be joining the Community. We do not see a substantial need for such a directive. On the contrary it can do a lot of damage to the image of the Community among people in Norway in the run up to the referendum' (Brundtland's Speech in Bonn, 23/3/1993). In Denmark, too, domestic conditions made it important that the 'concession' directive did not surface too much in the debate. The Danes were having a referendum on the Maastricht treaty in May 1993. Thus, the Danes could speak against the directive within the EU while the Norwegians lobbied both outside and inside the system. Their 'No-side' in the EU-debate used the proposed directives as 'proof' that the EU was seeking to get control over Norwegian energy resources, and there was a major public debate on this theme, which was easy to present as a move towards foreign 'dominance'. It therefore became imperative that the government achieve a 'success' in the negotiations with the EU on this issue in order to show that small countries like Norway also wielded power. The politicisation of the case of the 'concession directive' in the public debate probably contributed to the outcome of the negotiations with the EU and Norway: unless the issue were resolved reassuringly, there would be a negative reaction in the general populace, and this would have diminished the chances for a positive outcome of the referendum even more.

Professor Svein Andersen of the Norwegian Business School has conducted a detailed study of the Norwegian negotiations with the EU over the 'concession' directive (Andersen 1995). He concludes that Norway exerted a strong and unexpected influence on the outcome of the decision-making within the EU on the directive proposal. This may be due to several factors, but the domestic situation in Norway was probably of major significance.

Further, Norway's oil revenue has and will play a major role in the relationship with the EU. The influx of oil revenue since about 1977 has made it possible to stay aloof from international pressures and to subsidise the public and other sectors. In the period 1977 to the present 485 billion NOK in oil revenue has been spent on inland consumption, most of it on social programmes and subsidies, as well as on the growth in the public sector. This is the so-called 'Dutch disease', which entails that large sums of money generated as rent from natural resources are pumped into the national economy. In Norway the 'oil age' is estimated to last about twenty more years for a sufficient influx of money into the economy (oil proven reserves) and one hundred years for gas. There will thus be a sufficient influx of money into the economy to sustain a large public sector and subsidies to agriculture for several years to come. There is thus much less need for membership on economic grounds in Norway than in Sweden or Finland.

In the latter countries, energy policy did not figure much in the debate on EU membership, whereas in Norway it was a major concern in the public debate in one case, viz. in the debate on the 'concession directive'. This conclusion is not surprising, as energy is a relatively dull and technical policy field from the point of view of the general voter and politician. The choices are often extremely limited as energy reserves determine what one can do. Only in the case of nuclear energy is there a persistent political debate and in most countries, referenda, on whether to have nuclear energy or not. But nuclear energy is notably not yet an issue in the EU energy policy debate despite it being so in several member countries.

NOTES

1 This section draws upon the book *Energy Policy in the European Union* by J. H. Matlary, published as part of the Macmillan European Union Series in 1995.
2 The Norwegian Ministry of Industry and Energy publishes the so-called 'Fact Sheet' each year. This is a very valuable publication containing information on all aspects of petroleum activity as well as details of all concessions.

16 The Nordic neutrals

Facing the European Union

Lauri Karvonen and Bengt Sundelius

INTRODUCTION

While 1989 is often seen as the year of significant European transformation, for Finland and Sweden, the two Nordic neutrals, 1991 represented a similar qualitative shift. Both nations experienced domestic political transformations towards greater market oriented economic policies and, perhaps even more enduring, redirections of their classical security doctrines based on neutrality between East and West. At that time Sweden led the way in this external policy reorientation through its 1 July application for membership of the European Community (EC). Finland joined the bandwagon on 17 March 1992. However, over time Finland moved more quickly than Sweden to discard its old doctrines concerning security policy and European integration. On 19 October 1994, by a margin of 57 versus 43 per cent, the Finnish people voted to join the EU. The Swedish referendum of 13 November resulted in a much closer 52–48 per cent margin in favour of membership.

In this chapter, the dramatic reorientations since 1990 of Finnish and Swedish security policy doctrines, and orientations towards the EU, will be outlined. This analysis offers the necessary background to any understanding of the national debates and policy controversies now confronting these two new members of the EU and of their involvement in its Common Foreign and Security Policy (CFSP). Although many issues were raised during the years of rapid redirection before entering the EU, an abundance of controversies remain to be settled as Finland and Sweden are pulled into the wider debates over the future course of the evolving European security posture. The 1996 Intergovernmental Conference (IGC) is only the first stop on this journey into uncharted waters.

1991: THE YEAR OF CHANGE

Sweden: rapid redirection

During the autumn of 1990 the Swedish debate over the future relationship towards the EC intensified. Many independent commentators argued that the traditionally strict interpretation of the incompatibility between the credibility of neutrality and EC membership had been overtaken by the sea-changes in European security relations. The classic formulation in this area had already been articulated in 1961 by then Prime Minister Tage Erlander, who argued that Sweden must avoid those ties which served to limit her chance of fulfilling, and winning support for, her policy of neutrality. It was noted 30 years later that such a restrictive view towards the European integration process might lead to serious national economic losses without any comparable gains in security. To some, the credibility of neutrality between East and West seemed less vital as a national objective when the two military blocs of Europe no longer confronted each other as they did during the Cold War period (see Sundelius 1987; Hakovirta 1988; Papacosma and Rubin 1989; Kruzel and Haltzel 1989; and Bissell and Gasteyger 1990).

Within the non-socialist opposition, questioning of the traditional neutrality posture argued for a policy change. The pattern from the earlier European debates in the 1960s seemed to reappear. Prominent liberal debaters pushed the question of the necessity of future membership. For quite some time, the conservative party leader, Carl Bildt, had been stressing in parliamentary foreign policy debates the need to 'emphasise a European identity and give Sweden a permanent place in the dynamic European cooperation' (18 March 1987). 'Sooner or later we have to examine whether a Swedish membership in the EC is compatible with our policy of neutrality' (*Utrikesutskottets betankanden* 1989).

Spokesmen for Swedish industry proposed initiatives concerning the necessity of membership to obtain fully the economic advantages of the post-1992 emerging Single European Market (SEM). The early expectations of the inchoate EEA agreement had diminished considerably during the drawn out negotiations. Additionally, several prominent union leaders realised the material costs for their members of continued political isolation from an economically more dynamic EC. This reversal of the official position of the Swedish Confederation of Trade Unions and the Swedish Central Organization of Salaried Employees occurred before a corresponding pro-EC approach started dominating the Social Democratic Party's leadership.

However, internal discussions occurred within the Social Democratic government party as well. These informal debates were clearly influenced by the changing perspective of the labour movement. Additionally, viewpoints from experts within the ministries were of importance.

Certain civil servants stressed the economic advantages of abandoning the traditional political separation from the EC. As early as 1989 the currency regulations had been abandoned to allow for free capital movements between Sweden and the rest of Europe. One could then maintain that the logical and perhaps necessary consequence of these politically uncontroversial steps would be now to participate fully in the shaping of the developing economic cooperation efforts in Western Europe.

At the September 1990 Social Democratic Party Congress a more positive view towards EC cooperation and possible Swedish participation was informally conveyed. However, the official statements were still cautious and vague. Ingvar Carlsson, the party leader, made his introductory speech on 15 September containing the following passage: 'In a Europe where the blocs have vanished the traditional obstacles to uniting membership and neutrality policy would disappear.'[1] An expectant attitude characterised the debate during this party congress, which took place just a month before the dramatic government initiative towards membership on 26 October.

Among the proponents of neutrality within the Foreign Ministry the evolving processes of the new European security scene were observed with great caution. The internal discussions, however, were influenced by the peaceful and unexpectedly rapid reunification of Germany in October 1990. Despite apprehensions about a negative reaction, the Soviet Union did not react negatively to what in reality became an East German incorporation in the German Federation. This important event radically changed Europe's security map. The economic and political centre of power had been re-located to *Mitteleuropa*. Previous cautious Swedish statements concerning Europe's future security structures soon changed to a more optimistic tone. A related event that inspired additional confidence was the signing of a new binding CSCE treaty in November, the Charter of Paris.

At the opening of the Swedish Parliament on 2 October 1990, Prime Minister Ingvar Carlsson introduced a vision of a developing Europe without dividing blocs. According to him in such a future situation Swedish EC membership would be compatible with the Swedish policy of neutrality. As part of an economic crisis package, on 26 October the government suddenly announced that 'Swedish membership in EC while retaining Swedish neutrality is in our national interest' (*Regeringsskrivelse* 1990/1991: 50). The stated ambition now was to begin preparations for membership negotiations.

The immediate motivation for this somewhat unusual format for one of the most significant foreign policy shifts during the postwar period is said to have been an urgent need to control quickly the vast capital flight. In the short term this unambiguous trend threatened the value of the Swedish currency. In the longer term it was a threat to Swedish employment. With the promise of membership, an important incentive for the capital drain of the nation would be removed. At the beginning of December, after the CSCE ceremony in Paris, the Parliament overwhelmingly approved the new position concerning EC membership. An application could be justified by the improved security situation in Europe. The new pan-European Paris Charter was said to be of particular importance to the expected positive development.

The parliamentary statement in December 1990 (*Utrikesutskottets betankanden* 1991: UU8) stimulated a minor public debate on the consequences of the expressed desire of combining membership with a continued credible policy of neutrality. A thorough review of this problem was demanded by several critical voices, among others the former Permanent Under Secretary of State for Foreign Affairs ambassador Sverker Astrom. In February 1991, after this first mini-debate the Prime Minister promised that membership would be preceded by a public referendum. This would probably be held in 1994. The spring was devoted to internal discussions within the corridors of government and among the party leadership, centring on the design and justification of an application. Two difficult remaining questions were how the big leap out into an uncertain Europe could be explained in terms of security policy and also find wide support in Parliament.

Within the Foreign Ministry intense discussions were held about the pros and cons of the developments in Europe and particularly in Eastern Europe. Behind closed doors questions were raised on the stability of developments in the Soviet Union. One concern was how Sweden could return to a policy of strict neutrality if a European common structure did not come to pass. These expert analyses emphasised the multiple futures that were possible and indicated caution in outlining a revised policy. The scope for suitable interpretations of these more or less optimistic analyses among the politically responsible leaders remained considerable.

The expected change of the official policy line needed support in the parliamentary groups before the summer break leading up to the September general election. Outside the government, the Green Party and the Left Party were the most reluctant to take the big step towards the EC. However these small fringe parties were not needed for a joint parliamentary declaration on the question. Instead, the Centre Party was critical for this purpose. Within this traditional agricultural party there was a strong identification with the national heritage and with the neutrality policy. As in the leading circles of the foreign affairs establishment and inside the Social Democratic Party, it was important to the Centre Party to include a provision in the application that formulated the intention to maintain a policy of neutrality. The current uncertain European security situation demanded such a safeguard, it was argued. In May and at the beginning of June 1991, the representatives of the major parties completed negotiations for the text of a governmental declaration on the membership issue.

On the last day of the parliamentary calendar, 14 June, the Prime Minister in a speech enumerated the motivations for the announced membership application.[2] The speech stressed that the desired membership could indeed be combined with a credible policy of neutrality. 'The overall judgement of the government is that a Swedish membership in the EC is compatible with the demands of a policy of neutrality.' Thus, through the lengthy internal discussions of Spring 1991, a new multi-party premise for Swedish security policy had been reached: due to the new European security order, the classic and previously supreme demand for upholding the credibility of neutrality was no longer an obstacle to membership within the dynamic West European economic integration process. This political metamorphosis had been reached in less than a year.

The Swedish EC application was submitted in the Hague on 1 July 1991. This landmark step was built on multi-party support, only excluding the marginalised Left and Green Parties. Thus, the Social Democratic government could look forward to the parliamentary elections in September with a certain confidence. In any case the EC membership question had been eliminated as a possible reason for voting against the government. Throughout the election campaign all the major parties seemed to take a pro-EC stance and this shared devotion to Europe did not become a divisive campaign issue. On the other hand, the Liberals and the Moderates tried to remind the voters that they had pushed for membership a long time ago when the Social Democrats had remained uncommitted to the most salient issues of the 1990s. The Social Democratic Party asked for votes to be able to spread their version of the good society in the new Europe. The small parties that were hostile to the EC lost ground in the election while two additional pro-EC parties gained seats in the new parliament. In the autumn of 1991 the rapid shift, from being outside Europe to becoming part of Europe, appeared to be settled in Sweden.

Finland: the EEA; an EC in sheep's clothing

Finnish policy concerning European integration had throughout the post-war period been a very difficult balancing act between two seemingly incompatible demands. First, to convince the Kremlin that Finland's trustworthy relationship with the Soviet Union was its highest priority, and second to assure the Finnish export industry the same good terms of trade within the vital European Market as its main competitors (especially Sweden) had.

In 1991 these two cornerstones of Finnish foreign policy underwent fundamental change. In July Sweden acted on its declared intention and submitted an application for EC membership. The August coup attempt in Moscow initiated the final dissolution of the Soviet Union. One of the consequences of this process, which although less important to the overall context was highly significant to Finland, was that the Friendship, Co-operation and Mutual Assistance Treaty of 1948 was abolished and replaced by a virtually non-binding Friendship Treaty with Russia.

Despite these fundamental changes around Finland the President and the government kept insisting on the viability and exclusivity of the 'EEA track'. From the start Finland had been strongly engaged in this attempt to create a common market for the EFTA and EC countries. Most of 1991 was dominated by the Finnish leadership patiently repeating their position that Finland saw the EEA as an end in itself, and not as a transitional arrangement or a gateway to EC membership.

However, from early autumn 1991 these statements acquired a more defensive tone. The main argument was that the EEA was still needed to guarantee an entrance into the Single European Market in 1993. 'Concerning our economic interests the EEA seems to be adequate; however, if this goal cannot be fulfilled we will have to find other ways to secure our interests' (ULA 1991: 173).

The uncertainty was dispelled once and for all when President Koivisto in connection with the opening of the 1992 session of Parliament on 7 February, stated that:

> Our Western relations are faced with new decisions. Integration is progressing in Western Europe, and we too have to make our own choice. Our freedom of choice is best utilised by applying for EC membership according to what is known as the short formula. Meanwhile, it is imperative that the Parliament be kept well informed about the course of the negotiations.
>
> (Koivisto 1992)

It is noteworthy that the President did not make reference to the country's security doctrine in this statement. When he did touch upon details they only concerned agricultural politics and foreign trade. With a characteristic formulation where he turned conventional opinion on its head, he maintained that only by being strictly embedded in a European framework would there be a long-term guarantee that 'the whole country remains inhabited and agriculturally vital'. He underlined that 'right now it seems uncertain whether they will succeed in creating a common area of European economic cooperation – EEA – an alternative which is important to us'.

From this moment there was hardly anyone who doubted that a satisfactory EC membership was Finland's real goal regarding European integration issues. Despite all assurances the EEA had proved to be the opposite, merely foreplay. A few weeks later the government's 'message to the parliament concerning application for EC membership' was presented; the message had the status of a manifesto for which the government sought parliamentary blessing, manifested in a decisive vote.

The parliamentary vote in the middle of March 1992 actually became an overwhelming manifestation for EC membership. Although the government's motion received only 108 of the 196 counted votes, the majority of the remaining votes supported the Social Democratic opposition's proposal, which in several ways could be categorised as even more EC-friendly than the government's position. From a situation where only a few individual representatives had taken clear EC stances, within just a few short months Finland's Parliament had been transformed into one of Europe's most EC-friendly legislatures. Immediately, on the day following the parliamentary vote, Finland submitted its membership application to Brussels. It had the shape of a 'clean' application with no reservations or clarifications attached.

FINIS NEUTRALITATIS?

Sweden: remaining tensions

The 1991 September parliamentary elections resulted in a minority government with the Moderate Party leader Carl Bildt as the new Prime Minister. In addition to the conservatives, the coalition government consisted of the Liberal Party, the Centre Party and Christian Democratic Party. The positions of prime minister, foreign minister, European minister, and defence minister were filled by members of the Moderate Party. Thus, this large party of the right was expected to dominate the field of security and European policy. In his government declaration on 4 October 1991, Prime Minister Bildt emphasised the importance of completing the road towards EC membership. He also repeated the traditional phrase of no alliances in peace, aiming for neutrality in the event of war, as an important cornerstone of security policy. The impression given from this initial public statement by the new government leader was one of continuity stressing EC membership and neutrality.

However the tension between the two components of the earlier EC application, membership and preserved neutrality, came to characterise the management of the European integration question during Carl Bildt's three years in government. For certain target groups, mainly those abroad, the clear goal of fully participating in all aspects of European cooperation was highlighted. In other circumstances the so-called neutrality commitment made in Ingvar Carlsson's earlier speech to Parliament was stressed. In particular, in announcements where the coalition Centre Party and the opposition's more traditional outlook figured prominently, the latter component was found in government declarations and in parliamentary multi-party committee reports.

The emphasis on neutrality was retained in the first governmental declaration in the autumn of 1991. In later statements the Prime Minister emphasised only the importance of preserving the policy of military non-alignment. In other words, 'the hard core of neutrality'. In a parliamentary debate on 15 January 1992, Carl Bildt introduced the quickly adopted phrase 'Nobody else defends Sweden, and we defend only Sweden' (*Utrikesutskottets betankanden* 1992: UU19, 52). In the spring of 1992 the parliamentary committee on foreign affairs formulated the multi-partisan line that 'preserving the policy of no alliances does not pre-suppose that Sweden in any other respects would have to impose restrictions on itself regarding participation in the growing and multi-dimensional European cooperation' (*Utrikesutskottets betankanden* 1992: UU19).

While the core element of no military alliances remained in policy statements with multi-party support, the traditional neutrality edict disappeared. Already in the second governmental declaration on 6 October 1992 this portion of the traditional formula was deleted after receiving critical scrutiny by the European Commission. In its evaluation report of 31 July

1992 before the forthcoming membership negotiations it was noted that neutrality could become a problem for Sweden's participation in the European Union. Thus, the new government statement in October 1992 ran: 'Sweden stands outside of military alliances' (Government Declaration to Parliament 6/10/1992). Through this short verification of the existing facts, a commitment to possible future ties to, or dissociation from, the EU's demands for cooperation on security policy and in the long run defence cooperation, was avoided.

A compromise among the non-socialist coalition parties and also with the Social Democratic opposition had been reached by this elegant but meaningless formulation. Sweden's introductory speech to the EC Council of Ministers on 1 February 1993 was also illustrative of internal national problems concerning this delicate subject. European Minister Ulf Dinkelspiel expressed the Swedish promise not to obstruct the development of future defence cooperation within the EU. Implicitly he also informed the EC leaders that there was no intention of actively promoting this new common defence area either. The Swedish line can be seen as a compromise between the ambitions of not unnecessarily irritating the important negotiation partners and simultaneously reaching a national consensus on a delicate policy issue. Also the second high level meeting in Brussels, in November 1993, was preceded by intense domestic discussion before a joint, multi-party speech could be presented by the moderate European Minister.

The tension between the deeply rooted neutrality posture and a politically active commitment to common West European security cooperation remained unsolved in the Swedish discussions. In the spring of 1992 the Parliament's Foreign Policy Committee stipulated in a multipartisan statement that in the future Sweden would retain the option of maintaining neutrality in the case of war. 'Sweden's policy of non-alliance with the possibility of neutrality in the case of war in its vicinity remains' (*Utrikesutskottets betankanden* 1992: UU19). It seemed unnecessary to rule out any alternative in advance, including the traditional solution – neutrality in war. At the same time government representatives were constantly making overtures towards future Swedish commitments in the EU as well as in the West European Union (WEU). These subtle differences reflected an underlying tension within the coalition government and within Parliament concerning Sweden's proper security role in the new Europe.

In a speech at Brussels in September 1993, Prime Minister Bildt tried to avoid these political pitfalls by concentrating on Sweden's traditional involvement in, and commitment towards, international cooperation. 'Sweden will be an active and committed participant in the evolution of the common foreign and security policy. Foreign observers who think otherwise have not really understood the Swedish mentality. When we join international cooperation, we intend to have an influence, and we want to make a difference.'[3]

The fear that Sweden, due to its heritage of neutrality, would take advantage of other states with regard to European security was repudiated in this way. However, European common defence was not directly mentioned by Bildt. Instead he stressed what Sweden had already performed militarily in support of European security even before membership had been agreed to: 'We have also taken on a greater military burden in former Yugoslavia than most Community countries.' According to the Prime Minister the Swedish military contribution in Croatia, Macedonia, and Bosnia showed 'the limited relevance of dividing countries into those which are part of a military alliance and those which are not'.

In the third annual government declaration on 6 October 1993 the Prime Minister once again soberly maintained that Sweden stands outside of military alliances. But Bildt also claimed, in reference to his Brussels speech, that 'we are serious about wanting to contribute to European common security' (Government Declaration to Parliament 6/10/1993). An expression of this good intent was the Nordic battalion in Bosnia, Nordbat. Thus, the earlier clearly limiting statement from January 1992, that Sweden only defends Sweden, seemed to have been superseded. On the other hand, the government did consider a public discussion of a possible membership in the WEU as inappropriate before Sweden became a member of the EU.

Much seems to have changed since 27 May 1990 when Ingvar Carlsson wrote: 'If the EC actually evolves into such an advanced community it will not be possible for Sweden to push for membership. That is definitely past our limits' (Carlsson 1990). It seems, even after the positive 13 November 1994 referendum, that this matter of limits is still relevant to the future Swedish security profile as a member in an interlinked security system in Western Europe. Certain parties, organisations and prominent individuals have consistently pushed forward the Swedish position in Europe. In other, and at least as politically important circles, the resistance against an active and overarching EU engagement remains strong.

The high point of a supportive public opinion and a positive political engagement seems to have been at the time of the Swedish EC application, the 1991 parliamentary election and shift in government. At that point there were no obvious limits in a dynamic Europe. Today, many Swedes have shown by their votes that they are concerned over the erosion of 'the definite limits' for Sweden's participation in the European cooperation experiment. Advocates of such a limiting perspective on the nation's engagement in the European Union have been included in the new Social Democratic cabinet under the leadership of Ingvar Carlsson. Thus, this tension has been built into the internal government deliberations over the future direction of Swedish policy as a member of the EU.

Finland: pressing ahead

During the period after applying for membership, Finland's foreign policy leadership pursued with great skill the art of having its cake and eating it too. Neutrality, now reformulated as 'military non-alliance combined with an independent defence', continued to appear as a public description of the country's security policy. Simultaneously, the variability over time has been included in the description of the doctrine as a central element: Finland is neutral 'for the present'.

At once these signals found fertile ground in Brussels. The EC's so-called notification of Finland's membership application in November 1992 expressed – contrary to the previous public notification about the Swedish application – no reservations regarding Finland's willingness to participate fully in the common foreign and security policy (*Dagens Nyheter* 12/11/1992). When the membership negotiations opened in Brussels a few months later the Finnish opening statement strove after securing this impression. In his address, Foreign Trade Minister Pertti Salolainen underlined that the Finnish government did not expect to encounter problems related to foreign and security policies. Quite to the contrary, the Finns share both the fundamental values underlying EU foreign policies and the major goals of the Union in world affairs, Salolainen argued. He defined the core of post-Cold War Finnish foreign policy as 'military non-alignment combined with an independent defence'. However, Salolainen underlined that the Finns looked to the future even in this respect 'with an open mind' and clearly signalled a will to contribute to the defence dimension of the Union.[4]

While agriculture was highlighted as the only real problem *vis-à-vis* Brussels, the tide turned in security politics through which the connection to Western defence cooperation was not only presented as possible but also as a particularly weighty argument for membership. A statement by the Under Secretary of State, Jaakko Blomberg, in February 1993 can be described as an authoritative speech in this context (*Ulkosiainministerio* 1993: 2–4). Blomberg is the highest ranking civil servant concentrating on security policies at the Foreign Ministry.

First, Blomberg maintained that Finland's independent influence on security policy questions is not at all diminished by EC membership: 'On the contrary, the specific importance of our policies increases.' Second, membership is an advantage, not a disadvantage, regarding Finland's relations with Russia. Blomberg stresses that Finland fully supports the EC's goal to create a common defence in the future. He admits that 'outside of a small inner circle' it can be difficult to understand that Finland partly describes itself as non-aligned and partly strives for a common defence. But: 'Our attachment to freedom from alliances is related to the point in time and to the prevailing conditions. These conditions may change, and we can therefore not exclude a membership in a common defence system in the future.'

However, it is not only a European defence that Blomberg has a vision of: 'No one can in the Europe of today – let alone tomorrow – undertake unilateral measures, be they in the form of diplomatic pressure, threats, direct aggression or alliance formation, without affecting the entire Euro-Atlantic Community.'

The binding commitment to the West's security policy included in EC membership was increasingly being presented as a central advantage from Finland's point of view. At the same time more energy was spent on agriculture, 'the only real problem'. Conspicuously, Heikki Haavisto, chairman of the Agricultural Producers' Central Organization MTK, was appointed Foreign Minister in May 1993. In the months before the EC application MTK had started a widespread 'No to EC' campaign and Haavisto had come forward as a leading advocate of 'No'. Many saw the choice of Haavisto as a stroke of genius, whereby the farmers – the nucleus in the Finnish EC resistance – were attached to the negotiation result.

After the autumn of 1993 security policy became the most central theme in the Finnish EC debate. The arguments for membership more often became linked to the concerns over military security, which the attachment to the West would enhance. This gave rise to the point of the EC opposition about the vulgarity of raising the 'Russian threat' argument to intimidate people to support EC membership (*Hufvadstadsbladet* 22/8/1993).

At the same time the debate for direct NATO membership intensified. At the time of writing the conception of neutrality seems more like a relic of the past, which is tolerated as a provisional arrangement preceding a definite security commitment to the West. Apparently, Finland will accept that form of its security policy which can be combined as smoothly as possible with EU membership. Already it includes observer status in the Western European Union (WEU). A future NATO membership option has not been officially closed in Finland.

LEADERSHIP FROM ABOVE

From a bird's eye perspective, Sweden and Finland's paths from the neutrality policies of the Cold War towards more ties to the West seem almost identical. The same arguments return during the various phases of decision, and in major ways the same steps have been taken in Stockholm and in Helsinki. This is natural considering that the two countries have been influenced to a high degree by each other's policy.

However, a closer look reveals that the Swedish foreign policy course contains a greater variety of meanings and its doctrinal status is more uncertain than in the case of Finland. Certain key questions still seem unresolved even at the elite level of security policy-making. To a certain extent the government has been forced to speak with different emphases to Brussels and to national public opinion. The decisive difference between these two countries is that Swedish security policy decision-making, to a larger extent, is a part of ordinary domestic political decision-making than is the case in Finland.

At a relatively early stage, leading Swedish politicians opted for an open debate on the European issue. Carl Bildt, during his time as opposition leader, had the political integration debate initiative in his hands for longer periods. The Social Democratic leadership was forced to define its standpoint in a public debate. When the Carlsson government declared its intention to apply for EC membership in the autumn of 1990 this was also a part of the domestic political tug of war between government and opposition: 'It's better to pro-act than to react', as the saying goes.

Thus, the first indication of membership was prepared (October 1990) in connection with an economic crisis package where the target groups were Swedish industry, unions, and international currency traders. The Finance Ministry's declaration of intent was followed up in a more democratically orderly fashion by the Parliament's Foreign Policy Committee. In December it presented a multi-party statement supporting a membership application.

In opposition, the Social Democrats embarked on a two part strategy. On one hand, the entire party leadership declared itself for EU membership. In this manner, Swedish industry, the pro-EU public, and Brussels all received a clear signal that they had nothing to fear if there should be a shift of government. At the same time, the party members were given a free reign in forming their own opinions on the EU question. An active anti-membership network was established among party members and media sympathisers. Public opinion polls clearly showed that Social Democratic voters in particular were sceptical towards Swedish EU membership. None the less, they were prepared loyally to support the pro-EU Social Democratic leadership's return to governmental power in September 1994. Strategically it was of course an advantage for the Social Democrats that the strong EU resistance among the voters could be channelled into voting against the Bildt government.

In many ways, Prime Minister Carl Bildt in his European ambitions faced an unsolvable dilemma. To reach a majority for Swedish membership in the November 1994 EU referendum he needed the participation of the Social Democrats in shaping public opinion. The Social Democrats, however, could reach two goals at the same time: letting the Bildt government fall in September and then, from a position of governmental leadership, guide Sweden into the EU. The gameplan succeeded in both respects but at the cost of deep divisions and some bitterness inside the party.

In Sweden foreign policy has been part of the party game between government and opposition. Although all governments have tried to control the currently acceptable doctrines they have not always succeeded in doing so. A certain degree of pluralism has existed also in the area of security policy. A major base for support behind the establishment viewpoints of the government has been the ability to mobilise the rank and file of voters at critical junctures, such as in the EU referendum.

Within Finnish foreign policy this domestic pluralism is very hard to trace. Finland's road from 'No to EC' to 'Yes to EC', including the common foreign and security policies, has been a process even more controlled from above than in Sweden. The central strategy has been to tie the political and social elite to a specific aim, which the foreign policy leadership has chosen: they have not been willing to discuss publicly any alternatives outside of the elite consensus. Finland has persisted in holding on to one position at a time: in public all other alternatives have been treated as 'irrelevant'.

Thus, Finland's position has been outwardly highly unambiguous. When the EEA was appropriate it was that goal that this country worked for 100 per cent. Once EC membership became appropriate, the foreign policy leadership wanted to remove all doubt about the country's comprehensive loyalty to Brussels. This decision strategy is undeniably effective; at the same time it is far from the democratic ideal of an active and open debate before an important decision is made. When a new consensus at the elite level has been reached, what was previously considered 'irrelevant' suddenly becomes 'unproblematic'. The public at large has been served a series of *faits accompli.*

Both constitutional factors and postwar foreign policy practices have assisted in making this extremely centralised foreign policy possible. The Finnish President has wide constitutional powers within foreign policy. The foreign policy authority which in a strict parliamentary system belongs to the cabinet rests in the hybrid Finnish system to a large extent with the President. At the same time he has been a central domestic political actor primarily due to his deciding role in appointing the Prime Minister. Additionally the individual ministers have been appointed to their posts by the President. The cabinet, as a decisive decision unit for central issues of foreign policy, has been reduced in authority. Instead, the pre-eminent role of the foreign ministry, as the President's designated practitioner of foreign policy, has been emphasised. The political elite in Finland – the members of government, parliamentarians, political party and organisation representatives – early on in their careers have been socialised into a way of thinking whereby independent security policy initiatives are akin to political suicide.

The axis of foreign policy power which runs from the President to the foreign ministry does not in itself automatically mean a certain position in questions of substance (for example towards EU membership and preserved neutrality). On the other hand, a central procedural demand is that any ambiguity or uncertainty over Finland's correct foreign policy line at a particular moment must be avoided. Foreign policy consensus is not created through open debate but through closed discussions at the elite level. Representatives of the central political, economic and social groups are socialised into a certain mode of procedural thinking.

The only important group which did not let its EU position become dictated from above was the farmers, primarily represented by MTK. The farmers had, despite representing only 6 per cent of the population, a key position in the largest government party, the Centre Party. Therefore the Finnish EU negotiations concentrated on pushing through an optimal solution regarding Finnish agriculture at the same time as Finland in most other areas acceded to the EU's demands. That the farmers 'stand under the nation's special protection' became especially obvious when the MTK leader, Haavisto, was appointed as the new Foreign Minister. Haavisto naturally realised that he had not received the President's mandate to sabotage the government's negotiations with the EC. Instead he was given an opportunity to push the farmers' interests as effectively as possible.

Thus Finland's foreign policy leadership has held a centralised decision-making capacity which many state leaders would envy. EU membership became a Finnish reality partly due to this capacity to control the political elites and thereby public opinion. Paradoxically, the Finnish shift on the EU issue will probably be the last political project to be carried out in this centralised fashion. Recent years have witnessed major constitutional changes away from semi-presidentialism towards fully-fledged parliamentarianism. Adaptation to the EU's internal decision-making procedures has been one important driving force behind these changes. At present, the recently elected President Ahtisaari is conducting what seems to be a losing battle over whether the President or the Prime Minister should represent Finland at summit level EU meetings. Stripped of even this main foreign policy power, the Finnish President would become a mere political figurehead, as in many other European democracies.

The differences between Sweden's and Finland's debate and decision-making processes obviously should not be exaggerated. None the less, it is clear that the heritage left over from the Cold War – a more open Swedish domestic debate climate – and constitutional factors still influenced the political handling of the EU question in these two countries. The question remains whether these differing national traditions will weigh heavily also on their national postures and internal policy shaping processes inside the European Union. Perhaps their common heritage as the Nordic neutrals will mean less than what is widely assumed, as Finland and Sweden move forward within the evolving Common Foreign and Security Policy.

Both Nordic states today pursue parallel courses away from their traditional neutrality and towards increasing integration with the Western security system. Official neutrality doctrines were already modified prior to joining the EU. During the membership negotiations no objections to the development of the Foreign and Security Policy were raised. They have also joined NATO's Partnership for Peace and have become observers of the Western European Union. In both nations the continued importance of a US presence in Europe is emphasised, in contrast with past public silence on that pivotal issue.

Still, important differences of emphasis remain in the way these national security questions have been addressed in domestic political discourse.

A division can be noted in Sweden between a more traditionally oriented and neutrality focused posture within the ruling Social Democratic Party as well as by the Centre and Left Parties, and on the other hand the views of the Liberal and Conservative Parties, which argue for a greater formal commitment to the Western security community. Some intense party quarrels occurred in early 1995 over the proper balance between the continued unilateralism of non-alliance membership and the regional multilateralism of a European security commitment. While the parties to the right wanted to examine the consequences of alliance membership, the parties to the left objected to such hypothetical excursions. In Finland only marginal opposition against a future full WEU or even NATO membership has been voiced.

The stronger domestic tradition in Sweden of a partisan dimension to considerations of national security policy seems to be operative here. The Finns continue to be true to their 'geo-political imperative' and welcome a policy alignment with the West as a historical opportunity to strengthen their national security and Western identity. After all, during the Cold War era Finnish neutrality was an important political step away from the Soviet orbit, while Swedish neutrality was a symbolic gesture of separation from Western security links. These different national traditions have left their marks also on the posture of these two Nordic states inside the EU. Most likely, the older EU members will find Finland to be a more flexible partner when it comes to developing further the Foreign and Security Policy dimension of the evolving European Union.

NOTES

1 Opening Address by party leader Ingvar Carlsson at the 1990 Social Democratic Party Congress.
2 Prime Minister Carlsson's 14 June 1991 declaration regarding Swedish membership of the EC (Carlsson 1992).
3 Statement by Carl Bildt to the Spaak Foundation in Brussels, 16 September 1993.
4 Address by Foreign Trade Minister Pertti Salolainen on 1 February 1993 in Brussels.

17 The NATO Nordics and the CFSP

Clive Archer

INTRODUCTION

Norway and Denmark are two small, rich, democratic, Nordic founder members of the North Atlantic Treaty Organisation (NATO). The world outlook of the leaders of these countries has been similar in the postwar period, and their security problems have often be seen in tandem. It might be a fair assumption, then, that the two states would approach the prospect of participation in the EU's Common Foreign and Security Policy (CFSP) in a similar manner. However, this has not necessarily been the case. Because of the intermix of geo-strategic differences and domestic political factors, Danish and Norwegian policy makers have not always seen eye-to-eye on foreign and security matters, though these differences were often overwhelmed by similarities. Developments in European security since 1989 have, if anything, helped to open up the divisions between the two main Nordic members. Their response to the EU's Common Foreign and Security Policy has been shaped by Danish founder membership of the European Union (EU) and the failed Norwegian attempt to join the Union by 1995. However, the two states' previous foreign and security policies have also affected their approach to the CFSP, as has the new external environment faced by the countries.

The third Nordic member of NATO is Iceland. From the beginning Iceland had different security and foreign policy considerations than those of Denmark and Norway. It was tied more to nearby North America than to the European continent and did not have its own armed forces. It was also a country with a very small population – a quarter of a million people as against Denmark's five million and the four million or so Norwegians – and a history of cultural isolation. This chapter will deal mainly with Denmark and Norway, because they are the main Nordic NATO members and the ones with the closest relations with the CFSP. Where necessary Iceland will be covered.

Any relationship between the Nordic NATO members and the future development of the CFSP will depend on the way that the European Union develops that policy. Norway will not have a direct input into it, though it may be able to influence it on certain issues. However, the reaction of the two states to the CFSP also relies on the more general foreign and security environment and on the domestic situation within the two countries.

The foreign and security policies of Denmark and Norway also have to be seen in the context of the policies of the other Nordic countries, especially those of Finland and Sweden (see Chapter 16). Whilst the Nordic states do not have, and in recent history have not had, a common foreign and security policy, there has been a degree of co-ordination of elements of these policies (for example, in foreign aid and within the United Nations) and, overall, the Nordic countries have considered that their security policies formed a pattern, sometimes described as the Nordic balance (Brundtland 1966: 30–63). The nature of this configuration of Nordic policies is contended, but it is generally accepted that, in foreign and security policies, the five states have a closeness that not only allows their policies to be compared easily (Sundelius 1982) but which is also a result – to some extent – of deliberate effort.

This chapter will first outline the foreign and security policies of Denmark and Norway prevailing in the period before 1989. It will examine the changes and continuity in those policies after the major upheavals in the politics of Europe after November 1989. The following two sections will look at how Denmark and Norway (with a note on Iceland) are adapting to the creation of the CFSP, and how they may continue in the future. The conclusion will seek to place the two countries in a wider context of the developing European framework.

FOREIGN AND SECURITY POLICIES PRE-1989

Nils Andrén has defined the security goal of the Nordic states in the post-war period of East–West confrontation as 'making the environment, regional or global, more "peace prone", by helping to dissolve tensions, to increase the respect for international law, and to create more social and economic equality in the international system as a whole' (Andrén 1982: 73). Furthermore the Nordic states have had – as small exposed countries – to tie their foreign policies to their security interests. The instruments of security policy became their foreign and defence policies, as well as their foreign trade, economic and disarmament policies. It is thus difficult to disentangle the foreign policies of the Nordic states from wider security considerations.

After the Second World War, all the Nordic states placed their faith in the creation of a universal system of international peace and security based on the United Nations Organisation, of which Denmark and Norway where founder members. Sweden joined in 1946 after debating whether membership was compatible with neutrality (Sundelius 1990: 118). Both Denmark and Norway had part of their territory liberated from Germany by the Soviet Union and were anxious not to alienate that country by moving too close to the United Kingdom or the United States. Also their immediate postwar governments had representatives of all the parties in their parliaments, including the communist parties.

However, they remained within the 'sphere of influence' of the victorious Western countries. Likewise Finland was seen to be within the Soviet 'sphere' despite avoiding occupation by the Red Army. Instead the Finnish army liberated the country from the German army (Mannerheim 1954: 363–89). The postwar government, a coalition including the Finnish communist party, had to negotiate a peace treaty with the victorious allies, the cost for being co-belligerents with Germany. Sweden had to adjust to a new strategic situation in the Baltic – one where the Soviet Union dominated the sea after the defeat of Germany. All the Nordic states hoped to 'build bridges' between the Soviet Union and the Western powers (Andrén 1982: 99).

These hopes were dashed in early 1948 when, in rapid succession, the Soviet Union placed pressure on Finland, the Brussels Treaty was signed by the United Kingdom, France and the three Benelux states, and Czechoslovakia was subjected to a communist coup. There was even a feeling in Denmark and Norway that they could be on a list for a Soviet takeover. The two countries were unable to defend themselves against any outside intervention and looked abroad for extra security. After failing to form a defence union with Sweden, Denmark and Norway turned to their war-time allies in the west, the United States and Britain. By April 1949, the two countries, together with Iceland, were founder signatories of the North Atlantic Treaty.

Signing the North Atlantic Treaty did not bring immediate assistance in the form of foreign troops to Denmark, Norway and Iceland. This was neither requested nor, at that time, offered. Indeed both Norway and Denmark issued unilateral statements that agreeing to the terms of the treaty would not lead to the stationing of foreign troops on their soil in peacetime. This was done partly to quieten public opinion, that still remembered the unhappy experience of wartime occupation, and in particular members of the ruling social democratic parties who had reservations about giving up neutrality. It was also meant to assure the Soviet Union that the two countries' subscription to the treaty would not bring US and British troops closer to their borders. There was the implication that this would prevent the Soviets from placing greater pressure on Finland.

Denmark, Iceland and Norway also joined the Organisation for European Economic Cooperation (OEEC) in 1948, thereby assisting their receiving Marshall Aid; and in 1949 Denmark and Norway became founder members of the Council of Europe (Iceland joined in 1950) which brought together the democratic countries of Europe. So by 1950 the three countries were part of the 'Western World' and economically, politically and strategically were tied to the USA and the United Kingdom.

From 1950 the policies that emerged in the 1947 to 1949 period were continued and refined. In the security field the three countries trod a fine line between greater integration with what became NATO and establishing a distance between themselves and the major powers in the organisation. These reactions reflected the need of the countries to 'buy in' security from outside in the forms of promises to assist in times of crisis, military infrastructure and exercises, and their wish not to allow the Nordic area to become too militarised or a source of tension between the sides in the Cold War. Denmark and Norway were thus prominent in promoting détente in the late 1960s and 1970s and in opposing the siting of US nuclear missiles in Europe in 1957. In the 1980s, public opinion in the two states also expressed reservations about the placing of US intermediate-range missiles in Western Europe (though they were not to be deployed in Denmark, Iceland or Norway). At the same time both Norway and Denmark were becoming more a part of NATO's integrated military command structure than ever before.

All three states showed some reservations about the political and economic integration of Europe. The intergovernmental cooperation of the OEEC and the Council of Europe (even with the latter's parliamentarians' meeting) did not undermine the sovereignty of the states, but the three saw no reason to become involved in the building of 'Community Europe', either in the European Coal and Steel Community (ECSC) in 1951 or the European Economic and Atomic Energy Communities (EURATOM) in 1957. Instead Denmark and Norway followed the British lead and, in 1960, became founder members of the European Free Trade Association (EFTA), an organisation with none of the supranational characteristics of the Communities.

However, once the United Kingdom decided to join the European Communities (EC), Denmark and Norway also negotiated settlements. Denmark joined the EC, together with the UK and Eire, in 1973, but Norwegian membership was rejected in a referendum in September 1972. Even within the EC, Denmark has shown a scepticism about some aspects of European integration, in particular when it came to handing over powers to EC institutions in the form of the Single European Act of 1986. A grouping opposing further integration – and indeed EC membership – was successful in returning members to the European Parliament in elections from 1979. Meanwhile the political scars caused by the 1972 referendum in Norway prevented the membership issue from surfacing in that country, and governments contented themselves with developing their free trade and other functional links with the EC.

During the early postwar period, Norway, Iceland and Denmark were recipients of Marshall Aid, helping them to rebuild economies adversely affected by the war. Sweden did not have such a need, and Finland had to pay reparations to the Soviet Union. By the 1960s all the Nordic states were comparatively prosperous and were candidates for giving assistance to the emerging Third World. None of them had colonies (since 1953 when Greenland was incorporated into Denmark), but all had active church missionaries in Africa and Asia. Aid throughout most of the 1960s was aimed, ostensibly, at raising 'poor people's standard of living' (Barnes 1980: 142), but other factors – for instance, missionary connections – made some strange links, such as that between socialist Sweden and feudal Ethiopia (Barnes 1980: 143). While Swedish aid policy in the 1970s tended to be more radical, supporting 'progressive' governments such as those in Cuba and North Vietnam (Barnes 1980: 144), Norwegian policy was more generally aimed at the broad perspective of North–South relations (Stokke 1993: 91). Danish policy remained 'low-key' and passive in its response to the Third World (Holm 1979: 95–7). Nevertheless, Denmark and Norway joined the other Nordic countries and the Netherlands in forming 'the Like-Minded Countries' group in 1975, being a meeting of those states that took a 'constructive and responsive attitude towards Third World demands for a New International Economic Order' (Dolman 1979: 57).

Continuity tended to typify the two states' policy towards the Third World during the 1980s (Stokke 1993: 92), though Danish policy also had to be seen in the context of that of the European Communities.

NEW PERCEPTIONS

After the collapse of the communist regimes in Central and Eastern Europe in late 1989, the security position of the NATO Nordic states – and of NATO itself – changed considerably.

At the same time as the Soviet Union was collapsing – at the end of 1991 – Western Europe was trying to integrate more closely. At the Maastricht summit of the EC, held in December 1991, it was agreed to create the European Union, which would include the EC, economic and monetary union and cooperation on justice and home affairs and on foreign and security policies. However, the forces of disintegration that had wracked the Soviet bloc were also to undermine West European efforts towards greater unity.

The response of Denmark and Norway to these historic events in Europe showed some differences. In examining the security policies of the two states during the post-1989 period, it can be seen that they both analysed the new situation in similar terms. Defence commissions and committees in the two states were initially cautious about the turn of events in Central and Eastern Europe, but then recognised that the old threat of a possible invasion from the East had disappeared. They also accepted that the threat had been replaced by new uncertainties, not least those of insecurity and instability in Europe (Archer 1994a). However, the Danish response was somewhat more relaxed than that of Norway, which still identified Russia as a source of direct threat to itself.

The response of the two states to Maastricht was also different. That of the Danish people was to reject the Treaty on European Union in a referendum in 1992, and only to accept the agreement once it had been revised at the EC Edinburgh Summit later that year. This allowed Denmark to hold back on defence and justice cooperation, and also to have the possibility of opting out of economic and monetary union. The Norwegian response was to come closer to the proposed Union, first by negotiating – together with other EFTA states – a European Economic Area agreement that allowed Norway to be part of the EC's Single European Market, and then, in November 1992, to apply for full membership of the Union. However, the Norwegian electorate – as in 1972 – rejected membership.

Why were there these differences? In the case of their security response, the two countries were reflecting both their contrasting geo-strategic positions and the internal debates on defence.

The end of the Cold War had left Denmark without any obvious threat to its frontiers. The Soviet Union and Warsaw Treaty Organisation – previously on its doorstep – had disappeared, and even the uncertainties of the newly-independent Baltic states were at the other side of the Baltic Sea. However, Norway still had a northern frontier with Russia, a country awash with insecurity. Furthermore, that frontier bordered on what was still the largest concentration of military bases in the world, the Kola Peninsula. This led Denmark and Norway to see the question of the threat to their security after 1989 in different terms. While both agreed that general insecurity in Europe had replaced the old threat, Norway was more concerned by a continuation of a threat from the east, albeit in a different form than before (Archer 1994a).

It was also this security uncertainty that helped to fashion Norway's new approach to the EC and the emerging European Union. Whereas during the Cold War Norway had relied upon NATO and the US to provide it with extra security resources from outside in times of crisis, the ending of the Cold War meant an increased opportunity for US withdrawal of its troops and presence from Europe. At the same time, the states forming the EU were discussing giving it a defence dimension, and in the 1992 Treaty on European Union the Western European Union (WEU) was recognised as an interim institution for West European defence co-ordination. Norwegian politicians were willing to associate their country with this process and, for some of them, the security element was an important reason for joining the Union.

On the other hand, Denmark had no such security imperative and there was a feeling that the country should try to distance itself from any defence arrangements leading to the further integration of their armed forces with those of the other EC states, especially Germany. This was seen as a threat to Danish sovereignty. The responses of the two states will now be examined in more detail.

DENMARK AND THE CFSP

As has been indicated above, there were differences between the Danish approach towards the EC and European Political Cooperation (EPC) and subsequently the EU and CFSP – all of which Denmark was a part – and that of the outsider, Norway. Clearly a sizeable part of both states' populations had – and have – reservations about the concept of European Union, but this scepticism has not extended to the CFSP and the WEU as much in Norway as in Denmark. What have been Denmark's reservations in the post-1989 period and what accounts for their cool attitude?

The member states of the European Communities developed European Political Cooperation, the forerunner of CFSP, at just the point when Denmark joined the EC. As it was intergovernmental by nature, the Danish government did not demur, though they saw the EC primarily as a trade and economic association. The separation of EPC from the institutions of the EC, and its exclusion of defence and military aspects, suited Denmark. Denmark had not been a founder member of the WEU and saw no reason during the 1980s to join. Defence and security matters were considered best dealt with by NATO.

In the period immediately after the collapse of communism in central and east Europe in 1989, Denmark was placed in a new geo-strategic position. Two major factors changed. First, the adversary alliance of the Warsaw Treaty Organisation disappeared and Denmark found that it controlled the approaches to a Baltic Sea of friendly states rather than potentially hostile ones. Second, Germany was united. This led to the centre-right government placing a heavier emphasis on European Political Cooperation as a means of controlling unified Germany through European institutions (Mouritzen 1993: 379).

However, this government had already had a warning about Danish lukewarm feelings on European integration at the time of the ratification of the Single European Act. This was opposed by two mainstream parties – the Social Democrats and the Radical Liberals – as well as the usual anti-EC forces. A referendum was 56 per cent in favour on a 75 per cent turnout, compared with 63 per cent in favour of EC membership on a 90 per cent turnout in 1972 (Schou 1992: 337–8). In the period before the Maastricht summit, the Danish parliament discussed Denmark's stance and there was broad agreement that any Common Foreign and Security Policy should be based on intergovernmental cooperation, that security cooperation should more be the task of NATO and the CSCE than of the European Union, and that Denmark should not be involved in the WEU or any plans for a European army (Schou 1992: 346–58). The Foreign Minister, Uffe Ellemann Jensen, seemed more positive about an EU involvement in security, including military, matters but what he accepted at the Maastricht summit was accepted by most of the other parties in the Danish parliament, which supported the Treaty on European Union by 130 votes to 25 (*Udenrigsministeriet* 1992: 42). The Conservative and Liberal coalition were joined by the Social Democrats, the Radical Liberals and the Centre Democrats (Schou 1992: 361).

A subsequent referendum on the ratification of the Treaty by Denmark resulted in a 50.7 per cent 'No' vote, and a Common Foreign and Security Policy was one of the elements to which Danish voters responded negatively. When the Danish government came to negotiate a settlement with the other EC governments that they could place before the Danish people, defence was one of the major issues. In the 'National Compromise' worked out between the main Danish political parties, it was required that Denmark should not participate in the defence policy dimension (Petersen 1993: 93). The agreed statement at the Edinburgh Summit of EC leaders in December 1992 was that Denmark would not be obliged to become a member of the WEU and would not participate in 'the elaboration and implementation of decisions and actions of the Union which have defence implications', though Denmark could rescind such a constraint at any time (Petersen 1993: 100). However, Denmark took up observer status with the WEU in November 1992 and indeed the question of full membership was one that caused a split in the opposition Social Democrats just before they changed leader in April 1992 (Schou 1992: 362).

Since the establishment of the European Union in November 1993, Denmark has participated in the CFSP. The priorities that have been agreed by the ministers – humanitarian assistance in Yugoslavia, support for the democratic process in Russia and South Africa, the stabilisation process in Europe – have all been fully supported by the new Social Democrat–Radical Liberal government in Denmark. This government, like its Nordic neighbours, has also given full support to the CSCE process but this has not proved incompatible with CFSP activity.

Denmark has been silent over the development of Europe's defence. The WEU has developed its relations with NATO and has started to emerge as the European pillar of the Atlantic Alliance, as well as the defence institution of the EU. The United States' disengagement from the defence of Europe has continued apace and 1994 did not see any diminution of the security challenges and uncertainties around the EU. Membership of the EU by Austria, Finland and Sweden from 1 January 1995 means that the Union contains three neutral (or non-aligned) states that could become members of the WEU. Membership by Finland gives the Union a long frontier with the Russian Federation. Russian involvement in Chechenia has brought further uncertainty in Europe.

All these factors would suggest that the time is now ripe for full Danish membership of the WEU, allowing it a full voice in the negotiations about the EU's defence aspect and the future of the WEU. Concerns about being brought into a European army could certainly be calmed and Denmark could consider on what conditions it would contribute to a European defence within the EU as well as within NATO. A paper by the Board of the Danish Commission on Security and Disarmament suggested – already in early 1992 – that by remaining outside WEU 'Denmark runs the risk of weakening its membership of NATO. Denmark is close to becoming isolated on this question.' In particular, doubt was expressed about the long-term structure of NATO (SNU 1992: 50). However, the Danish electorate might want to strike out any result of the 1996 Intergovernmental Conference that they consider moves too far towards a more unified EU, especially in the area of defence. Danish governments may find their hands tied on this issue for some time to come.

NORWAY AND THE CFSP

Norway has been on the outside while the Treaty on European Union, containing the development of the Common Foreign and Security Policy, was fashioned. This has not meant that Norway has held back from having an active foreign policy itself or from cooperating with the EU over foreign policy issues. From 1980, Norway had twice-yearly informal meetings with the EPC's presidency at foreign minister level, and in 1988 these meetings were formalised and assisted by meetings at the official level. However, whilst this kept Norway informed of the main points of EPC activity, influence over the process was limited (*Utenriksdepartementet* 1994: 337). NATO membership was anyhow the keystone of Norwegian security policy.

In the post-1989 period Norway has continued to stress the importance of NATO but has also realised that 'in the coming years, to a greater degree Europe must take a larger responsibility for its own security' (Brundtland 1994: 426, author's translation). Meanwhile Norway quietly took up associate membership of the WEU which was offered to the NATO-Europe non-EC states after the Maastricht Intergovernmental Conference of December 1991.

In opening its membership negotiations, Norway's Trade Minister, Bjorn Tore Godal, pointed out that NATO membership and cooperation between Europe and North America would continue to be of importance for Norway's security, and that Norway shared the same foreign policy aims as its European partners. He pointed to Norway's strategic position in Europe's northern corner, with its common border to Russia (*Utenriksdepartementet* 1994: 432). Indeed, the issue of the EU's Common Foreign and Security policy was quickly agreed between Norway and the Union negotiators, who were anyhow more concerned with Austria, Finland and Sweden in that area.

During the internal debate before the Norwegian referendum on EU membership, the major issues were ones of sovereignty, fisheries, regional policy and agriculture. In launching her campaign for membership, Mrs Brundtland stressed that this would provide Norway with security in an uncertain world (EIU 1994: 8). However, for the rest of the campaign security policy was a marginal issue, coming to the fore when some of the 'Yes' campaigners implied that a 'No' vote would be a vote against NATO. This was immediately denied by those anti-membership campaigners who had always backed Norwegian membership of NATO.

The start of membership negotiations with the EU, Norway – like the other applicants – had a more intensive dialogue with EPC and its successor in the institutions of the CFSP, which included increased contact with about half of the 25 working groups associated with the CFSP process (*Utenriksdepartementet* 1994: 337).

What has Norway to offer the CFSP? It is noticeable that the CFSP priorities of the European Council outlined in their Brussels meeting in October 1993 were ones that have also been Oslo's:

- to further stability and peace in Europe by supporting the democratisation process and strengthening regional cooperation in Central and Eastern Europe;
- support for the work for peace in the Middle East, especially the Oslo Treaty on Palestinian home rule;
- support for the development towards democracy and majority rule in South Africa;
- support for the peace process and humanitarian aid in former Yugoslavia;
- underpinning of the democratisation process in Russia (*Utenrikesdepartementet* 1994: 340).

Norwegian foreign policy since 1989 has given strong support to the process of democratisation in Central and Eastern Europe, in particular in the Baltic states and in CSCE forums. Norwegian participation in talks between the PLO and the Israelis was instrumental in bringing together the two sides, a task that the international conference sponsored by the EC and the USA had failed to achieve (Egeland 1994: 349–51). Norway, like its Nordic neighbours, had given strong support to the ANC in South Africa, often through secret contacts. The Norwegians are also present in the peace-keeping operations in former Yugoslavia and have given generously in humanitarian aid. In all these fields, Norway has proved that it is not only willing to participate in the CFSP but has something to contribute beyond what could be expected from a country its size.

However, it is in its – and the EU's – relations with Russia that Norway has a special point to make. Norway is the only NATO country to have a common frontier with Russia, for which the northern areas have increased military significance. It is thus important that Russia does not offer a military threat to Norway in the north. Norwegian membership of the EU was thus seen as a way of linking Russia to the EU and as increasing European involvement in the northern areas. In particular the threat posed to the environment by Russian nuclear power stations and waste is seen as a problem needing a common European solution (*Utenriksdepartementet* 1994: 84–5). For these reasons, Norway was in the forefront of the initiative to establish a Barents Euro-Arctic Council in 1992 together with Russia, the other Nordic states and the European Communities. This initiative has encouraged regional cooperation and placed an emphasis on environmental matters (Stokke and Tunander 1994). It allowed Norway to present a strong northern and Arctic profile to the EU in its membership negotiations. This had the added advantage of multilateralising Norway's non-military relationship with the Russians in the north and encouraging the regional basis of the reform process in the latter country.

The CFSP was seen by Norway as one of the instruments available in the effort to produce a secure Europe. Norway has been active in the UN – including its peacekeeping operations – in the CSCE and in NATO. It is now an associate of the WEU and came to the brink of EU membership. Life outside the Union will not see Norway denuded of forums to pursue its particular view of security. However, it will place it aside from a central element in European security and foreign policy of the 1990s and beyond, and will limit its influence on the development of the EU's policy in Northern Europe.

A NOTE ON ICELAND

Iceland's foreign and security policy was determined by two factors before the end of the Cold War. One was its strategic position in the North Atlantic, in between North America and Western Europe. The presence of US military installations on Iceland dominated Icelandic security policy. This and its membership of NATO tied it firmly to the Atlantic Alliance. A series of agreements between Iceland and the USA allowed the United States to operate out of the Keflavik defence area while the Icelanders limited the cultural impact of the base and kept a civilian presence there.

The second element was the domination of Icelandic foreign policy by its dependence on fisheries. Iceland extended its fisheries limits from the 1950s to the 1970s, thereby leading to 'Cod Wars' with the United Kingdom, its NATO ally though competitor for fish stocks. Since then Iceland has attempted to maintain its access to fish stocks and to open the world market for the sale of its produce. While the European Economic Agreement with the EU provides certain market benefits for Iceland fish exports, these could be endangered after three EEA states have joined the EU and the EEA is left with only Norway and Iceland as members. Already an Icelandic foreign minister has talked about his country applying for membership of the EU, but this does not seem to be the policy of the coalition government nor of a majority of the *Althingi*. However, it is possible that Iceland could reconsider its position and apply for membership at a later stage, maybe when the Maltese and Cypriot applications are under consideration. Icelandic interests in any future CFSP would be those specifically associated with the development of the law of the sea and with the security situation in the North Atlantic.

CONCLUSIONS

The post-Cold War period has opened up a number of foreign and security policy options for the Nordic NATO states. They are no longer so constrained by the demands of bloc politics as before. Their external policies are not dominated by the existence on their doorstep of a hostile superpower bloc. Their security environment is anyhow now more complicated with the one large presumed threat being replaced by a range of uncertainties and insecurities. There are a wide range of often inter-locking security institutions available to the three states, the main ones being the UN, the Organisation for Security and Cooperation in Europe (OSCE – formerly the CSCE), NATO and the North Atlantic Cooperation Council (NACC), and the WEU. Other institutions have a security dimension, such as the EU, the Nordic Council, the Baltic Sea Council and the Barents Euro-Arctic Council. Foreign policy can be conducted unilaterally or on a cooperative basis through the institutions named.

The preference structures of the three states in the foreign and security field has, however, been constrained by domestic factors. All three states have limited their activities within NATO, not least as a response to domestic concerns. Norwegian public opinion has shown a continued reluctance to join the EC and EU, and important Danish political parties have been against involvement in the WEU. Iceland's concerns in any forum are fairly uni-dimensional, those of fisheries.

It is possible that this wider choice for the foreign policy makers of the three states, coupled with domestic constraints, will lead to less commitment internationally, or commitments spread more thinly. What are their likely hierarchies of preferences in their foreign and security policies in the latter part of the decade?

All three Nordic NATO states will continue their commitment to the UN, and Denmark and Norway will underpin this with troops for UN peacekeeping, though not for any operation that looks like becoming peace enforcement. In this they will be joined by Sweden and Finland who hold a similar view on peacekeeping. The last few years have seen an intensification of Nordic peacekeeping cooperation (Archer 1994b). The same urge to make their international environment more 'peace prone' will lead all the Nordic states to continue their active support of the OSCE.

Norway is faced with the reality of carrying out its own foreign and security policies in the shadow of those of the EU. Although it has maintained close co-ordination with the CFSP process, it is not a member. In particular, this may cause some difficulties in its relations with Russia. Should it try to associate itself with EU policy, thereby hoping to have the advantages of the weight of the EU in international affairs, or should it carve out its own niche with the danger that this could leave it isolated on some questions? One possibility could be to follow the Union in broad foreign and security matters but to make a distinctive Norwegian contribution on northern and Arctic matters. This would be a change from the existing pattern of initiatives in areas such as South Africa, Central America and the Middle East, but it would follow the initiative of the Barents Euro-Arctic Council.

Norway's – and Iceland's – problem with NATO is that its Atlantic element may be fast disappearing. In late 1994 Canada informed Norway that it would no longer be able to provide reinforcements for Norway, and the USA has been running down its pre-positioned stocks and collocated bases in Norway. Should both states estimate that they still need the promise of external assistance to bolster their security, where will this come from in the future? The hope of the Norwegian government was that a link with the EU would help provide an answer. It may be that Norway is close enough to its European neighbours, both geographically and politically, that it can anyhow expect such support through NATO and its associate status within the WEU.

Denmark's foreign and security preferences are different. It is, of course, concerned with the general insecurity in Europe. More specifically, the Danish people have shown a desire not to be integrated too far within the EU. Their reservations about a European army reflect this point and a more specific fear of greater control by Germany. The task of Danish politicians has thus been less that of finding the ties that bind – the Norwegian concern – and more one of loosening the connections.

It may be that, within a decade, the distinction between NATO and non-NATO Nordic states will be replaced by that between EU and non-EU Nordic states or between those that are within the WEU (or whatever replaces it) and those that stay outside. Once again the Nordic area will be shown to have a fault line on security matters.

Part V

Conclusion

18 Conclusion

Lee Miles

Much of the research on the European Union and the Nordic countries has so far focused upon the individual Nordic countries and their attempts at achieving EU accession. Indeed, this book also incorporates this methodology. Yet, little has been written on the implications for the European Union of wider Nordic membership and vice-versa. To some extent, this book will contribute to redressing this situation as it provides a review of EU–Nordic relations using chronological, state-centred and issue-based approaches.

Several important themes are prevalent within the evaluation undertaken here. There will be significant impacts for the Nordic countries resulting from wider EU membership both in terms of determining their domestic outcomes and by influencing their international relations. To a limited extent, these are the external consequences of the European Union's growing size and increased dynamism since the mid-1980s. In particular, the Single European Market (SEM) programme and the later Treaty on European Union (TEU) transformed the nature of relations between the EU and non-member states.

THE IMPLICATIONS OF EU MEMBERSHIP FOR THE NORDIC COUNTRIES

There has been a noticeable movement by the Nordic countries from informal to formal integration in relation to the European Union. During the 1980s, EC initiatives were merely 'shadowed' by the Nordic governments. Domestic legislation based on EC principles or policies was approved by the Nordic legislatures in order to avoid any competitive disadvantages for their firms when trading within the EU's market.

However, this informal shadowing of EU legislation was soon deemed to be insufficient, as the EU was beginning to embark on even more advanced policies. At this point, formal integration (which often included common supranational structures) was adopted to allow non-member states further access to the SEM, such as through the European Economic Area (EEA). Yet, the EEA proved to most of the Nordic countries that formal integration must also include full participation in decision-making structures if it is to be successful in governing EU–Nordic relations in the longer term. In sum, there are no comprehensive alternatives to full EU membership for the Nordic countries if they require complete political as well as economic access to future EU policy development.

The economic benefits for the Nordic countries of SEM access were mostly felt through the EEA. The main benefits of full EU membership for the Nordic countries must, therefore, mostly be in policy areas outside the SEM or covered in detail by the EEA. Agricultural and regional policies and environmental and social affairs are some of the first to spring to mind. In all these areas there has been strong domestic support within the Nordic countries for active state intervention and control and it is here that EU membership will have a direct impact. In some areas this will be positive, such as allowing Nordic consumers greater choice and lower prices. However, this will not always be fully appreciated within the Nordic countries as their acceptance of free competition has usually been qualified by an equivalent commitment towards maintaining stringent Nordic social protection, welfare provision and the prioritising of full employment policies.

Some of the effects will also be negative. Concerns over the continuation of high environmental standards in the Nordic countries is still an area of anxiety. Despite the agreement on the 'third option', it still remains unclear to what extent Nordic environmental policies will need to be overhauled. The experience of twenty years of Danish EU membership does not indicate that Swedish or Finnish standards will have to be lowered as the Danes have maintained strict environmental laws, irrespective of the weakness of EU environmental policy.

Perhaps the greatest impact of EU membership for the Nordic countries is psychological. EU membership is neither a single, self contained act nor an end in itself. It is instead part of a wider transition taking place in several Nordic countries. Their declining growth rates, the growing size of their public sectors and problems of budgetary imbalances during the 1980s were the first signs that their successful consensual and corporate systems needed widespread reform. Severe recession forced Sweden and Finland to consider that increased competition was now essential for their long-term survival. Full EU membership was seen by most Nordic governments as a way of accelerating domestic change by meeting new international obligations. Wider Nordic EU membership is an integral part of a new, albeit limited, era of austerity and liberalisation within the Nordic countries.

However, it is clear from the analysis within Part III that the Nordic domestic populations do not always share the view that this process is desirable. Although wider Nordic EU membership has gained momentum because of the domestic economic problems in the Nordic states, this has also facilitated a deep-seated domestic resistance in some quarters against

EU membership. Despite it being argued that full membership may be part of the solution to the economic ills of the Nordic countries, this does not make the antidote any more palatable or easy to bear. The issue of EU membership within the Nordic region has become subsumed within a wider domestic debate over the future of some kind of 'Nordic model' itself.

To the anti-EU campaigners, full membership continues to be seen as an effective governmental weapon to lead the attack upon welfare provision, stringent social and environmental standards, generous levels of agricultural support, women's rights and Nordic democracy. In practice, the EU membership issue has emphasised and will continue to emphasise traditional North and South, urban and rural and left and right divisions already present within the Nordic countries. EU membership strikes at the very heart of domestic debates regarding the integrity of these countries and raises sensitive issues such as national sovereignty, open government and neutrality. Much of the threat may be perceived rather than real, but the implications for developing domestic consensus on the merits of EU membership remain as challenging as ever.[1] From this perspective, the European Union must be willing to incorporate Nordic concerns about transparency in EU decision-making and a stronger EU commitment towards environmental and social affairs.

However, wider EU membership has very positive implications for the Nordic countries in terms of foreign affairs. The Nordic countries are ardent activists with respect to arms control, confidence-building measures and aid to the Third World. The United Nations is seen by them as a suitable framework for managing conflict, supporting international law and promoting human rights (Archer 1994b). Already by June 1995 – and as a case in point – Carl Bildt had been appointed as the EU's new chief negotiator for the former Yugoslavia (Miles 1995c). Their membership of the EU will strengthen the effectiveness of Nordic 'internationalism' as they may be able to harness the EU for collective support. Traditional Nordic values may have a greater bearing on the international scene, if the three Nordic full members can convince other member states to follow their path.

One question mark does, however, arise from the complexity of intra-Nordic relations. Some Nordic countries are EU full members while others remain outside. Problems do emerge from this situation regarding, for example, the short-term future of specialised Nordic arrangements. In the short term, the Nordic Passport Union and the Common Nordic Labour Market and in the longer term the relationship between the Nordic Council and the European Union will be affected. In spite of previous arrangements, the external barrier of the European Union will now run along the Swedish-Norwegian border, presenting technical problems for the common commercial policy (CCP) and an EU immigration and asylum policy. Part of these problems may be solved by wider Nordic membership of the Schengen agreement (Watson 1995: 1).

Nevertheless, the harmonisation of EU policy with Norway and Iceland must continue. This will be essential if the Nordic Passport Union and the Common Nordic Labour Market are to remain and if the external borders of the EU are to be effectively policed. Intra-Nordic cooperation will continue to be paramount regardless of the division between full and non-member states as the interests of the Nordic region and the European Union are inseparably inter-linked.

Thus, in terms of foreign relations, wider full EU membership will reinforce existing trends within the Nordic countries rather than lead to a radical reorientation of policy. The accessions of Sweden and Finland in 1995 are the result of political and economic pressures over two decades which became irresistible after the imposition of severe recession in the early 1990s. The national interests of the Nordic countries have been and always will be heavily influenced by a mixture of intra-Nordic relations and economic interdependence with the rest of mainland Europe.

THE IMPACT OF THE NORDIC COUNTRIES ON THE EUROPEAN UNION

Judging the impact of the accessions of Sweden and Finland on the European Union is very difficult. The EU has embarked on yet another critical stage in its development. The 1996 Intergovernmental Conference (IGC) on the TEU aims to cover both institutional and policy reform and further enlargement to include Central and Eastern Europe will be on the agenda.

The 1995 enlargement was more symbolic than important as an EU event, due to the high level of compatibility between the Twelve and the new member states. The 1995 accessions represented the last of the classical enlargements. The EU simply absorbed the new members by swelling the size of its institutions and tweaking existing policies to incorporate a wider multiplicity of national interests. Yet, the accessions of Austria, Finland and Sweden have brought the EU to an 'enlargement threshold' of fifteen members. They have numerically increased the EU to such a large size that any future convoys of applicants cannot be seriously considered without prior or simultaneous radical reform of the EU's decision-making structures and policy areas. The 1995 enlargement did not actually force widespread reform, but has made the EU such a large critical mass that future reform is now inevitable and essential. The forthcoming 1996 review of the TEU does provide the Nordic members with an opportunity to influence the future development of the European Union and to force new issues to the fore. All three Nordic EU members have stated that they intend to cooperate to force three issues to be given a higher profile.

The two existing areas of social and environmental policy will be targeted. These governments wish to see the continued development of an EU strategy for full employment in Europe based around the two EU White

Papers on Growth, Competitiveness and Employment (1993) and Social Policy (1994). As the Swedish European Affairs Minister, Ulf Dinkelspiel noted in April 1993, they 'looked forward to actively contributing to the further development of . . . the working environment and the dialogue of social partners'. The impact of the new Nordic EU members in the social policy area has been quickly felt. The Swedish government, for example, proposed in September 1995 that a new 'employment chapter' should be added to the EU Treaties at the forthcoming 1996 IGC and that fighting unemployment should become a major priority for the EU. The Nordic members will also 'expect that the highest level of ambition will apply in the environmental area and there will be no lowering of standards' (Dinkelspiel 1993: 4). The first Finnish EU Commissioner, Erkki Liikanen, in 1995 estimated that EU environmental policy would take up a place comparable to that of economic and monetary union on the EU's political agenda.

The Nordic EU members will also agitate for greater transparency in EU decision-making. Pressure has been brought to bear since Sweden and Finland became full members in January 1995. In April 1995 the Swedish, Finnish and Danish delegations jointly proposed to the Council of Ministers that its minutes and voting outcomes should be published for public consumption.

To some extent, the championing of these issues by the Nordic governments is both an offensive and defensive strategy. These are natural areas for these governments to focus upon given their domestic policies. In these fields they are the European pace-setters and can provide expert leadership. Yet, their insistence on high EU standards and speedy progress towards them also reflects their national interests and their concern that their own stringent standards should not be compromised.

Their impact on some of the European Union's future flagship policies is hard to gauge; although this is mainly due to the embryonic nature of many of the new TEU based policies. The economic weakness of the two new Nordic members makes it unlikely that they will be able to participate in the first batch of countries to move to the third stage of economic and monetary union (see Chapter 11). Their high levels of budgetary deficits and national debt combined with the relative instability of the Swedish Krona and the Finnish Markka mean that they will probably be unable to meet the convergence criteria for moving to fixed exchange rates and an eventual single currency. Domestic political support for EMU is also questionable.

In terms of the EU's Justice and Home Affairs (JHA) pillar, these countries may play a role. The Swedish Social Democratic government's attempts at tightening up immigration controls seems to strike a chord with policy changes in several other member states. It will probably enhance the prospect of achieving a common immigration and asylum policy. The Nordic countries seem to be moving away from their traditional and open immigration policy towards the mainland European trend of restricting future immigration. EU membership will probably reinforce the existing domestic public opinion on immigration issues within Sweden and Finland. A question also concerns the role of non-aligned Sweden and Finland in the development of a Common Foreign and Security Policy (CFSP). As previous chapters have shown, many of the difficulties with their participation in the CFSP have been removed as Sweden and Finland have moved away from strict interpretations of neutrality. Their future full membership of the Western European Union (WEU) and any defence structure is far less certain though. The existing Swedish and Finnish policy view is that they will review full WEU membership in the future.

For the European Union, the inclusion of two additional Nordic countries will be beneficial in the longer term. These countries will contribute to EU finances and be active in the development of policy – for instance, Sweden's strong pressure to have new safety and health restrictions placed on the movement of live animals across borders in 1995. On both policy and institutional questions, they will have much to say and great experience to offer, especially given their high previous levels of cooperation in the Nordic Council and EFTA.

Yet, the inclusion of Sweden and Finland will have a larger psychological impact on the European Union than many anticipate. The three Nordic member states share a basic intergovernmental and economic based perspective regarding the merits of EU membership. Although they will seek the development of supranational policies in a few key areas, such as in environmental matters, these are mostly based on the defensive motives of protecting their own high standards. For the most part, the Nordic EU members will resist any radical extensions of the powers of the EU's institutions and especially the European Parliament. These countries have only reluctantly accepted supranationalism and do not share a commitment to a federalist view of European integration. They will alter the balance within the existing EU–15 in favour of a more cautious approach towards European integration. They could also weaken the influence of the existing member states pushing for federal solutions. From this perspective, it is likely that the accessions of Sweden and Finland will strengthen the demands for a multi-speed development of the EU. Their accessions should also help to redress the Mediterranean bias prevalent in the EU since the 1981 and 1986 enlargements. This will have obvious implications, such as providing greater resistance to the demands of the Mediterranean member states for further economic and social cohesion monies and probably a more EU cautious approach regarding its future financial commitments.

The 1995 Nordic enlargement should also bolster the international profile of the EU. By increasing its size, and by their claim to be the spokesmen for Europe, the Nordic countries will enhance the EU's international status. In the short term, the Nordic member states will sponsor the Baltic states as future EU applicants and insist on this region being given a prominent place on the EU's agenda. All three Nordic EU members, for example, were quick to welcome the full membership applications of Estonia, Latvia and Lithuania in late 1995. It is also likely that the developing world will find sympathy among the Nordic members in any future re-negotiations of the Lomé Conventions. The psychological influence of the Nordic countries on the EU will be political. However, this will be qualified by the reluctance of the Nordic countries to absorb any large EU financial liabilities due to their relative economic fragility.

DETERMINANTS OF THE LEVELS OF NORDIC INFLUENCE

In practice, the impact of EU membership on the Nordic countries and their effectiveness within the EU will depend on a number of important factors.

- *The success of Nordic cooperation*
  Denmark, Sweden and Finland will need both to champion their own Nordic interests within the EU and co-ordinate with the remaining Nordic non-member states on EU issues. This will require high levels of consultation between the governments and a visible intention to act as a unified three-state Nordic bloc within the EU's decision-making process. There is evidence to suggest that this already operates within the EU (see Chapter 2). Yet, formal and informal Nordic cooperation both inside and outside the EU and the relationship between the Nordic Council and the EU will need to be further developed.
- *The role of Norway and Iceland as 'EU Quasi-Members' by means of EEA membership*
  It will be essential that Norway's interests are also considered by the European Union due to the existence of specialised Nordic arrangements, the EEA, and that the EU's formal external border will run between Norway and Sweden. Regardless of the Norwegian rejection of EU membership in November 1994, specialised agreements on fisheries and the liberalisation of the energy sectors would still be advantageous (see Chapters 14 and 15).
- *Continued domestic opposition to EU membership within Sweden, Finland and Norway*
  Norway rejected EU membership in November 1994 mainly because of the outright opposition of important sectors of Norwegian society. In addition, despite Swedish and Finnish accession, there remains large opposition to EU membership in their Northern rural communities. In all cases, their respective governments will be sensitive to domestic criticism regarding EU policies for the foreseeable future and will resist attempts at undermining their welfare, social and environmental provisions. The speed of 'domestic naturalisation' to EU membership will be slow. Any future EU reforms or treaty ratification will have to be handled carefully due to the lack of domestic consensus within these

countries on EU issues. Danish style 'opt-outs' may not have appeared during the accession negotiations, but they cannot be ruled out for the Nordic countries in the future TEU review.

- *The speed of Swedish and Finnish economic recovery*
  The relative economic fragility of Sweden and Finland will inhibit their ability to participate fully in some of the EU's future key policies. At the government level, this will at least partially limit their influence on the EU's future development. At the domestic level, it will bolster concerns regarding the financial costs of EU membership for Sweden and Finland. For the moment, Sweden and Finland will remain 'EU middle-rankers' with a somewhat weaker level of influence as long as their economic problems continue. Only once these economic problems have been sufficiently addressed can Sweden and Finland fully utilise their new role as EU members.

Regardless of these factors, the combined membership of three Nordic states will guarantee that the interests of the Nordic region are represented as the EU enters a period of re-examination, revision and reform. The forthcoming 1996 TEU review will provide an opportunity for the Nordic countries to influence the development of EU policies. They could, however, provide another role as pivotal players in the review. In political and economic terms the three Nordic member states are situated between the supranational 'hard core' of the EU and the poorer members who constitute the Union's periphery. On some issues they will strengthen the dominance of the core, such as in environmental policy, by adding middle range powers to policy initiatives. On the other hand and on institutional issues in particular, they will provide numerical weight to those aiming to restrict the speedier integration of the EU core and to protect the interests of the periphery. Their role will be critical in determining the level of supranational advancement that the EU will undertake in the 1990s and in which areas.

In conclusion, wider Nordic EU membership should be viewed positively by both the Union and the Nordic countries. However, given their concerns over levels of supranationalism and maintaining national sovereignty their membership will not be an easy ride. For the Nordic region, the EU has become the dominant institutional framework influencing them and pressurising those Nordic countries who are not full members to join the fold. By 1995 the balance had tipped decisively in favour of wider Nordic full EU membership. Yet, although many may view complete Nordic EU membership as inevitable in the long term, the division between Nordic EU and non-EU members will remain for the foreseeable future, given the problems with Norwegian and Icelandic domestic support for full membership.

Nevertheless, this division has always been somewhat artificial. After all, the Nordic non-members have already secured specialist arrangements with the EU and complete exclusion for Norway and Iceland from EU affairs is virtually impossible. Their interests will still be partially guaranteed by their Nordic neighbours and by EEA participation. Yet, as the EU grows ever larger and as Norwegian oil and Icelandic fisheries resources become further depleted, there may be increasing demands for further attempts at full EU membership. Comprehensive membership of the EU for the entire Nordic region may remain as elusive as ever. However, the high degree of interdependence between the Nordic countries and the EU means that their futures remain permanently entwined.

NOTE

1 Indeed, the problems of maintaining domestic support even once an EU member is illustrated by the Swedish case. By the time of the Swedish European parliamentary election (17 September 1995), the majority of domestic public opinion had returned to being opposed to EU membership. In the election, the anti-EU Left Party and Greens made considerable gains (12.9 per cent and 17.2 per cent of the vote respectively compared to the previous 1994 general election outcomes of 5 per cent and 6.2 per cent), while the governing Social Democrats saw their share of the vote fall dramatically by a third (from 45.3 per cent to 28.1 per cent). By November 1995, some twelve months after the original referendum on EU membership, public opinion polls showed that only 26 per cent of Swedes were now in favour of EU membership compared to 52 per cent a year earlier.

Bibliography

Aaltonen, S. (1993) 'Agriculture and Food Industries in the Finnish National and Regional Economy', in L. Kettunen (ed.) *Finnish Argiculture and European Integration* 71, Helsinki: Agricultural Economics Research Institute (MTTL).

Aardal, B. (1994a) 'Hvorfor skaper EU så sterk debatt i Norge?' *Nationen*, 19/9/1994: 7.

—— (1994b) 'The 1994 Storting Election: Volatile Voters Opposing the European Union' *Scandinavian Political Studies* 17, 2: 171–80.

Akerholm, J. (1994) 'Finland's Experience with a Floating Exchange Rate', *Bank of Finland Bulletin* 68, 3.

Åkström, S. (1971) 'Schweden und die europäische Integration', *Europa-Archiv* 26, 12: 421–8.

Alanen, P. and Forsberg, T. (1989) 'The Evolution of Opinion about Foreign Policy in Finland from the 1960's till the 1980's', *Yearbook of Finnish Foreign Policy* 1988–9: 29–33.

Allen, D. and Smith, M. (1990) 'Western Europe's Presence in the Contemporary International Arena', *Review of International Studies* 16, 1: 19–32.

Allen, H. (1979) *Norway and Europe in the 1970s*, Oslo: Universitetsforlaget.

Althingi (1990) *Ìsland of Evrópa,* Reykjavik: Althingi.

Andersen, S. S. (1995) *Naerkontakt av tredje grad: Eus lisensdirektiv og norsk parvirkning*, Report to the PETRO-programme, (January) Oslo: Norwegian Research Council.

Andrén, N. (1967) 'Nordic Integration', *Cooperation and Conflict* (1): 1–25.

—— (1975) 'Sweden and Europe', *Cooperation and Conflict* 10, 1, 1975: 51–64.

—— (1982) 'Changing Strategic Perspectives in Northern Europe', in B. Sundelius (ed.) *Foreign Policies of Northern Europe*, Boulder, Col.: Westview Press: 73–106.

Andrén, N. and Möller, Y. (1990) *Från Undén till Palme. Svensk utrikespolitik efter andra världskriget*, Stockholm: Norstedts.

Angell, V. (ed.) (1992) *Norway Facing a Changing Europe: Perspectives and Options*, Oslo: Norwegian Institute of International Affairs.

Antola, E. (1981) 'Finland and the Prospects for Western European Integration in the 1980s', *Yearbook of Finnish Foreign Policy*: 37–48.

Antola, E. and Tuusvuori, O. (1983) *Länsi-Euroopan integraatio ja Suomi*, Helsinki: The Finnish Institute of International Affairs.

Apunen, O. (1977) *Paasikiven – Kekkosen linja*, Helsinki: Tammi.

Archer, C. (1994a) 'New Threat Perceptions: Danish and Norwegian Official Views', *European Security* 3, 4: 587–615.

—— (1994b) 'Conflict Prevention in Europe: the Case of the Nordic States and Macedonia', *Cooperation and Conflict* 29, 4: 367–86.

Arter, D. (1993) *The Politics of European Integration in the Twentieth Century*, Aldershot: Dartmouth.

Asp, K. and Holmberg, S. (1984) *Kampen om Kärnkraften. En om om väljare, massmedier och folkomröstningen 1980*, Stockholm: Publica.
Austvik, O.-G. (ed.) (1991) *Norwegian Gas in the New Europe*, Oslo: Vett & Viten.
—— (1993) 'Norwegian Petroleum and European Integration', in B. Nelsen (ed.) *Norway and the European Community. The Political Economy of Integration*, London: Praeger: 181–209.
Avery, G. (1994) 'The European Union's Enlargement Negotiations', *The Oxford International Review* (Summer): 27–32.
Aylott, N. (1995a) *Swedish Social Democracy and European Integration*, Paper prepared for the annual conference of the Political Studies Association, York (UK), (April).
—— (1995b) 'Back to the Future: The 1944 Swedish Election', *Party Politics* 1, 3: 419–29.
Bach, M. (1992) 'Eine leise Revolution durch Verwaltungsverfahren', *Zeitschrift für Soziologie* Jg. 21. Heft 1. (February): 16–30.
Bachrach, P. and Baratz, M. (1970) *Power and Poverty. Theory and Practice*, New York: Oxford University Press.
Back, P.-E. and Berglund, S. (1978) *Det svenska partiväsendet* (4th ed.), Stockholm: Almqvist & Wiksell.
Baldwin, R. (1992a) *The Economic Logic of the EFTA Countries Joining the EC*, Occasional paper 41, Geneva: EFTA Economic Affairs Department.
—— (1992b) *Is Bigger Better? The Economics of EC Enlargement*, London: Centre For Economic Policy Research.
—— (1994) *Towards An Integrated Europe*, London: Centre For Economic Policy Research.
Baragiola, P. (1991) *EC/EFTA: The Future European Economic Area*, Brussels: Club de Bruxelles.
Barnes, I. (1980) 'The Changing Nature of the Swedish Aid Relationship during the Social Democratic Period of Government', *Cooperation and Conflict* 15, 3: 141–50.
Bayoumi, T. and Eichengreen, B. (1992) *Is There a Conflict Between EC Enlargement and European Monetary Unification?*, Discussion Paper 646, London: Centre for Economic Policy Research.
Bechtoldt, H. (1979) 'Finland and its Specific Neutrality', *Aussenpolitik* 30, 3: 247–57.
Bennulf, M. (1994) 'Sensation att milljöpartiet kom tillbaka', *Göteborgs-Posten*, 21 September.
Berg, U. (1994) 'Norwegian Economic Policy on a Steady Course', *Financial Review* 4, Oslo: Norwegian Bankers' Association.
Berge, O. (1972) 'The Expectations of the Government, Administrations and the Organizations Toward EFTA', in Nils Örvik (ed.) *Fears and Expectation: Norwegian Attitudes towards European Integration*, Oslo: Universitetsforlaget: 134–77.
Bergquist, M. (1969) 'Sweden and the European Economic Community', *Cooperation and Conflict* 4, 1: 1–12.
—— (1971) 'Research Communications: Sweden and the EEC: A Study of Four Schools of Thought and their Views on the Swedish Common Market Policy in 1961–62', *Cooperation and Conflict* 6, 1: 39–56.
Bernitz, U. (1986) 'The EEC–EFTA Free Trade Agreements with Special Reference to the Position of Sweden and other Scandinavian EFTA countries', *Common Market Law Review* 23, 3: 567–90.
Bille, L. (1992) 'Denmark', in R. Katz and P. Mair (eds) *Party Organizations: A Data Handbook*, London: Sage: 199–272.
Binswanger, H. and Mayrzedt, H. (1970) *Die Neutralen in der europäischen*

Integration: Kontroversen, Konfrontationen, Alternativen, Wien: Wilhelm Braumüller.
—— (1972) *Europapolitik der Rest-EFTA-Staaten*, Zurich: Polygraphischer Verlag.
Bissell, R. and Gasteyger, C. (eds) (1990) *The Missing Link: West European Neutrals and Regional Security*, Durham: Duke University Press.
Bjørklund, T. (1982) 'The Demand For Referendum: When Does it Arise and When Does it Succeed?', *Scandinavian Political Studies* 5, 3: 237–59.
—— (1994a) 'En reprise fra 1972?', *Dagbladet*, 30/11/94: 3.
—— (1994b) *Public Opinion in Norway, Sweden and Finland Towards Membership in the EU Prior to the Referenda in the Autumn 1994*, Working Paper 2/94, Oslo: Institute of Political Science.
Bonham, G. M. (1969) 'Scandinavian Parliamentarians: Attitudes toward Political Integration', *Cooperation and Conflict* 4, 3: 149–61.
Boyens, J. (1963) 'Integrationsprobleme für Schweden und Finnland', *Aussenpolitik* 14, 6: 401–10.
Branner, H. (1992) 'På Vagt eller på Spring?', in N. B. Thomsen (ed.) *The Odd Man Out? Danmark og den Europæiske Integration 1948–1992*, Odense: Odense Universitetsforlag.
Brown-Humes, C. (1995) 'A Bridge over Troubled Waters', Sweden Survey, *Investors Chronicle*, 24 February: 83.
Brundtland, A. O. (1966) 'The Nordic Balance – Past and Present', *Cooperation and Conflict* 2, 2: 30–63.
—— (1968) 'Norwegian Foreign Policy – Cooperation in Three Overlapping Circles', *Cooperation and Conflict* 3, 3: 169–83.
Brundtland, G. H. (1992) *Statement to the Storting Concerning the Norwegian Application For Membership of the EC*, Oslo: UD, 16 November.
—— (1994) 'Statsministerens redegjorelse for Stortinget om norsk soknad om medlemskap i EF, 16 November 1992', in *Om medlemskap i Den europeiske union. Stortingsmelding nr. 40 (1993–1994)*, Oslo: Utenriksdepartementet: 424–30.
Camps, M. (1964) *Britain and the European Community 1955–1963*, London: Oxford University Press.
Carlsnaes, W. and Smith, S. (1994) *European Foreign Policy – the EC and Changing Perspectives in Europe*, London: Sage.
Carlsson, I. (1990), in *Dagens Nyheter*, 27/5/1990, p. 2.
—— (1992) 'Prime Minister Carlsson's 14 June 1991 Declaration Regarding Swedish Membership in the EC', *Documents on Swedish Foreign Policy 1991*, Stockholm: Swedish Institute.
Cerny, P. G. (1993) 'Plurilateralism: Structural Differentiation and Functional Conflict in the Post-Cold War World Order', *Millennium* 22, 1: 22–51.
Childs, M. (1980) *Sweden: the Middle Way on Trial*, New Haven, Mass.: Yale University Press.
Christensen, J. (1992) 'Danmark, Norden og EF', in N. B. Thomsen (ed.) *The Odd Man Out? Danmark og den Europæiske Integration 1948–1992*, Odense: Odense Universitetsforlag: 135–53.
Church, C. (1991) *EFTA and the European Community*, London: University of North London Press.
Closse, W. (1964) 'Les Pays Scandinaves et la C.E.E.', *Chronique de la Politique Étrangère* 17, 6: 697–768.
Commission of the ECs (1981) *Answer given by Mr Haferkamp on behalf of the Commision on 1 April 1981 to the Written Question No 1620/80 by Mrs Walz of 25 November 1980*, OJ No C 103, 6/5/1981, Brussels.
—— (1983) *The EC and EFTA liberalise industrial trade on 1 January 1984. Statement by Vice-President Wilhelm Haferkamp*, Spokesman's Group, Brussels, December 1983.

—— (1985) *Completing the Internal Market*, COM (85) 310, Brussels.
—— (1988) *Proposal for a Council Directive on the Procurement Procedures of Entities providing Water, Energy and Transport Services*, COM (88) 377, Brussels.
—— (1989a) *Background Report*, ISEC/B25/89, 11/10/89, London.
—— (1989b) *Transparency of Consumer Energy Prices*, COM (89) 123, Brussels.
—— (1989c) *Draft Directive on Natural Gas Transportation*, COM (89) 334, Brussels.
—— (1989d) *Draft Directive on Electricity Transportation*, COM (89) 336, Brussels.
—— (1989e) *Communication from the Commission Concerning its Action Programme Relating to the Implementation of the Community Charter of Basic Social Rights for Workers*, COM (89) 568, Brussels.
—— (1992a) *Treaty on European Union*, Brussels.
—— (1992b) Europe and the Challenge of Enlargement, *Bulletin of the EC*, Supplement 3/92, Brussels.
—— (1992c) The Challenge of Enlargement: The Commission's Opinion on Sweden's Application for Membership, *Bulletin of the EC*, Supplement 5/92, Brussels.
—— (1992d) The Challenge of Enlargement: The Commission's Opinion on Finland's Application for Membership, *Bulletin of the EC*, Supplement 6/92, Brussels.
—— (1992e) *The Internal Market after 1992: Meeting the Challenge: Report by the High Level Working Group on the Operation of the Internal Market*, Sutherland Report 28/10/1992, Brussels.
—— (1992f) *Towards Sustainability. A Community Programme of Policy and Action in Relation to the Environment* (Fifth Environmental Action Programme), COM (92) 23 FINAL, Brussels.
—— (1992g) COM (92) 110 FINAL, Brussels.
—— (1993a) *Council Directive 93/104/EEC* 23/11/93 concerning certain aspects of working time, OJ L 307 – 13.12.93, Brussels.
—— (1993b) *Reinforcing the Effectiveness of the Internal Market*, COM (93) 256 FINAL, 2/6/1993, Brussels.
—— (1993c) *Green Paper – European Social Policy: Options for the Union*, COM (93) 551, Brussels.
—— (1993d) COM (93) 600 FINAL, Brussels.
—— (1993e) *Making the Most of the Internal Market: the Strategic Programme*, COM (93) 632 FINAL, Brussels.
—— (1993f) *Administrative Structures for Environmental Management in the European Community*, Brussels: European Environment Agency Task Force.
—— (1994a) *The EEA Agreement*, ISEC/B19/94, Brussels.
—— (1994b) 'Contribution to the Preparatory Work for the White Paper on Social Policy', *Social Europe*, 2: 94, Brussels.
—— (1994c) *European Social Policy – A Way Forward for the Union – A White Paper*, COM (94) 333 FINAL, Brussels.
—— (1994d) *Treaty on the Accession of Austria, Finland and Sweden to the European Union*, OJ C241 37 (August), Brussels.
—— (1994e) *Financial Perspective With a View to Enlargement of the European Union*, COM (94) 398 FINAL, Brussels.
—— (1994f) *Eleventh Report on the Application of Community Law*, COM (94) 500 FINAL, 22/4/1994, Brussels.
—— (1995) *Impact of the Three New Member States on the European Union*, background Report, B/06/95, Brussels.
Committee on Foreign Affairs and Security (1994a) *Report on Finland's Application to Join the European Union*, Titley Report (April), Brussels: European Parliament.

—— (1994b) *Report on Norway's Application to Join the European Union*, Jepsen Report (April), Brussels: European Parliament.

—— (1994c) *Report on the Outcome of the Negotiations on Sweden's Application for Accession to the European Union*, Rossetti Report (April), Brussels: European Parliament.

Committee on the Environment, Public Health and Consumer Protection (1994a) *Report on the Environmental Aspects of the Enlargement of the Community to include Sweden, Austria, Finland and Norway*, Bjornvig Report, (January), Brussels: European Parliament.

—— (1994b) *Report on the Need to Assess the True Costs to the Community of the Non-Environment*, Pimenta Report (February), Brussels: European Parliament.

Council of the ECs (1984) *Preliminary Report from the Ad-Hoc Committee on Institutional Questions to the European Council* (3–4 December), Brussels.

—— (1992) *Conclusions of the Presidency in Edinburgh 11–12 December 1992*, Brussels.

Dagens Nyheter, 12/11/1992.

Dalsager, P. (1972) 'Derfor siger jeg Ja', *Ringkøbing Amts Dagblad*, 16.9.1972.

Damgaard, E. (ed.) (1992) *Parliamentary Change in the Nordic Countries*, Oxford: Scandinavian University Press/OUP.

De Clercq, W. (1985) *Speech at the EC–EFTA Ministerial Meeting*, Interlaken, 20 May 1987, *The Community and the EFTA Countries: Implementation of the Joint Declaration issued at Luxemburg on 9 April 1984. Communication from the Commission to the Council*, COM (85) 206 FINAL (13 May), Brussels.

—— (1987) in 'Joint Conclusions, Reykjavik, 5 June 1986', *Twenty-Sixth Annual Report of the European Free Trade Association 1986*, Geneva: EFTA Secretariat: 50.

Delegation of Finnish Business Life (1995) *Suomalaisten EU-kannanotot*, 1987–1994, Helsinki: The Delegation of the Finnish Business Life.

Delors, J. (1989) 'Statement on the Broad Lines of Commission Policy', *Bulletin of the European Communities*, Supplement 1/89, Brussels: 17.

—— (1990) 'Introduction of the Commission's Programme for 1990 by the President of the Commission of the European Communities', *Bulletin of the European Communities*, Supplement 1/90, Brussels: Commission of the ECs.

Derry, T. K. (1979) *A History of Scandinavia: Norway, Sweden, Denmark, Finland and Iceland*, Minneapolis: University of Minnesota Press.

Dinan, D. (1994) *Ever Closer Union?*, London: Lynne Rienner/Macmillan.

Dinkelspiel, U. (1994) *Statement at the Opening of Sweden's Accession Negotiations*, Stockholm, Ministry of Foreign Affairs: 4.

Dolman, A. J. (1979) 'The Like-Minded Countries and New International Order: Past, Present and Future Prospects', *Cooperation and Conflict* 14, 2/3: 57–85.

Economic and Social Committee (1994) *Opinion of the Committee on the Annual Report on the Functioning of the Internal Market* (September), Brussels.

Economic Commission for Europe (1993) *Economic Bulletin For Europe* 44, New York: United Nations.

—— (1994) *Economic Survey of Europe in 1993–94*, New York: United Nations.

Economist (1992a) *Join the Club*, 322, 22/2/1992.

—— (1992b) *Nightmare on ERM Street, II*, 325, 23/11/1992.

—— (1993) *Farewell Welfare*, 329, 23/10/1993.

—— (1995) *Sweden and Finland*, 330, 14/1/1995: 12.

Economist Intelligence Unit (1994) *Country Report Norway*, 3rd quarter 1994, London: EIU.

Egeland, J. (1994) 'Norway's Middle East Peace Channel – an Insider's View', *Security Dialogue* 25, 3: 349–51.

Eggertsson, T. (1975) 'Determinants of Icelandic Foreign Relations', *Cooperation and Conflict* 10, 1/2: 91–9.

Eide, E. B. (1990) 'Europa-debatten i Arbeiderpartiet: Forholdet mellom "Konfoderale" og "foderale" posisjoner', *Internasjonal Politikk* 48, 3.

Elaissen, K. A. (1993) *Norwegian Membership of the EC: Why is it so Controversial?*, Working Paper 51, Oslo: Norwegian School of Management.

Elder, N., Thomas, A. H. and Arter, D. (1988) *The Consensual Democracies? The Government and Politics of the Scandinavian States*, revised edition, Oxford: Blackwell.

European Communities/European Free Trade Association (1985) 'Joint Declaration of the Ministerial Meeting between the European Community and its Member States and the States of the European Free Trade Association, Luxembourg, 9 April 1984', in *Twenty-Fourth Annual Report of the European Free Trade Association 1984*, Geneva: EFTA Secretariat: 54.

—— (1988a) 'Joint Conclusions of the Meeting between EFTA Ministers and Mr Eilly De Clercq, Member of the EC Commision, Interlaken, 20 May 1987', in *Twenty-Seventh Annual Report of the European Free Trade Association 1987*, Geneva: EFTA Secretariat: 44.

—— (1988b) 'Joint Communique from the Meeting between Ministers of the Member States of EFTA and Mr Willy De Clercq, Member of the EC Commission, Geneva, 29 November 1988', in *Twenty-Eighth Annual Report of the European Free Trade Association 1988*, Geneva: EFTA Secretariat.

—— (1989a) 'Joint Declaration of the Ministerial Meeting between the European Community, its Member States and the States of the European Free Trade Association on the Internal Market, Brussels, 2 February 1988', in *Twenty-Eighth Annual Report of the European Free Trade Association 1988*, Geneva: EFTA Secretariat: 32.

—— (1989b) 'Joint Communique from the Meeting between the Ministers of the member states of EFTA and Mr Willy De Clercq, Geneva, 29 November 1988', in *Twenty-Eighth Annual Report of the European Free Trade Association 1988*, Geneva: EFTA Secretariat: 48–51.

—— (1990a) 'Final Declaration of the Meeting of the EFTA Heads of Government, Oslo, 14–15 March 1989', in *Twenty-Ninth Annual Report of the European Free Trade Association 1989*, Geneva: EFTA Secretariat: 36–7.

—— (1990b) 'Joint Declaration of the Ministerial Meeting between the European Community and its Member States and the Countries of the European Free Trade Association, Brussels, 19 December 1989', in *Twenty-Ninth Annual Report of the European Free Trade Association, 1989*, Geneva: EFTA Secretariat: 55.

European Free Trade Association (1977) 'Declaration of the Meeting of the EFTA Heads of Governments and Ministers, Vienna, 13 May 1977', in *Seventeenth Annual Report of the European Free Trade Association 1976–1977*, Geneva: EFTA Secretariat: 53.

—— (1987) *The European Free Trade Association*, Geneva: EFTA Secretariat.

—— (1989) 'Communique of the Ministerial Meeting of the EFTA Council, Tampere, 14–15 June 1988', in *Twenty-Eighth Annual Report of the European Free Trade Association 1988*, Geneva: EFTA Secretariat, 1989: 24.

—— (1990) 'Communique of the Meeting of the EFTA Council at Ministerial Level, Geneva, 11–12 December 1989', in *Twenty-Ninth Annual Report of the European Free Trade Association 1989*, Geneva, EFTA Secretariat: 51.

—— (1991) *EFTA Trade 1990*, Geneva: EFTA Secretariat.

European Parliament (1977), *Report on Behalf of the Committee on External Economic Relations on Economic Relations between the European Communities and the Nordic Countries*, Maigard, J, Doc. 184/77 (1 July).

Eurostat (1992) *Basic Statistics of the Community*, Brussels.

—— (1994) *Basic Statistics of the Community*, Brussels.
Fagerberg, J. and Lundberg, L. (eds) (1994) *European Economic Integration: A Nordic Perspective*, Aldershot: Avebury.
Financial Times (1993) 11/6/1993: 13.
—— (1994) *Survey of Finland 9: Agriculture Faces Shake-up and the Likely Impact of Joining Europe*, 9/11/1994.
—— (1995a) *Fish May Hinder SDP plans to net Iceland's Pro-EU Voters*, 3/4/1995: 3.
—— (1995b) *Danish Banking and Finance*, VIII, 29/3/1995.
—— (1995c) *Survey of Finland 9: Agriculture Faces Shake-up – The Likely Impact of Joining Europe*, 9/11/1994.
Folketing (1972) *Folketingets Forhandlinger*, 1971–1972, Copenhagen: Folketing.
—— (1984) *Folketingets Forhandlinger*, 1983–1984, Copenhagen: Folketing.
—— (1990) *Folketingets Forhandlinger*, 1989–1990, Copenhagen: Folketing.
—— (1991) *Folketingets Forhandlinger*, 1990–1991, Copenhagen: Folketing.
Freestone, D. (1992) 'The 1992 Maastricht Treaty – Implications for European Environmental Law', *European Environmental Law Review* 1, 1: 23–6.
Fullerton, B. and Knowles, R. (1991) *Scandinavia*, London: Paul Chapman.
Gahrton, P. (1988) *Vad vill de gröna?*, Göteborg: Korpen.
Gellner, M. (1960) 'The Outer Seven – Buying Time in the European Trade Dispute', *The World Today* 16, 1: 15–23.
Gidlund, G. (1992) *Partiernas Europa*, Stockholm: Natur och kultur.
Gilljam, M. (1994) '*Folkomröstningar är ett elände!*', speech delivered to the 4th Jörgen Westerståhl seminar, Department of Political Science, Göteborg University, 1 December 1994 (printed in 'Funderingar kring valet och folkomröstningen', Working Paper, Department of Political Science, Göteborg University).
Gilljam, M. and Granberg, D. (1994) 'Sverige är inte kluvet', *Dagens Nyheter* (23 November).
Gilljam, M. and Holmberg, S. (1993) *Väljarna inför 90-talet*, Stockholm: Norstedts juridik.
Gíslason, G. T. (1971) 'Iceland', *EFTA Bulletin* 12, 1: 20–1.
Goldmann, K. (1986) 'Change and Stability in Foreign Policy', *World Politics* 34: 230–66.
Goldstein, M. (1993) *International Capital Markets: Part 1. International Monetary Fund*, Washington DC: IMF.
Gourevitch, P. (1978) 'The Second Image Reversed: the International Sources of Domestic Politics', *International Organization* 32, 4 (Autumn): 881–911.
—— (1984) 'Breaking with Orthodoxy: the Politics of Economic Policy Responses to the Depression of the 1930s', *International Organization* 38, 1 (Winter): 95–129.
—— (1988) *Finland och den vasteuropeiska integrationen*, Helsinki.
Granell, F. (1995) 'The European Union's Enlargement Negotiations with Austria, Finland, Norway and Sweden', *Journal of Common Market Studies* 33, 1: 117–42.
Greenaway, D. and Whalley, J. (1994) 'Mini Symposium on the Accession of the Nordic Countries to the European Union', *The World Economy* 17, 5 (September): 639–794.
Gstöhl, S. (1994) 'EFTA and the European Economic Area or the Politics of Frustration', *Cooperation and Conflict* 29, 4: 333–66.
Haagerup, N. J. (1973) 'Skandinavien und die Europäische Gemeinschaft', *Europa-Archiv* 28, 9: 291–9.
Haahr, J.-H. (1993) *Looking to Europe*, Aarhus: Aarhus University Press.
Haas, E. B. (1958) *The Uniting of Europe*, London: Stevens & Sons Ltd.
—— (1964) *Beyond the Nation State*, Stanford: Stanford University Press.

Hakovirta, H. (1988) *East–West Conflict and European Neutrality*, Oxford: Clarendon Press.

Hancock, M. D. (1972) 'Sweden, Scandinavia and the EEC', *International Affairs* 43, 3: 424–37.

—— (1974) 'Swedish Elites and the EEC: Models of the Future', *Cooperation and Conflict* 9, 4: 225–42.

Hannibalsson, J. B. (1989–90) 'Iceland: 20 years in EFTA – the Challenges Ahead', *EFTA Bulletin* 4/89–1/90: 15–17.

Hansen, P. (1969) 'Denmark and European Integration', *Cooperation and Conflict* 4, 1: 13–46.

Hanssen, H. J. and Sandegren, K. (1969) 'Norway and Western European Economic Integration', *Cooperation and Conflict* 4, 1: 47–62.

Haparanta, P. and Heinonen, T. (1993) 'Finland and the EMS' in J. Fagerberg and L. Lundberg (eds) *European Economic Integration: A Nordic Perspective* Aldershot: Avebury.

Hardarson, O. T. (1993) 'Iceland', *European Journal of Political Research* 24.

Hasselberg, P. A. G. (1994) 'KdS och den europeiska integrationen – en studie av ståndpunkter och argumentation över tid', unpublished mimeograph, Göteborg: B-uppsats, Department of Political Science, Göteborg Universitet.

Hermann, C. (1990) 'Changing Course: When Governments choose to Redirect Foreign Policy', *International Studies Quarterly* 34, 1: 3–21.

—— (1994) Symposium: 'The End of the Cold War and Theories of International Relations', *International Organization* 48, 2 (Spring): 155–344.

Hermansson, J. (1988) 'A New Face for Swedish Communism: The Left Party Communists', in M. Waller and M. Fennema (eds) *Communist Parties in Western Europe: Decline or Adaptation?,* Oxford: Basil Blackwell.

Holm, H.-H. (1979) 'Danish Third World Policy: The Feed-Back Problem', *Cooperation and Conflict* 14, 2/3: 87–103.

Holmberg, S. (1994) *SVT/VALU94EU, Rapport nr 23 med resultat från Sveriges Televisions vallokalsundersökning i november 1994*, Valu94EU. Stockholm: Sveriges Television.

Holst, J. J. (ed.) (1985) *Norwegian Foreign Policy in the 1980s*, Oslo: Norwegian University Press.

House of Lords Select Committee on the EC (1990) *Fourteenth Report of the Select Committee on the European Communities, Relations between the Community and EFTA*, London: HMSO, HL Paper 55-I (22 May).

—— (1993a) *Fifth Environmental Action Programme: Integration of Community Policies*, Session 1992–1993, Eighth Report, London: HMSO.

—— (1993b) *Implementation and Enforcement of Legislation*, Session 1992–1993, Ninth Report, London: HMSO.

Hoyer, K. (1993) *Nordic and EC Environmental Policies: Differences and Similarities*, Paper presented to European Environment Conference, University of Nottingham, 20/21 (September).

Hufvadstadsbladet, 22/8/1993.

International Monetary Fund (1993) *International Capital Markets: Part 1 Exchange Rate Management and International Capital Flows*, Washington DC: IMF.

Jacot-Guillarmod, O. (ed.) (1990) *L'avenir du libre-echange en Europe: vers un Espace économique européen?*, Zurich: Schulthess Polygraphischer Verlag/Bern, Stampfli.

Jamar, J. and Wallace, H. (eds) (1988) *EEC–EFTA: More than Just Good Friends? CEE–AELE: Mariage en vue?*, Bruges: De Tempel/Tempelhof.

Jerneck, M. (1993) 'Sweden – the Reluctant European?', in Teija Tiilikainen and Ib Damgaard Petersen (eds) *The Nordic Countries and the EC*, Copenhagen: Copenhagen Political Studies Press: 23–42.

Johansson, B. A. W. (1970) 'Sweden and the EEC. An Approach to the Study of the Political Process', *Cooperation and Conflict* 5, 4: 286–92.

Johansson, G. (1985) *Kristen demokrati på svenska. Studier om KDS tillkomst och utveckling 1964–1982*, Malmö: CWK Gleerup.

Johnson, C. and Collogon, S. (eds) (1994) *The Monetary Economics of Europe: Causes of the EMS Crisis*, London: Pinter.

Jonnergård, G. (1985) *Med Gunnar Hedlund i politiken*, Stockholm: LT.

Karvonen, L. and Sundelius, B. (1987) *Internationalization and Foreign Policy Management*, Aldershot: Gower.

Katz, R. and Mair, P. (1995) 'Changing Models of Party Organization and Party Democracy: The Emergence of the Cartel Party', *Party Politics* 1, 1: 5–28.

Kelstrup, M. (ed.) (1992) *European Integration and Denmark's Participation*, Copenhagen: Copenhagen Political Studies Press.

—— (1993) 'Small States and European Political Integration', in Teija Tiilikainen and Ib Damgaard Petersen (eds), *The Nordic Countries and the EC*, Copenhagen: Copenhagen Political Studies Press: 136–62.

Keohane, R. and Nye, J. (1989) *Power and Interdependence* (Second edition), Glenview: Scott, Foresman and Company.

Kersaudy, F. (1987) *Norway 1940*, Paris: Editions Talladier; London: Arrow Books.

Kettunen, L. (1993) *Finnish Agriculture and European Integration*, 71, Helsinki: Agricultural Economics Research Institute (MTTL).

—— (1994) *Finnish Agriculture in 1993*, 73, Helsinki: Agricultural Economics Research Institute (MTTL).

—— (1995) *Finnish Agriculture in 1994*, 76a, Helsinki: Agricultural Economics Research Institute (MTTL).

Koivisto, M. (1992) 'Opening Address to Parliament', *Parliamentary Record*, Helsinki.

Krag, J. O. (1961) 'European Integration – The Danish View', *EFTA Bulletin* 2, 11: 3.

—— (1962) 'Skandinavien und die wirtschaftliche Einigung Europas', *Österreichische Zeitschrift für Aussenpolitik* 2, 2: 67–71.

Kragh, J.-O. (1972) 'Før Afgørelsen', *Aarhus Stifttidende* (1 October).

Kristensen, O. (1993) 'Norway – Europe's Energy Partner', in *Energy in Europe*, 21/7/1993.

Kristinsson, G. H. (1987) 'Iceland: Vulnerability in a Fish-based Economy', *Cooperation and Conflict* 22, 4: 245–53.

—— (1989) 'Iceland's Interests and Options in Europe', in K. Möttölä and H. Patomäki (eds) *Facing the Change in Europe: EFTA Countries' Integration Strategies*, Helsinki: Finnish Institute of International Affairs: 22–30.

—— (1990) *Evropustefnan. Adlogun Islands ad throun Evropubandalagsins*, Reykjavik: Öryggismalanafnd.

—— (1991) 'Iceland', in H. Wallace (ed.) *The Wider Western Europe: Reshaping the EC/EFTA Relationship*, London: Pinter: 159–78.

—— (1994) 'Iceland and Norway: Peripheries in Doubt', in J. Redmond (ed.) *Prospective Europeans: New Members for the European Union*, Hemel Hempstead: Harvester-Wheatsheaf: 86–109.

Kristinsson, G. H., Jonsson, H. and Sveinsdottir, H. (1992) *Atvinnustefna aa Isalndi*, Reykjavik: Felagvisindastofnun.

Kruzel, J. and Haltzel, M. (eds) (1989) *Between the Blocs: Problems and Prospects for Europe's Neutral and Non-Aligned States*, Cambridge: Cambridge University Press.

Kuhnle, S. (1991) 'Das skandinavische wohlfartsstaaliche Modell im Zeitalter der europäischen Einigung', *Zeitschrift für Sozialreform* 37: 601–19.

Lambert, J. R. (1962a) 'Enlargement of the Common Market: Denmark, Norway and Ireland', *The World Today* 18, 8: 350–60.

—— (1962b) 'The Neutrals and the Common Market', *The World Today* 18, 10: 444–52.

Lane, J.-E. (ed.) (1991) *Understanding the Swedish Model*, London: Frank Cass.

Lange, G. (1962a) 'Erklärung des schwedischen Handelsminister, Gunnar Lange, vor dem EWG-Ministerrat in Brüssel an 28 Juli 1962', *Europa-Archiv* 17, 17: 414–19.

—— (1962b) 'Schweden erstrebt die Assoziierung mit der EWG', *Aussenpolitik* 13, 7: 438–43.

Laursen, F. (ed.) (1990) *EFTA and the EC: Implications of 1992*, Maastricht: European Institute of Public Administration.

—— (1994) 'Denmark and the Ratification of the Maastricht Treaty', in F. Laursen and S. Vanhoonacker (eds), *The Ratification of the Maastricht Treaty: Issues, Debates and Future Implications*, Maastricht: European Institute of Public Administration: 61–87.

Laursen, J. N. (1992) 'Mellem Fællesmarkedet og Frihandelszonen', in N. B. Thomsen (ed.) *The Odd Man Out? Danmark og den Europæiske Integration 1948–1992*, Odense: Odense Universitetsforlag: 65–9.

Levy, J. S. (1994) 'Learning and Foreign Policy', *International Organization* 48, 2 (Spring): 279–312.

Lewin, L. (1988) *Ideology and Strategy. A Century of Swedish Politics*, New York: Cambridge University Press.

Linbeck A. *et al.* (1994) *Turning Sweden Round*, Cambridge: MIT Press.

Lindahl, R. (1991) 'Alla ombord: EG-tåget går!', in S. Holmberg and L. Weibull (eds) *Politiska opinioner* (SOM report 6), Göteborg: Department of Political Science and School of Journalism and Mass Communication.

—— (1992a) 'Massmedierna, medborgarna och EG-frågan' in S. Holmberg and L. Weibull (eds) *Åsikter om massmedier och samhälle* (SOM report 7), Göteborg: Department of Political Science and School of Journalism and Mass Communication.

—— (1992b) 'När opinionen vände: Åsikter i EG-frågan', in S. Holmberg and L. Weibull (eds) *Trendbrott?* (SOM report 8), Göteborg: Department of Political Science and School of Journalism and Mass Communication.

—— (1993) 'Ekonomiska förhoppningar och EG-medlemskap', in S. Holmberg and L. Weibull (eds) *Pespektiv på krisen* (SOM report 9), Göteborg: Department of Political Science and School of Journalism and Mass Communication.

—— (1994) 'Inför avgörandet: Åsikter om EU', in S. Holmberg and L. Weibull (eds) *Vägval* (SOM report 11), Göteborg: Department of Political Science and School of Journalism and Mass Communication.

Lindberg, L. and Scheingold, S. (eds) (1971) *Regional Integration: Theory and Research*, Cambridge, Mass.: Harvard University Press.

Lindfelt, E. (1991) *Moralpartiet. En bok om KDS*, Stockholm: Carlssons.

Lisein-Norman, M. (1974) *La Suède face à l'intégration européenne*, Bruxelles: Université Libre de Bruxelles.

Lonnroth, M. (1992) *Sweden and the European Environment*, Stockholm: Swedish Institute.

Ludlow, P. (ed.) (1994) *The Fourth Enlargement. Public Opinion on Membership in the Nordic Countries*, CEPS Paper 56, Brussels: Centre for European Policy Studies.

Lyck, L. (ed.) (1992) *Denmark and EC Evaluated*, London: Pinter.

Mäentakanen, E. (1978) 'Western and Eastern Europe in Finnish Trade Policy, 1957–1974: Towards a Comprehensive Solution?', *Cooperation and Conflict* 13, 1: 21–41.

Mair, P. (1994) 'Party Organizations: From Civil Society to the State', in R. Katz and P. Mair (eds) *How Parties Organize: Change and Adaptation in Party Organizations in Western Democracies*, London: Sage: 1–22.

Mannerheim, G. (1954) *Marskalkens Minnen. Nationalupplaga av G. Mannerheim: Minnen I–II*, Esbo: Schildts Forlags Ab.

Marschang, E. *Der 'Luxemburg Prozess' als eine Komponente der EFTA–EG Zusammenarbeit*, unpublished PhD dissertation.

Matlary, J.-H. (1993) 'Norway and European Integration: A Theoretical Discussion', in B. F. Nelsen (ed.) *Norway and the European Community: The Political Economy of Integration*, London: Praeger: 63–86.

—— (1995) *Energy Policy in the European Union*, London: Macmillan.

Miles, L. (1993) *Scandinavia and European Community Enlargement: Prospects and Problems for Sweden, Finland and Norway*, 1/93, Hull: Centre for European Union Studies, University of Hull.

—— (1994a) 'Sweden and Finland – From EFTA Neutrals to EU Members', in J. Redmond (ed.) *Prospective Europeans*, London: Harvester-Wheatsheaf: 59–85.

—— (1994b) 'The 1993–1994 Enlargement Negotiations', *European Access* 3: 8–11.

—— (1994c) *The 1993–1994 Enlargement Negotiations: A Critical Appraisal*, CEUS Paper 1/94, Hull, University of Hull.

—— (1995a) 'Enlargement of the European Union', Dossier No. 36, London: University of North London Press.

—— (1995b) 'The European Union and the Nordic Countries: Impacts on the Integration Process', in C. Rhodes and S. Mazey (eds) *The State of the European Union, Volume III: Building a European Polity?*, USA: Lynne Rienner: 317–34.

—— (1995c) *Sweden, Security and Accession to the European Union*, Occasional Papers in Nordic Studies, 1, Hull: University of Humberside.

Miles, L. and Widfeldt, W. (1995) 'The Swedish Non-Socialist Parties and the European Union', in J. Lovenduski and J. Stanyer (eds) *Contemporary Political Studies 1995, Volume III*, Exeter: Short Run Press/Political Studies Association: 1513–19.

Miljan, T. (1977) *The Reluctant Europeans – The Attitudes of the Nordic Countries Towards European Integration*, London: Hurst.

Milner, H. (1990) *Sweden: Social Democracy in Practice*, Oxford: Oxford University Press.

—— (1994) *Social Democracy and Rational Choice – The Scandinavian Experience and Beyond*, London: Routledge.

Milward, A. (1992) *The European Rescue of the Nation State*, London: Routledge.

Ministry of Finance (1995) Press Release, 12/6/1995.

Ministry of Foreign Affairs (1993a) *Position Paper on the Enlargement Negotiations – Labour Market Situation and Labour Market Policy Measures in Finland*, 27/7/93, Helsinki.

—— (1993b) *Position Paper on the Environment*, Helsinki.

—— (1995) *Guidelines of Finland's European Policy*, 14/2/95, Helsinki.

Ministry of the Environment and Natural Resources (1993) *Swedish Position Paper on the Environment*, Stockholm.

Moravcsik, A. (1993) 'Preferences and Power in the European Community', *Journal of Common Market Studies* 31, 4 (December): 473–524.

Mortensen, J. V. (1995) 'Sverige og EF', unpublished MA thesis, Aarhus: Institute of Political Science, Aarhus University.

Möttölä, K. and Patomäki. H. (eds) (1989) *Facing the Change in Europe: EFTA Countries' Integration Strategies*, Helsinki: The Finnish Institute of International Affairs.

Mouritzen, H. (1988) *Finlandization. Towards a General Theory of Adaptive Politics*, Aldershot: Avebury.

—— (1993) 'The Two Musterknaben and the Naughty Boy: Sweden, Finland and Denmark in the Process of European Integration', *Cooperation and Conflict* 28, 4: 373–402.

Mousson-Lestang, J.-P. (1990) *La Scandinavie et L'Europe de 1945 à nos jours*, Paris: Presses Universitaire de France.

Moxon Browne, E. (1973) 'The Special Relations Agreements', *The World Today* 29, 8: 337–42.

Muoser, T. (1986) *Finnlands Neutralität und die Europäische Wirtschaftsgemeinschaft*, Baden Baden: Nomos.

Nell, P. (1988) 'Strategie des ays de l'AELE face au marché interne de la CE: de la voie universelle a l'adhésion', *Revue du Marché Commun* 1988, 322.

Nelsen, B. F. (1993a) 'The European Community Debate in Norway: The Periphery Revolts Again', in B. Nelsen (ed.) *Norway and the European Community: The Political Economy of Integration*, London: Praeger: 41–62.

—— (ed.) (1993b) *Norway and the European Community: The Political Economy of Integration*, London: Praeger.

Nicholson, F. and East, R. (1987) *From the Six to the Twelve: The Enlargement of the European Communities*, London: Longman.

Nicolaides, P. and Armand, C. (1994) 'The Process and Politics of Enlargement', *European Trends* (1st quarter): 70–9.

Norberg, S. *et al.* (1993) *EEA Law: A Commentary on the EEA Agreement*, Stockholm: Publica/Fritzes.

Nordic Council (1995a) *Political Premises* (March), Copenhagen: Nordic Council of Ministers.

—— (1995b) 'Nordisk och europeisk passunion via ESS?', *Nordisk Kontakt* 20: 8–9.

Nordisk Ministerråd, *Nordiska Samarbetsorgan 1992,* Copenhagen: Nordic Council of Ministers.

Noreng, O. (1972) 'La Norvège après le "non"', *Politique Étrangère* 38, 1: 27–40.

Nørgaard, A. S. (1994) 'Institutions and Post-Modernity in IR: The "New" EC', *Cooperation and Conflict* 29, 3: 245–87.

Norros, M. (1994) 'Finland Becomes the 14th Member of the European Union', *FINNFAX* (March) Helsinki: Finland Promotion Board: 1–2.

Nydegger, A. (1962) 'Die Einstellung der drei EFTA-Neutralen gegenüber der EWG', *Wirtschaft und Recht* 14, 1: 1–15.

Nye, J. S. (1971) 'Comparing Common Markets. A Revised Neo-Functionalist Model', in L. N. Lindberg and S. S. Scheingold (eds), *Regional Integration: Theory and Research*, Harvard: Harvard University Press.

Oddsson, D. (1994) *Avarp forsaetisradherra a aoalfundi LIU, 28. okt.*, Reykjavik: Prime Minister's Office.

Odell, J. S. (1982) *US International Monetary Policy. Markets, Power and Ideas as Sources of Change*, Princeton: Princeton University Press.

OECD (1993a) *Environmental Performance Review – Norway*, Paris: OECD.

—— (1993b) *Taxation and the Environment*, Paris: OECD.

—— (1994) *Agricultural Policies, Markets and Trade: Monitoring and Outlook 1994*, Paris: OECD.

—— (1995) *Economic Survey of Finland*, Paris: OECD.

Ólafsson, S. (1990) *Lifskjor of lifshaettir a Islandi*, Reykjavik: Felagsvisindastofnun.

Olesen, T. B. and Laursen, J. (1994) 'Det Europæiske Markedsskisma', in T. Swienty (ed.) *Danmark i Europa 1945–93*, København: Munksgård: 93–127.

Örvik, N. (ed.) (1972) *Fears and Expectation: Norwegian Attitudes towards European Integration*, Oslo: Universitetsforlaget.

Papacosma, V. and Rubin, M. (eds) (1989) *Europe's Neutral and Non-Aligned States*, Wilmington: Scholaly Resources Inc.

Pedersen, T. (1988) *The Wider Western Europe: EC Policy towards the EFTA Countries*, London: The Royal Institute of International Affairs.

—— (1993) 'Den Europæiske Integration', in *Danmark efter den kolde krig*, København: SNU.

—— (1994a) 'Demokratiformer og Institutional Udvikling i den Europæiske Union', in Bertel Heurlin (ed.), *Danmark og den Europæiske Union*, København: Forlaget Politiske Studier: 57–90.

—— (1994b) *European Union and the EFTA Countries. Enlargement and Integration*, London: Pinter.

—— (1995a) 'Denmark', in Wolfgang Wessels and D. Rometsch (eds), *Decision Making in the European Union*, Manchester: Manchester University Press: 37.

—— (1995b) 'Sub-systems and Regional Integration: The Case of Nordic and Baltic Cooperation', in C. Wellmann (ed.), *Nation-States, International Organizations and Sub-State Actors*, Kiel: Christian Albrechts Universität.

—— (1995c) 'Europa – Tysklands anden nation', in H. Gottlieb (ed.) *Tyskland i Europa*, København: SNU: 69–102.

Pesonen, P. (ed.) (1994) *Suomen kansanäänestys 1994*, Helsinki: Painatuskeskus oy.

Pesonen, P. and Sänkiaho, R. (1994) 'The Finnish Referendum on Membership in the EU', *Yearbook of Finnish Foreign Policy*, 1994: 52–9.

Petersen, N. (1991) *EF, den Politiske Union og Danmark*, København: SNU.

—— (1993) '"Game, Set, and Match", Denmark and the European Union after Edinburgh', in T. Tiilikainen and I. D. Petersen (eds) *The Nordic Countries and the EC*, Copenhagen: Copenhagen Political Studies Press: 79–106.

Petersen, N. and Elklit, J. (1973) 'Denmark enters the European Communities', *Scandinavian Political Studies* 8, 2: 198–214.

Petersson, O. (1982) *Väljarna och världspolitiken*, Stockholm: Norstedts.

—— (1994a) *The Government and Politics of the Nordic Countries*, Stockholm: Publica/ Fritzes.

—— (1994b) *Swedish Government and Politics*, Stockholm: Publica/ Fritzes.

Pierre, J. (1986) *Partikongresser och regeringspolitik*, Lund: Kommunfakta.

Pierre, J. and Widfeldt, A. (1992) 'Sweden', in R. Katz and P. Mair (eds) *Party Organizations: A Data Handbook*, London: Sage: 781–836.

—— (1994) 'Party Organizations in Sweden: Colossuses on Clay Feet or Flexible Pillars of Government?', in R. Katz and P. Mair (eds) *How Parties Organize: Change and Adaptation in Party Organizations in Western Democracies*, London: Sage: 332–56.

Pittelkow, R. (1990) 'EF-modstanden bør få en værdig død', *Politiken*, 31/8/1990.

Putnam, R. (1988) 'Diplomacy and Domestic Polities: The Logic of Two-Level Games', *International Organization* 42, 3: 427–60.

Regeringsskrivelse 1990/91: 50.

Rehn, O. (1993) 'Odottavasta ennakoivaan integraatiopolitiikkaan? Suomen integraatiopolitiikka kylmän sodan aikana ja sen päätösvaiheessa 1989–92', in T. Forsberg and T. Vaahtoranta (eds) *Johdatus Suomen ulkopolitiikkaan*, Helsinki: Gaudeamus.

Reymond, C. (1993) 'Institutions, Decision-Making Procedure and Settlement of Disputes in the European Economic Area', *Common Market Law Review* 30, 3: 449–80.

Richardson, J. (ed.) (1982) *Policy Styles in Western Europe*, London: Allen and Unwin.

Richardson, N. R. (1987) 'Dyadic Case Studies in the Comparative Study of Foreign Policies', in C. Hermann, C. W. Kegley and J. N. Rosenau (eds) *New Directions in the Study of Foreign Policy*, Boston: Allen and Unwin.

Riksdag (1988) 'Annual foreign policy debates', *Parliamentary Record* 3, 1986/87, Stockholm.

—— (1990) 'Annual foreign policy debates', *Parliamentary Record* 5, 1988/89, Stockholm.

—— (1992) *Parliamentary Record* 1991/92 Stockholm: Riksdag: 52.

Rommetveldt, H. (1992) 'The Norwegian Storting: The Central Assembly of the Periphery', *Scandinavian Political Studies* 15, 2: 79–97.

Rosenau, J. and Czempiel, O. (eds) (1992) *Governance Without Government: Order and Change in World Politics*, Cambridge: Cambridge University Press.

Rosenau, J. N. (1971) 'Pre-Theories and Theories of Foreign Policy', in James N. Rosenau, *The Scientific Study of Foreign Policy*, New York: The Free Press: 95–116.

Ross, J. F. L. (1991) 'Sweden, the European Community, and the Politics of Economic Realism', *Cooperation and Conflict* 26: 117–28.

Royal Ministry of Foreign Affairs, (1987) 'Norge, EF og europeisk samarbeid', *Stort. meld*, 61 (1986–1987), Oslo: 3–4.

—— (1988) *UD-informasjon*, 28/10/88, Oslo: 3.

—— (1992) *UD-informasjon*, 43/92, Oslo: 101.

—— (1994a) 'Fisheries Agreement', *Norway Now* 1, 6, Oslo: 7–8.

—— (1994b) *The Norwegian Referendum Result*, 29/11/94, Oslo.

—— (1994c) UD-informasjon, 41/94, Oslo: 3.

—— (1995) *UD-informasjon*, 2/95, Oslo: 3.

Ruin, O. (1986) *Tage Erlander 1946–1969*, Stockholm: Tiden.

Sæter, M. (1991) 'European Integration and Energy Policy: Consequences For Norway', in O.-G. Austvik (ed.) *Norwegian Gas in the New Europe*, Oslo: Vett & Viten: 13–34.

—— (1993) 'Norwegian Integration Policy in a Changing World: The Primacy of Security', in B. Nelsen (ed.) *Norway and the European Community. The Political Economy of Integration*, London: Praeger: 21–40.

Sæter, M. and Knudsen, O. F. (1991) 'Norway', in H. Wallace (ed.) *The Wider Western Europe: Reshaping the EC/EFTA Relationship*, London: Pinter: 179–93.

Salovaara, J. (1993) 'Finnish Integration Policy – from an Economic to a Security Motivation', *Yearbook of Finnish Foreign Policy*, 16–23.

Sandström, A. (1979) *KDS. Partiet bakom fromhetsvallen*, Stockholm: LT pocket.

Särlvik, B. (1959) *Opinionsbildningen vid folkomröstningen 1957*, 24 Stockholm: Statens offentliga utredningar (SOU): 10.

Sauerberg, S. (1992) 'Parties, Voters and the EC', in L. Lyck (ed.) *Denmark and EC Membership Evaluated*, London: Pinter: 60–76.

Schmitter, P. (1971) 'A Revised Theory of Regional Integration', in L. Lindberg and S. Scheingold (eds) *Regional Integration: Theory and Research*, Cambridge, Mass.: Harvard University Press.

Schou, T.-L. (1986) 'EF-Unionsdebatten i Danmark', *Dansk Udenrigspolitisk Årbog 1985*, København: DJØF.

—— (1992) 'The Debate in Denmark 1986–91 on European Integration and Denmark's Participation', in M. Kelstrup (ed.) *European Integration and Denmark's Participation*, Copenhagen: Copenhagen Political Studies Press: 328–64.

Simmonds, K. R. (1964–5) 'The Community and the Neutral States', *Common Market Law Review* 2, 1: 5–20.

Singleton, F. (1974) 'Finland, Comecon, and the EEC', *The World Today* 30, 2: 64–72.

SNU (The Danish Commission on Security and Disarmament) (1991) 'Memorandum from the Danish Government concerning the Political and the Economic-Monetary Union, 4 October 1990', in N. Petersen, *EF, den Politiske Union og Danmark*, København: SNU.

—— (1992) *The Future of NATO*, Copenhagen: SNU.

Social Democratic Party of Denmark (1987) *An Open Europe*, English version, Brussels.

Social Democratic Party of Sweden (1990) *Tiden* 82, 8.

—— (1993a) *Motions*, 1993 Congress, 4, Stockholm.

—— (1993b) *Aktuellt i Politiken*, Special Congress edition, Stockholm: SAP.

Solem, E. (1977) *The Nordic Council and Scandinavian Integration*, New York and London: Praeger Special Studies.
Soloveytchik, G. (1970) 'Nordek: its Hopes and Pitfalls', *National Westminster Bank Quarterly Review* (February): 22–32.
Sørensen, C. L. (1978) *Danmark og EF i 1970-erne*, København: Borgen.
Sørensen, G. and Holm, H. H. (1995) *Whose World Order?*, Boulder, Col.: Westview Press.
Sørensen, H. and Væver, O. (1992) 'State, Society and Democracy and the Effect of the EC', in L. Lyck (ed.) *Denmark and EC Membership Evaluated*, London: Pinter: 3–25.
Sorsa, K. (1974) 'Finnland zwischen EWG und RWG', *Europa-Archiv* 29, 14: 461–72.
Sparring, A. (1972) 'Iceland, Europe, and NATO', *The World Today* 28, 9: 393–403.
Stålvant, C.-E. (1973) 'Sweden: The Negotiations with the EEC', *Scandinavian Political Studies* 8: 236–45.
—— (1974) 'Neutrality and European Integration: A Comparison of Finland's and Sweden's EEC Policies', *Scandinavian Studies* 46, 4: 405–28.
—— (1982) 'Nordic Policies Towards International Economic Cooperation', in B. Sundelius (ed.) *Foreign Policies in Northern Europe*, Boulder, Col.: Westview: 107–42.
—— (1989) 'How a Non-EC Member Copes with the Internal Market: the Case of Sweden', in K. Möttölä and H. Patomäki (eds) *Facing the Change in Europe: EFTA Countries' Integration Strategies*, Helsinki: Finnish Institute of International Affairs: 42–54.
Steininger, R. (1993) '1961: Europe at Sixes and Sevens – Die EFTA und Großbritanniens Entscheidung für die EWG', in M. Gehler and R. Steininger (eds) *Österreich und die europäische Integration 1945–1993*, Wien: Böhlau Verlag: 201–25.
Stephensen, O. (1994) *Afangi a Evropufor*, Reykjavik: Centre for International Studies.
Stokke, O. (1993) 'Norsk bistandspolitikk mot ar 2000: Veivalg og verdier', *Internasjonal Politikk* 51, 1: 91–114.
Stokke, O. S. and Tunander, O. (eds) (1994) *The Barents Region. Cooperation in Arctic Europe*, London: Sage.
Storting Finance Committee (1989) *Innstilling fra finanskomiteen om norsk tilpasning til EFs indre marked*, Innst.S.nr. 38 (1989–90), Oslo: Storting (28 November).
Sundelius, B. (ed.) (1982) *Foreign Policies of Northern Europe*, Boulder, Col.: Westview Press.
—— (1987) *The Neutral Democracies and the New Cold War*, Boulder, Col.: Westview Press.
—— (1990) 'Sweden: Secure Neutrality', *The Annals of the American Academy of Political and Social Science* November, 512: 116–24.
—— (1994) 'When Sweden chose to join the EC', in Walter Carlsnaes and Steve Smith (eds) *European Foreign Policy. The EC and Changing Perspectives in Europe*, London. Sage: 177–201.
Sundelius, B. and Wiklund, C. (1979) 'The Nordic Community, the Ugly Duckling of Regional Co-operation', *Journal of Common Market Studies* 18, 1: 59–75.
Svåsand, L. (1992) 'Norway' in R. Katz and P. Mair (eds) *Party Organizations: A Data Handbook*, London: Sage.
Svensson, M. (1993) *Riksdagspartierna och EG – en studie av de svenska riksdagspartiernas representativitet i EG-frågan*, unpublished mimeograph, Göteborg: B-uppsats, Department of Political Science, Göteborg Universitet.
Svensson, P. (1994) 'The Danish Yes to Maastricht and Edinburgh. The EC Referendum of May 1993', *Scandinavian Political Studies* 17, 1: 69–82.

Svensson, P., Siune, K. and Tonsgaard, O. (1992) *Det blev et nej*, Aarhus: Aarhus University Press.

—— (1994) *Fra et Nej til et Ja*, Aarhus: Aarhus University Press.

Swedish Board of Agriculture (1993) *The Swedish Agricultural Reform*, Stockholm.

Swedish Green Party (1991) *Miljöpartiet de gröna* (Green Party congress) 1991, documents 7.

Swedish Ministry of Foreign Affairs (1992) *Government Declaration to Parliament 6 October 1992*, Stockholm.

Taggart, P. (1993) 'The New Populism and the New Politics: Transformations of the Swedish Party System in Comparative Context', unpublished PhD thesis, University of Pittsburgh.

Taggart, P. and Widfeldt, A. (1993) *'1990s Flash Party Organization: The Case of New Democracy in Sweden'*, Paper presented to the Political Studies Association of the UK Annual Conference, University of Leicester (20–22 April).

Thomsen, B. N. (ed.) (1992) *The Odd Man Out? Danmark og den Europæiske Integration 1948–1992*, Odense: Odense Universitetsforlag.

Thune, C. (1987) 'Denmark, Europe and the Creation of EFTA', in EFTA, *EFTA From Yesterday to Tomorrow*, Geneva: EFTA Secretariat: 74–83.

Tiilikainen, T. (1994a) 'Det finländska folket inför det historiska beslutet – EG-opinionens utveckling i Finland från 70-talet till medlemsförhandlingarna', in J. Bingen and R. Lindahl (eds) *Nordiske skjebnevalg?*, Oslo: Europa-programmet.

—— (1994b) 'The Finns as Constructors of a United Europe; Reflections upon the European Political Heritage of Finland', *Yearbook of Finnish Foreign Policy*, 1994: 20–8.

Tiilikainen, T. and Petersen, I. D. (eds) (1993) *The Nordic Countries and the EC*, Copenhagen: Copenhagen Political Studies.

Törnudd, K. (1969) 'Finland and Economic Integration in Europe', *Cooperation and Conflict* 4, 1: 63–72.

Turner, B. and Nordquist, G. (1982) *The Other European Community: Integration and Cooperation in Nordic Europe*, London: Weidenfeld & Nicolson.

Udenrigsministeriet (1992) *Hvidbog om Danmark og Maastricht-Traktaten*, Copenhagen: Udenrigsministeriet.

Ueland, G. K. (1975) 'The Nordek Debate – An Analysis of the Attitudes of Nordic Elites toward the Relationship between Nordek and the EC', *Cooperation and Conflict* 10, 1: 1–19.

Ulkoasiainministerio, *Eurooppa* (1993) 1: 2–4, Helsinki: Ulkoasiainministerio: 20.

Ulkopoloottisia lausuntoja ja asiakirjoja (ULA) 1991: 173.

Urwin, D. W. (1991) *The Community of Europe: A History of European Integration since 1945*, London: Longman.

Utanríkismál (1992) *Skyrsla Jons Baldsvins Hannibalssonar utanrikísráðherra til Alþingis*, Reykjavik: Utanríkismál.

Utenriksdepartementet (1987) (Government Report to Parliament) *Norge, EF og europeisk samabeid*, St.meld. No. 61 (1986–87), Oslo: Utenriksdepartementet (22 May).

—— (1994) *Om medlemskap i Den europeiske union. Stortingsmelding nr. 40 (1993–1994)*, Oslo: Utenriksdepartementet.

Utrikesdepartementet (1987) *Sverige och den vasteuropeiska integrationen*, Prop. 1987/88: 66, Stockholm: Utrikesdepartementet (17 December).

Utrikesutskottets betankanden (1991) *Parliamentary Record*, 1990/91: UU8, Stockholm.

—— (1992) *Parliamentary Record*, 1991/92: UU19, Stockholm.

—— (1993) *Parliamentary Record*, 1992/93: UU19, Stockholm.

Valen, H. (1994) 'Norge sa nei for annen gang', *Aftenposten*, 2/12/1994, Oslo: 13.

Valen, H. and Aardal, B. (1993) *Aftenposten*, 23/12/1993, Oslo: 3.

—— (1994a) 'Opinion' *Aftenposten*, 15/4/1994, Oslo: 2.

—— (1994b) 'Opinion' *Aftenposten*, 14/10/1994, Oslo: 5.

—— (1994c) 'Opinion' *Aftenposten*, 15/10/1994, Oslo: 5.

—— (1994d) 'Opinion' *Aftenposten*, 13/11/1994, Oslo: 4.

—— (1994e) 'Opinion' *Aftenposten*, 1/12/1994, Oslo: 9.

Väyrynen, P. (1979) 'Finnish Foreign Policy in Today's World', *Aussenpolitik* 30, 1: 3–14.

Viklund, D. (1989) *Sweden and the European Community: Trade, Cooperation and Policy Issues*, Stockholm: The Swedish Institute.

Wæver, O. (1992) 'From Nordism to Baltism', in Mare Kukk, Sverre Jervell and Pertti Joenniemi (eds) *The Baltic Sea Area – A Region in the Making*, Århus: Institutt for Statskundskab.

Wallace, H. (ed.) (1991) *The Wider Western Europe: Reshaping the EC/EFTA Relationship*, London: Royal Institute of International Affairs/Pinter.

Watson, R. (1995) 'Scandinavians Queue Up to Join Schengen', *The European*, 259, 28/4/1994: 1.

Webb, C. (1983) 'Theoretical Perspectives and Problems', in H. Wallace, W. Wallace and C. Webb (eds) *Policy Making in the European Community* (Second edition), Chichester: John Wiley & Sons.

Wellenstein, E. (1973) 'The Free Trade Agreements between the Enlarged European Communities and the EFTA Countries', *Common Market Law Review* 10, 3: 137–49.

—— (1983) 'The Relations between the European Communities and Finland', *Common Market Law Review* 20, 4: 713–25.

Wendt, F. (1959) *The Nordic Council and Co-operation in Scandinavia*, Copenhagen: Munksgaard.

Widfeldt, A. (1992) 'The Swedish Parliamentary Election of 1991', *Electoral Studies* 11, 1.

—— (1995) 'The Swedish Parliamentary Election of 1994', *Electoral Studies* 15, 2.

Widgren, M. (1995) *National Interests, EU Enlargement and Coalition Formation*, A20, Helsinki: ETLA.

Wieslander, H. (1974) *De politiska partiernas program* (4th ed.) Lund: Prisma.

Wijkman, P. M. (1990) *Patterns of Production and Trade in Western Europe: Looking Forward after Thirty Years*, Geneva: EFTA.

—— (1992) *The European Free Trade Area Expanded? The European Community, EFTA and Eastern Europe*, Occasional Paper 43, Geneva: Economic Affairs Department.

World Commission on Environment and Development (1987) *Our Common Future* (The Brundtland Report), Oxford: Oxford University Press.

Worre, T. (1995) 'First No, then Yes: The Danish Referendums on the Maastricht Treaty 1992 and 1993', *Journal of Common Market Studies* 33, 2: 235–58.

Wright, W. E. (1971) 'Comparative Party Models: Rational-Efficient and Party Democracy', in W. E. Wright (ed.) *A Comparative Study on Party Organization*, Columbus: C.E. Merrill.

Index

Aaltonen, S. 226
Aardal, Bernt 134, 138, 144, 145, 148n, 149n
Aarhus 86
Accession Treaty (1972) 46n; (1994) 71, 77
Act of Self-Government (1991) 8
Act on Changes for Environmentally Hazardous Batteries (Sweden) 212
African Development Fund 29
Agrarian parties 6; Finland 118, 119; Norway 137
agriculture 45–6nn, 55, 70, 85, 87 121, 128; common policy not to be considered 148n; common positions 71; concessions in trade 58; cooperation 50, 52; environmental protection 212, 214; exclusion from EFTA's rules 35; exports 33–4, 85; failure to reform 233; final challenge to 130; Nordic enlargement and 222–9; policy 21, 26, 276; powerful organisations 162, 163; primary economy 161; problem 254, 255; quotas 71; strong alliances between farmers and fishermen 138; strong interest organisations in 160; subsidies 68, 76, 244; support 67, 68, 73–4, 226–7, 277; support for EU membership 125; *see also* CAP
Aho, Esko 76, 132n
Ahtisaari, Martti 29, 131, 258
Akerholm, J. 170
Åkström, S. 41
Åland Island 8, 23, 27, 31n, 71, 72; EU membership (1995) 9, 28; referendum (1994) 9
Alanen, P. 132n
alcohol 71, 113; monopolies 58, 72, 108
Allen, H. 36, 37, 40, 42, 44, 135
Allied Powers 19
Alpine countries 54; 'Alpine/Scandinavian gap' 58
Althingi (Icelandic parliament) 39, 66, 150, 154, 270; majority of seats held by regions 161
Andersen, Svein 243
Andrén, Nils 16, 39, 40, 101, 103, 261, 262
Anglo-Nordic grouping 85
animals 280
Antarctic 15
'anti-authoritarian' movements 138
anti-dumping measures 57, 191, 192
anti-EC/EU movements Denmark 36, 86, 92, 93; Finland 120, 128; Norway 137, 143
Antola, Esko 44, 118, 119
Apunen, O. 118
aquaculture 230, 233
Archer, C. 264, 265, 277
Arctic 29, 269–70, 272; agriculture 73, 223; medicine 25
Armand, C. 67
Arter, D. 7, 15, 39, 42, 46n, 64
Asgrimsson 164, 165
Asian Development Bank 29
Asp, K. 115
Astrom, Sverker 248
'Atlantic' relationship 136
Atlantic Treaty (1949) 20
Auken, Sven 91
Austria 40, 58, 227, 268; associate agreement with EC 37; convergence criteria for EMU 181; EC/EU membership 56, 60, 67, 69, 143, 267, 278; EEA customs union favoured by 59; EFTA membership 35, 52; ERM membership 170; real effective exchange rates (1988–93) 173; referendum (1994) 22, 107; social protection 188; unionisation 190
Austria-Prussia 18
autonomous regions 8, 9, 15, 17, 72
autonomy 170; decision-making 57, 59; wealth 61
Axis Powers 19
Aylott, N. 111

Bachrach, P. 165n
Bach, M. 96
Bakke, Hallvard 144
balance of payments: deficits 182, 184; surpluses 174, 182, 184
Baltic region 71; argument to enlarge Nordic Council to accommodate republics 30; cooperation with states 29; Finland developed relations with republics 19; marine environment 26; NC sponsorship of future EU entry 280–1; newly independent states 265; stronger international role for EU 68; suuport for democratisation 269; Sweden/Denmark conflict for dominance 17; *see also* Estonia; Latvia; Lithuania
Baltic Sea 26, 29, 30, 262, 265, 266
Baragiola, P. 55
Baratz, M. 165n
Barents Euro-Arctic Council 269, 272
Barents Sea 29, 232
Barnes, I. 264
Basic Agreements 189, 201n
Baunsgaard, Hilmar 21, 22
Belgium 173, 181, 188, 190, 216, 262
Bennulf, M. 114
Berge, O. 46n
Bergquist, M. 37
Bernitz, U. 41
Bildt, Carl 64, 76, 95, 104, 112, 246, 251–3 *passim*, 256, 277
Bille, L. 115
Binswanger, H. 41, 45n

Bissell, R. 246
Berregaard, Ritt 91
Bjørklund T. 149n
Blomerg, Jaakko 254–5
Bonham, G. M. 39
Borten government (Norway) 40
Bosnia 253
Branner, H. 85
Bratelli, Trygve 40, 138
Britain *see* UK
Brown-Humes, C. 26
Brundtland, A. 0. 38, 261
Brundtland, Gro Harlem 55, 56, 65, 141, 145, 192, 243, 268
Brussels 23, 252, 253, 262, 269; Spaak Foundation 259
budgetary issues 71, 183, 204, 222, 227; contributions 67, 68, 73, 74; deficits 174, 176, 181, 189, 279; provisions 70; surpluses 176
Bundesbank 172
bureaucracy 82, 83

Camps, M. 35, 36, 46n
Canada 272
CAP (Common Agricultural Policy) 35, 36, 40, 58, 73, 222; aim 223; cost of farming increased 227; maintenance of principles 89; prices 229; problems facing 233; reforms (1992) 214;
capital 52, 55, 189; flight of 247; free movement of 50, 56, 70, 152; international flows 178; inward flows 172; productive, exodus of 97
capitalism 30, 174
Carlsson, Ingvar 64, 102, 104, 106, 111, 247, 251, 253, 259n
CCP (Common Commercial Policy) 58, 277
CEEC (Central and Eastern Europe) 29, 104, 119, 131, 147, 233, 278; clamour for EC membership 95; closer cooperation with 91; collapse of communism 264; collapse of Finnish exports to 177; confrontation and militarisation 30; environmental problems 205; strengthening regional cooperation 269
Central Europe *see* CEEC
Central Organisation of Finnish Trade Unions 76
Centre parties 24; Finland 6, 43, 119, 120, 121, 125, 129–30, 131, 258; Norway 6, 37, 137, 142, 143, 148n, 149n; Sweden 37, 44, 102, 103, 107, 111–13 *passim*, 115, 116, 248, 251, 259
Centre-Left coalition (Denmark) 86
Centre-Right parties: Denmark 89, 266; Iceland 152
Cerny, P. G. 100
certificates 52; of conformity 55
CET (Common External Tariff) 33, 35
CFP (Common Fisheries Policy) 9, 45, 54, 58, 155, 222; conservation management 223; Denmark and 265–8; Finland and 232–3; Iceland and 66, 151, 154, 232; Norway and 229, 230–2; Portugal and Spain integrated 75; problems facing 233; Sweden and 232
CFSP (Community Foreign and Security Policy) 48, 67, 131, 132n, 280; NATO Nordics and 260–74
Chambers of Commerce (Iceland) 162, 163
Charter of Paris 247
chemicals 211–12, 213
Cheysson, Claude 49
Christensen, J. 86
Christian Democratic Party (Sweden) 111, 112, 113, 115, 116, 251
Christian People's Party (Norway) 37, 42, 137, 142, 143, 148n, 149n
Christian Union (Finland) 130
Church, C. 45
citizenship 28, 93, 187
class 114
Closse, W. 36, 37
CMEA (Council for Mutual Economic Assistance) 41
coal 238, 240; *see also* ECSC
Cockfield, Lord 98
'Cod Wars' 270
cohesion 58; economic 51; social 51, 280
'Cohesion Fish' 230
Cold War 54, 60, 139, 246, 255, 263, 265, 270; heritage left over from 258; non-alignment a product of 103
collective bargaining 190
Comecon 22; *see also* CMEA
Commission of the ECs 49, 50, 55, 56, 62n, 69; Community Charter of Fundamental Social Rights of Workers 193; Danish membership 85; directives 195, 199, 201n; energy issues 237, 239, 240, 241, 242; environmental issues 205, 206; evaluation report (July 1992) 251–2; fishery issues 232, 233; general strategy for enlargement of EU 66; Green Paper on European Social Policy (1993) 189–90, 194, 201n; national farm package 73–4; new role 95; opinions on NC applications 67; Social Action Programme 186, 193, 194; Task Force 217; White Papers 140, 193, 194, 196, 198, 199, 201n, 202n
Commissions of Inquiry (Sweden) 7
Common Customs Tariff 55
Common Labour Market Treaty (1954) 25
Common Market 85, 152
Common Nordic Labour Market 8, 277, 278
commonalities 7
communism 30, 119, 174; collapse of 108, 264
Communist parties 6; Denmark 36, 262; Finland 43; Norway 262; Sweden 37, 102
company law 52, 56, 70
competition: common rules of 57; policy 55, 70
confederalism 93
Confederation of Finnish Industry and Employers 76
Conservative parties 6, 24; Britain 113; Denmark 37; Finland 43; Norway 137, 138, 142, 143, 144; Sweden 42, 101, 102, 246, 251, 259; *see also* Moderate Party
constitutions: Denmark 5, 46n; Finland 117, 122, 129, 132n, 257; Norway 5, 135, 148n
consumer protection 50, 52, 70, 90
convergence criteria 74, 170, 175, 180, 181, 183–5 *passim*, 189
Copenhagen 23, 26; anti-EC movement 86; Convention (1968) 29; decision to establish EEA 217; Nordic Cultural Fund 25; Summit of EC leaders (1982) 44
Corfu 71, 77
Council of the Baltic States 30
Council of Europe 262, 263, 269
Council of Ministers 24, 49, 59, 88, 90 96; adoption of TEU 91; Enlargement Task Force 67; environmental legislation 207; French Presidency 45; pulication of minutes 279; Sweden's introductory speech to 252; voting rights 77
Croatia 253
CSCE (Conference on Security and Co-operation

in Europe) 29, 247, 267, 269, 270; *see also* OSCE
Cuba 264
Culture Fund 26
currency: gold-based union 18; strict regulations 152; union disintegrated 20; *see also* ECU; EMI; EMS; EMU; ERM; monetary issues
Currency Act (Finland, 1977) 178
customs: barriers 146–7; control 28; posts 23; regulations 108; union 39, 40, 59, 62n, 70, 71
Cyprus 147
Czechoslovakia 262
Czempiel, O. 84

Dalsager, Poul 87, 88
Davignon Report (1970) 39
decentralisation 29
decision-making 51, 85, 91, 96, 121, 165n; common 55, 56; consensual 7; difficult for small countries to influence 218; environmental 207, 215, 221; formal 134; full participation 276; integrated 24, 97; internal procedures 258; joint 57, 58–9; model emphasising the role of 83–4; new procedures 89; parliamentary 128; security 255–6; supranational 61; transparency in 68, 199
De Clerq, Willy 51, 62n
defence 17, 18, 121, 146, 262, 265, 266; commissions and committees 264; cooperation 107, 254; Nordic bloc 103; 'opt–outs' on 93; policy 7, 24, 267; relatively independent 108; Scandinavian regional agreement proposed 19–20; US disengagement from Europe 267
deficits 174, 176, 180–1, 189, 279; balance of payments 182, 184
Delors, Jacques 55, 56, 57, 67, 193
Derry, T. K. 19, 20
devaluation 173, 175, 178, 179, 180, 182
dialects 15
Dinkelspiel, Ulf 252, 279
disintegrative factors 17–18
divergence 169–70; national interests 17, 54; security/defence interests 18–19, 20, 30; US-EC 139
Dolman, A. J. 264
Dooge committee (1984) 89
drug-trafficking 108
'Dutch disease' 243

EAPs (Environmental Action Programmes) 206, 210
East, R. 40
Eastern Europe *see* CEEC
EC (European Community) *see under various headings, e.g.* Commission of the ECs; Council of Ministers; EP (European Parliament); 'Luxembourg Process'
ECE (Economic Commission for Europe) 26, 177; agreement on Long Range Trans-Boundary Air Pollution 208
ECJ (European Court of Justice) 59, 65, 142
economies of scale 53
Economist 174, 176
ECSC (European Coal and Steel Community) 85, 239, 263
ECU (European Currency Unit) 73, 103, 170, 172
Edinburgh Summits: (1992) 67, 215, 264, 267; (1993) 23, 82, 93
education 27, 56, 70, 129
Eduskunta (Finnish parliament) 43, 122, 128–9, 132n, 250, 257
EEA (European Economic Area) 3, 4, 22, 28–9, 47–62, 65, 69, 121, 140–3, 148n, 246, 250, 257, 265, 270, 275–6, 283; agreement into effect 215; chapters almost fully and partly covered by 70; decision to establish 217; fishery issues 231, 232; formation 150; governmental frustration at slowness of negotiations 64; gradual entry to single market through 81; Icelandic reaction to 66, 152, 153, 154, 165n; natural progression in Finnish pragmatism 119; negotiations between EC and EFTA 103; Norwegian parliamentary support for EEA/EU policy 134; resented by some 104; seen as an end in itself by Finland 249–50; solution for Denmark 92; Swedish abandonment 97; treaty into operation 107
EES (European Economic Space) 50, 56, 62n
EEZs (exclusive economic zones) 229, 230
EFTA (European Free Trade Association) 16, 32–46, 52, 54, 66, 87, 107, 136, 148n, 265, 280; adapting to EC 141; anti-EU side weakend by enlargement 93; clamour for EC membership 95; closer cooperation with 91; departure of several important members 102; EC arrangement 22; environmental issues 215, 217; Finland's membership 177; formation 21; founder members 3, 35, 101, 263; free trade 139–40; Iceland becoming marginalised within 66; Iceland joined 152; Iceland's failure to participate in membership negotiations 163; intensified cooperation with 89; intergovernmental policy 88; international law-based approaches 142; membership complementary to all main NCs 4; membership negotiations 153; Oslo summit (1989) 56, 65, 150; overshadowed plans for Nordic Common Market 86; relations with EEA 57–62; 'rights' in shaping SEM legislation 121; trade with Finland 178
Egeland, J. 269
Eggertsson, T. 38, 39
Eire *see* Ireland
Elder, N. 7, 16
electricity 237, 238, 239, 240, 241
Elklit, J. 87
EMAS (EU eco-management scheme) 220
EMCF (European Monetary Cooperation Fund) 171
EMI (European Monetary Institute) 171
employment 160, 161, 187, 192; educationally handicapped 198; full 68, 88, 193, 276, 278; higher levels 6; threat to 247
EMS (European Monetary System) 69, 169, 170–1, 173–5 *passim*, 184
EMU (Economic and Monetary Union) 48, 60, 70, 71, 90, 169–85; convergence criteria 74, 170, 180; link between EMS and 169
energy 50, 70, 89, 235–44; liberalisation 68; policy based on rules of SEM 146; stockpiling 71; tax on 210; *see also* nuclear power
environmental issues 26, 56, 70, 148n, 238, 276, 277; cooperation in 50; policy 68, 203–21; protection 57, 58; standards 7, 58, 68, 90, 108; *see also* environmental standards
environmental standards 7, 58, 68, 90, 108, 203, 204, 207; differing 210–11, 215, 216–17; high 209, 219, 276; pressure to improve 217
Environmental Protection Convention (1974) 25
EP (European Parliament) 43, 49, 55, 72, 89, 96, 141, 226; approved accession treaty 77; Danish grouping opposing further integration 263; environmental proposals 211, 219–20; levels of

cooperation in 280; Pimenta Report (1994) 209; powers extended 207; sceptics 116
EPC (European Political Cooperation) 44, 53, 139, 265–6, 267, 268
Erlander, Tage 101–2, 246
ERM (Exchange Rate Mechanism) 169, 170–61 178–81, 184, 229
ESA (EFTA Surveillance Authority) 59
Eskimo-Aleutic languages 15
Estonia 30, 281
EURATOM (European Atomic Energy Community) 58, 239, 263
EURES database 199
European Energy Charter 146, 241
European Round Table of Industrialists 49
European Social Fund 198, 201n
exchange rates *see* ERM
Executive Council 8
exhaust emissions 210–11
exports 41, 57, 63, 145, 177, 213; agricultural 33–4, 85; energy 235; fish 232; manufacturers' shares 53; NCs to EC 22, 45; oil 184, 236; percentage of GDP 33; wood, heavy reliance on 183
external relations 70

Froes 8, 23; elected to remain outside EU 9, 46n; free trade agreements 4; North Atlantic links between Norway, Iceland, Greenland and 30; salmon farmers 27
Far East 193
Farmers' Union (Finland) 121
farmers/farming *see* agriculture
federalism 280; Denmark's scepticism regarding 5
Fenno-Ugric 15
fertilisers 214
finance 67, 68, 71; largely state-run system 152; Sweden's predominance 22; *see also* capital; monetary issues
Financial Times 175, 176, 178, 181, 192, 227
FINEFTA (Fenno-EFTA) Agreement 3, 21, 36
Finnish Agricultural Policy 226
Finnish Forest Industries Association 214
Finnmark 144
First World War 18
First World War 20
fishery issues 39, 44, 65, 70, 76, 271; access to resources 54; chapter 40; common positions 71; concessions 58; cooperation 50; depletion of stocks 229, 283; enlargement of EU and 229–33; exports 33, 57, 145; grounds 21; Icelandic problem 164; importance of 157–8; liberalisation 68; limits 41; major competitor in European markets 157; management of stocks 223, 230–1, 233–4; national conference (Iceland 1994) 150–1; policy 21, 27; powerful organisations 162, 163; primary economy 161; products 41, 57; protection 73; quotas 66, 75, 154, 229, 231, 232; rights 44, 46n; salmon farmers 27; strong interest organisations in 160; zones 15; *see also* CFP
fjords 15
Folketing (Danish parliament) 8, 36, 46n, 88, 89, 90, 91; discussion before Maastricht 266; legislation discussed in secrecy 96; Memorandum on IGCs supported by 94
food 108, 218–19, 224, 225, 232
foreign exchange reserves 171
foreign ministers 19, 145
Foreign Ministry (Sweden) 248
foreign policy 24, 70, 84, 88, 97, 117–18, 137; changes 82, 96–8, 125; common 252, 254, 257, 258; comparative 100; consensual tradition 102; developing 259; economic 44–5, 152; incompatibility between democracy and 99; leadership 258; logical progrssion for 122; NATO-based and pro-Atlanticist 34; 'normal' 97; open discussion and disagreement 130; post-Second World War 136; question of competence to handle 134; redirection in 81; relatively independent 108; sensitive area 151; small states 94, 95, 99; stailisers 96; structural effects upon 83; supported by public 123; *see also* CFSP
forestry 26, 27, 53, 58, 213
Forsberg, T. 132n
Fourth Environmental Action Programme (1987) 64
France 38, 240; change in attitude to supranationality 88; convergence criteria for EMU 181; lost jobs 201n; policy towards EC 39; progress in implementing directives applicable to environment 216; real effective exchange rates (1988–93) 173; referendum on TEU 178; regulation 190; social protection 188; unionisation 190; vetoes on British EC membership 86, 136
free movement: capital 50, 56, 70, 152; goods 52, 54, 56, 70; persons 55, 56, 58, 70, 201n; services 56
free trade: agreements 4, 42–3, 44, 45, 110, 140, 152; global economy 8; industrialisation programme dependent on 40; non-EC NCs negotiated with EC 16; prevented 152; reciprocal 41; treaty 123, 138, 139; UK proposal for European area 35; *see also* EFTA; FINEFTA
fylker 144

Gahrton, P. 114
gas 53, 236, 240, 241; licences for 242; reliance on imports 237, 238; reserves 243
Gasteyger, C. 246
GATT (General Agreement on Tariffs and Trade) 29, 177, 228; Kennedy Round 86, 152; Uruguay Round 222, 223
Gaulle, Gen. Charles de 22, 38, 39, 46n, 87, 136
GDP (gross domestic product) 7, 33, 187, 196; Denmark 197; Finland 174, 177, 180, 218, 233; Iceland 232; Norway 184; Sweden 174, 176, 218
Gellner, M. 35
gender 108, 114, 125
Geneva 49
Germany 30, 88, 94, 95, 180, 240, 265; 'absorption' of Denmark 85; access to Icelandic waters 41, 44; agricultural aid 228; alternative to unilateral dependence on 91; convergence criteria for EMU 181; currency 170, 173, 174, 175, 176; environmental issues 203, 210, 211, 216, 219; exports/imports 176; Finnish-USSR treaty against aggression 22; interest rates 184; markets 22; real effective exchange rates (1988–93) 173; regulation 190; rise of Nazism 19; second most important trading partner for Denmark Norway after 21; social protection 188; strategic interests 20; trade with Finland 178; unification 95, 99, 175, 247, 266; unionisation 190; wartime occupation of Norway and Denmark 18, 19, 34, 261
Gidlund, G. 101, 102, 112
Gilljam, M. 104, 108, 110, 114
Gíslason, G. T. 40, 41
Glasgow 201n
globalisation 194

GNP (gross national product) 19, 29, 236
Godal, Björn Tore 145, 268
gold 18
Goldmann, K. 83
goods: end use of 213; free movement of 52, 54, 56, 70; industrial, quantitive restrictions 55; investment 177, 213
Gorbachev, Mikhail S. 82
Göteborg 26
Gourevitch, P. 151
Gradin, Anita 116
Granberg, D. 114
Granell, F. 69, 71, 77
Greece 43, 89, 181, 188; fish 231; progress in implementing directives applicable to environment 216
Green parties: Finland 119, 125; Sweden 104, 107, 113–14, 115, 248, 249
Greenland 27; EU question 4; granted home rule from Denmark (1979) 46n; incorporated into Denmark (1953) 263; languages 15; left EC (1984) 46n; legislative assembly delegates to Nordic Council 23; North Atlantic links between Norway, Faeroes, Iceland and 30; plebiscite to leave EC (1982) 4, 9; referendums (1979 and 1982) 8, 46n; status as part of Danish crown 8; US bases 20
Grunnloven (Norwegian constitution) 5
Gstöhl, S. 58
Guardian, The 30n

Haahr, J.-H. 90, 95, 96, 100n
Haakon VII, king of Norway 19
Haas, E. B. 96
Haavisto, Heikki 255, 258
Haferkamp, Wilhelm 62n
Hague, The 249
Hakovirta, H. 41, 246
Halonen, Tarja 131
'Halving' programme (Sweden) 212
Hammarskjöld, Dag 29
Hancock, M. D. 37, 40, 42
Hannibalsson, J. B. 39, 154, 165n
Hansen, P. 35, 36, 38, 46n, 84, 87
Hanssen, H. J. 37, 38
Hansson, Per Albin 19
Hardarson, O. T. 165n
Hartling, Poul 29
Hasselberg, P. A. G. 112
health 25, 27, 70, 148n, 188, 206; protection 208; and safety 58, 186, 187, 192–6 *passim*, 200, 280
Hedtoft, Hans 23
Hellström, Mats 49
Helsinki 238; Nordic Arts Centre 26
Helsinki Protocol (1957) 118
Helsinki Treaties (1962) 23; (1971) 24, 25
Hermann, Charles 81, 82–4, 96, 97, 99, 100
Hermansson, J. 114, 150, 155
historical affinities 17
HLCG (High-Level Contact Group) 51
HLIG (High-Level Interim Group) 60
HLNG (High-Level Negotiating Group) 57, 60
HLSG (High-Level Steering Group) 56, 57
Holkeri, Harri 132n
Holm, H.-H. 264
Hølmberg, Soren 104, 108, 109, 110, 115
home affairs 70
Home rules Bill (1948) 8
Hoover 201n
hospitals 25, 27
human rights 7
humanitarian organisations 8
Hungary 19
hydroelectric power 236

Icelandic Election Study 157
identity 8; common 17; European, political conditions of 66; national 17, 34, 122; Western 259
IEA (International Energy Agency) 237
IEM (Internal Energy Market) 236, 239, 240, 241
IGCs (Intergovernmental Conferences) 29, 56, 90, 96, 169, 207, 245, 268, 278; Memorandum 94
IMF (International Monetary Fund) 29; Bretton Woods System 178
immigration 28, 279–80
imports 22, 63, 177, 213, 226; energy 235, 236, 237, 238, 239; high tariffs 225; surcharge on 38
independence: Finland (1917) 18, 19; Iceland (1944) 17, 34, 150; Norway (1905) 34, 135
Independence Party (Iceland) 150, 152, 153, 154, 155, 158–64 *passim*
Independent Front of the Finnish People 120
industrial policy 70, 153
industrial property rights 52
industrial relations 189, 190, 191, 199
industrialisation 21, 39, 40, 137–8
industry 37, 89, 161–2, 213–14; agriculture 226; complacency 177; fishing 230, 232; large 53
inflation 173, 178, 179, 181, 182; low 185
information exchange 52
institutions 70, 266, 280; credit 71; national 182
integration theory 96–8
intellectual property 50
interdependence 96, 97, 99, 283
interest rates 172, 174, 181, 184
intergovernmentalism 97
'Interlaken principles' 51
internationalism 8, 29, 277
Inter-Parliamentary Union 23
Inuits 15
Ionnina Compromise (1994) 78n
IR (International Relations) level 242
Ireland 263; convergence criteria for EMU 181; EC membership 16, 22, 40, 140; fish 231; progress in implementing directives applicable to environment 216; real effective exchange rates (1988–93) 173; social protection 188
Israel/Arab relations 29
Italy 173, 181, 188, 190, 216

Jacot-Guillarmod, O. 55
Jamar, J. 55
Jansson, Jan-Magnus 120
Japan 170
Jerneck, Magnus 64, 81, 83
JHA (Justice and Home Affairs) 146–7, 279
Johansson, Olof 112
Joint Declaration on Nordic Co-operation (1994) 71
Jonnergård, G. 102
Jonsson, H. 152
judges 62n; foreign, fear of 59
justice 70, 146, 264

Kalmar Union 17
Karelia 19, 238; Northern 129
Kautokeino 25–6
Kekkonen, Urho 20, 30n, 117, 118, 119, 130, 132n
Kelstrup, M. 94
Kenya 29

Keohan, R. 165n
Kettunen, L. 74, 233
Kiel 30
Kleppe, Per 49
Knud (Canute), Viking king of England 17
Knudsen, O. F. 139
Kohl, Helmut 84
Koivisto, Mauno 132n, 250
Kola peninsula 27, 265
Korhonen, Keijo 120
Korvald government (Norway) 138
Kragh, Jens Otto 87–8
Kristensen, O. 237
Kristinsson, G. H. 44, 45, 66, 152, 154
Kuhnle, Stein 6
Kuopio 129
Kværner 23

labour markets 152, 187; active policies 196–8; widely organised 190
Labour Party (Norway) 37, 42, 65, 133–5 *passim*, 137–9 *passim*, 141–5 *passim*, 148n
Lambert, J. R. 36, 37
Landting (island government parliament) 8
Lange, G. 37
language 15, 26; affinities 17
Lapland 129, 226
Lapps 15, 26
Latvia 30, 281
Laursen, J. N. 85, 86, 91
law 199; company 52, 56, 70; environmental 206, 276; labour 190, 194
Law of Accessio 87
League of Nations 8, 19
Left parties 24; Finland 119, 125; Iceland 152; Norway 37, 137, 141, 142, 143, 147, 148n, 149n; Sweden 102, 104, 107, 113–14, 115, 248, 249, 259, 283n
Leonardo programme 198
Levy, J. S. 99
Lewin, L. 115
LFA (Less Favourable Area) status 227
liberal democracies 68, 122
Liberal parties 6; Denmark (Radical) 21, 46n, 90, 266, 267; Finland 43; Norway 37, 137, 138, 149n; Sweden 37, 42, 101, 102, 103, 111–13 *passim*, 115, 251, 259
Liberalist Group (Norway) 24
Lie, Trygve 29
Liechtenstein 22, 58, 62n
life assurance 70, 71
Liikanen, Erkki 279
'Like-Minded Countries' group 264
Lindahl, R. 104, 105, 106, 110
Lindberg, L. 16
Lipponen, Paavo 131
Lisbon European Council Summit (1992) 66, 67, 77
Lisein-Norman, M. 37, 40
literature 26
Lithuania 30, 281
LO (Swedish Trade Union Confederation) 64, 201n, 246
Lomé Conventions 43, 281
London 23; Declaration of EC States (1961) 36; money markets 172
Ludlow, P. 69
Lutheran Christianity 15
Luxembourg 151, 216, 262; converqence criteria for EMU 181; social protection 188
Luxembourg Compromise (1966) 39
'Luxembourg Process' (1984) 45, 47, 48–54, 57, 61, 140; Swedish judge at 62n
Lyck, L. 201n
Lyseby Declaration 148n

Maastricht 100, 145, 243; chapters 70, 71, 72; EC summit (1991) 264, 266; exemptions 28; IGC Conference (1991) 169, 268; negotiations 60
Macedonia 253
macroeconomic policy 50
MacSharry reforms (1992) 222
Mäentakanen, E.. 40, 41, 43
Malmö 18
Malta 147, 151
Mannerheim, G. 262
manual workers 161, 162
Margrethe, queen of Denmark 17
Mariehamn 31n
maritime links 71
market economies: competitive 7; functioning 66; highly industrialised and open 53
market liberalisation 96
Marshall Aid 118, 262, 263
Marxism 114
Matlary, J.-H. 146, 244n
Maudling, Reginald 86
Mayrzedt, H. 41, 45n
Mediterranean 5, 218, 280
Metal Industry Workers' Union (Sweden) 101
Middle East 269
Miles, Lee 63, 65, 68, 69, 77, 113, 277
Miljan, Toivo 5, 33, 38, 39, 40, 42, 44, 45, 46n
Milward, A. 85
Ministry of the Environment and Natural Resources (Sweden) 215
Ministry of Finance (Sweden) 183
Ministry of Foreign Affairs (Finland) 197, 199, 219, 254; Guidelines on European Policy 192
Ministry of Industry and Energy (Norway) 244
Ministry of Labour (Denmark) 190, 197, 200, 201n
Mitterrand, François 88
Moderate Party (Sweden) 102, 103, 106, 111–13 *passim*, 115, 251
Moller, Y. 101, 103
monarchies 6, 15
monetary issues 279; integration 93, 169–85; policy 88; union 94, 102
monopolies: alcohol 58, 72, 108; energy 237, 240, 241; national 241; 'natural' 237
Moravcsik, A. 97
More county (Norway) 144
Mortensen, J. V. 96, 99, 100n
Moscow (August 1991 coup attempt) 249
motor vehicles 210, 218; fiscal incentives for 71
Mouritzen, H. 94, 100n, 266
Mousson-Lestang, J.-P. 39
movement *see* free movement
Moxon Browne, E. 41
Mozambique 29
MTK (Central Union of Agricultural Producers, Finland) 76, 227, 255, 258
multinational companies 89
Muoser, T. 41
Murmansk 27
music 26

NACC (North Atlantic cooperation Council) 271
Namibia 29
Napoleonic wars 17
nation states/status 5, 17, 18, 97, 121

National Coalition (Finnish right-wing party) 119, 131, 132n
'National Compromise' (Denmark) 267
Nationalbank (Denmark) 175
nationalism: Denmark 17, 18; Iceland 151, 160; Norway 18, 136
NATO (North Atlantic Treaty Organisation) 7, 8, 20, 34, 53, 98, 103; accelerating reduction of military functions 146; 'Atlantic' relationship built around 136; France's withdrawal from military structure 39; Nordic members and CFSP 260–74; Norwegiam reliance on 265; Norwegian external policy 139; Partnership for Peace 258; security position of Nordic states 264
natural resources *see* energy; fishery issues; forestry; gas; nuclear power; oil; petroleum
Nell, P. 55
Nelsen, B. F. 138
Netherlands 173, 181, 188, 216, 262, 264; unionisation 190
neutrality 277; Denark 18; Finland 119, 121, 124, 132, 245, 249–50, 254–9 *passim*; Norway 18; Sweden 7, 18–20 *passim*, 22, 37, 39, 40, 47, 64, 108, 245–53, 255, 256, 258, 259; UK 45
NHO (Confederation of Norwegian Business and Industry) 144
NIB (Nordic Investment Bank) 21, 26, 27
Nicholson, F. 40
Nicolaides, P. 67
non-alignment 7–8, 101, 103, 108, 113, 280; military 254
Norberg, Sven 58, 62n
Nordbanken 183
Nordek (Nordic Organisation for Economic Cooperation) 16, 21, 22, 25, 39, 86; Danish-initiated plan for 136; recent failure 124
Norden Association 18
Nordic Action Plans 208
Nordic Arts Centre 26
'Nordic Balance' 20, 30
Nordic Common Market 39, 85; EFTA overshadowed plans for 86
Nordic Council 8, 16, 17, 22, 28, 29, 271, 277; achievements 27; arguments to enlarge 30; environmental action 208, 218; Finland joined 118; formation and function 23–4; Iceland becoming marginalised within 66; literature prize 26; proposal for treaty which would confirm and codify Nordic cooperation 86; various meetings 31n
Nordic Council of Ministers 16, 20, 24, 25, 31n
Nordic Cultural Agreement (1971) 25
Nordic Cultural Fund 25
Nordic Customs Union 16, 20–1, 35
Nordic Economics Research Council 25
Nordic Environmental Protection Convention (1976) 26
Nordic Fund for Technology and Industrial Development 26
Nordic Gene Bank 26
Nordic Institute for Studies in Urban and Regional Planning 26
Nordic Passport Union (1952) 8, 25, 28, 277, 278
Nordic School of Public Health 25, 26
Nordic Social Security Convention (1955) 25
Nordiska samarbetsorgan (Directory of Nordic cooperation) 6, 25
Nordkalotten 27, 30
Nordquist, G. 17, 22, 37, 38, 43, 44
Noreng, O. 42
Nørgaard, A. S. 100
Norrack, Ole 131
Norros, M. 76
Norsk Hydro 23
North Atlantic links 30; *see also* NACC; NATO
North Sea 236
nuclear power/energy 115, 236, 238, 239, 240, 244, 269
nuclear weapons 20, 29
Nydegger, A. 37
Nye, J. S. 96, 165n
Nygaard, Kristen 144
nynorsk 1 5

Oddsson, David 28, 150–1
Odell, J. S. 82
OECD (Oranisation for Economic Cooperation and Development) 174, 176, 186, 187, 196, 201n, 217, 218, 228
OEEC (Organisation for European Economic Cooperation) 35, 45–6nn, 85, 118, 262, 263
oil 236, 237, 238; derivatives 53; exports 184; first shock (1973–4) 240; fuel 213; licences for 242; prices 53, 177; reserves 243; second crisis (1979–81) 177
Ólafsson, S. 160
Old Norse 15
Olesen, T. B. 86
OPEC (Organisation of Petroleum Exporting Countries) 237
Oporto (EEA Agreement, May 1992) 59, 142
'opt-outs' 93, 193–4, 195, 215, 282
Oscar I, king of Sweden–Norway 18
OSCE (Organisation for Security and Cooperation in Europe) 145, 271
Oslo 23, 92; EFTA summit (1989) 56, 65, 150; Fjord 144; Nordic Council meeting (1993) 31n; Treaty on Palestine home rule 269
Ostfold 144
Ostrobothnia 129
ozone layer 212

Paasikivi, J. K. 117, 130, 132n
Palme, Olof 44, 102
Pangalos, Theodorus 76
Papacosma, V. 246
Paris 247
parliaments *see Althingi*; *Eduskunta*; *Folketing*; *Landting*; *Riksdag*; *Storting*
passport queues 23; *see also* Nordic Passport Union
Pedersen, T. 45, 49, 58, 81, 91, 95, 96, 97, 99, 100
People's Alliance (Iceland) 152, 153, 159, 165
People's Democratic League (Finland) 43
People's Movement against the European Community (Denmark) 43, 92
Persson, Göran 114
Pesonen, P. 129
pesticides 212, 214
Petersen, N. 87, 93, 267
Petersson, Olof 5, 6, 7, 64, 110
petroleum 53, 236, 237, 244n
Pierre, J. 112
Pittelkow, Ralf 91
PLO (Palestine Liberation Organisation) 269
Poland 19, 210
political parties 7, 183; *see also under various headings, e.g.* Centre; Christian; Communist; Conservative; Independence; Liberal; Progress; Social Democratic; Socialist
political union 94, 102
pollution *see* environmental issues

Portugal 21, 75, 171; 'Cohesion Fish' 231; convergence criteria for EMU 181; currency 175; EC membership 62n; EFTA membership 35; progress in implementing directives applicable to environment 216; social protection 188
prices 179, 180, 276; agricultural 73–4, 87, 222, 225–9 *passim*; energy 53, 177, 240, 241
privatisation 183, 237
Progress parties: Denmark 24; Norway 24, 148n, 149n
Progressive Party (Iceland) 40, 150, 152, 153, 155, 159, 164–5
public sector: debt 183; growing 276; large 6, 244
public spending 187
pulp industry 29, 213
Putnam, Robert 242

qualifications 25; mutual recognition 192
Queen Maud Land 15
quotas: agricultural 71; fishing 66, 75, 154, 229, 231, 232

radioactivity 71
'Rainbow government' (Finland) 131
raw materials 213
recession 278; Finland 60, 187; Sweden 60, 63–4, 110
recycling 29, 204, 208, 213
referendums 28, 38, 244; Åland islands 9; Austria 22, 107; Denmark 42, 46n, 67, 87, 90, 92, 93, 97, 243, 264, 266–7; Finland 22, 107, 117, 121–3 *passim*, 125, 128–31 *passim*, 245; France 178; Greenland 8, 45n; Iceland 154; Norway 4–5, 16, 22, 23, 42, 45, 65, 133–5 *passim*, 143–8 *passim*, 218, 231, 237, 243, 263, 265, 268; Sweden 22, 101, 104, 106, 107–15 *passim*, 128, 238–9, 245, 248, 253, 256, 283n
regional divisions 114
regional policy 57, 73, 74
Rehn, 0. 119
religious affinities 17
'Remiss Procedure' (Sweden) 7
republics 6, 15
research 89; and development 57; technology 70
Reykjanes 153, 160–4 *passim*
Reykjavik 24, 153, 160–4 *passim*
Reykjavik Nordic Council meetinq (1995) 31n
Reymond, C. 58
Richardson, J. 16, 97
rights 7; establishment 70; exclusive 72; fishing 44, 46n; migrant 196; property 52; social 6, 25; voting 77; workers 186, 187, 190, 193, 201n
Riksdag (Swedish parliament) 6, 42, 64, 102, 104, 247–8 ; Advisory Committee on EU Affairs 183; agricultural policy changed as a result of reforms 228; decision to submit application 112; election (Sept 1991) 251, 253; election (Sept 1994) 106, 107, 111, 114, 115, 116; Foreign Policy Committee 252, 256; Government Declarations 252, 253
riksmål 15
Romania 19
Romsdal 144
Rosenau, J. 84, 95
Ross, J. F. L. 44, 63
Royal Ministry of Foreign Affairs (Norway) 75, 140, 143, 145
RSFSR (Russian Soviet Federated Socialist Republic) 19
Rubin, M. 246
Russia 29, 122, 123, 128, 132n; Danish support for democratic process 267, 269; environmental degradation 204; fish stocks 231; Friendship Treaty with Finland (1991) 249; Imperial, Grand Duchy of 18; NC frontiers 265, 267, 268, 269; Norway's relationship with 270, 271; stability 248; trade/relations with Finland 178, 187, 236, 237–8, 239, 254, 255, 263; *see also* Soviet Union

Saab-Scania 211
Sæter, Martin 139, 142
SAF (Swedish Employers' Confederation) 65, 201n
safety belts 70, 71
St Petersburg 30
Salolainen, Pertti 254, 259n
Salovaara, J. 123
Sami people: cultural institute 26; exclusive rights 72; languages 15
Sandegren, K. 37, 38
Sänkiaho, R. 129
SAS (Scandinavian Airlines Sysytem) 25
Sauerberg, S. 38, 43
Scheingold, S. 16
Schengen agreement 23, 28, 277
Schleswig-Holstein 228
Schlüter, Poul Holmskov 90
Schmitter, P. 16
Schou, T.-L. 89, 267
science 25
SEA (Single European Act, 1986) 90, 95, 140, 195, 198, 203, 206, 220, 263
Second World War 19, 136
secondary residences 71
security 17, 121, 122, 123, 132n, 141; commitment to 259; divergent interests 18–19, 30, East-West 60; large party of the right expected to dominate 251; new European structure 131; policy 16, 70, 136, 137, 252–5 *passim*, 257–9 *passim*; sea-changes in 246; *see also* CFSP
SEM (Single European Market) 49, 50, 51, 53, 54, 172, 207, 275; access to 57, 121, 230, 276; agreement which basically extended 58; avoiding economic marginalisation by taking part in 56; completion 60, 179; determining future legislation 64; distortion of 205; EFTA countries' 'rights' in shaping legislation 121; emerging 246; EMS central to 170; energy policy 146, 240; extensive economic cooperation centring on 92; gradual entry 81; imbalances 95; implementation 55; integration built around 103; introduction 186; liberalisation introduced by 194; may suffer as a result of fragmentation 185; measures to complete 215; national legislation relevant for 52; ratification 266; removal of trade barriers 204; services 50, 56, 70
'set aside' 225
SF (Socialist People's Party, Denmark) 36, 92, 95
shipbuiliding 23
shocks: asymmetrical 183; external 83, 91, 94–5, 97, 99; oil 177, 237, 240; symmetrical 182
Sigurðadóttir, Jóhanna 159, 163
Single Market *see* SEM
Singleton, F. 43
'Skandek' 22
skerries 15
skilled workers 162
Snellman, J. V. 132n
SNU (Danish Commission on Security and Disarmament) 90, 267, 268

Social Chapter 113, 192, 193
Social Charter 64, 186, 194
Social Democratic parties 24; Denmark 6, 46n, 86–91 *passim*, 95, 100n, 266, 267; Finland 43, 119, 131, 132n; Iceland 152–5 *passim*, 159, 160, 161, 163, 164, 232; Norway 6, 55, 144; Sweden 6, 37, 38, 55, 64, 101–7 *passim*, 109–16 *passim*, 246–9 *passim*, 2561 259n, 279, 283n
social issues 148n, 277; dumping 191, 192; policy 52, 57, 68, 70, 186–7, 190, 191–200 *passim*; protection 50, 187, 188, 276; states with lower provision 183; *see also* standards; welfare
Socialist parties: Denmark 36, 92, 95; France 55; Iceland 152; Norway 137, 141, 142, 143, 147, 148n, 149n
Society for Finnish Independence 120
Socrates programme 198
Solem, E. 16
Soloveytchik, G. 21
Sørensen, C . L . 88
Sørensen, Georg 100
Sørensen, H . 43
Sorsa, K. 36, 41, 43
Sound protection 26
South Africa 267, 269, 272
sovereignty 8, 17, 20, 34, 61; attachment to 7; fishing limit 232; national 136, 141, 142, 182, 265, 282; natural resources 243; operational 100; threat to 265
Soviet Union 262; Denmark and Norway liberated from Germany by 261; dissolution/ disintegration 53, 103, 247, 249, 264; Finland and 8, 18–23 *passim*, 34, 35, 38, 41, 44, 53, 55, 117–18, 177, 182, 249, 262; strategic interests 20
Spain 50, 62n, 75, 77, 171; 'Cohesion Fish' 231; convergence criteria for EMU 181; currency 175; progress in implementing directives applicable to environment 216; real effective exchange rates (1988–93) 173; social protection 188; unemployment 187
Sparring, A. 39, 40, 41
Spinelli report 88
Spitzbergen 15
Stålvant, C.-E. 34, 38, 41, 42
standards 280; health 58, 192; labour 190–1; living 187, 201n; safety 58, 71, 192; social 7, 183, 187, 191, 200; technical 55; *see also* environmental standards
state intervention 6, 25, 171, 190, public confidence in 7
Statoil (Norway) 236
Steininger, R. 36
Stephensen, O. 165
Stockholm 27, 239; Nordic Council meeting (1994) 31n; Nordic Council of Ministers Secretariat 24; Nordic Institute for Studies in Urban and Regional Planning 26; UN Conference on the Environment (1972) 208; 'Yes' voters 114
Stockholm Convention (1959) 35, 46n
Stokke, O. S. 264, 269
Storting (Norwegian parliament) 6, 37, 38, 40, 42, 135, 147, 148n; Brundtland's November 1992 address 65; clear majority for membership 137; clear maority in favour of maintaining EEA 146; EEA treaty ratified 143; elections (1993) 144; Finance Committee 57; foreign policy statement (Jan. 1995) 145; support for EEA/EU policy 134
Strasbourg 90
strikes 152–3
Structural Funds 74, 198, 227, 230
subsidiarity 93, 190, 191, 200, 207
subsidies 206, 208; agricultural 68, 76, 228, 244; recruitment 197
Sundelius, Bengt 16–17, 18, 21, 81, 246, 261
supranationalism/supranationality 32, 34, 37, 45, 81, 96, 136; change in French attitude to 88; effective instrument in the pursuit of national interests 85; environmental legislation 210; general concessions to 94; integration 61, 95–6; political 87; reluctantly accepted 280; shifting loyalty towards 98
surpluses 174, 176, 182, 184; agricultural 223–4, 228; fishing 233
sustainable development 68, 206, 207
Svåsand, L. 115
Sveinsdottir, H. 152
Svensson, P. 92, 93, 97
Swedish Central Organisation of Salaried Employees 246
Swedish Environmental Protection Agency 208
Swedish Party (Finland) 43, 119, 124, 125, 131
Switzerland 22, 40, 56, 62n, 163; associate agreement with EC 37; EEA Agreement 60, 143; EFTA membership 35, 53; free movement of persons 58

Taina, Martti 131
Tanzania 29
tariffs 35, 43, 46n, 55; barriers 21, 41, 491 50; envisaged reductions 38; high 215
taxation 70, 183; environmental/energy 206, 210, 211, 237, 239; falling revenues 176; highest in OECD 186; indirect 52, 240; system reformed 208
TEC (total energy consumption) 238
technology 89, 195, 229; information 70; research 70
TEU (Treaty on European Union) 5, 11n, 56 58, 69, 77, 97, 131, 169, 265, 275; change as a result of endorsement 82; convergence criteria 170, 175, 189; criticism of Social Chapter 113; Danish and Swedish acceptance 99; Danish referendums 67, 266–7; Danish rejection of 106, 143, 264; Denmark negotiated 'opt-outs' 93; environmental issues 203, 204–5, 206–7, 220; European Council adopted 91; *finalité politiques* 66; Finnish acknowledgement 132n; forthcoming review (1996) 278, 282; 'Maastricht' chapters 70, 71, 72; Norway on the outside of 268; rejected draft 89; Social Protocol 113, 186, 193–4, 195; 'White Paper' on 92
Third World 88, 113, 263–4, 277
Thomas, A. H. 7, 16
Thomsen, B. N. 84
Thune, C. 85
Tiilikainen, T. 121, 123, 124, 126, 127
tobacco 72
Törnudd, K. 36, 38
tourism 27, 50
trade 213; agreements 22, 112; barriers 52, 204, 205; benefits for 182; dependence 98; distortions 215, 216–17; extensive relationship 238; favourable relations 150; foreign, restrictions on 152; illiberal policy 46n; imbalances 177; international cooperation 152; inter-Nordic 16; intra-industry 53; liberalisation 36, 108, 152; NCs' largest partner 21; promotion of 35; 'snus' tobacco 72; terms of 53; traditional reliance on 33; westwards 19, 181–2; *see also* free trade
trade unions 199; Austria 190; Belgium 190; Denmark 190; Finland 76, 121, 227, 255, 258;

France 190; Germany 190; Italy 190; Netherlands 190; Norway 190; Sweden 7, 37, 64, 101, 186, 190, 201n, 246, 256; UK 190
transit 58
transport 55, 239; cooperation in 50; policy 70
Treaty of Friendship, Cooperation and Mutual Assistance (USSR-Finland, 1948) 19, 22, 249
Treaty of Rome (1957) 78n, 90, 101, 158, 192, 198, 201n, 205–6, 222, 229
Tunander, O. 269
Turku/Åbo county (Finland) 27
Turner, B. 17, 22, 37, 38, 43, 44
Tuusvuoril 0. 118

Ueland, G. K. 39
UK (United Kingdom) 20, 34, 89, 261, 262; access to Icelandic waters 41, 44; centrality to NCs' European policies 36; convergence criteria for EMU 181; directive on working time subject to legal challenge from 195–6; EC/EU membership 16, 22, 32, 36, 37, 38–9, 40, 86, 140, 263; EFTA membership 35; environmental issues 203, 216; Euro-sceptics 113; exports/imports 176; Finland's need to retain access to market 40; French vetoes on membership 86, 136; industrial relations 190; large and important market for NCs 21; NCs' most important trading partner 33; neutrality policy 45; occupation of Iceland 19; 'opt-outs' 193–4, 195, 215; Presidency of EU 67; proposal for free trade area 35; real effective exchange rates (1988–93) 173; social protection 188; strong reliance on 136; surcharge on imports from EFTA countries 38; trade with Finland 178
Ulvskog, Marita 111
UN (United Nations) 8, 85, 261; Commission on the Environment (1987) 206; Secretary General's special representative 29; High Commissioner for Refugees 29; *see also* ECE
unemployment 50, 108, 177–8, 180, 218; cyclical 194; determined effort to combat 89; escalating 186; high 110, 130; lowest in OECD 187; mass 192; pay/benefits 25, 174, 183; regional 204; serious problem 197; strategy to deal with 131; Sweden's remarkable record 176; Union of the Left (Finland) 125
universities 26
University of Iceland, Social Sciences Research Institute 157, 158, 161, 162, 163, 164n
Uralic languages 15
urbanisation 160
Urwin, D. W. 35, 38
USA (United States of America) 139, 261, 262, 269; bases in Greenland 20; currency 170, 175; disengagement from defence of Europe 267; exports/imports 176; military inrtallations in Iceland 19, 270; running down bases in Norway 272; trade with Finland 178
USSR *see* Soviet Union
Utanríksmál 165n

Væver, O. 43
Val Duchesse 193
Valen, Henry 137, 144, 145, 148n, 149n
Väyrynen, P. 44
Vehicles Emissions Ordnance (Sweden) 210
veterinary questions 71
Vienna Summit (1977) 43
Vietnam 264
Viking age 17
Viklund, D. 44
Volvo 211
voting behaviour 129

Wæver, O. 30
'wait and see' policy 37, 38, 40, 85
Wallace, H. 55
Waltzean neo-realism 83
Warsaw Treaty Orqanisation 265, 266; Pact disintegration 103
waste 71, 208, 212, 269
Watson, R. 277
Webb, C. 151
welfare 6, 64, 88, 110, 122, 138; burden 183; comprehensive 7, 187; consequences for states 189; general crisis 60; generous provisions 68, 186; loss of 87; social 196, 200; stringent provision 276; threats of cuts 116; universal 187
Wellenstein, E. 41, 44
Wendt, F. 18
West European Free Trade Area 85
WEU (Western European Union) 91, 146, 253, 265–7 *passim*, 270–2 *passim*l 280
White Papers 278–9; *see also* Commission of the ECs; TEU
Widfeldt, A. 111, 112, 113
Wieslander, H. 103, 112
Wijkman, P. M. 33
Wiklund, C. 16–17, 18, 21
Winberg, Margareta 111
Winter War (1939–40) 18
women 122, 125–8, 145, 218; equal pay and treatment in the workplace 193, 201n
Women's Alliance (Iceland) 153, 159
Work Environment Act (Sweden, 1978) 195
working conditibns 50, 190–5 *passim*
World Bank 29
World Commission on the Environment 208
Worre, T. 67
Wright, W. E. 112

Yugoslavia (former) 147, 252, 267, 269, 277